COLLECTED PAPERS OF KENNETH J. ARROW

Volume **3** Individual Choice
under Certainty and
Uncertainty

COLLECTED PAPERS OF KENNETH J. ARROW

Individual Choice under Certainty and Uncertainty

The Belknap Press of Harvard University Press

Cambridge, Massachusetts   1984

This book is printed on acid-free paper,
and its binding materials have been chosen
for strength and durability.

Library of Congress Cataloging in Publication Data
(Revised for volume 3)

Arrow, Kenneth Joseph, 1921 –
  Collected papers of Kenneth J. Arrow.

  Includes bibliographical references and index.
  Contents: v. 1. Social choice and justice —   —
v. 3. Individual choice under certainty and uncertainty.
    1. Welfare economics — Addresses, essays, lectures.
2. Social choice — Addresses, essays, lectures.   3. Social
justice — Addresses, essays, lectures.   4. Distributive
justice — Addresses, essays, lectures.   I. Title.
HB846.A7725 1983   330.1   83-2688
ISBN 0-674-13760-4 (v. 1)
ISBN 0-674-13762-0 (v. 3)

Preface

Individual choice as a basic element of the theory of economic equilibrium has been a dominant theme of economics since the neoclassical "revolution" of the 1870s, as formulated in different ways by the pioneers, W. Stanley Jevons, Carl Menger, and Leon Walras. They initiated (subject to the usual precursors of any major discovery) the hypothesis that demand for goods could be interpreted as maximization of utility subject to a budget constraint. They treated primarily the case in which there was no uncertainty, although a corresponding theory of choice under uncertainty had been available since 1738 in the work of Daniel Bernoulli. The subsequent rich development of this hypothesis and its reinterpretation in ordinalist terms is too well known for recapitulation here.

I have had a variety of motivations for studies in the theory of individual choice. Chapter 6 was collateral to the theory of social choice, although it has independent interest. Several of the chapters (4, 8, and 13) are expositions which seek to bring together the interests in choice shown in economics and in other social and behavioral sciences. During the last thirty years psychologists in particular have been increasingly interested in the processes of individual decision making in a way which complements that of economists. A major interest of mine over the years has been extension of the theory of individual choice to the case in which the consequences of actions are uncertain (Chapters 2, 9, 10, 11, and 12). The remaining chapters (1, 3, 5, and 7) are responses to miscellaneous questions.

In addition to their original place of publication, Chapters 2, 9, and 10 have already been reprinted in a volume of essays on risk bearing (K. J.

Arrow, *Essays in the Theory of Risk-Bearing,* Chicago: Markham, and Amsterdam: North-Holland, 1977).

I should like to thank Mary Ellen Geer for her careful and thorough editing and Michael Barclay and Robert Wood for preparation of the index.

Contents

1 Homogeneous Systems in Mathematical Economics: A Comment *1*

2 Alternative Approaches to the Theory of Choice in Risk-Taking Situations *5*

3 The Determination of Many-Commodity Preference Scales by Two-Commodity Comparisons *42*

4 Utilities, Attitudes, Choices: A Review Note *55*

5 The Measurement of Price Changes *85*

6 Rational Choice Functions and Orderings *100*

7 Additive Logarithmic Demand Functions and the Slutsky Relations *109*

8 Utility and Expectation in Economic Behavior *117*

9 The Theory of Risk Aversion *147*

10 Exposition of the Theory of Choice under Uncertainty *172*

11 The Use of Unbounded Utility Functions in Expected-Utility Maximization: Response *209*

12 Optimal Insurance and Generalized Deductibles *212*

13 Risk Perception in Psychology and Economics *261*

Index *271*

Individual Choice
under Certainty and
Uncertainty

1   Homogeneous Systems in Mathematical Economics: A Comment

In a paper published in *Econometrica* in 1950,[1] Gerhard Tintner developed some highly useful general theorems bringing together the various problems in economic theory which lead to relations homogeneous of degree zero in certain variables. These theorems were derived by Tintner under the assumption that the various functions involved are differentiable twice.[2] Modern mathematical economics seeks to avoid assumptions of differentiability which seem to have no economic relevance and which frequently are unnecessary. Indeed, the use of methods of the differential calculus occasionally leads to unnecessarily complicated derivations and exposition.[3] It is the purpose of this chapter to show that Tintner's chief

---

1. G. Tintner, "Homogeneous Systems in Mathematical Economics," *Econometrica,* vol. 16, October, 1948, pp. 273–294.

2. Ibid., p. 277.

3. This point has been especially stressed by Samuelson. See P. A. Samuelson, *Foundations of Economic Analysis,* Cambridge, Massachusetts: Harvard University Press, 1947, pp. 70–76, 107–112; and "Comparative Statics and the Logic of Economic Maximizing," *Review of Economic Studies,* vol. 14 (1), 1946–47, pp. 41–43. It is true, however, as pointed out by one of the reviewers of Samuelson's book, that the differentiability or nondifferentiability of the utility or revenue function or of the constraints on behavior is of importance in characterizing the behavior of the decision variables with respect to variations in the initial conditions. See K. E. Boulding, "Samuelson's *Foundations:* The Role of Mathematics in Economics," *Journal of Political Economy,* vol. 56, June, 1949, p. 194.

Reprinted from *Econometrica,* 18 (1950):60–62. I wish to thank J. Marschak, Cowles Commission for Research in Economics and the University of Chicago, and G. Tintner, Iowa State College, for their very helpful comments and criticism.

results can be obtained without any assumptions of differentiability and in a simpler manner. It will consequently be noted that some remarks of Tintner implying that differentiability is a necessary condition for homogeneity are misleading.

The tools used by Tintner are the following two theorems, his Theorems 5 and 6. Let the behavior of some individual be described by saying that he maximizes $g(x,x^*,x^{**})$ with respect to x and x^* subject to the restrictions, $h^{(k)}(x,x^*,x^{**}) = 0$, $(k = 1,2, \ldots , N)$. Here x, x^*, x^{**} are vectors; let x_1, $\ldots , x_p$ be the components of x.

THEOREM 5. *If the function g which is to be maximized and the side conditions $h^{(k)}$ are all either independent of the variables that are components of x^{**} or homogeneous of some arbitrary degrees in the same variables, then the solutions $x_1, \ldots , x_p$ are homogeneous of zero degree in these variables.*

THEOREM 6. *If the function g which is to be maximized and the side conditions $h^{(k)}$ are either independent of the variables that are components of x^* and x^{**} or homogeneous of some arbitrary degrees in the same variables, then the solutions $x_1, x_2, \ldots , x_p$ are homogeneous of zero degree in the variables that are components of x^{**}.*

Following Tintner, a function $f(u,u^*)$ of two vectors u, u^* is said to be homogeneous of degree K in u if $f(tu,u^*) = t^K f(u,u^*)$ for every *positive* value of t.[4] It may be observed that if f is independent of u, it is homogeneous of degree zero in u.

Theorem 5 will first be derived from Theorem 6.

Proof of Theorem 5. Let $x' = (x,x^*) = (x_1, \ldots , x_r)$, and let x'' be a vector whose components are variables not appearing in g or in any of the functions $h^{(k)}$. Under the assumption of Theorem 5, g and $h^{(k)}$ are each homogeneous of some degree in x'', x^{**}, or independent of them. Then, Theorem 6 applies, with x', x'' replacing x, x^*, respectively, so that the solutions $x_1, \ldots , x_r$, and, in particular, $x_1, \ldots , x_p$, are homogeneous of degree zero in x^{**}.

Proof of Theorem 6. Let $\hat{x}$, $\hat{x}^*$ maximize g subject to $h^{(k)} = 0$ for a given x^{**}.

---

4. Tintner, "Homogeneous Systems," p. 274. The term "positive homogeneity" is frequently used in the above sense, "homogeneity" being reserved for the case where $f(tu,u^*) = t^K f(u,u^*)$ for all t.

Then, by definition of maximum,

(1-1) $g(\hat{x}, \hat{x}^*, x^{**}) \geqq g(x, x^*, x^{**})$

for all x, x^* such that

(1-2) $h^{(k)}(x, x^*, x^{**}) = 0.$

Take any $t > 0$. Assume g homogeneous of degree K_0 in x^*, x^{**}, $h^{(k)}$ homogeneous of degree K_k in x^*, x^{**}. Multiply through both sides of (1-1) by $t^{K_0} > 0$. By the definition of homogeneity, it follows easily that

(1-3) $g(\hat{x}, t\hat{x}^*, tx^{**}) \geqq g(x, tx^*, tx^{**})$

for all x, x^* satisfying (1-2). Multiply through in (1-2) by t^{K_k}; by the definition of homogeneity, (1-2) is equivalent to

(1-4) $h^{(k)}(x, tx^*, tx^{**}) = 0.$

Therefore, (1-3) holds for all x, x^* satisfying (1-4). Replace x^* by (x^*/t) in (1-3) and (1-4); this is permissible since $t \neq 0$. We then have

(1-5) $g(\hat{x}, t\hat{x}^*, tx^{**}) \geqq g(x, x^*, tx^{**})$

for all x, x^* satisfying

(1-6) $h^{(k)}(x, x^*, tx^{**}) = 0.$

Clearly, $\hat{x}$, $t\hat{x}^*$ satisfy (1-6) so that from (1-5) and (1-6) and the definition of a constrained maximum, $\hat{x}$, $t\hat{x}^*$ maximize $g(x, x^*, tx^{**})$ subject to $h^{(k)}(x, x^*, tx^{**}) = 0$. Since $\hat{x}$ is unchanged by multiplying all the components of x^{**} by a positive constant, the solutions $x_1, \ldots, x_p$ are homogeneous of degree zero in x^{**}.

It has also been proved, incidentally, that the components of the solution x^* are homogeneous of degree one in x^{**}. Thus, in Tintner's discussion of monopoly,[5] it can be shown that the prices charged by a monopolist are homogeneous of degree one in the prices charged on atomistic markets.

Since differentiability has been shown to be irrelevant for the validity of the basic theorems on homogeneous functions, it cannot be, as Tintner states in several places, that lack of differentiability explains lack of homogeneity. In the case of the kinked demand curve in oligopoly,[6] the point seems

---

5. Ibid., pp. 284–285.
6. Ibid., p. 287.

to be that the established price must be taken as a variable distinct from price as a decision variable; since it is a datum it is to be included, along with the prices on atomistic markets, in the components of x^{**}. The analysis of oligopoly then proceeds as in Tintner's paper, so that output is homogeneous of degree zero in all the components of x^{**}; but of course, output need not be homogeneous of degree zero in the prices on atomistic markets alone.

Similarly, it cannot be that the existence of lumpiness disturbs homogeneity simply because of the lack of differentiability.[7] Mathematically, lumpiness may be represented by letting certain variables assume only integer values. The previous definitions of homogeneity do not have any meaning in this case.

---

7. Ibid., p. 294.

2 Alternative Approaches to the Theory of Choice in Risk-Taking Situations

I was invited by W. Allen Wallis, then at the University of Chicago and later president of the University of Rochester, to give a survey to a meeting of the American Statistical Association on new developments in the theory of choice under uncertainty. It was a very exciting period, in which the expected-utility theory introduced by John von Neumann and Oskar Morgenstern as part of the foundations for the theory of games (1947) was gradually becoming accepted and Leonard J. Savage was developing his theory of personal or subjective probability. It was a very useful time to make a historical survey linking the newer developments to the previous discussions in the history of probability theory, going back to Daniel Bernoulli's work of 1738. (References will be found at the end of this chapter.)

1. Introduction

There is no need to enlarge upon the importance of a realistic theory explaining how individuals choose among alternate courses of action when the consequences of their actions are incompletely known to them. It is no exaggeration to say that every choice made by human beings would meet this description if attention were paid to the ultimate implications. Risk and

Reprinted from *Econometrica,* 19 (1951):404–437. I wish to express my gratitude to J. Marschak, of the Cowles Commission for Research in Economics and the University of Chicago, and L. J. Savage, University of Chicago, for many helpful comments.

the human reactions to it have been called upon to explain everything from the purchase of chances in a "numbers" game to the capitalist structure of our economy; according to Frank Knight, even human consciousness itself would disappear in the absence of uncertainty.

I seek to survey here the present status of this theory, particularly in relation to choices in economic situations, as we ordinarily understand that term. The point of view will be that of a theory of choice, as it is usually conceived. The general picture of such a theory is the following. There is a set of conceivable actions which an individual could take, each of which leads to certain consequences. The individual has in mind an ordering of all possible consequences of actions, saying, for each pair of consequences, either that he prefers one or that he is indifferent between them; these relations of preference and indifference have the property (known as transitivity) that if consequence A is preferred to consequence B and B to C, then A is preferred to C, and similarly with indifference. In a given situation, the range of actions open to an individual is limited in some way; thus, in the theory of consumers' demand under perfect competition, the actions possible are the purchases of bundles of consumers' goods whose cost does not exceed the available income. Among the actions actually available, then, that action is chosen whose consequences are preferred to those of any other available action.[1] In the theory of consumer's choice it is not customary to differentiate between actions and their consequences, since the two stand in one-to-one correspondence; but in the static theory of the firm we do distinguish between the actions — input-output decisions — and the consequences — varying levels of money profit. In the theory of choice under risky conditions, one of the chief problems is the description of consequences which are not certain and therefore certainly not uniquely related to the actions; the distinction between the two will be carefully maintained.

The range of actions available is, in a sense, no different from that in the theory of choice under certainty, particularly if the latter includes planning for the future, as in the theory of capital. However, as A. G. Hart (1942) has shown, certain distinctions among types of actions that are important for an understanding of choice in risk-taking situations are irrelevant under certainty and have therefore been ignored. Limitations of space prevent our entering upon this subject.

There has been a steady, if slow, development in the formalization of the

---

1. It is assumed that there exists a unique maximum; the more general case of none or many could be included by an obvious reformulation.

theory of choice under uncertainty and its relation to many business phenomena. However, three developments in past decades have represented dramatic breaks in continuity and have given hopes of a much clearer understanding of the problem: (1) the axiomatic treatment of choice among probability distributions by von Neumann and Morgenstern (1947), leading to a new understanding of the rule of maximizing the expected utility (in this, however, they were anticipated by Ramsey, 1931); (2) the development of the modern theory of statistical inference, by Neyman and Pearson (1933) and Wald (1939, 1950), which is a special form of the problem of (rational) behavior under uncertainty; and (3) Shackle's new formulation of the whole problem of uncertain anticipations and actions based on them; see Shackle (1949, 1949–50). This seems, therefore, to be an especially propitious time to take stock, to compare the various new developments with each other and with the whole background of the subject.

Two methodological remarks may be made at this point. (1) The uncertainty of the consequences, which is controlling for behavior, is understood to be that existing in the mind of the chooser. Of course, such subjective uncertainty or risk may very well stem from observations on the external world; thus, the behavior of an insurance company is derived from its observations on mortalities. I do not wish to face here the question of whether or not there is any "objective" uncertainty in the economic universe, in the sense that a supremely intelligent mind knowing completely all the available data could know the future with certainty. The tangled web of the problem of human free will does not really have to be unraveled for our purpose; surely, in any case, our ignorance of the world is so much greater than the "true" limits to possible knowledge that we can disregard such metaphysical questions.

(2) Some of the theories discussed here purport to explain the actual behavior of individuals under conditions of uncertainty, some to give advice as to rational behavior, and some, by implication at least, to do both. In its broadest sense, rational behavior simply means behavior in accordance with some ordering of alternatives in terms of relative desirability, that is, a theory of choice as described above. In some situations, however, there are additional conditions which appeal to the intuition as being rational. Almost all the theories discussed here seem to be rational in the first sense, but not all in the second. In view of the general tradition of economics, which tends to regard rational behavior as a first approximation to actual, I feel justified in lumping the two classes of theory together.

The plan of this study is dictated by the above outline of the structure of a theory of choice. A comparative discussion of the various ways proposed of *describing* uncertain consequences will be followed by the different theories of how they are ordered. Preceding these discussions will be a brief outline of certain facts of common experience in economic behavior which have been regarded as being related to the existence of risk, together with a sketch of the relation between scientific and statistical inference, on the one hand, and behavior under uncertainty, on the other.

In my limited space here the coverage of the subject matter cannot be expected to be complete. Although the whole mathematical theory of probability has been, in a sense, a development of material relevant for behavior under uncertainty, the actual technical developments of recent decades have not been concerned with the principles of such behavior. Indeed, the currently prevalent axiomatic treatment of probability as a branch of measure theory (see Kolmogorov, 1950) seems designed to keep the technical development of the theory from being bogged down in the difficulties of the foundations. Also, incidental references by economists to problems of risk bearing in the course of works on other subjects have for the most part not been discussed here; and treatments before the beginning of the century have largely been omitted. Finally, of course, there are doubtless many studies even within the proper bounds, especially in foreign languages, which I have not encountered.

2. The Basic Evidence

2.1. Among economic phenomena which have in some way been tied up with the existence of uncertainty, three classes may be distinguished: (1) those which by their very definition are concerned with uncertainty; (2) those which are not related to uncertainty by definition but nevertheless have no other conceivable explanation; (3) those whose relation to uncertainty is more remote and disputable.

2.1.1. Gambling and insurance are the obvious examples of the first type. In both cases, the consequences of the action involve a mathematical expectation of loss (as compared with nonperformance of the action), yet those actions are in fact undertaken. Gambling is exemplified by preferring the small probability of a large gain and the large probability of a small loss to the certainty of an income greater than the mathematical expectation of the gamble; insurance means preferring a certain small loss to the small chance of a large loss (see Friedman and Savage, 1948, pp. 289–291). A theory of uncertainty must account for the presence of both.

Several writers have observed that the analysis of insurance just depicted is far from typical. Usually, the individual insured would have indirect losses in addition to those insured against; for example, an uninsured fire would probably entail a loss of credit rating (see Hardy, 1923, p. 57; Hart, 1951, pp. 68 – 69). Hence, it might well be that insurance is profitable, in the sense of mathematical expectation, to both parties.

One particular imaginary gamble, the St. Petersburg game, has played an important part in the history of uncertainty theory. A fair coin is tossed until a head appears; the individual is then paid 2^n ducats, where n is the number of tosses. How much should the individual pay for this gamble? It is easy to see that the mathematical expectation, $\Sigma_{n=1}^{\infty}(2^n)(1/2^n)$, is infinite, so that he "should" be willing to pay any finite stake. Introspection tells us that he will not, and this "fact" will have to be explained.

2.1.2. Among the economic phenomena of the second type are the existence of legally guaranteed incomes, variations in the rate of return on securities, and the holding of inventories beyond those demanded by pure transfer cost considerations. In a world of certainty, contractual obligations such as leases, bonds, and long-term labor contracts would have no significance, except possibly as a protection against dishonesty.

It is an obvious fact that securities and other contracts, which on their face promise the same returns, will have different market values, and these values are correlated in some sense with the risk that the contracts will not in fact be fulfilled. An extreme case is the fact that some individuals hold money, which brings no return, in preference to securities which promise some. (This phenomenon could, of course, still occur in a world of subjective certainty where individuals had differing price expectations.)

The holding of inventories is a more complicated matter since in a given firm it is usually impossible to distinguish among inventories due to indivisibilities in the cost of acquisition, unintended inventories, and inventories held for genuinely speculative motives. Only in transactions on the commodity markets do we have a relatively clear separation.

In summary, the observations just described have in common the following: they would not arise in the absence of risk, and they indicate that the reactions of individuals to a given risk situation are not all the same. Beyond that, probably little can be inferred without more definitely quantitative investigations.

2.1.3. The more recondite phenomena associated with the occurrence of risk in the minds of many economists include the existence of profits (in the "pure" sense of a residual after all factor payments including contract interest and imputed interest on the capital of the entrepreneur), the limitation on the size of the firm, and the characteristic form of the free-enterprise system.

It cannot be said that the evidence on any of these questions is at all clear. It has long been vaguely contended that "profits are the reward of risk taking," in the sense that the expectation of profits is a necessary inducement for risk bearing. However, after a long book devoted to establishing a variant of this proposition, Knight (1921, pp. 362–366) suggests that perhaps profits in aggregate are negative. While negative profits call for explanation as much as positive ones do, it cannot be said that most of the current theories would really seem to have this possibility in mind. In any case, of course, the statistical evidence on the magnitude of pure profits can only be described as negligible.

The problem of limitation of the size of the firm arises because of the argument that under perfect competition in all markets there would be no limit to the size of the firm. The restriction is found in the unwillingness of the entrepreneur to borrow so much as to risk the wiping out of his equity and in the imperfection of the capital market, due to the unwillingness of individuals to lend more than a limited amount to any one firm, again because of risk feelings (see Kalecki, 1937). The whole subject is wrapped up in the abstruse mysteries of capital theory and the coordinating function of the entrepreneur, and there is probably little point in pursuing the matter here. It is interesting to note, however, that as early as 1896 E. A. Ross argued that one of the chief motives for the *increase* in the size of the firms was the reduction in risk due to the operation of the law of large numbers (quoted by Hardy, 1923, pp. 20–21); and Irving Fisher (1906, pp. 408–409) and Knight (1921, p. 257) express similar views.

Most authors agree that many of our characteristic institutions are shaped by the existence of risk; Knight (1921, chap. 9) goes so far as to maintain that the free-enterprise system as such arises as a reaction to the existence of uncertainty. Since the phenomenon of uncertainty must certainly have preceded the capitalist era, it would still have to be shown what differences between the present and the past explain the different social organization for meeting risk. The phenomena discussed in this section are not likely, therefore, to be immediately useful in discriminating among various theories of uncertainty.

2.2. The businessman may be compared with two other types of individuals who are essentially concerned with behavior under uncertainty—the scientist and the statistician. The scientist must choose, on the basis of limited information, among the innumerable logically conceivable laws of nature, a limited number. He cannot know whether his decisions are right or wrong, and, indeed, it is none too clear what is meant by those terms. There is a long history of attempts to reduce scientific method to system, including many which introduce probability theory, but it cannot be said that any great formal success has attended these efforts. If we were to compare the businessman to the scientist, we would be forced to the melancholy conclusion that little of a systematic nature can be said about the former's decision-making processes.

The statistician typically finds himself in situations more similar to that of the businessman. The problem of statistics can be formulated roughly as follows. It is known that one out of a number of hypotheses about a given situation is true. The statistician has the choice of one of a number of different experiments (a series of experiments can be regarded as a single experiment, so that drawing a sample of any size can be included in this schema), the outcome of any one of which is a random variable with a probability distribution depending on which of the unknown hypotheses is correct. On the basis of that outcome, the statistician must take some action (accept or reject a hypothesis, estimate the mean of a distribution to be some particular value, accept or reject a lot of goods, recommend a change in production methods, and so on), the consequences of which depend on the action taken and on the hypothesis that is actually true.

Equivalently, we could describe the statistician as choosing, before performing the experiment, what experiment to perform and what action he would take for each possible outcome of the experiment. The actual action taken would be a random variable, depending on the outcome of the experiment. The consequences, therefore, of the initial decision would have a double uncertainty, depending on what outcome is observed and on which hypothesis is true. The statistician's problem is of the same general type as the businessman's, and even the information-getting aspects have their economic counterparts. The various theories which have been proposed from time to time as foundations for statistical inference are therefore closely related to theories of economic behavior under uncertainty.

3. The Description of Uncertain Consequences

With some inaccuracy, descriptions of uncertain consequences can be classified into two major categories, those which use exclusively the language of probability distributions and those which call for some other principle, either to replace or to supplement. The difference in viewpoints is related, though not perfectly, to the dispute between those who interpret probability as a measure of degree of belief (for example, Fisher or Keynes; see Sections 3.1.1, 3.2.1) and those who regard probability as a measure (objective) of relative frequency. The most careful formulations of this view stem from the work of R. von Mises (see, for example, von Mises, 1941). The latter concept clearly cannot encompass certain types of ignorance. For example, in the problem of statistical behavior (see Section 2.2), in any given situation the unknown hypothesis cannot be regarded as having a probability distribution in the frequency sense; just one hypothesis is true and all others false. Frequency theorists are therefore compelled to accept the view that probability statements cannot describe all kinds of ignorance (see Keynes, 1921, pp. 95–99). This is indeed the viewpoint that has predominated among statisticians (see Section 3.2.3).

It is understood that in economic situations the consequences about which uncertainty exists are commodity bundles or money payments over future dates. Thus, in a probability description, the consequences of an action would be described as the *joint* probability distribution of commodities received or delivered over various points in the future. For many of the general principles, the fact that the actual consequences of an action form a multidimensional random variable is irrelevant.

The principal importance of the difference between the two types of description lies in the usefulness of the data on gambling and insurance (see Section 2.1.1) for a theory of uncertainty; accepting a pure probability description means that the more easily accessible information on such genuine probability questions is relevant for the theory of business risks.

3.1. Among those who describe uncertainty by means of probability, several groups may be distinguished: (1) those who treat the probability distributions of the consequences of alternative actions as subjectively given to the individual and who do not attempt further analysis; (2) those who derive all probability judgments from a limited number of a priori probabilities; (3) those who attempt to relate the degree-of-belief and frequency theories to each other through the law of large numbers.

3.1.1. Irving Fisher's theory (1906, chap. 16 and appendix; 1930, chaps. 9 and 14) is typical of those who regard uncertainty as expressible by probability distributions. His typical example is that of a bond promising a series of interest payments and a final repayment of principal. For each time period there is a certain probability that the payment will be defaulted; in his more general analysis these probabilities are not independent, since a default of one payment usually entails the default of all subsequent payments.

In Fisher's view (1930, p. 221), probability is simply an expression of ignorance; "risk varies inversely with knowledge." In the sense that the probability of an event is always measured relative to the available evidence, this proposition would be acceptable to virtually all schools of thought. Fisher further implies, as Laplace did before him, that with sufficient knowledge there would be no probability distributions, only certainty; the truth or falsity of this statement is certainly hardly relevant to the actual economic world.

Marshall, as usual, was not very explicit on the formulation of risk situations; however, it seems clear that he fully accepted the probability description in the same manner as Fisher did (see Marshall, 1948, pp. 135 fn., 398–400, 843).

Hicks (1931), Friedman and Savage (1948), and Lange (1944) make use of the simple probability description. Their motives seem to be not so much a philosophical position as a view that the relevant phenomena can be explained by theories using only probability language, such theories being preferred on grounds of simplicity. Lange seeks somewhat more generality by supposing the individual to be able to form judgments only about the ordering of probabilities of different outcomes (this view bears some relation to that of Keynes; see Section 3.2.1 below) but not about the actual values of the probabilities. In application, however, cardinal probabilities reappear, so that Lange's attempt must be judged a failure (see Section 4.1.2).[2]

3.1.2. In the whole calculus of probabilities, there is a process of evaluating the probabilities of complex events on the basis of a knowledge of the probabilities of simpler ones. This process cannot go on indefinitely; there must be a beginning somewhere. Hence, in the study of games of chance, an a priori judgment is usually made as to certain probabilities. But in the usual types of events which occur in insurance or business affairs, there is no natural way of making these judgments; instead, the appeal is to past observations, if anything. The first systematic study of the inference of probabilities from empirical evidence was the justly famous contribution of Thomas Bayes (1763). Understand by the symbol $P(A|B)$ the probability that A is true given that B is true. Suppose that it is known that one of the mutually exclusive hypotheses $B_1, \ldots, B_n$ is true, and suppose that an

---

2. As a matter of fact, if it is assumed that probabilities of various events can be ordered, it follows easily that they can be measured by comparison with a random machine capable of producing an event B with any given known probability. I am indebted to A. G. Hart, Columbia University, for an interesting discussion of this point, and to J. Marschak for this simplification of my earlier proof.

event A has occurred. Then the probability of the hypothesis B_i on the evidence A is given by

$$P(B_i|A) = P(A|B_i)P(B_i)/\left[\sum_{i=1}^{n} P(A|B_i)P(B_i)\right].$$

The a posteriori probabilities $P(B_i|A)$ then depend on the a priori probabilities $P(B_i)$ of the various hypotheses and on the probabilities $P(A|B_i)$ of the occurrence of the observed event A under the various hypotheses. (The latter probabilities are sometimes referred to as the *likelihoods* of the various hypotheses given A.)[3]

Bayes's theorem shows clearly how a new piece of information, such as a price quotation or sales figures for a month, will modify the previous judgments as to the uncertainties of a situation. In a given context, the a priori probabilities are the judgments of the relative uncertainty of various hypotheses made on the basis of all past information; the a posteriori probabilities are the judgments made with the aid of new information.

The general problem of behavior under uncertainty can be formulated in this language as follows. Suppose there are m possible mutually exclusive events $C_1, \ldots, C_m$, one of which will occur in the future. (An event might be an entire income stream over several future time points.) The probabilities of these events depend in a known way upon which of the hypotheses $B_1, \ldots, B_n$ is true; that is, $P(C_j|B_i)$ varies with i for each given j. Finally, we have an a priori probability distribution for the hypotheses, $P(B_i)$ ($i = 1, \ldots, n$). This is the formulation used by Tintner (1941a and b, 1942a and b) and Hart (1942).[4]

3.1.3. How are the a priori probabilities appropriate to the above formulation obtained? In any particular context, of course, the a priori probabilities are the a posteriori probabilities of the preceding time period. But this process must have a start somewhere. At this point, the Principle of Insufficient Reason has been called into play. First formulated by Jacob Bernoulli in the seventeenth century, it states that if there is no evidence leading us to believe that one of an exhaustive set of mutually exclusive events is more likely to occur than another, then the events should be judged equally

---

3. Here, and in most of the discussion, it will be assumed that the number of alternative possible events or hypotheses is finite. Most of the principles can be illustrated without considering the case of infinite sets of alternative events.

4. However, the basic point of Hart's work is largely independent of this particular description.

probable. Thus Bayes, in applying his theorem, postulated that in the absence of further knowledge the hypotheses B_i ($i = 1, \ldots, n$) could be judged equally probable, and therefore $P(B_i) = 1/n$ for each i.[5] It follows then that the a posteriori probabilities are proportional to the likelihoods of the various hypotheses.

According to Keynes (1921, chap. 4), the contradictions flowing from this principle were first pointed out by J. von Kries (1886). Suppose we have a coin with completely unknown bias, and two tosses are made. In our assumed ignorance, we have no evidence for or against the hypothesis that the event of two heads will occur, and we must therefore assign it probability one-half, since the probability of the hypothesis equals the probability of its contradictory. But similarly, the probabilities of a head followed by a tail, a tail followed by a head, and two successive tails would each be one-half. This is impossible, since the events are exclusive and their probabilities cannot therefore add up to more than one.

Keynes proposed to resolve these contradictions by restricting the application of the principle to the case where each of the events considered is incapable of further analysis. More precisely, an event A is said to be divisible if there are two exclusive events, A_1 and A_2, of the same "form" as A such that A occurs if and only if one of A_1, A_2 occurs; then the Principle of Insufficient Reason is applied only to a set of indivisible events. By the term "the same form" is probably meant "describable using the same language."[6]

It is hard to judge how satisfactory this theory is. It does avoid the paradox previously mentioned; however, it makes probability judgments depend on the form of the language, which may or may not be regarded as an objection. From a technical point of view, a greater deficiency is its failure to avoid the corresponding paradoxes which arise when there is a continuum of events rather than a finite number to consider.[7]

---

5. Bayes himself seems to have had his doubts about this postulate, and indeed the paper was not published until after his death.

6. Carnap (1950) advanced a new formulation of the theory of probability as a rational degree of belief. As in Keynes's work the assignment of a priori probabilities depends on consideration of indivisible events; however, the method preferred by Carnap (1950, pp. 562–577) does not give them equal probability. An excellent account of Carnap's theories, with applications to statistical problems, is given by Tintner (1949).

7. Keynes's full theory of the description of uncertainty is, I believe, to be more properly classed with those which hold that probability statements alone are insufficient (see Section 3.2.1).

Keynes's form of the Principle of Insufficient Reason leads to a different judgment of a priori probabilities in applications of Bayes's theorem than that usually made. Consider, for example, a finite population of n elements and let m be the unknown number of them with some quality

3.1.4. Brief mention may be made here of another development of the concept of a priori probabilities. In this version the fundamental description of uncertainty is couched in terms involving other than probability statements (actually, along lines similar to those used by Neyman, Pearson, and Wald; see Section 3.2.3), but certain postulates are placed on the behavior of individuals under those conditions, and it is shown that they then act as if there were an a priori distribution of probabilities. Discussion of this viewpoint properly belongs with theories of ordering uncertain consequences and will be deferred until these are taken up; see Section 4.2.3.

3.1.5. Finally, mention must be made of a group which seeks to relate empirical observations to probability judgments via the law of large numbers. In its simplest form, due to Jacob Bernoulli, the law states that in a sequence of *independent* trials in each of which a given event E may occur with a constant probability p, the probability that the relative frequency of occurrence of E in n trials differs from p by more than any assigned positive quantity can be made as small as desired by making n sufficiently large. It is still true, of course, that in any finite number of trials, no matter how large, we cannot with certainty identify relative frequency with true probability. However, Buffon (quoted in Menger, 1934, p. 471n) and Cournot (see Fréchet, 1948, p. 62) have suggested as a general principle that events whose probability is sufficiently small are to be regarded as morally impossible. Hence, in a sufficiently long series of trials, relative frequencies could be equated to probabilities. This theory therefore tends to lead to the same conclusions as the frequency theory.

The principle of neglect of small probabilities was used by Buffon to resolve the St. Petersburg problem (see Section 2.1.1). The probability that a head will not appear until the nth toss becomes very small for n sufficiently large; if the occurrence of that event is regarded as impossible for all n beyond a certain value, then the mathematical expectation of return becomes finite, and the paradox is resolved.

This principle seems extremely arbitrary in its specification of a particular critical probability and also runs into much the same difficulties of classification as does the Principle of Insufficient Reason. In an extreme case,

---

A; m may be any value from 0 to n. The usual treatment of this problem by Bayes's theorem would be to set the a priori probability of each value of m equal to $1/(n + 1)$. Keynes's assumptions, however, would imply that m has a binomial distribution based on $p = \frac{1}{2}$. Carnap (1950, p. 565) points out that Keynes's rule has a very undesirable consequence: after drawing any sample without replacement from a finite population (short of the whole population), the a posteriori probability that the next observation has the quality A is one-half regardless of the sample observed. Carnap's rule avoids this difficulty.

suppose that we find an exhaustive set of mutually exclusive indivisible events, each of which has a probability less than the critical value. It would be contradictory to say that all of them were impossible, since one must occur. This case actually occurs when a continuous random variable is considered.

The application of the neglect of small probabilities to Bernoulli's theorem also requires a knowledge that successive trials are independent, itself an a priori probability judgment. Hence, the principle does not supply a sufficient basis for probability reasoning.

3.1.6. The neglect of small probabilities is related to another question which has agitated the more philosophically minded. Even if we describe uncertainty by probabilities, what significance do they have for conduct if the event occurs only once? Both Knight (1921, p. 234) and Shackle (1949–50, p. 71) argue that if the individual does not have the ability to repeat the experiment indefinitely often, the probabilities, being essentially long-run frequency ratios, are irrelevant to his conduct.

This argument would obviously have no validity in the degree-of-belief theory of probability. It is more serious in the frequency theory. It has sometimes been argued that even if an individual does not have the opportunity to repeat that particular experiment, he can nevertheless expect stability through the operation of a generalized Bernoulli's theorem in which the chance fluctuations in one trial are offset by those in others. This last argument is not entirely valid. In any one person's life the number of trials he can perform is finite; unless the neglect of small probabilities is invoked, the effect of a finite number of trials is, in principle, the same as one trial, the only difference being the quantitative one that the probability distributions are apt to be much more concentrated. Further, as Shackle has argued, in such a situation as a large investment, the number of comparable events in an individual's life is likely to be very small by anybody's standards.

While it may seem hard to give a justification for using probability statements when the event occurs only once, except on the interpretation of probability as degree-of-belief, the contrary position also seems difficult to defend. If an individual were told to predict whether or not two heads would come up in successive throws of a fair coin and further informed that he would lose his life if he guessed wrong, I find it very hard to believe that he would disregard the evidence of the calculus of probability. As is seen in Section 4.1.3, an extension of this reasoning suggests that in almost any reasonable view of probability theory the probability of a single event must still be the basis of action where there are genuine probabilities.

3.2. A number of writers maintain either that not all risky situations can properly be described by probability statements or that the latter do not provide a complete description.

3.2.1. Keynes, although an advocate of a degree-of-belief theory of probability (see Section 3.1.3), differs in certain ways from the various schools discussed in Section 3.1. Probability is for him, as for most others, a relation between the evidence and the event considered; but it is not necessarily measurable. He does not even consider that in general it is possible to order the probabilities of different events. It is true that every probability is considered to belong to some ordered sequence of probabilities, but they do not all belong to the same sequence.[8] The view that probabilities are not necessarily measurable seems to have some relation to Knight's distinction between measurable risks and unmeasurable uncertainties (see Section 3.2.2), and indeed they arise because Keynes is anxious to describe all uncertainties as probabilities. The actual effect of this extension of the probability concept is not clear since no applications are made.

Keynes, however, evidently does not regard the probability description as complete. He suggests, though tentatively, that in addition we must consider the *weight* of the evidence relative to which the probability is formed. Weight has the property that it increases with the evidence available, though it is not necessarily measurable. In Keynes's theory, then, uncertainty has the two dimensions, probability and weight, neither of which need be measurable. It is to be noted that weight is not necessarily related to the dispersion of a distribution; thus, in applications of Bayes's theorem, the a posteriori distribution of a numerical variable may have a larger standard deviation than the a priori, though the former must certainly have a greater weight. In ordinary problems of statistical inference from random samples, however, increase in weight and decrease in variance generally accompany each other (see Keynes, 1921, chap. 6).

3.2.2. Knight (1921, chap. 7) denies that all types of risks can be described by probability statements. His views stem from a functional view of uncertainty in relation to the problem-solving methods of the human mind. Because of the difficulties of reasoning, it is necessary for the mind to simplify matters by grouping cases. The relations between events derived from such an analysis will usually be uncertain rather than invariant. Some of these, of course, can be described by probability statements, which Knight

---

8. See Keynes (1921, chap. 3). Since the particular ordered sequences of probabilities need not be continuous, the argument given in note 2 cannot be applied here to establish a measurable probability.

classifies in the customary way as a priori and statistical; the two differ in the degree of homogeneity of the grouping. The classification upon which a statistical probability is based is partly empirical. Although Knight's analysis is so lacking in formal clarity that it is difficult to be sure, he appears to derive statistical probabilities from experience with the aid of the a priori in the manner of Bayes's theorem.[9]

Sharply distinguished from both a priori and statistical probabilities are true uncertainties or estimates. These arise when there is no valid basis for classification and are usually applied to situations which are in some sense unique. In such cases, according to Knight, the habit of the mind is not only to form an estimate of the situation but also to make a judgment as to its reliability, also on an intuitive basis.

No formal method of describing uncertainties or estimates is given by Knight, but some of their properties are discussed. He states that the estimates are generally based on some classification either of objective circumstances or, more often, of ability of individuals to judge or of subjective confidence in one's own judgment. Later he refers to "probable" or "improbable" outcomes of events about which uncertainty judgments have been made and argues that there is some tendency for the degree of uncertainty to be reducible by consolidation of many cases, analogously to the law of large numbers (see Knight, 1921, chap. 8). In brief, Knight's uncertainties seem to have surprisingly many of the properties of ordinary probabilities, and it is not clear how much is gained by the distinction.

Knight appears to be worried about the seemingly mechanical nature of the probability calculus and its consequent failure to reflect the tentative, creative nature of the human mind in the face of the unknown. In a fundamental sense, this is probably correct, though it seems to lead only to the conclusion that no theory can be formulated for this case, at least not of the type of theory of choice discussed here (see the discussion of the scientist in Section 2.2; see also Section 4.3). The remark that estimates differ from statistical probabilities in that no valid principles of classification exist for the former may lead in a more definite direction; it might be interpreted to mean that the a priori probabilities needed for Bayes's theorem are unknown. If this is correct, Knight's concept of uncertainty leads into the statistical theories discussed in the next section; and it should be noted that

---

9. "It must be emphasized that any high degree of confidence that the proportions found in the past will hold in the future is still based on an a priori judgment of indeterminateness" (Knight, 1921, p. 225)

these theories seek to represent at least part of the knowledge-seeking propensities of human beings.

3.2.3. Hardy (1923, pp. 46, 53–55) suggested that Knight's case of uncertainty really belongs with statistical methods, though, of course, actual business judgments are apt to be biased. He therefore held that Knight's distinction was not a sharp one and, further, that the possibility of a more definite theory than Knight allowed existed. At the time Hardy wrote, the foundations of statistical inference had been discussed chiefly in terms of inverse probability (Bayes's theorem), so it is not clear what he had in mind. However, contemporaneously with Hardy, R. A. Fisher (1922) was arguing that statistical inference required new principles not contained in the classical theory of probability. More recently there has been a formulation of the statistical problem due to Neyman and Pearson and modified by Wald (see Neyman and Pearson, 1933; Wald, 1939, 1950, sec. 1.1). In the description of the statistical problem given in Section 2.2, the set of possible hypotheses is assumed known, but there are no judgments of a probability nature or otherwise which discriminate among the possible hypotheses in the range as to their truth. Thus, in an economic context, in the simplest case, there may be two possible hypotheses, of which it is known that one is true. For each action, then, we can associate an *income function* specifying for each possible true hypothesis what the consequences will be of that action. The problem is then to choose among the income functions. In a more general case, the income arising from a given action under a given hypothesis may itself be a random variable with a probability distribution specified by the hypothesis. The problem is then to choose among these possibly random income functions.

In this description there are two types of uncertainty: one as to the hypothesis, which is expressed by saying that the hypothesis is known to belong to a certain class or *model,* and one as to the future events or observations given the hypothesis, which is expressed by a probability distribution. If the model contains just one hypothesis, the uncertainty would be completely expressed by a probability distribution; if each hypothesis is a certainty, in the sense that given the hypothesis the future event is no longer uncertain, then the uncertainty is expressed by saying that the future event is one of a certain class without further information. It is to be noted that the Neyman-Pearson description does not eliminate all a priori elements, since the model must still be chosen.[10] However, it does involve the

---

10. It is possible to use as a model the class of *all* logically possible hypotheses; but only meager statistical inferences could be drawn in that case.

elimination of a priori probabilities. It is also to be noted that, unlike Knight, Neyman and Pearson do not consider the uncertainties of the nonprobability type to be eliminable in any way by consolidation. If one model says that any income can be received from 0 to a and another, concerning an independent event, says that any income from 0 to b is possible, then the two models together say only that any income from 0 to $a + b$ is possible.[11]

3.2.4. Shackle's formulation of uncertainty starts from a rejection of all probability elements, at least as applied to "large" decisions (see Shackle, 1949, pp. 6–7, chap. 7). He rejects the degree-of-belief theory of probability, since a distribution can never be verified even ex post, while the frequency theory is inapplicable where indefinite repetition is impossible (see Section 3.1.6). His own theory is a generalization of the Neyman-Pearson formulation in the case where the hypotheses determine the future events uniquely rather than via a probability distribution (see Shackle, 1949, pp. 10–17, 43–58, 128–133). Neyman and Pearson divide hypotheses into two categories, possible and impossible; Shackle permits a continuous gradation from one case to another. To each possible future event he assigns a degree of *potential surprise,* the extent to which the individual would be surprised if the event occurred. Potential surprise is an ordinal concept;[12] the alternative possibilities are arranged on a scale from a minimum possible degree of potential surprise, such as might attach to a tautology, to a maximum, which is assigned to events deemed impossible.

Analogously to probability theory, rules are established for combining potential surprises; but the rules are of a nonadditive nature. Let $\eta(E)$ be the potential surprise of event E, and $E_1 \cup E_2$ be the occurrence of one or another of E_1 and E_2. Then if E_1 and E_2 are mutually exclusive events, $\eta(E_1 \cup E_2)$ is equal to the smaller of $\eta(E_1)$ and $\eta(E_2)$; this proposition corresponds to the addition rule of probabilities. Further, let $\eta(E|F)$ be the potential surprise of E given that F has occurred, and let $E \cap F$ be the occurrence of both E and F. Then, analogous to the multiplication rule for compound probabilities, it is assumed that $\eta(E \cap F)$ is the larger of $\eta(E|F)$ and $\eta(F)$. It would be natural to say that E is independent of F if $\eta(E|F) = \eta(E)$; for such events, $\eta(E \cap F)$ is the larger of $\eta(E)$, $\eta(F)$. This shows that in Shackle's system, as in the Neyman-Pearson theory, there is no

---

11. The importance of the Neyman-Pearson-Wald description for economic behavior has been chiefly stressed by Marschak (1938, pp. 323–324; 1946, pp. 108–110; 1949, pp. 183–184, 192–195).

12. At some points Shackle implies that degrees of potential surprise are measurable and even interpersonally comparable, but his whole theory can be developed without any such assumption.

law of large numbers or elimination of risks by consolidation of independent events, for the potential surprise attached to a sequence of unfavorable outcomes is as large as to any one.

This last point shows that the elimination of all probability elements from Shackle's theory cannot be regarded as satisfactory. Since, in a single event, a probability distribution is irrelevant according to Shackle (see Section 3.1.6), the situation is described by a potential surprise function. But then no amount of repetition in independent trials would lead to reduction of risks, whereas even Shackle concedes that in long runs probability rules would be applicable. In other words, Shackle's theory does not lead, even in the limit, to the probability theory.[13]

This argument can be given another form by means of an example. Consider the event of a fair coin's coming up heads twice. It certainly seems reasonable to assert that the potential surprise of this event must be greater than that of its not occurring. On the other hand, the potential surprise of a head on any given toss would be the minimum possible.[14] Under the assumption of independence of successive tosses, the potential surprise of two or any number of successive heads would be the same as of one, that is, the minimum possible.

It would seem more reasonable, though this is not Shackle's view, to consider his concept of potential surprise as a straightforward generalization of the Neyman-Pearson theory; that is, to attach the potential surprise to the hypotheses which define the probability distributions of future events. In that case, the Neyman-Pearson theory would appear as the special case where all potential surprises are either the maximum possible or the minimum possible.

4. The Ordering of the Consequences

After having described uncertain consequences in some manner or another, it is necessary to set up a theory which will discuss the way in which an individual orders these consequences. Some theories say little more than that the consequences are orderable in some fashion; others make more

---

13. Some of the observations here and in Section 4.2.4 concerning Shackle's views have already been made by Graaf and Baumol in their excellent review article (1949).

14. Let A be the event of a head, $\overline{A}$ a tail, and, following Shackle, let 0 be the minimum possible degree of potential surprise. Since $A \cup \overline{A}$ is a tautology, $\eta(A \cup \overline{A}) = 0$; since A and $\overline{A}$ are mutually exclusive, $\min[\eta(A), \eta(\overline{A})] = 0$. Since there are no grounds for preferring one of them to another, $\eta(A) = \eta(\overline{A}) = 0$.

definite assertions. The theory of preference among possible uncertainty situations will, of course, depend on the mode of description adopted.

4.1. Among those who describe uncertainties in terms of probability distributions, several theories of conduct have successively held the stage: the concept of maximizing the expected utility, the maximization of more general functionals, the Ramsey–von Neumann–Morgenstern revival and reinterpretation of expected utility, and a new stage, also originating with Ramsey, in which a priori probabilities are derived from behavior postulates. Except for the last group, all writers consider the case where the probabilities themselves are known directly.

4.1.1. As a solution of the St. Petersburg game (see Section 2.1.1), Daniel Bernoulli (1738) advanced the proposition that the utility of a sum of money was proportional to its logarithm or at least that the marginal utility of money was decreasing. It followed that the mathematical expectation of utility (rather than of money) in the game was finite, so that the individual would be willing to pay only a finite stake.

With the development of the utility theory of value in the 1870s, Bernoulli's proposal was found to fit in very well, especially in view of the common assumption of a diminishing marginal utility of income. Marshall (1948, pp. 398–400) ascribes the risk aversion he observes in business to this cause. However, Marshall also notes (1948, pp. 135n., 843) that under this hypothesis, gambling must be regarded as an economic loss. The practice of gambling then could only be explained by other considerations, such as the excitement derived therefrom. Menger (1934, pp. 479–480) argued that this showed that the Bernoulli theory was an insufficient resolution of the paradox.

Menger gave a further argument against the Bernoulli theory. Let $U(x)$ be the utility derived from a given amount of money x, and suppose that $U(x)$ increases indefinitely as x increases (for example, if $U(x) = \log x$, as in Bernoulli's own theory). Then, for every integer n, there is an amount of money x_n such that $U(x_n) = 2^n$. Consider the modified St. Petersburg game in which the payment when a head occurs for the first time on the nth toss is x_n. Then, clearly, the expected utility will be the same as the expected money payment in the original formulation and is therefore infinite. Hence, the player would be willing to pay any finite amount of money for the privilege of playing the game.[15] This is rejected as contrary to intuition.

---

15. Menger (1934, pp. 464–469). The resolution of the St. Petersburg paradox by means of a bounded utility function was first proposed by the eighteenth-century mathematician Cramer in a letter printed in D. Bernoulli's original paper (see Bernoulli, 1738, pp. 57–58).

4.1.2. Though the preceding argument would suggest that requiring the utility function to be bounded would overcome the paradox, Menger argues that in fact the discrepancy between actual behavior and that based on the mathematical expectation of return is explained not solely by undervaluation of large returns (through diminishing marginal utility) but also through undervaluation of small probabilities (a generalization of the neglect of small probabilities discussed in Section 3.1.5). He finally concludes that the ordering of different probability distributions (in the sense of the amount that an individual would be willing to pay for the various chances) depends on the diminishing marginal utility of money, the ratio of the initial size of his fortune to the minimum subsistence level in comparison with the chances of gain, and the systematic undervaluation of both very large and very small probabilities (and consequent overvaluation of medium probabilities).

A natural generalization of Menger's viewpoint is to consider simply that there is some ordering of probability distributions. If desired, this can be accomplished by assigning to each probability distribution a number representing its desirability. Such an assignment of numbers may be termed a *risk preference functional,* to use a term of Tintner's;[16] it is analogous to the assignment of numbers to commodity bundles in order of their desirability, which we call a utility function.

Tintner seems to have been the first to use this formal description, but the general idea goes back at least to Irving Fisher.[17] He argued that the value of a security will tend to depend on the probabilities of repayment. Usually, though not always, an uncertain income will be valued at less than its mathematical expectation. This risk aversion leads to devices for reducing the burden. The existence of guaranteed incomes such as bonds, as contrasted with stocks, is a device for reducing the risks for those guaranteed. Such devices do not reduce total risks but rather redistribute them; they come into being because different individuals have different risk aversions. Measures which serve to reduce total risk are inventory holding, increase of knowledge, and insurance and speculation. Insurance is applicable only when the risks can be reduced to a statistical basis; otherwise it is the

---

16. See Tintner (1941a and b, 1942a and b). The term "functional" is used because the measures of desirability are assigned to whole probability distributions rather than to variables in the ordinary sense.

17. I. Fisher (1906, chap. 16 and appendix to chap. 16). The discussion of Pigou (1924, appendix I) is similar, though he puts it by saying that uncertainty bearing is a factor of production, a form of wording that is, at best, a confusing figure of speech.

function of speculators to assume the risk. This specialization is a social gain, both because speculators normally have greater knowledge of the uncertainties than the average individual and because of the operation of the law of large numbers. However, if the speculators' forecasts tend to be interdependent, this law, which depends on the independence of the random events consolidated, may be inoperative and the situation may actually be worse than without speculation.

In considering incomes which may assume a wide range of values, such as dividends, Fisher suggested that the purchaser would consider the expected value and the standard deviation of possible incomes as derived from his subjective probability distributions. Fisher himself seems to have had in mind the situation where the probability distributions are normal, in which case, of course, knowing the mean and standard deviation amounts to knowing the entire distribution. However, the idea that the desirability of a probability distribution may depend solely on a limited number of parameters and not on the whole probability distribution became widely held, at least as a first approximation (see Marschak, 1950, pp. 118–119). Thus Hicks (1934) uses the mean and standard deviation, though his earlier discussion of uncertainty used only a generalized ordering of the probability distributions (see Hicks, 1931); the utility of a distribution increased with its mean and decreased as the standard deviation increased. In connection with the theory of insurance, Cramér suggested the probability that income will fall below some critical level as the criterion for ordering (see Cramér, 1930, pt. 3, as cited by Marschak, 1950, p. 120); the higher this probability, the less desirable the distribution. Domar and Musgrave (1944) suggested that the utility of a distribution depends on its *risk* and its *yield,* defined as follows: if $x_1, \ldots, x_n$ are the possible incomes with probabilities $p_1, \ldots, p_n$, respectively, with $x_1, \ldots, x_m$ negative and $x_{m+1}, \ldots, x_n$ positive, then the risk is $\Sigma_{i=1}^{n} p_i x_i$, while the yield is $\Sigma_{i=m+1}^{n} p_i x_i$. Lange (1944, chap. 6), in accordance with his general principle of avoiding measurable probabilities (see Section 3.1.1), suggests the mode and the range, utility increasing with the first and decreasing with the second. However, he shortly agrees that it is the "practical" range that is really relevant; this may be defined as the interval between the fifth and ninety-fifth percentiles of the distribution (or any other similar pair of percentiles). Such a definition, of course, depends on measurable probability. Marschak (1938, pp. 320–325) also suggested the use of the mean and variance as a first approximation, though other parameters, such as the skewness, are also considered to be relevant. Finally, Keynes (1921, chap. 25) also thought that conduct should be guided not only by the expectation of utility but also by some measure of risk; in accordance with his views on the description of uncertainties (see Section 3.2.1), he also regarded the weight of the evidence on which the probability distribution is based as still another variable in determining the utility of a given uncertainty situation.

4.1.3. The underlying intuitions which led to the rejection of the Bernoulli theory of maximizing expected utility stemmed from regarding utility as some objectively measurable quality in goods. It therefore seemed reasonable to say that not only the mean but also the dispersion of the possible utilities was relevant. This argument, however, was undermined by the rise of the indifference-curve view of utility, due to Pareto, where utility ceased to have any objective significance and in particular diminishing marginal utility had lost its meaning (see Friedman and Savage, 1948, pp. 280–281). The immediate effect of this development on the theory of risk was, as is natural, to actually hasten the trend toward a general ordinal theory of risk bearing. But it was first observed by Ramsey (1931)[18] that, by starting from an ordinal theory of risk bearing and adding a few reasonable assumptions, one could derive a utility function such that the individual could be said to behave in such a way as to maximize the expected value of his utility.

Ramsey's work was none too clear and attracted little attention. It remained for von Neumann and Morgenstern (1947, appendix) to enunciate a clear set of axioms on choice among probability distributions which led to the assumption of maximizing expected utility and which were convincing. Subsequently Marschak (1950) gave a simplified treatment, which will be followed here.

The key point turns out to be that no matter how complicated the structure of a game of chance is, we can always describe it by a single probability distribution of the final outcomes. Thus, suppose there are two gambling machines, one of which yields outcomes x_1 and x_2 with probabilities p and $1 - p$, respectively, while the second yields outcomes x_3 and x_4 with probabilities q and $1 - q$, respectively. Suppose now the choice of which machine is to be played is made by a preliminary gamble, in which machine 1 will be selected with probability r and machine 2 with probability $1 - r$. Then, of course, we have a complicated game with four possible outcomes x_1, x_2, x_3, x_4, with probabilities rp, $r(1 - p)$, $(1 - r)q$, $(1 - r)(1 - q)$, respectively. It obviously should make no difference for conduct, at least for the rational individual, whether he is told that he is playing the

---

18. I am indebted for this reference to N. C. Dalkey, RAND Corporation.

two-stage game or a single-stage game with the probabilities just described.

Suppose, for convenience, that the total number of possible outcomes is finite, say n in number. Then, denote by $p = p_1, \ldots, p_n$ a probability distribution where p_i is the probability of the ith possible outcome; $p_i \geqq 0$ for each i, $\Sigma_{i=1}^{n} p_i = 1$. If p and q are two probability distributions and a a real number with $0 \leqq a \leqq 1$, then by $ap + (1 - a)q$ we shall mean the distribution in which the probability of the ith outcome is $ap_i + (1 - a)q_i$. From the preceding paragraph it is easily seen that, from the viewpoint of behavior, the risk situation described by the distribution $ap + (1 - a)q$ is the same as that of the two-stage game in which a choice is made between the distributions p and q by means of a random device which chooses the first with probability a and the second with probability $1 - a$. We will refer to such a distribution as a *mixture* of p and q.

Von Neumann and Morgenstern start with the general principle that probability distributions are ordered. However, it is argued that the above considerations on the structure of probability distributions suggest certain further reasonable postulates on the choice among probability distributions. For example, since a mixture of p and q may be regarded as a game in which one of those two distributions is chosen by chance, the desirability of such a mixture should lie between that of p and that of q. It is natural, therefore, to assume, as Marschak does, that if p is preferred to q and q to r, then there is some mixture of p and r which is just indifferent to q. Further, suppose that p is indifferent to q. Then it is reasonable to assume that a mixture $ap + (1 - a)r$ with any other distribution r is indifferent to the same mixture of q with r, $aq + (1 - a)r$. For, in the two-stage game, we have in one case a probability a of getting p and $1 - a$ of getting r; in the other, a probability a of getting q and $1 - a$ of getting r. Since it makes no difference to the individual whether he receives p or q, by assumption, it seems reasonable to hold that the individual would be indifferent to the two gambles.

From these very reasonable assumptions,[19] a remarkable theorem follows: There is a method of assigning utilities to the individual outcomes so that the utility assigned to any probability distribution is the expected value under that distribution of the utility of the outcome. The numbers assigned are said to be utilities because they are in the same order as the desirability of the distribution or outcome (desirability itself being merely an ordinal

---

19. Actually, these assumptions are not quite adequate. An additional one which would enable the theorem to be proved is, for example, that there are at least four probability distributions, no two of which are indifferent (or all are indifferent).

concept). The method of assigning utilities, furthermore, is unique up to a linear transformation.

A few remarks may be made about this result. First, the utilities assigned are not in any sense to be interpreted as some intrinsic amount of good in the outcome (which is a meaningless concept in any case). Therefore, all the intuitive feelings which led to the assumption of diminishing marginal utility are irrelevant, and we are free to assume that marginal utility is increasing, so that the existence of gambling can be explained within the theory. Second, the behavior postulates appear to be reasonable even under the frequency or any other definition of probability. The von Neumann–Morgenstern theorem then leads to the conclusion that the probability distribution is relevant even when only one event is to be observed; that is, any definitin of probability leads to a degree-of-belief interpretation. The objections, therefore, to the use of the probability concept in the absence of indefinite repetition seem to fall to the ground (see Section 3.1.6).

Some of the literature on the ordinal theory of risk bearing can be interpreted within the present framework. Menger's objection to the Bernoulli theory in the case of unbounded utility functions (see Section 4.1.1) can be reformulated as follows: If the utility function is unbounded, then there is a probability distribution with infinite utility. If, as seems natural, we demand that all utilities be finite,[20] then Menger's argument leads to the conclusion that no utility should exceed some fixed upper bound.

The characterization of probability distributions by mean and variance would be valid, at least in a special case, under the present theory if the utility function of income were quadratic; in that case the utility of a probability distribution would be the same quadratic function of the mean plus a term proportional to the variance. Finally, the rule of minimizing the probability that the income falls below some critical level would be a special case of the von Neumann–Morgenstern theory where the utility was 0 for all incomes below the critical level and 1 for all incomes above it.

Friedman and Savage (1948) have used the von Neumann–Morgenstern construction to arrive at some information about the utility function for income. Members of lower-income groups both take out insurance and gamble. Insurance is rational if the utility function has a decreasing deriva-

---

20. Pascal, of course, considered the hope of heaven to be of infinite value compared with any earthly reward. But I doubt that he would have regarded any version of the St. Petersburg game as entitled to such a special place.

tive over the interval between the two incomes possible (decreasing on the average but not necessarily everywhere), while gambling is rational if the utility has a predominantly increasing derivative over the interval between the possible incomes. In view of the structure of gambles and insurance (see Section 2.1.1), this requires that the utility function have an initial segment where marginal utility is decreasing, followed by a segment where it is increasing. The fact that lotteries generally have several prizes instead of one grand prize equal to the sum indicates that the willingness to gamble does not rise indefinitely; therefore, there must be a final segment of high incomes in which marginal utility decreases again.

These results were anticipated in part by L. Törnqvist (1945). Arguing from the fact that some lottery tickets will be unsold and therefore the lottery owner is also running a risk, it follows that the utility function must be such as to explain the behavior of both lottery buyers and sellers. He suggests on this basis the following as a utility function for income:

$$U(x) = x\{1 + k[x/(K + x)]^2\},$$

where k and K are constants, and where there is diminishing marginal utility for small values of x and increasing marginal utility for other values.

4.2. We may now turn to the theories of behavior under uncertainty held by those who do use other than probability statements in their description. I will include in this group, for convenience, those who use a priori probabilities not as a fundamental assumption but as a derivation from postulates on behavior (see Sections 3.1.4 and 4.2.3).

4.2.1. As already indicated (see Section 3.2.2), Knight has not given a formal description of uncertainty situations in his sense (as opposed to risks or probability distributions) and correspondingly has given no definite set of assumptions concerning their ordering. Actually, his uncertainties produce about the same reactions in individuals as other writers ascribe to risks. For example, the list of devices which are used to reduce uncertainty is about the same as that given by Irving Fisher when starting from a strictly probability point of view (see Knight, 1921, chap. 8).

There is, however, one analytic point of considerable interest in Knight's theory. He asserts as a basic theorem that if all risks were measurable, then risk aversion would not give rise to any profit (see Knight, 1921, pp. 46–47). The argument is that, in that case, the law of large numbers would permit the wiping out of all risks through insurance or some other form of consolidation of cases. This proposition, if true, would appear to be of the greatest importance; yet, surprisingly enough, not a single writer, as far as I know, with the exception of Hicks (1931), has mentioned it, and he denies its validity.

Knight's argument does not seem to be a rigorous proof by even a generous stretch of the imagination. His proposition, of course, depends not only on the behavior of individuals in risk-taking situations but also on the workings of the economic system as a whole and the way in which random events, such as technological uncertainty, enter. Knight gives no indication of how such a fundamental concept as constant returns would appear under uncertainty, though he is most meticulous in his corresponding discussions under certainty.

Some indications of what might happen are contained in a paper by C. Palm (1947; discussed in Feller, 1950, pp. 379–383). Palm considers the case of a number of automatic machines which need tending only when out of commission, an event which is supposed to occur in a random manner. The time needed for repair is also a random variable. Palm then calculates the probability distribution of the length of time the machines are operating for a given number of machines and a given number of repairmen. (The conditions of the problem are that when all the repairmen are busy, any machine which then breaks down must remain idle until one of the men finishes repairing the machine he is working on.) It is shown that the expected amount of operating time would more than double if both men and machines were doubled. This suggests that under conditions most favorable to Knight's assertion, that is, independent technological risks, there would be a universal tendency toward increasing returns, which would be incompatible with his basic assumption of perfect competition.

A somewhat more obvious criticism of Knight's result is the argument that in fact the risks occurring are mutually correlated, so that the law of large numbers may not operate. This point was already made by Irving Fisher (see Section 4.1.2) and was used by Hicks (1931, pp. 175, 188) as a criticism of Knight's proposition. Hicks also observed that contractual guarantees can never constitute a complete shifting of risks, since there is always some risk of default (see Hicks, 1931, p. 178).

Finally, it may be observed that even if Knight's proposition were true, the use he makes of it would not be justified. He argues that this proposition, in conjunction with the existence of profits, shows that there must be other types of uncertainty. But, of course, the consolidation of risks would not proceed to the limit if there were a predominance of risk-preferring attitudes,[21] and we would have on the aggregate negative profits (though by chance individual firms would have positive profits). Since Knight concludes by suggesting that aggregate profits are in fact negative (see Section 2.1.3), he argues that there must be some preference for uncertainty bearing in his sense; but there seems to be no reason why he could not have used the simpler theory of postulating risk preference in regard to probability distributions and dispensed with the distinction between the two types of uncertainty.

4.2.2. Neyman and Pearson did not have a unique principle for choosing among actions under their formulation of uncertainty (see Section 3.2.3). We may consider as a typical illustration their discussion of behavior when there are only two possible hypotheses H_1 and H_2 in their model, and an action is considered to be a rule for choosing, for any possible observation, one of the two hypotheses. For a given observation, the action may be described as right or wrong. If H_1 is true, for a given rule of action, there is a certain probability that the observation will call for a wrong action, and similarly with H_2. Neyman and Pearson suggest the following rule: Fix some probability α; then, among all actions for which the probability of error if H_1 is true is α or less, choose an action which minimizes the probability of error if H_2 is true.

This rule is arbitrary in that there is in general no criterion for choosing α, and there will be a different best action for each α. The economist will notice immediately the analogy to Pareto's weak definition of an optimal economic state, and the above criterion has been generalized to a form even more like Pareto's by Lehmann (1947). We will say that one action *dominates* another if the (expected) return[22] to the first action is at least as great as to the second action under each of the alternative possible hypotheses, and actually greater for at least one hypothesis. Then an action A is said to be *admissible* if there is no other available action which dominates A.

---

21. Consider the following example: Individuals A and B, facing independent risk situations, each have a probability p of receiving 0 and a probability $1 - p$ of receiving 1. If they consolidate and share the returns equally, they each have a probability p^2 of receiving 0, $2p(1 - p)$ of receiving $\frac{1}{2}$, and $(1 - p)$ of receiving 1. Assume that they act so as to maximize the expected utility; then consolidation will be preferred if and *only if* $U(\frac{1}{2}) > \frac{1}{2}[U(0) + U(1)]$, a situation of diminishing marginal utility of income, or risk aversion.

22. For a given action and a given hypothesis, the return (consequence) is a random variable with a known probability distribution. Each such distribution can be given a numerical utility in accordance with the von Neumann–Morgenstern theorem (see Section 4.1.3).

The rule that one should restrict oneself to admissible actions is extremely reasonable, but, like the corresponding rule in welfare economics, it rarely leads to definite decisions as to which action to take. Wald (1939, 1950, pp. 18, 26–27) has suggested the following rule: For each action consider the minimum of the expected returns possible under the alternative hypotheses; choose that action which maximizes the minimum return.[23] This means, in effect, that that action should be chosen about which the best certain statement can be made. This rule can be interpreted as making behavior under uncertainty analogous to a zero-sum two-person game with the individual and Nature as the two players; the individual chooses the action, Nature chooses the hypothesis (each without knowing the opponent's "move"), and the individual then receives the expected return determined by the two choices.

Wald's theory is intuitively highly appealing in that it reflects fully the idea of complete ignorance about the hypotheses. However, the theory of the zero-sum two-person game is based on the idea of an opponent with a definite interest in reducing one's gains (see von Neumann and Morgenstern (1947, pp. 98–100, 220). No such motive can be ascribed to Nature. A difficulty arising in connection with Wald's principle naively stated, as well as a possible resolution of it, was first suggested by L. J. Savage.[24] Suppose that there are two possible actions, A_1 and A_2, and two possible hypotheses, H_1 and H_2. Suppose that if A_1 were chosen, the utility would be 100 under H_1 and 0 under H_2, while if A_2 were chosen, the utility would be 1 under either hypothesis. Wald's criterion would call for choosing A_2; yet, since it can hardly be said that Nature would choose H_2 deliberately to prevent the individual from realizing the gains he would receive with A_1 under H_1, it does not seem reasonable that the hope of a small gain under H_2 should outweigh the possibility of a large gain under H_1, especially since it can be shown that the choice would not be altered by any accumulation of observations. Savage and, independently, J. Niehans (1948, p. 445) argued that the statistician or businessman is only responsible for doing as well as he can under the hypothesis which actually prevails. For each possible hypothesis, therefore, he should find the best he could expect if he knew the hypothesis

---

23. Wald himself refers to losses rather than gains, and so he states the rule as that of minimizing the maximum loss. The criterion is therefore frequently referred to as the *minimax principle.*

24. In his course in mathematical statistics (oral lectures), winter 1948; see also Marschak (1949, pp. 192–195); Savage (1951, pp. 58–62).

were true, that is, the maximum of the returns of all possible actions under that hypothesis. If he takes action A and it turns out that hypothesis H is correct, the statistician should be given a penalty (which has been given the not altogether felicitous name of *regret*) equal to the difference between the reward to A under H and the maximum income possible under H if known. The regret is computed in this way for each possible action and hypothesis; the individual is then supposed to choose his action so as to minimize the maximum regret.

Like Wald's, Savage's principle expresses the idea of complete ignorance of the true hypothesis and at the same time seems to get around the assumption of a malevolent universe. But there is another difficulty, pointed out by Chernoff (1950a). Suppose the incomes accruing under various combinations of three actions and two hypotheses are given by the following table:

Action	Hypothesis	
	1	2
1	0	10
2	3	6
3	6	0

Under hypothesis 1, the best action would yield 6; therefore, the regrets of the different actions under hypothesis 1 are the differences between the numbers in the first column and 6, and similarly with the regrets under hypothesis 2. The regret matrix is, then,

Action	Hypothesis	
	1	2
1	6	0
2	3	4
3	0	10

Under the principle of minimaxing regret, action 2 would be chosen.[25] But now suppose that action 3 were no longer allowed. Then a new regret matrix would have to be formed, since, for example, the best available action under hypothesis 1 would now yield only 3.

	Hypothesis	
Action	1	2
1	3	0
2	0	4

Now, however, action 1 would be chosen. In other words, even though action 2 would be preferred when both 1 and 3 are available, action 1 would be chosen over 2 if 3 is no longer available. This result does not seem compatible with rational behavior; the difficulty is that the Savage minimax principle does not and is not intended to give rise to a genuine ordering in the usual economic sense (see also Savage, 1951, p. 64).

4.2.3. The preceding discussion suggests the possibility of setting down axioms for rational behavior under uncertainty starting with the Neyman-Pearson description, that is, axioms on the ordering of income functions (see Section 3.2.2). Ramsey (1931), de Finetti (1937), and Savage (1950) start with a particular class of actions, namely, betting on outcomes of events (see, in particular, Ramsey, 1931, pp. 179–184; de Finetti, 1937, pp. 4–11). Thus de Finetti says that if an individual is willing to exchange the sum of money pS but no more for the privilege of receiving S when the event E occurs, then p is the "subjective" probability of E. A similar definition can be given for conditional probability. Then, if it is postulated simply that there is no system of bets of the above type by which the individual feels sure of winning regardless of the actually observed event, then all the usual theorems of probability can be deduced. This particular formulation is unacceptable since it is implicitly postulated that p is independent of S, an assumption contradicted by the everyday experience that individuals will not make indefinitely large bets at the same odds. Ramsey's construction is similar, except that he substitutes utility (see Section 4.1.3) for money as the medium of betting. To define the utility itself requires some probability

---

25. This is not true if randomized actions are permitted, but a similar paradox will obtain.

elements; it is presupposed that there exists an event which the individual would as soon bet for as against, that is, in effect an event with probability one-half.

Subsequently there have been other discussions by Rubin (1949a and b) and Chernoff (1950a and b).[26] Their starting point is the concept of a mixture of income functions, analogous to a mixture of probability distributions in the von Neumann – Morgenstern theory (see Section 4.1.3). If x and y stand for two income functions, then the mixture $ax + (1 - a)y$, where $0 \leqq a \leqq 1$, is the income function derived by choosing x with probability a and y with probability $1 - a$. It can also be obtained by mixing the returns for each possible hypothesis corresponding to x and y; for any given hypothesis, this mixing is of the type already described. Then it is argued that the von Neumann – Morgenstern axioms already described for probability distributions are equally reasonable when applied to income functions. That is, it is assumed (1) that income functions can be ordered;[27] (2) that if x is preferred to y and y to z, there is a mixture of x and z indifferent to y; (3) if x is indifferent to y, then any mixture of x and a third alternative z is indifferent to the same mixture of y and z.[28] If we further add the condition that an income function which is not admissible (see Section 4.2.2) will not be used, then it can be shown there exists an assignment of nonnegative numbers $p_1, \ldots, p_n$ to the various hypotheses $H_1, \ldots, H_n$ and of utilities to the probability distributions defined by the actions and hypotheses such that the desirability of an income function x is measured by the utility function $\sum_{i=1}^{n} p_i U(x, H_i)$, where $U(x, H_i)$ is the von Neumann – Morgenstern utility of the outcome specified by the income function x for the hypothesis H_i. We can so choose the p_i's that $\sum_{i=1}^{n} p_i = 1$; then it is natural to interpret them as a priori probabilities. The theorem, in effect, says that in order for an individual to act rationally, he must act as if he had a set of such probabilities in mind.

Chernoff, like Jacob Bernoulli, argued that in the case of complete ignorance all the alternative hypotheses must be treated on a par, so that the a priori probabilities would all be equal to $1/n$. This argument supplies a justification for the Principle of Insufficient Reason (see Section 3.1.3).

It should be noted in passing that both the von Neumann – Morgenstern utility theory and the present extension to a priori probabilities are ideally

---

26. Savage has made important oral contributions to this development.

27. Rubin has shown that this condition can be considerably weakened.

28. The third assumption can be shown to eliminate the difficulty found by Savage in the Wald minimax principle.

capable of refutation. Both the utilities and the probabilities can be discovered by suitable formulations of choices in simple situations; then behavior in more complicated situations can be checked against that predicted by the theory, with the numerical data supplied by study of simple cases. Similar considerations apply to the minimax theories.

4.2.4. Shackle's theory (1949, chap. 2) of uncertainty bearing stems from his description in terms of potential surprise (see Section 3.2.4). The exposition is greatly complicated by his insistence on differentiating between gains and losses. It is completely unclear to me what the meaning of the zero-point would be in a general theory; after all, costs are usually defined on an opportunity basis only.

For a given action there is attached to each possible gain a potential surprise. The possible pairs of this type are ranked according to their power to stimulate the mind, and it is assumed that the effect of the most stimulating one will sum up the entire influence of possible gains on choice. The stimulation of an outcome is assumed to increase as the size of the gain increases and to decrease as the potential surprise increases. Similarly, the maximum stimulation associated with a loss is found. This pair of stimulations completely defines the effects of the given action; there is then an ordering among pairs of stimulations (referred to as the *gambler indifference map*) which determines which action is taken.[29] This theory is not based on considerations of rational behavior, which Shackle (1949–50, p. 74) specifically rejects, but on an alleged inability of the mind to consider simultaneously mutually exclusive events.

In the same way that the concept of potential surprise is a generalization of the Neyman-Pearson formulation of the statistical problem, so Shackle's theory of behavior under uncertainty generalizes the Wald minimax principle. Suppose (1) that only losses occur or else that the gambler's indifference map depends only on the standardized focus-loss, and (2) that for any outcome, potential surprise is either 0 or else the maximum possible. Then Shackle's theory leads to the rule of minimizing the maximum loss.

Shackle has the sound impulse to base a theory of uncertainty bearing on the necessity of the human mind to simplify a problem in order to be able to deal with it. However, his particular simplification seems to be purely

---

29. Shackle defines a *standardized focus-gain* as that outcome which, if potential surprise 0 were attached to it, would be as stimulating as the most stimulating gain, and a *standardized focus-loss* similarly. The gambler indifference map has as coordinates the pair of standardized focus-outcomes. These are obviously merely a method of attaching numbers to the maximum degrees of stimulation and have no special significance.

arbitrary. We have already seen that the complete rejection of probability elements cannot be regarded as successful (see Section 3.2.4). As a matter of fact, description *solely* in terms of probability distributions seems to me to be at least as plausible as Shackle's hypothesis, which is, further, lacking in the virtue of simplicity. (Why do we need both a stimulation function and a gambler indifference map to describe reactions to uncertainty?)

The theory can indeed be shown to lead to an odd result. Suppose an event has two possible outcomes, A and B. Then it follows from the assumptions about potential surprise (see Section 3.2.4) that one of them, say A, must have potential surprise 0. Suppose that under action 1 the individual gets one dollar regardless of what happens, while under action 2 he gains one dollar if A occurs and nothing if B occurs. Then in both cases he gains one dollar with potential surprise 0 and loses nothing with the maximum possible potential surprise, so that the two actions have the same standardized focus-outcomes (namely, focus-gain 1 and focus-loss 0) and are indifferent. Yet the second action is obviously not admissible (see Section 4.2.2).

This result also shows that the theory is, at least, a genuine theory in the sense of having refutable consequences. In fact, it is possible to construct a sequence of simple experiments which will enable us to actually find the potential surprise function, the stimulation function, and the gambler indifference map. I will briefly sketch the procedure. For any two hypotheses, H_1 and H_2, let A_1 be an action which yields one dollar if H_1 is true and nothing otherwise, and let A_2 be an action yielding one dollar if H_2 is true and nothing otherwise. Then H_1 has a lower potential surprise than H_2 if and only if A_1 is preferred to A_2. Since potential surprise is an ordinal concept, that function is completely defined. In particular, we may find a hypothesis H which has the same potential surprise as its contradictory; then both will have potential surprise 0. Consider an action for which the individual receives a if H occurs and loses b otherwise. Then the standardized focus-outcomes are a and b; by ordering all actions obtained by varying a and b, we can fill out the gambler indifference map. Finally, for any given degree of potential surprise y and any given gain c, choose a hypothesis H_1 with potential surprise y. Let action A_1 yield c if H_1 is true and 0 otherwise; let action A_2 yield d if H is true and 0 otherwise. Vary d until A_1 and A_2 are indifferent; then, since H has potential surprise 0, d is the standardized focus-gain corresponding to the pair (y,c). The stimulation function is therefore defined for gains; a similar procedure is applicable to losses.

Though the theory is therefore not empty, it has not actually given rise to much in the way of useful consequences. The discussion of the holding of assets under uncertainty (see Shackle, 1949, chap. 4) is vitiated by a logical error at the beginning of the argument. As a matter of fact, since there is no law of large numbers in the calculus of potential surprise, diversification of assets cannot be explained. His discussion of the bargaining process (see Shackle, 1949, chap. 6) amounts to the well-known proposition that the process is determinate if the reaction curves of the participants are known, the only difference being that the reaction curves constructed by Shackle include uncertain behavior.[30]

4.3. There is one body of opinion which argues that there can be no theory of rational behavior under uncertainty by the nature of the problem. As early as 1879, Cliffe-Leslie argued that the wiping out of profits by competition would not occur in reality since the profits of other firms were unknown (quoted by Hardy, 1923, pp. 35–37). Irving Fisher also doubted that a satisfactory theory of behavior under uncertainty was really possible (see I. Fisher, 1930, chaps. 9, 14), though his conclusion was that the theory of economic behavior under certainty afforded a good approximation to actuality. Knight and Shackle (see Sections 4.2.1 and 4.2.4) tend to somewhat similar viewpoints. Alchian (1950) has argued that the absence of definite criteria for action, corresponding to profit maximization in the theory of behavior under certainty, means that we should regard behavior under uncertainty as essentially random. The process of convergence to optimal behavior by trial and error is impossible when the basic conditions are changing and unknown. However, since there will be a process of selection in the economic struggle for existence, there will be some tendency toward optimal behavior.

References

Alchian, A. A., "Uncertainty, Evolution, and Economic Theory," *Journal of Political Economy,* vol. 58, June, 1950, pp. 211–221.

Bayes, Thomas, "An Essay toward Solving a Problem in the Doctrine of Chances," *Philosophical Transactions of the Royal Society of London,* vol. 53, 1763, pp. 370–418. (Reprinted in *Facsimiles of Two Papers by Bayes,* W. D. Deming, ed., Washington, D.C.: Graduate School, Department of Agriculture, 1940.)

---

30. An interesting suggestion of Shackle's is that when an event with high potential surprise has occurred, forcing a revaluation of the uncertainty situation, the effect will not take place all at once but only after an interval of time during which almost every possibility is assigned a low potential surprise (Shackle, 1949, pp. 73–75). This proposition could be reformulated in terms of other theories.

Bernoulli, D., "Specimen theoriae novae de mensura sortis," *Commentarii academiae scientiarum imperiales Petropolitanae,* vol. 5, 1738, pp. 175–192; translated by A. Pringsheim under the title, *Die Grundlage der modernen Wertlehre: Versuch einer neuen Theorie der Wertbestimmung von Glücksfallen,* Leipzig: Duncker and Humblot, 1896, 60 pp.

Carnap, Rudolf, *Logical Foundations of Probability,* Chicago: University of Chicago Press, 1950, 607 pp.

Chernoff, Herman, "Remarks on a Rational Selection of a Decision Function" (hectographed), Cowles Commission Discussion Papers: no. 326 and 326A, January, 1949; 346 and 346A, April, 1950a.

Chernoff, Herman, "Remarks on a Rational Selection of a Decision Function" (abstract), *Econometrica,* vol. 18, April, 1950b, p. 183.

Cramér, H., "On the Mathematical Theory of Risk," *Försäkringsaktiebolaget Skandias Festskrift,* Stockholm: Centraltryckeriet, 1930, pp. 7–84.

Domar, E., and R. A. Musgrave, "Proportional Income Taxation and Risk-Taking," *Quarterly Journal of Economics,* vol. 58, May, 1944, pp. 388–422.

Feller, W., *An Introduction to Probability Theory and Its Applications,* vol. 1, New York: John Wiley and Sons, 1950, 419 pp.

de Finetti, Bruno, "La Prévision: Ses Lois Logiques, Ses Sources Subjectives," *Annales de l'Institut Henri Poincaré,* vol. 7, 1937, pp. 1–68.

Fisher, I., *The Nature of Capital and Income,* New York and London: Macmillan Co., 1906, 427 pp.

Fisher, I., *The Theory of Interest,* New York: The Macmillan Co., 1930, 550 pp.

Fisher, R. A., "On the Mathematical Foundations of Theoretical Statistics," *Philosophical Transactions of the Royal Society of London,* pt. A, vol. 222, 1922, pp. 309–368.

Fréchet, M., "L'Estimation Statistique des Paramètres" (abstract), *Econometrica,* vol. 16, January, 1948, pp. 60–62.

Friedman, M., "Lange on Price Flexibility and Employment: A Methodological Criticism," *American Economic Review,* vol. 36, September, 1946, pp. 613–631.

Friedman, M., and L. J. Savage, "The Utility Analysis of Choices Involving Risk," *Journal of Political Economy,* vol. 56, August, 1948, pp. 279–304.

Graaf, J. de V., and W. J. Baumol, "Three Notes on 'Expectations in Economics' II," *Economica,* new series, vol. 16, November, 1949, pp. 338–342.

Hardy, C. O., *Risk and Risk-Bearing,* Chicago: University of Chicago Press, 1923.

Hart, A. G., *Anticipations, Uncertainty, and Dynamic Planning,* New York: Augustus M. Kelley, 1951, 98 pp.

Hart, A. G., "Risk, Uncertainty, and the Unprofitability of Compounding Probabilities," in *Studies in Mathematical Economics and Econometrics,* O. Lange, F. McIntyre, and T. O. Yntema, eds., Chicago: University of Chicago Press, 1942, pp. 110–118.

Hicks, J. R., "The Theory of Uncertainty and Profit," *Economica,* vol. 11, May, 1931, pp. 170–189.

Hicks, J. R., "Application of Mathematical Methods to the Theory of Risk" (abstract), *Econometrica,* vol. 2, April, 1934, pp. 194–195.

Kalecki, M., "The Principle of Increasing Risk," *Economica*, new series, vol. 4, November, 1937, pp. 440–447.

Keynes, J. M., *A Treatise on Probability*, London: Macmillan and Co., 1921, 466 pp.

Knight, F. H., *Risk, Uncertainty, and Profit*, New York: Houghton Mifflin and Co., 1921. (Reprinted, London: London School of Economics and Political Science, 1946, 381 pp.)

Kolmogorov, A. N., "Grundbegriffe der Wahrscheinlichkeitsrechnung," *Ergebnisse der Mathematik und Ihre Grenzgebiete*, vol. 2, 1933, translated as *Foundations of the Theory of Probability*, New York: Chelsea Publishing Co., 1950, 70 pp.

von Kries, J., *Die Principien der Wahrscheinlichkeitsrechnung*, Freiburg, 1886, 298 pp.

Lange, O., *Price Flexibility and Employment*, Cowles Commission Monograph 8, Bloomington, Ind.: Principia Press, 1944, 114 pp.

Lehmann, E. L., "On Families of Admissible Sets," *Annals of Mathematical Statistics*, vol. 18, March, 1947, pp. 97–104.

Marschak, J., "Money and the Theory of Assets," *Econometrica*, vol. 6, October, 1938, pp. 311–325.

Marschak, J., "Von Neumann's and Morgenstern's New Approach to Static Economics," *Journal of Political Economy*, vol. 54, April, 1946, pp. 97–115.

Marschak, J., "Role of Liquidity under Complete and Incomplete Information," *American Economic Review, Papers and Proceedings*, vol. 39, 1949, pp. 182–195.

Marschak, J., "Rational Behavior, Uncertain Prospects, and Measurable Utility," *Econometrica*, vol. 18, April, 1950, pp. 111–141.

Marshall, A., *Principles of Economics*, 8th ed., New York: Macmillan Co., 1948, 871 pp.

Menger, K., "Das Unsicherheitsmoment in der Wertlehre," *Zeitschrift für Nationalökonomie*, vol. 5, no. 4, 1934, pp. 459–485.

von Mises, R., "On the Foundation of Probability and Statistics," *Annals of Mathematical Statistics*, vol. 12, June, 1941, pp. 191–205.

von Neumann, J., and O. Morgenstern, *Theory of Games and Economic Behavior*, 2nd ed., Princeton: Princeton University Press, 1947, 641 pp.

Neyman, J., and E. S. Pearson, "The Testing of Statistical Hypotheses in Relation to Probabilities A Priori," *Proceedings of the Cambridge Philosophical Society*, vol. 29, 1933, pp. 492–510.

Niehans, J., "Zur Preisbildung bei ungewissen Erwartungen," *Schweizerische Zeitschrift für Volkswirtschaft und Statistik*, vol. 84, no. 5, 1948, pp. 433–456.

Palm, C., "The Distribution of Repairmen in Servicing Automatic Machines" (in Swedish), *Industrietidningen Norden*, vol. 75, 1947, pp. 75–80, 90–94, 119–123.

Pigou, A. C., *The Economics of Welfare*, 2nd ed., London: Macmillan and Co., 1924, 783 pp.

Ramsey, F. P., "Truth and Probability," in *The Foundations of Mathematics and Other Logical Essays*, London: K. Paul, Trench, Trubner and Co., 1931.

Rubin, H., "The Existence of Measurable Utility and Psychological Probability" (hectographed), Cowles Commission Discussion Paper: Statistics no. 331, July, 1949a, 5 pp.

Rubin, H., "Postulates for the Existence of Measurable Utility and Psychological Probability" (abstract), *Bulletin of the American Mathematical Society,* vol. 55, November, 1949b, pp. 1050–1051.

Samuelson, P. A., *Foundations of Economic Analysis,* Cambridge, Mass.: Harvard University Press, 1947, 447 pp. [enlarged ed., 1983].

Savage, L. J., "The Role of Personal Probability in Statistics" (abstract), *Econometrica,* vol. 18, April, 1950, pp. 183–184.

Savage, L. J., "The Theory of Statistical Decision," *Journal of the American Statistical Association,* vol. 46, March, 1951, pp. 55–67.

Shackle, G. L. S., *Expectation in Economics,* Cambridge: Cambridge University Press, 1949, 146 pp.

Shackle, G. L. S., "A Non-Additive Measure of Uncertainty," *Review of Economic Studies,* vol. 17, no. 1, 1949–50, pp. 70–74.

Tintner, G., "The Theory of Choice under Subjective Risk and Uncertainty," *Econometrica,* vol. 9, July–October, 1941a, pp. 298–304.

Tintner, G., "The Pure Theory of Production under Technological Risk and Uncertainty," *Econometrica,* vol. 9, July–October, 1941b, pp. 305–312.

Tintner, G., "A Contribution to the Non-Static Theory of Choice," *Quarterly Journal of Economics,* vol. 56, February, 1942a, pp. 274–306.

Tintner, G., "A Contribution to the Non-Static Theory of Production," in *Studies in Mathematical Economics and Econometrics,* O. Lange, F. McIntyre, and T. O. Yntema, eds., Chicago: University of Chicago Press, 1942b, pp. 92–109.

Tintner, G., "Foundations of Probability and Statistical Inference," *Journal of the Royal Statistical Society,* series A, vol. 112, pt. 3, 1949, pp. 251–279.

Törnqvist, L., "On the Economic Theory of Lottery Gambles," *Skandinavisk Aktuarietidskrift,* vol. 28, pts. 3 and 4, 1945, pp. 228–246.

Wald, A., "Contributions to the Theory of Statistical Estimation and Testing Hypotheses," *Annals of Mathematical Statistics,* vol. 10, December, 1939, pp. 299–326.

Wald, A., *Statistical Decision Functions,* New York: John Wiley and Sons, 1950, 179 pp.

3 The Determination of Many-Commodity Preference Scales by Two-Commodity Comparisons

The rather unusual subject of this paper arose from some discussions with a mathematician, J. W. T. Youngs, during the summer of 1950 at the RAND Corporation. The summer period in the Mathematics Division there was mostly devoted to the development of game theory; questions about individual choice theory appeared as part of the basis of the theory of games. I had been holding forth, in some context that I no longer remember, on the importance of specifying the alternatives being compared as vectors with a large number of dimensions, as is usual in economic theory. Youngs objected that no one was capable of making comparisons when all or many of the components differed. This chapter was an argument that one could always reduce such comparisons to a sequence of presumably easier comparisons of commodity vectors which differed in only two components.

If, as is customary in economics, it is assumed that the behavior of individuals is governed by a consistent pattern of preferences with respect to varying bundles of goods, it is natural to suggest that this pattern can be approximated by the answers to a questionnaire as to the preferences between pairs of such bundles. Against this it has been argued that although such a procedure might be satisfactory if only two or three commodities are involved, the procedure will be useless if there are several hundred commod-

Reprinted from *Metroeconomica*, 4 (1952):107–115.

ities involved, since the questionee will be unable to apprehend truly the situation, and his answers may be only distantly related to the choice he would actually make if the situation arose. It is the purpose of this chapter to show that, under the assumptions usually made in economic literature, the determination of a preference scale relating to many commodities can always be accomplished by means of comparisons involving the variation of only two commodities at a time. In this chapter, the procedure will be illustrated by showing how to pass from a knowledge of the preferences among bundles in which the quantities of only two commodities vary to a knowledge of preferences among three-commodity bundles. The procedure for more commodities is sketched, and some points of mathematical rigor are discussed in the appendix to this chapter.

This result suggests that there is no true gain in generality in considering more than two commodities. In principle, all properties of multicommodity indifference maps are deducible from those of two-commodity maps. Of course, in any given situation, it may be simpler to consider the problem in full generality directly.

Assumptions and Definitions

A commodity bundle will be denoted by a point X (or Y or Z), with coordinates $(X_1, \ldots, X_n)$, where X_i is the quantity of the ith commodity. It will be assumed that $X_i \geqq 0$ for all i; that is, we only consider the relations of preference and indifference as between two bundles both of which satisfy this restriction on their coordinates. For such commodity bundles, the relations of preference and indifference are assumed to have their usual properties, as listed in the following statement.

ASSUMPTION 1.　(a) *For all pairs of bundles X and Y, either X is preferred to Y or Y is preferred to X or X and Y are indifferent.*

(b) If X is indifferent to Y, then Y is indifferent to X; if X is indifferent to Y and Y is indifferent to Z, then X is indifferent to Z.

(c) X is preferred to Z if any of the following conditions hold: X is preferred to Y and Y is preferred to Z; X is preferred to Y and Y is indifferent to Z; X is indifferent to Y and Y is preferred to Z.

In addition, we shall make the following customary assumption.

ASSUMPTION 2.　*If $X_i \geqq Y_i$ for all i and $X_j > Y_j$ for some j, then X is preferred to Y.*

That is, other things being equal, an individual will prefer more of a good to less. This is equivalent to the usual, though sometimes only implicit, assumption in demand theory that the marginal utility of each commodity be positive. If some of the commodities entering into the bundles among which choice is to be made are irksome, one can always take their negatives and then change the origin to make them nonnegative; for example, replace the item "work" by "leisure," defined as the difference between the length of the day and the number of hours worked. Assumption 2 is only essentially contradicted when the preferences for varying quantities of one commodity (given the quantities of all other commodities) are neither always in the same nor always in the opposite direction to those quantities. This situation arises, for example, if there is a point of saturation on the indifference map, that is, if there is one bundle of goods which is preferred to all others, even to bundles having more of each commodity.[1] This case has not yet been adequately formalized in the literature on demand theory and will not be treated here.[2]

Under Assumption 2, the preference scale in the one-commodity case is completely defined, being simply that more of that commodity is preferred to less. Henceforth, it will be assumed that the number of commodities is at least two.

To state the next assumption, we shall define a linear combination of two commodity bundles. If X and Y are two commodity bundles, with X_i the amount of the ith commodity in bundle X and Y_i the amount of the ith commodity in bundle Y, we will use the symbol $aX + bY$ to denote the commodity bundle in which the amount of the ith commodity is $aX_i + bY_i$ for each commodity i. If each bundle is represented by a point in n-dimensional space whose coordinates are the quantities of the different commodities in the bundle, and if we consider the particular case where $a = t$,

---

1. The existence of a point of saturation in an indifference map was apparently first suggested by I. Fisher, *Mathematical Investigations in the Theory of Value and Prices,* "Transactions of the Connecticut Academy of Arts and Sciences," 9 (1894), pp. 68, 70–71. The idea is implicit in some of the Austrian discussion of diminishing marginal utility of a single commodity; this marginal utility, it was held, might become zero as the quantity of the commodity became indefinitely large. See, for example, C. Menger, *Grundsätze der Volkwiertschaftslehre,* Vienna, 1871, pp. 57–60.

2. For example, points of saturation are not handled by H. Wold in his classic restatement of the field, *A Synthesis of Pure Demand Analysis,* "Skandinavisk Aktuarietidskrift," 1943, pp. 85–118, 220–263; 1944, pp. 69–120.

$b = 1 - t, 0 < t < 1$, then $tX + (1 - t)Y$ is represented by a point between X and Y on the straight line segment joining them.

ASSUMPTION 3. *If X is preferred to Y and Y is preferred to Z, then there is a number t such that $0 < t < 1$ and $tX + (1 - t)Z$ is indifferent to Y.*

Assumptions 1–3 are essentially equivalent to Wold's axioms I–V.[3] Assumption 1 is exactly equivalent to his axioms I–III; Assumption 2 is slightly stronger than his axiom IV; Assumption 3 is somewhat weaker than his axiom V.

The essential role of Assumption 3 is to establish the continuity of the indifference map. More precisely, an indifference map satisfying Assumptions 1–3 admits of a continuous utility indicator.[4] From this point on, we shall assume without special discussion that our indifference maps have all the usual continuity properties. For the purposes of this chapter it is unnecessary to make the usual assumptions of differentiability of the utility function and convexity of the indifference surfaces.

By a *rationed collection of commodity bundles,* we shall mean a collection consisting of all bundles in which certain commodities occur in fixed quantities but all other commodities can occur in any nonnegative amount; for example, the set of all commodity bundles containing just five units of the first commodity, or the collection of all bundles containing exactly three units of the first commodity and exactly six units of the third. Particular interest centers on rationed collections in which all but two of the commodities are fixed in amount; such collections will be termed *ration planes.* Among the bundles in a given rationed collection, there will still hold relations of preference and indifference, and these relations will still satisfy Assumptions 1–3 in the restricted space, Assumption 2 holding with respect to the coordinates which are not restricted. This statement is obvious for Assumptions 1 and 2. To see that 3 still holds within a rationed collection, suppose that collection defined, for example, by prescribing $X_1 = c$. If X, Y, and Z are bundles in the collection such that X is preferred to Y and Y to Z, then there is a number such that $tX + (1 - t)Z$ is indifferent to Y and $0 < t < 1$. But the first coordinate of $tX + (1 - t)Z$ is $tX_1 + (1 - t)Y_1 = tc + (1 - t)c = c$, since X and Z both have c as a first coordinate. Hence, all

---

3. Wold, *Pure Demand Analysis,* pp. 221–223.
4. Ibid., p. 226.

the usual properties of indifference maps hold on the rationed collections as well as on unrestricted collections of bundles.

The Case of Three Commodities

In this section we will assume that there are only three commodities altogether. In this case, a ration plane is defined by fixing the amount of one commodity. We assume that for each ration plane we know the relations of preference or indifference as between any pair of bundles on that plane. That is, we consider that between any two bundles which have the same quantity of one commodity, we can ask the individual whether he is indifferent between the two or prefers one to the other, and, in the latter case, which he prefers. We are not permitted, let us say, to ask these questions as between two bundles in which the quantities of each commodity differ. It will turn out that we can infer the preferences in the latter case from the preferences as between pairs of bundles having the same quantity of some commodity.

Let X and Y be any two given bundles, and let $U = (u_1, u_2, u_3)$ be a variable bundle. If $X_3 = Y_3$, both X and Y lie on the ration plane $u_3 = X_3$, and from knowledge of the indifference curves on every ration plane we can certainly infer the proper preference or indifference relation as between X and Y. Hence, we need only consider the case $X_3 \neq Y_3$; since it does not matter which bundle we call X and which Y, we may assume that $X_3 > Y_3$.

Our procedure will be to derive, for each of the propositions, X is preferred to Y, X is indifferent to Y, and X is disfavored to Y, the respective necessary implications concerning the indifference maps on each of various ration planes; then it will be easily seen that the conditions in question are also respectively sufficient. Let I_1 be the indifference curve through X on the ration plane $u_3 = X_3$; by assumption this curve is known. We will derive the conditions in question separately for the two cases where the projection of I_1 on the u_1-axis is unbounded and where it is bounded.

Case 1. The projection of I_1 on the u_1-axis is unbounded. Consider the bundles represented by points on the ration plane $u_3 = Y_3$ which are indifferent to X; these points, if there are any, form an indifference curve I_2. Since $Y_3 < X_3$ the curve I_2, if it exists at all, must lie further away from the origin than the curve I_1, if we imagine them plotted together (see Figure 3.1). In particular, I_2 must also be unbounded.

Suppose X is, in fact, preferred to Y. Consider the intersection, if any, of

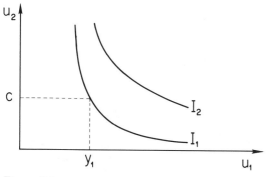

Figure 3.1

the line $u_1 = Y_1$ with I_1 on the plane $u_3 = X_3$; let the u_2-coordinate of the point of intersection be c. On the ration plane $u_1 = Y_1$, this point of intersection has the coordinates $u_2 = c$, $u_3 = X_3$; let I_3 be the indifference curve on this plane through the indicated point (see Figure 3.2).

Consider the intersection, if any, of I_3 with the line $u_3 = Y_3$; let Z be the bundle designated by this point of intersection. By construction, $Z_1 = Y_1$, since Z is on the ration plane $u_1 = Y_1$, and $Z_3 = Y_3$; also, Z is indifferent to the bundle (Y_1, c, X_3), which in turn is indifferent to X. Since X, and hence Z, is preferred to Y, $Z_2 > Y_2$. That is, *if X is preferred to Y, then either Z is not constructible by the above procedure or $Z_2 > Y_2$.*

Suppose Z is, in fact, not constructible. This means either that the line $u_1 = Y_1$ does not cut I_1 on the plane $u_3 = X_3$, or that the curve I_3 does not intersect the line $u_3 = Y_3$ on the plane $u_1 = Y_1$. Since I_1 is unbounded in the

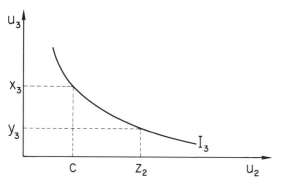

Figure 3.2

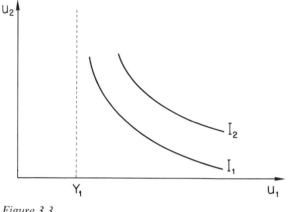

Figure 3.3

u_1-direction by assumption, the first contingency can only arise if I_1 is separated from the origin by the line $u_1 = Y_1$ (see Figure 3.3). But then either I_2 does not exist at all or I_2 must also be separated from the origin by the line $u_1 = Y_1$, since it must lie still further away from the origin than I_1. If I_2 does not exist at all, there are no points on the plane $u_3 = Y_3$ which are indifferent to X; since $X_3 > Y_3$, this means that X is preferred to all the points on the plane $u_3 = Y_3$, and hence in particular to Y. If I_2 is separated from the origin by the line $u_1 = Y_1$, on which Y lies, the points of the plane $u_3 = Y_3$ which are indifferent to X are preferred to Y, and again X must be preferred to Y.

Now suppose that the line $u_1 = Y_1$ does intersect I_1, but that I_3 does not intersect the line $u_3 = Y_3$. Since any point of I_2 for which $u_1 = Y_1$ would lie on the intersection of I_3 with the line $u_3 = Y_3$, there can be no such points of I_2. Either I_2 does not exist, in which case X is preferred to Y as before, or, since I_2 is unbounded, it must be separated from the origin by the line $u_1 = Y_1$, so that again X is preferred to Y.

If Z is not constructible, then X is preferred to Y. Therefore, if X is indifferent to Y, Z must be constructible and must be indifferent to Y; since $Z_1 = Y_1, Z_3 = Y_3$, we must have $Z_2 = Y_2$. Similarly, if X is disfavored to Y, Z is constructible, and $Z_2 < Y_2$.

If I_1 is unbounded in the x_1-direction, then we may ascertain the preference or indifference relation between X and Y, where $X_3 > Y_3$, by the following criterion: Try to construct the point Z. If it is not defined, then X is preferred to Y. If Z is defined, then X is preferred, indifferent, or disfavored to Y according as $Z_2 > Y_2$, $Z_2 = Y_2$, or $Z_2 < Y_2$.

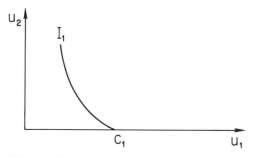

Figure 3.4

It is to be observed that the question of whether or not Z is defined and of finding the value of Z_2 if it is defined can be answered solely from a knowledge of the indifference maps on certain ration planes; in fact, not more than two such planes need be considered.

Case 2. The projection of I_1 on the u_1-axis is bounded. In this case, I_1 cuts the u_1-axis; let the u_1-coordinate of the point of intersection be c_1 (see Figure 3.4). Suppose X is preferred to Y. On the plane $u_1 = c_1$, let I_4 be the indifference curve through the point with $u_2 = 0$, $u_3 = X_3$. This point represents the bundle $(c_1, 0, X_3)$, which is the point of intersection of I_1 with the u_1-axis on Figure 3.4, and hence I_4 represents points indifferent to X. If I_4 intersects the line $u_3 = Y_3$, let the point of intersection be Z. Then $Z_3 = Y_3$, so that Z and Y are on the same ration plane; since X is preferred to Y, so is Z. If Z is not defined, then I_4 must be unbounded in the u_2-direction (see Figure 3.5). Since I_4 does cut the line $u_2 = 0$, there is a point on I_4 with

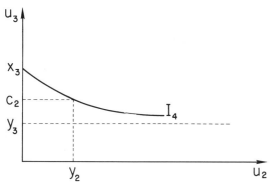

Figure 3.5

any preassigned (nonnegative) value of u_2 and in particular a point with $u_2 = Y_2$. Let the u_3-coordinate of this point of intersection be c_2. On the ration plane $u_2 = Y_2$, the point of intersection just found has the coordinates $u_1 = c_1, u_3 = c_2$. Draw the indifference curve through this point on the plane $u_2 = Y_2$; let W be its intersection, if any, with the line $u_3 = Y_3$. $W_2 = Y_2$, and $W_3 = Y_3$; also W is indifferent to X, by construction. Hence, W is preferred to Y since X is; therefore, $W_1 > Y_1$.

If X is preferred to Y, then either Z is preferred to Y or $W_1 > Y_1$ or neither Z nor W is defined.

Suppose neither Z nor W is defined. Since Z is not defined, it follows, as above, that there is a point on the plane $u_2 = Y_2$ which is indifferent to X. If there were a point on the plane $u_3 = Y_3$ which was indifferent to X and for which $u_2 = Y_2$, that point would be W; since W is not defined, either I_2, which contains all points on the plane $u_3 = Y_3$ indifferent to X, does not exist, or I_2 does not cross the line $u_2 = Y_2$. If I_2 does not exist, then, as before, X must be preferred to Y. If I_2 does not cross the line $u_2 = Y_2$, then either I_2 is separated from the origin by the line $u_2 = Y_2$, in which case, again as before, X is preferred to Y, or I_2 is on the same side of that line as the origin, in which case every bundle for which $u_2 = Y_2, u_3 = Y_3$ is preferred to X. This last case is impossible, however; for, in particular, the bundle (c_1, Y_2, Y_3) would be preferred to X, but it is disfavored to the bundle (c_1, Y_2, c_2) by Assumption 2, since $c_2 > Y_3$, and this last bundle is indifferent to X by construction.

If neither Z nor W is defined, then X is preferred to Y.

If X is indifferent to Y, then either Z or W must be defined; in the first case, Z must be indifferent to Y, in the second, $W_1 = Y_1$. Similarly, if X is disfavored to Y, either Z is defined and disfavored to Y or W is defined and $W_1 < Y_1$.

If I_1 is bounded in the u_1-direction, then we may ascertain the preference or indifference relation between X and Y, where $X_3 > Y_3$, by the following criterion: Try to construct the point Z as indicated; if it is not defined, try to construct W. If neither Z nor W is defined, then X is preferred to Y. If Z is defined, then X is preferred, indifferent, or disfavored to Y according as Z is preferred, indifferent, or disfavored to Y. If W is defined, then X is preferred, indifferent, or disfavored to Y according as $W_1 > Y_1$, $W_1 = Y_1$, or $W_1 < Y_1$.

It is to be observed again that all the processes implied in the above statement can be carried out with a knowledge of the indifference maps on certain ration planes separately; in this case, the indifference maps on three ration planes are needed.

Thus it has been shown that a comparison of any two bundles of three commodities can be carried through by means of a knowledge of all comparisons of two bundles in which the same quantity of one commodity appears in the two bundles.

The development of indifference maps for more than three commodities from the indifference maps on the various ration planes will be illustrated by the case of four commodities. The crucial point here is that each rationed collection of bundles obtained by fixing the quantity of just one commodity is essentially a world of three commodities, and the indifference surfaces in each such rationed collection can be derived from the indifference curves on the individual ration planes by a comparison of any two three-commodity bundles.

Let X and Y be any two bundles; as before, we may assume $Y_4 < X_4$. Let I_1 be the indifference surface in the ration hyperplane $u_4 = X_4$ through the point X; let I_2 be the indifference surface, if any, in the ration hyperplane $u_4 = Y_4$ of points indifferent to X.

First, suppose I_1 to be unbounded in the u_1-direction. Find a point in I_1, if any, for which $u_1 = Y_1$; if there is one such point, there will in general be many. Find the indifference surface through this point on the ration hyperplane $u_1 = Y_1$ and then a point Z of this surface with $u_4 = Y_4$. As before, if Z is not defined, X is preferred to Y. If Z is defined, then the preference or indifference relation of X to Y is the same as that of Z to Y. But the latter relation is known, since Z and Y are both in the ration hyperplane $u_4 = Y_4$, and we have said that we may assume the indifference surfaces known on each ration hyperplane.

Next, suppose I_1 to be bounded in the u_1-direction. It must then contain a point with $u_2 = 0$, $u_3 = 0$, and, of course, $u_4 = X_4$. Let the u_1-coordinate of this point be c_1. This point is, then, on the hyperplane $u_1 = c_1$; consider the indifference surface through the given point on the indicated hyperplane. If there is a point on the indifference surface for which $u_4 = Y_4$, call that point Z. If there is no such point Z on the indifference surface, there must be one point for which $u_2 = Y_2$. Consider the indifference surface through this point in the hyperplane $u_2 = Y_2$. If there is a point on this indifference surface for which $u_4 = Y_4$, call it W. Then, if neither Z nor W is defined, X must be preferred to Y. If either Z or W is defined, then X bears the same preference or indifference relation to Y that Z or W does, respectively.

By this method, the indifference hypersurfaces in four-commodity spaces may be built up out of the indifference surfaces in three-commodity spaces, and hence ultimately out of the indifference curves in two-commodity spaces. By mathematical induction, we can pass to any number of dimensions.

Appendix

Certain propositions about the nature of indifference surfaces deducible from Assumptions 1–3 which have been used implicitly in the above analysis will here be brought out into the open. A repeatedly used theorem is the following.

PROPOSITION 1. *The projection of an indifference curve or surface on the* x_1*-axis is an interval (finite or infinite).*

Proof. Let I be the given indifference surface. It suffices to show that if $a_1 < a_2 < a_3$ and if there are points in I for which $u_1 = a_1$ and $u_1 = a_3$, respectively, then there is a point in I for which $u_1 = a_2$.

Let X be a point in I for which $X_1 = a_1$, Y a point in I for which $Y_1 = a_3$. Define points X' and Y' by their coordinates as follows: $X'_1 = a_2, X'_i = X_i$ for $i \neq 1$; $Y'_1 = a_2$, $Y'_i = Y_i$ for $i \neq 1$. Since $X'_i = X_i$ $(i \neq 1)$, $X'_1 > X_1$, X' is preferred to X, by Assumption 2; similarly, Y is preferred to Y', so that X, which is indifferent to Y, is preferred to Y'. Hence, by Assumption 3, there is a number t such that $Z = tX' + (1 - t)Y'$ is indifferent to X and hence belongs to I. But $Z_1 = tX'_1 + (1 - t)Y'_1 = a_2$, so that there is a point of I for which $u_1 = a_2$.

This proposition alone suffices to justify the procedure indicated for deciding the relation between X and Y, with $X_n > Y_n$, in the case where I_1, the indifference surface in the hyperplane $u_n = X_n$ through X, is unbounded in the u_1-direction. If the point Z is defined, then the procedure clearly determines the relation between X and Y. If Z is not defined, then either I_1 has no points for which $u_1 = Y_1$, or I_2, the surface of points in the hyperplane $u_n = Y_n$ indifferent to X, has no points for which $u_1 = Y_1$, or I_2 does not exist. In the last case, certainly X is superior to some point for which $u_n = Y_n$, since $X_n > Y_n$ by Assumption 2; if X were not preferred to Y, there would, by Assumption 3, be a point for which $u_n = Y_n$ which is indifferent to X. But there can be no point for which $u_n = Y_n$ which is indifferent to X if I_2 does not exist.

Now suppose that I_1 has no points for which $u_1 = Y_1$. Since I_1 is unbounded in the u_1-direction, there are points for which $u_1 > Y_1$. By Proposition 1, then, there cannot be any points on I_1 for which $u_1 < Y_1$, for if there were, there would have to be a point on I_1 for which $u_1 = Y_1$. Hence $u_1 > Y_1$ for every point of I_1; every point for which $u_n = X_n$, $u_1 = Y_1$ must be disfavored to the points of I_1 and hence to X. Since $Y_n < X_n$, any point for which $u_n = Y_n$, $u_1 = Y_1$ must be disfavored to X a fortiori, by Assumption 2; in particular, X must be preferred to Y.

Finally, suppose that I_2 has no points for which $u_1 = Y_1$. Since I_1 is unbounded, there is a point of I_1 with $u_1 > Y_1$. Consider the bundle obtained by replacing the u_n-coordinate of this point, which is X_n, by Y_n. Since $Y_n < X_n$, the new bundle must be disfavored to I_1 and hence X. That is, there is a point disfavored to X on the hyperplane $u_n = Y_n$ for which $u_1 > Y_1$. The projection of I_2 on the x_1-axis is an interval not containing the number Y_1. Hence, either $u_1 < Y_1$ for all points of I_2 or $u_1 > Y_1$ for all such points. If the first alternative held, all points on the hyperplane $u_n = Y_n$ for which $u_1 > Y_1$ would be preferred to points of I_2 and hence to X; but we know this to be false. Hence, $u_1 > Y_1$ for all points of I_2, so that any point for which $u_1 \leqq Y_1$, $u_n = Y_n$ must be disfavored to X. In particular, X is preferred to Y.

The case where I_1 is bounded in the u_1-direction requires another proposition.

PROPOSITION 2. *If an indifference surface is bounded in the u_1-direction, it contains a point for which $u_i = 0$ for all $i \neq 1$. That is, the indifference surface must cut the u_1-axis.*

Proof. Since the u_1-coordinates of the points on I are bounded from above, they must possess a least upper bound c; that is, for all points on I, $u_1 \leqq c$, while for any number $c' < c$, there is a point on I such that $u_1 > c'$. Let X be the bundle $(c, 0, \ldots, 0)$; it will be shown that X belongs to I.

Suppose it did not. Then either X is preferred to the points of I or is disfavored to them. In the first case, let X' be any point in I, so that $X_1' \leqq c$. Since $X_i' \geqq 0 = X_i$ for $i \neq 1$, if also $X_1' = c$, we would have X' preferred or indifferent to X, contrary to assumption. Hence, $X_1' < c$. Define X'' as follows: $X_1'' = X_1'$, $X_i'' = 0$ for $i \neq 1$. Then X' is preferred or indifferent to X''; since X is preferred to X' by assumption, there is a linear combination $Y = tX'' + (1 - t)X$, $0 < t \leqq 1$, which is indifferent to X' and hence belongs to I. Clearly, $Y_1 < c$, $Y_i = 0$ ($i = 1$). As noted above, there is a point Z in I for which $Z_1 > Y_1$; as $Z_i \geqq 0 = Y_i$ ($i \neq 1$), Z is preferred to Y, which is a contradiction since both are in I. Hence, X cannot be preferred to the points of I.

Now suppose that X is disfavored to the points of I. Again let X' be any point of I; $X_1' \leqq c$. Define X'' as follows: $X_1'' = c$, $X_i'' = X_i'$ $(i \neq 1)$. Then X'' is preferred or indifferent to X', which, in turn, is preferred to X. There is a linear combination $Y = tX + (1 - t)X''$ which is indifferent to X' and hence belongs to I; $Y_1 = c$. If $Y_i = 0$ for all $i \neq 1$, then $Y = X$, and X would belong to I, contrary to assumption. Hence $Y_j > 0$ for some $j \neq 1$. Choose numbers c', c'' so that $0 < c' < Y_j$, $c'' > c$. Define Y', Y'' as follows: $Y_j' = c'$, $Y_i' = Y_i$ $(i \neq j)$; $Y_1'' = c''$; $Y_i'' = Y_i$ $(i \neq 1)$. Then Y'' is preferred to Y and Y to Y'; hence, there is a linear combination $Z = tY' + (1 - t)Y''$, $0 < t < 1$ which is indifferent to Y and hence belongs to I. But $Z_1 > c$, which is impossible by definition of c. Hence, X cannot be disfavored to the points of I; it must belong to I. Q.E.D.

Proposition 2 establishes the validity of the procedure for deciding the preference as between X and Y, $X_n > Y_n$, when I_1 is bounded in the x_1-direction. If c is the least upper bound of the values of u_1 for points of I_1, then, by Proposition 2 applied to the ration plane or hyperplane $u_n = X_n$, the bundle $(c, 0, \ldots, 0, X_n)$ belongs to I_1 and hence is indifferent to X. Therefore, I_4, the surface in the hyperplane $u_1 = c$ of points indifferent to $(c, 0, \ldots, X_n)$, consists of points indifferent to X. Hence, if Z is defined, X bears the same relation to Y as Z does. If Z is not defined, there is no point of I_4 for which $u_n = Y_n$. Since there is a point of I_4 for which $u_n = X_n > Y_n$, there cannot be a point of I_3 for which $u_n = 0$, by Proposition 1. On the hyperplane $u_1 = c$, the coordinates which vary are $u_2, \ldots, u_n$. If I_4 is bounded in the u_2-direction, then by Proposition 2 there would have to be a point of I_4 for which $u_i = 0$, $(i = 3, \ldots, n)$; but there is no point which $u_n = 0$. Hence I_4 is unbounded in the u_2-direction; since there is a point of I_4 for which $u_2 = 0$, it follows from Proposition 1 that there is a point of I_4 with any assigned value of u_2 and in particular with $u_2 = Y_2$. For this point $u_n > Y_n$. Let I_5 be the indifference surface on the hyperplane $u_2 = Y_2$ of points indifferent to the one just found; I_5 consists of points indifferent to X. If W is defined, then the relation of X to Y is the same as that of W to Y. If W is not defined, then there is no point of I_5 with $u_n = Y_n$; since there is a point of I_5 with $u_n > Y_n$, we must have, by Proposition 1, that $u_n > Y_n$ for all points of I_5, and therefore any point for which $u_2 = Y_2$, $u_n = Y_n$ must be disfavored to the points of I_5 and hence to X. In particular, X is preferred to Y.

4   Utilities, Attitudes, Choices:
A Review Note

The appearance of two books of studies dealing with mathematical models in the social sciences[1] forms a convenient excuse for some remarks on the study of choice or decision making, a topic which is clearly basic to our own discipline and is receiving increasing study from psychologists and sociologists, with the aid of mathematics. Because of the excellent survey that has been made by Ward Edwards (1954), I will confine myself to certain tendencies in research of interest to economists, with no pretense of balanced or comprehensive coverage.

Speaking very broadly, almost any human action involves choice; the external environment delimits a range of possible actions at any given moment but does not usually reduce that range to a single alternative. The formulation of a theory of human action in some sphere as a theory of choice means its presentation as a functional relation associating with each possible range of alternatives a chosen one among them. Economic theory is a clear illustration; the attitudes expressed in polls are again examples of

---

1. Paul F. Lazarsfeld (ed.), *Mathematical Thinking in the Social Sciences,* Glencoe, Illinois: The Free Press, 1954, 444 pp., hereafter cited as MT; R. M. Thrall, C. H. Coombs, and R. L. Davis (eds.), *Decision Processes,* New York: John Wiley and Sons, 1954, viii + 332 pp., hereafter cited as DP. The genesis of these two books is rather different. The first consists of eight long invited papers, designed to give fairly thorough coverages of certain areas of research; the second consists of nineteen papers, many of a decidedly informal nature, presented during a seminar held during the summer of 1952.

Reprinted from *Operations Research,* 5 (1958):765–774.

choices from a given range of alternatives, which in this case are verbal expressions.

One might perhaps draw a distinction between *choices* and *decisions*. Psychologists frequently use the latter term only when conscious reflective choice is involved. Though economists are not always clear on this matter, I think it most consistent with the usual uses of choice theory to consider it applicable to unconscious or at any rate unreflective choices, as well as decisions in the narrower sense.[2] I will therefore speak of the theory of choice, rather than of decision making, in what follows, despite the current popularity of the latter phrase.

1. The Economists' Concept of Choice

1.1. Choice under Certainty

Pareto's "ordinal revolution" in utility theory amounts to recognizing that the subjective theory of value was a statement that choices made under different conditions are consistent. What may be termed a *rational model of choice* (or decision making) has the following well-known form: an individual is assumed to rank all alternative logically possible decisions in order of preference; in any given situation, only some of the logically possible alternatives are in fact available, due to budgetary or other limitations, and the individual is assumed to choose among the alternatives available that one which is highest on his ranking. The ranking or *ordering* is assumed to have the usual consistency properties so that, if alternative A is preferred to alternative B, and B to C, then A is preferred to C.

1.1.1. Such a theory is not empty in the logical sense, that is, it obviously has refutable consequences, but in general it seems to say very little. As Herbert Simon points out (MT, pp. 388–415), the more important part of the content of a rational model of choice in any particular context lies in the specification of the range of alternatives actually available, and, it might be added, in more specific hypotheses about the underlying ordering. The typical application of the rationality postulate in economics is to the ordering of commodity bundles. Here, it is customary to assume about the ordering that it depends solely on the quantities of each commodity in the bundles being compared and not on other conceivable variables such as

2. The distinction between habitual behavior and genuine decisions has been sharply drawn by G. Katona; see, for example, Katona, 1951, pp. 49–52.

prices, and that of two bundles which include the same quantities of all but one commodity, the one with the higher quantity of that commodity will be preferred. In the competitive theory of consumers' choice, the range of alternatives available to any given consumer is described by a budget restraint determined, at least in part, by prices which are taken as given by the consumer (the chooser or decision maker in this case). The rational model of choice then implies the familiar derivation of demand functions from utility-maximization considerations and the standard theorems about those functions.

1.1.2. There are several observations about this model which have relevance for decision making in other spheres of activity. For one thing, the choice is among commodity *bundles.* To describe two alternatives, it is necessary, at least in theory, to specify for each the quantities of all commodities, not just a few. There are two reasons for this: (1) the individual's choice between, for instance, bread and cake will not be independent of the amount of butter available to him; there are relations of complementarity and rivalry among the different commodities; (2) the different commodities are linked together through the budget restraint; all commodities compete for the dollar.

Both reasons may still hold when we consider values not embodied in commodities. An individual deciding whether or not to marry will certainly take into account his current income level for both of the above reasons; there are relations of complementarity between consumption and marriage, and they constitute alternative drains on income. Similar reasoning applies to the choice between national security and personal consumption.

We are thus led to a universal theory of choice where each decision is effectively a choice among total life histories. Such a theory is certainly impractical at our present state of knowledge, and we are forced to compartmentalize the different aspects of life, decisions in each area being treated in some sense independently. But at least we must be aware that such a breakup of the totality may be defective for either or both of the reasons cited above: the effect of one part on the individual's ordering with respect to another, which may be termed the *interdependence of values,* and the limitations imposed by reality on the simultaneous achievement of values in several areas, which may be termed *jointness of resource limitations.*

There may be situations in which neither of these factors operates. To take an example from economics, suppose in a war situation there is point rationing of clothing and of food but no transferability of points between the two. Then the resource limitations are not joint; the choice of alternatives among all clothing combinations is not restricted by a decision about food. Further, it is not unreasonable to suppose in this case that the individual's preferences with respect to clothing are more or less independent of his food consumption pattern. In this situation, it would be reasonable to formulate separate theories of choice for food and for clothing consumption.

In the usual situation in economics, the universal validity of money makes the jointness of resource limitations obvious. One has the feeling that in sociological and political analysis, there is a greater tendency to separate different value areas and to ignore their interrelations both on the value and on the resource sides. Thus separate studies may well be made of attitudes toward race and toward war, without thought being given to their possible correlation. It may well be, in fact, that an individual's attitude toward war is influenced by the presence or absence of racial segregation in the armed forces; this would be an example of interdependence of values. Jointness of resource limitations is less important in this case; the obstacles to achievement of one's racial attitudes are more or less independent of those to achievement of attitudes toward war. However, the political organization of society may lead to examples of jointness of resources. For example, suppose a political party which is anticlerical and favors economic interventionism lacks a majority. It may be confronted with a choice between coalition with a clerical interventionist party and an anticlerical laissez-faire party. Achievement of one goal is therefore at the expense of another.

1.1.3. Another aspect of the rational model of choice in consumption may be briefly mentioned. The choice in any given situation is to be made among a great many, strictly speaking infinitely many, alternative bundles. In attitude studies, on the other hand, the tendency is to consider only two or a few alternatives. There are frequently genuinely discrete alternatives in social and political affairs, while continuous sets of alternatives are more characteristic of economic choices (although occupational choice is discrete), but even where there are a great many alternatives in a political or social issue, the difficulty of quantifying them in the natural way available for commodities makes it very difficult to handle the full range for purposes of analysis.

1.1.4. Finally, we may notice that in both economics and the behavioral sciences, the choices studied may be *actual* or *potential.* In economics the study of actual choices would be exemplified by statistical analysis on family budget data. Potential choices would perhaps be exemplified by questionnaires which seek to establish how much an individual would buy, were conditions something other than they are now. The latter type of analysis has had little actual use in empirical economics, though one might say it is the chief content of the pure theory of demand. In the behavioral sciences there has, on the whole, been relatively little work on choices made in what might be termed natural settings, though considerable analysis of choices which are actual but made under controlled experimental situations. In addition, there is a considerable body of work on potential choices, in the form of attitude analyses.

The relation between potential choices and actual ones is, of course, rather tricky. One can easily see all sorts of reasons why the response to a question, always posing a potential choice, may be different from a choice made in the actual situation. Undoubtedly, depth interviews and questionnaires can go far in eliminating inconsistencies by elaborate sets of questions.

1.2. Choice under Uncertainty

Much recent work in economics as well as statistics has emphasized a rational model of choices made in the presence of uncertainty.

1.2.1. Uncertainty has been long discussed in economic literature, but usually only in a rather marginal way. Discussion rarely advanced beyond the point of the famous article by Daniel Bernoulli (1738), who argued that the individual acts in such a way as to maximize the mathematical expectation of his utility. Despite the elegance and simplicity of this theory, little real use was made of it in explaining the facts of the business world beyond the existence of insurance, at least until the work of Frank Knight (1921), which was continued somewhat belatedly by J. R. Hicks (1931) and Albert G. Hart (1942), who made the first fruitful applications of the theory of uncertainty to the behavior of business firms, particularly in regard to such questions as liquidity, the holding of inventories, and flexibility of production processes.

During the past half-century there has been a remarkably rapid growth in one form of behavior under uncertainty, namely, statistics. Statistics is concerned with the making of decisions, in the face of uncertainty, from information. Sometimes the decision making is of a very concrete nature, as in quality control or selection of drugs for use; at other times it is a tool of scientific inference. In either case it postulates a situation in which the observations are random representations of some underlying situation about which an inference must be made. Such an inference is intrinsically uncertain, and the problem is how to make the best decision in the face of this uncertainty.

1.2.2. In the last few years there has been a confluence of the ideas arising in both statistics and economics which has led to a widely accepted formulation of the problem of behavior under uncertainty.[3]

The rational model of choice under uncertainty can be summarized as follows: There are a number of possible states of nature and a number of possible actions we can take. We do not know which state of nature, among a certain class, is the true one. We have to take an action the consequences of which will depend upon which state of nature is the true one. The problem is to choose which action to take among those which satisfy the constraints of the situation. The consequences are completely determined by the action and the state of nature, and presumably are ordered as in the case of certainty.

For simplicity, let us suppose that there are only a finite number of possible states of nature and a finite number of possible actions. Let i denote an action, j a state of nature, and a_{ij} the consequences if action i is taken when state of nature j prevails. The space of possible consequences has already been assumed ordered so that the a_{ij}'s can be thought of as utilities. There have been a number of alternative attempts to axiomatize the behavior of a rational individual when faced with a problem of decision under uncertainty. (1) If it is assumed that uncertainty about the state of nature can be expressed in the form of probabilities, that is, an assignment of probabilities by the individual to each state of nature, then axiom systems stemming from Ramsey and von Neumann and Morgenstern suggest that the a_{ij}'s may be described as real numbers, with the choice among actions determined by the principle of maximizing the expected utility of the action. (2) Some writers, particularly Ramsey, Savage, and de Finetti, have held that there are always probabilities, that is, any individual will act in a manner which may be described by saying that he assigns probabilities to the different states of nature, and then chooses his action among those available so as to maximize expected utility. The probabilities so assigned are subjective in the sense that they may vary from individual to individual. (3) This position is not

---

3. One can mention the work of Frank Ramsey (1931), B. de Finetti (1937), J. Neyman and E. S. Pearson (1937), Abraham Wald (1950), John von Neumann and Oskar Morgenstern (1947, appendix), and L. J. Savage (1954); for a summary of these developments, see Arrow (1951a). The universality of the model is not always accepted. In particular Sir Ronald Fisher (1956) rejects the view that statistics, as used in scientific inference, can be reduced to a utilitarian basis.

universal; Knight, Wald, and Shackle have, in different ways, argued that not all uncertainties are reducible to probabilities. Without going into detail, I think that roughly the major line of distinction between the two schools is the applicability of the law of large numbers.

Reformulation of Bernoulli's hypothesis as sketched under (1) has stimulated a considerable amount of experimental work by social psychologists and others interested in the rational theory of choice. There has also been a limited amount of work on the subjective probability hypothesis.

Economists have been stimulated to seek to describe the shape of the utility function for money compatible with casual economic observations (Friedman and Savage, 1948; Markowitz, 1952), to relate the distribution of observed income to choices made by individuals among random variables (Friedman, 1933), and to continue Knight's investigation of the use of the market to achieve a redistribution of risks (Allais, 1953; Arrow, 1954).

1.2.3. Much work in both economics and statistics has stressed the sequential nature of many choice situations; choices are frequently extended in time, with a choice at one stage having an effect on choices at a later stage. For example, the nature of the machinery purchased by a firm in one period will obviously have an effect on the possibility of changing the scale of operations in a second period. If the demand conditions are to a certain extent random or unknown, a choice at period 1 should rationally take account of the possibility that a second decision will be made in period 2. Thus the proper policy within a firm must consist of a *strategy* rather than a single decision made for all time, that is, the decision to be made takes the form of a function which specifies the relation between the action taken at any time point in the future and the information available at that time, though not available at the time at which the initial decision is made.[4]

Wald's theory of the sequential analysis of statistical data is closely related to the economic theories of flexibility just mentioned. The observations are assumed to be collected one after the other; after each observation, one of two decisions must be made, to terminate the observations and to draw whatever inference is called for or to draw at least one more observation. Presumably there are costs to the observation, or at least to the delay in making it a terminal decision, but this incentive to stop must be weighed against the value of the additional information obtained. The choice is

---

4. See A. G. Hart (1942); J. Marschak (1949). The principle, applied to inventory policy and related fields, has led to the modern theory of dynamic programming; see P. Massé (1946), R. Bellman (1953), Arrow, Harris, and Marschak (1951).

somewhat similar to that of the firm between making a strong commitment under uncertainty or postponing the commitment for better information. Either policy has some gains and some losses, and they must be weighed against each other.

1.2.4. Learning, as studied by psychologists, closely resembles sequential analysis in some aspects. Learning experiments usually consist of a series of trials in which the subject's choices are sometimes rewarded and sometimes not. The individual, after making many choices, eventually begins to discriminate between the proper response and the improper one. At some point, presumably, he could terminate the experiment, at least in the sense of disregarding the further observations and making the same choice each time.

1.3. Multipersonal Choices

In many choice situations, complications arise because choices made by different individuals have some kind of mutual dependence. These have, as is well known, given rise to a good many largely unresolved problems in economics, and parallel problems exist elsewhere in the social sciences.

1.3.1. In this context we need, of course, refer only to the classic economic problem of oligopoly; the inability of economics to get a firm understanding of the rules governing such behavior is notorious. Bargaining among nations, as in the formation of alliances, has to a large extent the same characteristics as the behavior of economic units, each of which is relatively large, so that a choice made by one influences the opportunities for others.

1.3.2. Of course the theory of games, and particularly the theory of n-person games, has grown in an attempt to meet this situation. There has indeed been a highly sophisticated development: general concepts originating in economics have been refined and abstracted to where they can be applied in other areas and have even been given new interpretations within the field of economics itself. Thus Cournot's solution for duopoly, in which each person maximizes his profit, taking the quantity sold by the other as datum, has been generalized by John Nash (1950) into an equilibrium-point theory in which each individual chooses his strategy, which may be a quantity, a price, or a combination of the two, on the assumption that the other one's strategy is given. The Cournot solution and its generalization are applicable to the cases of noncollusive interaction; that is, the choices are interdependent, but there is no agreement by the parties to act as one to maximize the total profit or benefit. A genuine collusion makes the problem simpler, since the behavior of the total group is presumably one of monopoly. But there remains the problem of dividing up the spoils. This problem has been approached in different ways by von Neumann and Morgenstern (1947), Nash (1953), and others (see also Harsanyi, 1956).

The mathematical structure of a special part of the theory of games, namely zero-sum two-person games, has had a curiously multiple role in some developments of the theory of choice. In its literal interpretation it is a theory of pure conflict without any possibility of coalition formation. As such, it has found no important application in economics, which is primarily concerned with cases where cooperation can increase to the satisfaction of both parties. Indeed, its principal applications have been to the mathematical theory of social games and to military tactics.

However, it has played a role by reinterpretation in the theory of decision making under uncertainty. Wald (1950) has suggested that we may view the decision problem under uncertainty, as restated in the previous section, as a game in which one player, the statistician, chooses an action i, and a second player, nature, chooses a state j. The payoff of the game then consists in transferring the amount a_{ij} from nature to the player; the optimal policies recommended by the theory of games in this situation are therefore referred to as minimax rules. Among other consequences, a minimax rule frequently implies that the optimal strategy is mixed, that is, the statistician should not take a fixed action but should choose among several alternative actions with certain probabilities. An interesting application of this idea to anthropology is found in a paper by Omar Khayyam Moore (1957), who suggested that the universal practice of divination as a basis for action could be interpreted as the choice of a mixed strategy in accordance with minimax principles.

A third interpretation of the theory of zero-sum two-person games has been the identification of constrained maxima with such games. Thus there is a close relation between game theory and linear and nonlinear programming (see H. W. Kuhn and A. W. Tucker, 1951). A very closely related interpretation is the problem of choosing *vector maxima*. Supposedly there are a number of criteria for choice. Without wanting to weigh them together, we might at least say that we wish to avoid choosing alternatives which are inferior to some other alternative from the point of view of every criterion. Such a problem arises in welfare economics, where we seek to characterize the positions of the economy for which there is no other position such that everybody could be made better off by changing to it. An entirely analogous concept is that of admissible actions or strategies in statistics, where we wish to find those actions which are not inferior to some other action for any state of nature. Since vector maxima can usually be regarded as constrained maxima (Kuhn and Tucker, 1951), the theory of zero-sum two-person games has an important role to play mathematically in these problems.

1.3.3. The problem of welfare economics formulated in the last paragraph is a weak one. It avoids obviously inferior states, but it does not say which of the many possible economic states which are not thereby rejected is to be chosen. We have the problem of finding a technique for amalgamating, in some form, the preferences of different individuals. This problem has sometimes been termed that of establishing a social welfare function, or a constitution (see Arrow, 1951b; Weldon, 1952).

The problem here has some strong formal analogies with that of decision making under uncertainty. We may use i as before to represent the action, in this case a social action, but we will take j to represent individuals. Each individual will rank the possible actions, but of course the rankings will be different for different individuals. The problem is to amalgamate them in some way so as to arrive at a choice of social action.

It is also interesting to observe that in some formulations the problem of statistics is different from that of choice by an individual under uncertainty. Statistics and science in general are social enterprises, and their results are supposed to be interpersonally valid. It follows that even if one accepts the subjective or personal probability viewpoint as a guide to an individual's action, there is need for some method of combining the utility functions and subjective probabilities of different individuals. The statistical decision problem then becomes part of the social choice problem. It is in this form that the problem has been posed by de Finetti (1951) and Savage (1954), and the latter has reinterpreted the minimax principle, which does not depend on personal probabilities, as being an attempt to seek such a socially acceptable form of choice of actions.

2. Choice in the Behavioral Sciences

2.1. The Context of Choices

Obviously, the behavioral scientist is usually interested in different kinds of choices from those the economist is interested in, although purchasing goods is indeed one area of his interest. But a vote is also an expression of choice, and so indeed is the formation of a group. Attitudes are clearly potential choices. These decisions are frequently not quantitative, and the budgetary limitation at least does not play such an obvious role. It is not surprising, therefore, if the focus of interest in the methods of study of the behavioral scientists in choice situations is different from that of the economists.

2.2. The Structure of Choices

The economist is usually not interested in choices or preferences in themselves; the theory of choice serves as a background for empirical demand analysis or as a tool in welfare economics. There is little investigation of the utility function in itself, and what assumptions are made about it are of a very general nature. Only in side remarks do we find any attempt to develop an organized structure of choices.[5]

The sociologist and the social psychologist, on the other hand, are interested as much in the choices themselves as in the consequences which flow from a general theory of decision making. Thus research on attitudes has been concerned chiefly with the relationships among different attitudes. When social psychologists became interested in the utility of gambling, it was the possibility of measuring the utility curve that interested them, not the implications for behavior in economic situations.

Closely related to the difference in interest is a difference in the empirical methods used. Where the economist tends to rely on time-series data or on budget studies, the social psychologist tends to emphasize experimentation under controlled conditions. It is clear that the fine structure of the choice process can only be discussed in the light of such a situation, though there is certainly a possible loss of realism in that the choices made in the laboratory are on too small a scale to be relevant to real-life situations. Attitude analysis occupies a middle role between experimental situations and budget analysis, but questionnaires, too, frequently provide a more flexibly controlled type of probe than is usually employed by the economist.

2.3. Measurement

Because choices are studied directly, the behavioral scientist is under a much stronger compulsion to seek to measure his magnitudes. It is not a question

---

5. Georgescu-Roegen has argued that such a theory is needed and points to earlier precedents, particularly Banfield (Georgescu-Roegen, 1954, pp. 513–518).

here of the rather philosophical discussion that has taken place among economists, as between cardinal and ordinal utility. For empirical work, measurement, while not logically indispensable, is extremely convenient; the behavioral scientist will make many assumptions analogous to cardinal utility, and indeed to highly specific forms of cardinal utility, simply because they are usable for empirical work.

Coombs, Raiffa, and Thrall (DP, chap. 2) present an elaborate classification of possible types of measurement. Not only do we have the interval scale (exemplified by cardinal utility, where unit and origin are arbitrary) and the weak ordering (exemplified by ordinal utility) but also weaker measurements, such as partial orderings, and stronger ones, such as the ratio scale (only the unit is arbitrary).

2.4. Maximization and Adaptation

As we have seen, the rational model of choice in economics is dominated by the idea of achieving an optimum. Presumably, in its strict form, the model would argue that behavior in any moment of time can be described as the achievement of an optimal position. Even within economics we do not always stick strictly to this assumption, and Simon (MT, chap. 8) has shown how the behavioral sciences may depart even further than economics has.

The most immediate generalization of the simple maximization principle is to assume that the dynamics of behavior can be described as adaptation or movement to a maximum. The individual may be assumed at each moment to be changing the variables under his control in such a way as to increase his utility. Without going into details here, it may suffice to say that this is in effect the basis for most stability analysis in economics; the usual law of supply and demand can be thought of as a minimization of the aggregate value of excess demand.[6]

This hypothesis gives rise to a system of differential equations which describe the behavior of the system and which are usually assumed, eventually, to converge to the optimal position. This kind of adaptive argument has some resemblance to the notion of the struggle for life in the theory of evolution.

Simon suggests that for many purposes we may consider the dynamics of

---

6. See G. Debreu (1951), secs. 11 and 12; Arrow and Debreu (1954), pp. 271–272. In these articles the dynamics is only implicit, but it can be made explicit and in this form give rise to stability considerations.

social behavior as governed by differential equations which cannot be regarded as leading to an optimum at their equilibrium. A great many plausible hypotheses about human behavior, derived mostly from everyday observation, may be put in this more general form. A simple illustration in learning is provided by Simon. Let us assume that learning a new subject (for instance, a foreign language, in Simon's illustration) is governed by the following laws: (1) the difficulty D decreases logarithmically with the rate of practice x; (2) the pleasantness of the practice has a maximum up to a point $\bar{x}$ and decreases beyond that; (3) at any moment the individual is changing the rate of practice in such a way as to move toward the maximum of pleasure. The first assumption, about the nature of learning, can be written as a differential equation,

(4-1) $dD/dt = -a\,Dx.$

The second and third assumptions together can be written as

(4-2) $dx/dt = -b(x - \bar{x}).$

Notice that (4-2) is derived from a maximization assumption, but (4-1) is not. The behavior of the individual over time can be determined from the joint solution of the two equations.

We will see a number of other examples of this distinction between *purely adaptive* models and *maximizing* models. However, there is always a strong tendency to attempt to explain the first category by introducing more considerations into the maximization process. Thus in many cases a type of behavior may be explained as rational if one introduces uncertainty and the need for learning.

Constraints relevant for behavior are for the most part perceived rather than actual restraints. (Compare the usual discussion in economic theory of monopolistic competition, where a distinction is drawn between the demand curves imagined by the firm and those which it might actually experience.) If one introduces into a maximizing model perceptions or expectations which themselves change under the impact of experience, obviously a great variety of behavior is rationalizable if, perhaps, not explainable in a really scientific sense. A number of social psychologists argue that perceptions will change so as to bring them into agreement with those of a reference group (see, for example, Festinger, 1955, p. 173, and Section 5.4.1 later in this chapter).

Simon has also argued for a weaker form of optimization, in which the agent is presumed to seek a given level of satisfaction rather than the optimal level; this approach is related to the "level of aspiration" concept in psychology. Of course, if it is assumed that the level of aspiration changes with success, the process is a form of maximizing behavior, but with rather more stress on the process and less on the goal than is usual in economics.[7]

3. Decision Making under Uncertainty

Let us now turn to more specific examples of work on choices and attitudes in the behavioral sciences, particularly as drawn from the two examples mentioned in footnote 1.

3.1. Maximizing Models

3.1.1. An excellent exposition of the role of the probability concept in the social sciences is given by Jacob Marschak (MT, chap. 4). He first restates the hypothesis of the maximization of expected utility with subjectively given probabilities and then points to one particular form of behavior under uncertainty, namely, statistics as used as a tool of scientific inference in the social sciences. An exposition of the special problems connected there is followed by a discussion of the identification problem and its relation to policy. If a state of nature relevant to the evaluation of actions is specified by certain parameters, statistical inference, to be useful, must estimate those parameters. We may presume that the general outlines of these matters are familiar to the reader.

3.1.2. The sets of axioms which lead, in the hands of Ramsey and Savage, to the subjective-probability expected-utility theory are not the only ones possible. The minimax principle, as proposed by Wald (see Section 1.3.2) is an alternative one designed to reflect the idea of genuine ignorance, that is, no preference among the states of nature. Savage has shown that the minimax principle as applied to the original payoffs has certain consequences which seem unreasonable (see the Radner-Marschak remarks summarized below), and proposed a modification which has been termed the *minimax-of-regret principle* (a term which Savage himself does not particularly like). It reflects the idea that the aim of the statistician is to do the best he can as compared with the best possible situation if he knew what the state

---

7. Simon's views are expressed not only in the article just referred to, but in a number of other essays in a recent volume (Simon, 1957), especially chapters 6–8, 10, 11, 14, 15, and 16.

of nature were. This principle, in turn, has been shown by Chernoff (1954) not to lead to an ordering of all possible actions and so is not completely consistent with the usual rational model of choice. All these arguments essentially amount to introducing additional axioms of reasonable or rational behavior.

In an extraordinary paper, John Milnor (DP, chap. 4) has given an exhaustive listing of axioms for rational choice under conditions of uncertainty. The formulation of the statistical decision problem is that given earlier in Section 1.2. The axiom system taken as a whole is inconsistent.[8] But Milnor shows that by taking various subsets of the axioms one can derive any one of the various alternative criteria that have been proposed for solution of the problem of decision under uncertainty, as well as others.

The examination of possible criteria is also taken up by Roy Radner and Marschak (DP, chap. 5). By means of an example, they show that the minimax principle leads to the conclusion of not taking more than one observation even when it would be reasonable to take a good deal more, while the minimax of regret principle violates the condition of transitivity, as observed before.[9]

It is clear that we really do not have a universally valid criterion for rational behavior under uncertainty. Probably the best thing to be said is that different criteria are valid under different circumstances.

Stefan Valavanis-Vail has sought to reconsider different types of subjective probability by distinguishing the number of times an event referred to is supposed to be repeated, and also by distinguishing perceived from actual subjective probabilities. However, little is really done with these classifications, though the problems posed are very interesting.

3.1.3. The subjective-probability expected-utility hypothesis has given rise to a considerable amount of experimental work. If we think of an individual choosing among different bets, in which the stakes, prizes, and probabilities of winning differ, the hypothesis suggests the shapes of indifference surfaces among these three variables. Many possible combinations of conditions are possible, giving rise to different experiments. In an extensive survey of these possibilities made by Coombs and Beardslee (DP, chap. 17), a number of experiments carried out on this basis are described. The

---

8. Inconsistency of the requirements also occurs in the parallel problem for social choice (Arrow, 1951b; for the parallelism, see 1.3.3. above and 5.1. below).

9. Actually, they deal with the Hurwicz criterion, which is a generalization of the minimax principle.

results, as in the experiments of Mosteller and Nogee (1951), and more recently of Davidson, Suppes, and Siegel (1957), are generally consistent with the basic hypothesis but can hardly be said to confirm it in all the detailed applications one would like to make.

It is interesting to observe, however, the fruitfulness of a fairly definite hypothesis of this type. The revival of interest in the measurability of utility in its probabilistic and other aspects may have the salutary function of suggesting experiments and thereby bringing new data to bear beyond those already used in economics.

3.1.4. In virtually all developments of rational models of choice, whether under uncertainty or not, the following so-called Archimedean property is generally postulated. If *A, B,* and *C* are three alternatives such that *A* is preferred to *B* and *B* is preferred to *C*, then there is an alternative which is in some sense intermediate to *A* and *C*, and which is indifferent to *B*.[10] In a case of choice under uncertainty, the assumption would be that some random mixture of *A* and *C* is indifferent to *B*.

This hypothesis would be false if the satisfaction of *A* were in some sense incommensurably greater than that of *B* or *C*. As in Pascal's famous wager, it may be that *B* is preferred to *C*, but a mixture of *A* and *C* which gives any probability greater than 0 to *A* would be preferred to *B*.

The modification of the von Neumann – Morgenstern theory of utility to allow for dropping the Archimedean postulate is carried through in two papers by Hausner and Thrall (DP, chaps. 12 and 13). They show that instead of a single utility function to represent the preferences, there will be a sequence of utility functions, the choice between the two prospects being made in accordance with the first utility function in the sequence which gives different values to the two prospects. It is remarked that the theories of zero-sum two-person games and of linear programming are not essentially altered by this introduction of multidimensional utilities.

3.2. Adaptive Models

Learning is certainly one of the most important forms of behavior under uncertainty. Results found in this field should have very striking impact on economic thought. Most of the work to be described here is of an adaptive nature, and it suggests that there is not the convergence to an optimum that we would ordinarily expect in economics.

---

10. Georgescu-Roegen (1954) has raised objections to this view.

3.2.1. R. R. Bush, F. Mosteller, and G. L. Thompson (DP, chap. 8) have formulated a mathematical model to represent learning. It is assumed that the experimental subject is faced with a succession of trials, at each of which there is a set of alternatives on which the subject must choose, and a set of possible outcomes. In an experimental situation, the probability π_{jk} that outcome k will follow the choice of alternative j is chosen by the experimenter and assumed constant among trials. Let $p(n)$ be the vector of probabilities of different alternatives being chosen by the subject at the nth trial. As a result of choosing the alternative j, and observing the outcome k, this vector is transformed into $p(n+1) = T_{jk} p(n)$, where T_{jk} is symbolically an operator which transforms vectors. If we assume the operator is linear, it can be represented by a matrix. The authors assume that the operator T_{jk} will satisfy the "combining of classes" criterion, that if for each k the probabilities π_{jk} are the same for all j in a certain class, then the class can be regarded as a single alternative for all purposes. Under these conditions it is shown that any matrix T_{jk} can be expressed in the form

$$\alpha_{jk} I + (1 - \alpha_{jk}) \Lambda_{jk},$$

where I is the unit matrix, all the columns of Λ_{jk} are the same, and $0 \leq \alpha_{jk} \leq 1$.

This representation is very useful in interpreting experiments; in particular, it permits the development of a number of "trapping" theorems, which state regions in which the probability vector $p(n)$ will eventually lie.

3.2.2. W. K. Estes (DP, chap. 9) has considered a simple model of learning which is equivalent to a special case of the preceding, and applied it to the interpretation of a set of data. Individuals are asked to predict an event the occurrence of which is actually random with a constant probability π. If we assume that success and failure affect the individual in a symmetrical way, they lead to the following rules for the transformation of the individual's probabilities of response. If $p(n)$ is now the probability of predicting the event, so that $1 - p(n)$ is the probability that the individual predicts the failure of the event, then $p(n+1) = p(n) + \theta[1 - p(n)]$ if the event occurs and $p(n+1) = p(n) - \theta p(n)$ otherwise.

These relations are plausible if when the event occurs, the probabilities that it was predicted by the individual for the next time will be increased, and otherwise decreased. Let $\bar{p}(n)$ be the average of this number over a great many individuals; then in the experimental situation described we have

$$\bar{p}(n+1) = \bar{p}(n) + \theta[\pi - \bar{p}(n)].$$

It is easy to see that as n approaches infinity, $\bar{p}(n)$ will approach π. This result has been confirmed experimentally with a very high degree of success.

The remarkable thing about this is that the asymptotic behavior of the individual, even after an indefinitely large amount of learning, is not the optimal behavior. If, for example, π is greater than one-half, the optimal strategy of the individual is always to predict an event, since this gives him an expected outcome of π. To predict the event with probability π, and to predict its failure with probability $1 - \pi$, leads to a payoff of only $\pi^2 + (1 - \pi)^2$. Thus there is no indication that the individual is maximizing even in the sense of approaching a maximum. It is certainly reasonable enough from an economic point of view that he does not achieve an optimum immediately, since he does not know the situation. But it is usually assumed that after a certain amount of trial and error, the optimal behavior will in fact be found, and this reasoning is given implicitly and explicitly in most economics texts. We have here an experimental situation which is essentially of an economic nature in the sense of seeking to achieve a maximum of expected reward, and yet the individual does not in fact, at any point, even in a limit, reach the optimal behavior. I suggest that this result points up strongly the importance of learning theory, not only in the greater understanding of the dynamics of economic behavior, but even in suggesting that equilibria may be different from those that we have predicted in our usual theory.

3.2.3. There have been some attempts to reconcile the results of Estes and his colleagues with a rational model of choice. In particular, Flood (DP, chap. 18) has suggested two explanations. One is that the individuals are not seeking to maximize their expected score, but attach an unusually high utility to getting a perfect score. Second, they are not necessarily aware of the fact that the observations of success and failure are based on a random mechanism, but they believe that there is some nonstationary process at work. Suppose, for example, an individual believes that the observed successes and failures follow a deterministic principle. Then having observed that on the average a success occurs, say, three-quarters of the time, he will try to construct some deterministic hypothesis which will account for this. The simplest would, for example, be that every fourth trial yields a failure, and all others successes. This hypothesis could be easily refuted, but it is easy to construct a more complicated version which would not be so simple for the subject to overthrow. As an individual who was seeking to achieve a perfect score, he would attempt to predict in accordance with his deterministic hypothesis and in doing so would reproduce the probabilities of the actual occurrence, as predicted by the Estes experiments. Flood has attempted to design some experiments which would test this version of the hypothesis, but he was unable to achieve conclusive results.[11]

4. The Structure of Attitudes or Preferences

4.1. *Lazarsfeld's Latent Structure Analysis*

The idea of most structural analysis in psychology has been that a great many measurable variables can be regarded as functions of a relatively few variables which are, however, not directly measurable. One may refer to a *latent* structure in terms of which the *manifest* data are determined, at least in a probability sense. The most important application of this technique has been the factor analysis of tests, particularly intelligence tests. In its simplest form, the score on a particular type of test, which is for verbal or arithmetic ability, is regarded as a linear function of two variables, one a general factor of intelligence and the other a factor of the specific ability in question. From such assumptions it is possible to arrive at a rationale for estimating the value of the intelligence factor for any individual. A knowledge of the values of the factors will also serve to predict future test scores or future success in real-life situations.

The preceding discussion has been in terms of abilities, but the same principles are applicable to attitudes. However, their successful analysis depends on new mathematical techniques, because the responses to attitude questions are typically qualitative rather than quantitative. In their simplest form, attitude questions are dichotomies; the individual prefers one alternative to the other. The most general form of latent structure analysis for qualitative data is due to Paul Lazarsfeld (MT, chap. 7). Assume that we have a battery of questions (which are to be thought of, actually, as a sample of a whole universe of possible questions). If there are n questions, an individual may give a positive response to some subset, say S, of them, and a negative response to the remainder. In repeated testing, the individual may well not give the same responses to the same questions. So, over the long run, his response pattern will be measured by the probabilities, here denoted by p_S, of answering positively the questions in S and responding negatively to all others. It is assumed in Lazarsfeld's analysis that the response patterns

---

11. Simon has recently given a more formal treatment of Flood's propositions (1957, chap. 16).

are determined by the value of a latent variable, x, which may be discrete or continuous, one-dimensional or multidimensional, so that the probability of giving positive responses to the questions in S and negative responses to all others can be designated as a function of x with a notation p_S^x. It is finally assumed (and this is crucial) that for any individual or any class of individuals in which the latent variable is constant, the responses to different questions are independent in the probability sense. That is, the probability, for example, of a positive response to questions 1 and 2 is the product of the probabilities of a positive response on 1 and a positive response on 2. The reason is that any tendency toward association of positive responses is supposed to be already accounted for by the latent variable. This does not mean that correlation of responses to different questions in the population as a whole is zero.

Let p_S be the probability of the responses S in the population. Then $p_S = \int p_S^x f(x)\, dx$, where $f(x)$ is the density of a latent variable x. By making assumptions as to the nature of the functions p_S^x it is possible to infer from the manifest probabilities p_S the latent probabilities p_S^x. Notice that it is only the former that are directly observed in the population, since we cannot ask individuals to repeat, nor do we know the value of latent variables for any individual. It is, however, possible to use the above information to estimate the value of a latent variable for any individual.

In this way, the attitude structures are assumed to depend on a much smaller number of variables, perhaps one. In economic terms, we would assume that indifference maps in different individuals varied according to one parameter. A system of questions about the preference among commodity bundles would enable us to relate the utility function to the unobserved parameter and to estimate the value of that parameter for any individual. The latter information, in turn, would be helpful in predicting choices for future situations.

4.2. Guttman's Perfect Scale

A special case of the latent structure model is given by Louis Guttman's perfect scale.[12] It is assumed that for any given value of the latent variable

---

12. Historically, it should be observed that the perfect scale precedes the development of the general latent structure model.

the probabilities of responses are either zero or one. That is, the latent variable determines completely the responses. Further, by deciding which response is to be regarded as positive and which is negative for each question in an appropriate way, and by suitably reordering the questions and the individuals, it can be assumed that a later individual will give positive responses on every question to which an earlier individual will give such responses and possibly on additional questions as well. Such questions can be regarded as a sequence of increasing intensity of preference for one attitude over its opposite, the order of the questions having the same significance for all individuals. It appears from Guttman's evidence that the existence of such scales is more common than one might suppose a priori.

It is interesting to observe how Guttman seeks to make cardinal this essentially ordinal notion of a scale. He does this first by assigning numbers to individuals in such a way that on the average the differences in the mean values of individuals answering, giving positive or negative responses on each question, are maximized. That is, if x is the score assigned to individuals, $\bar{x}_{1j}$ is the average x score of the individuals giving a positive response on question j, and $\bar{x}_{2j}$ is the average score of individuals giving a negative response to question j, Guttman chooses the x scores so as to maximize $\Sigma (\bar{x}_{1j} - \bar{x}_{2j})^2$. This way of defining the scores thus increases their discriminatory power with respect to the average question. It is unique only up to linear transformations with positive coefficients and, of course, orders the individuals in the same way as they are ordered by the scale.

Guttman attempted to extend this analysis by looking at the maximization process more closely. The formula given above is a quadratic form, and the maximizing solution is the characteristic vector corresponding to the largest characteristic root. Additional information can be derived by looking at the remaining characteristic vectors. The characteristic vector corresponding to the second highest characteristic root which assigns another set of scores to individuals turns out to be highest for those at the two extremes and lowest somewhere in the middle. Guttman interprets it as intensity of feeling. Similar psychological interpretations are given to the additional characteristic vectors.

This cardinalization, which is somewhat different from the usual problems of cardinal utility, is based on an interpersonal comparison. The x scores can be thought of as the utilities attached by different individuals to an attitude, which can be thought of as a potential social choice, and we now have additional measurements which purport somehow to measure intensity. Of course, Guttman's development does depend on very restrictive assumptions.[13]

4.3. Coombs's Unfolding Technique

Clyde Coombs has used, in a number of places (see Coombs, 1952; DP, chap. 6), a technique for measuring strength of preferences which he terms the *unfolding technique.* In effect, Coombs considers the case in which the alternatives can be represented as the different values of a one-dimensional variable, whose value is not observed. The utility function of the ith individual is $-|d(x) - d_i|$, where x ranges over the alternatives, and $d(x)$, the unobserved score, is assumed to be the same for all. The utility function in terms of this score is the same for all except for the point d_i of maximum utility, about which the utilities of the other alternatives fall away linearly in the score. It is possible to discover the d scaling by a sufficient number of observations which take the form of expressed preferences among all possible alternatives by a sufficient number of individuals. The assumptions, of course, are very stringent.

4.4. Time Changes in Attitude

A set of attitudes or utility functions can be thought of as a set of answers to a specified set of questions. Let us suppose that there is only a finite number of attitude structures represented by a variable i. One problem which has received very little attention in economics has been that of changes in preference patterns. Theodore W. Anderson (MP, chap. 1) has suggested a model for studying such changes. He supposes that individuals having an attitude structure i at time t will have certain probabilities of changing their attitude structure to j at time $t + 1$. Let p_{ij} be the probability of such a change. Then we have a *stochastic process,* and it is possible to infer the probability that a given individual will have a given attitude structure after any given length of time, provided his initial attitudes are known. The original simple model can be extended in several directions without losing its basic computational simplicity.

---

13. In MP, chap. 6, Guttman presents a generalization and reorientation of factor analysis. The interpretations given, however, run in terms of abilities rather than in terms of attitudes and therefore are beyond the scope of this chapter.

Stochastic process interpretations have one very salutary effect; they emphasize a new kind of data based on following a single individual. A similar development has occurred in the field of income distribution theory. In the case of attitude analysis, such empirical observations are frequently referred to as panel studies; that is, there are repeated interviews with the same set of individuals. Anderson has illustrated his methods with reference to the voting preferences of potential voters.

4.5. *Utility Functions and Orderings*

Gerard Debreu (DP, chap. 11) studies a topic more in the classical vein of economic theory. We have been accustomed, in economics, to the identifying of preference orderings with utility functions. Clearly, if a utility function is defined over a commodity space, an ordering is defined by it. However, the converse is not true in general. Surprisingly enough, however, little attention has been paid to this point; the only writer who has considered the question previously has been Herman Wold (1953, p. 83), and his assumptions are rather restrictive. Debreu has considered the problem in great generality and has stated the topological conditions on the ordering needed to ensure the existence of the utility function which would be consistent with a predesigned ordering. If, as is usual, the commodity space is considered to be a subset of a finite dimensional Euclidean space, then Debreu's condition reduces to the statement that for every point x_0 in the set, the set of all points x which are at least as good as x_0 and the set of all points which are not preferred to x_0 are both closed sets. This clears up a major gap in the mathematical presentation of utility theory.[14]

5. Multipersonal Choice Problems

5.1. *Social Choice*

5.1.1. L. A. Goodman (DP, chap. 3) points out the analogy between the statistical decision problem and the social choice problem as formulated in Section 1.3.3. above. He also presents a general formula covering both

---

14. Reference should be made at this point to the paper by H. G. Bohnert (DP, chap. 15) on the logical structure of the utility concept. He points out difficulties in the empirical interpretation of a formal axiom scheme for utility, but his own counterproposals are difficult to understand.

problems which includes many previous suggestions. However, no properties of this formula are discussed.

5.1.2. Coombs (DP, chap. 6) has applied his unfolding technique (see Section 4.3) to social choice. He simply assumes that social utility is the sum of the individual utilities, that is, that the unit of utility of the different individuals is comparable. Two alternative methods of forming social utility, one based on equal voting rights for all and one on Thurstone's Law of Comparative Judgment, are briefly described and the results of the three methods compared in an experimental situation. Since all the methods involve the assumption of a common unit of utility, it is hard to see how the study of social choice has been enhanced; it is precisely the determination of the common unit that is the basic problem.

5.2. Rational Theory of Organization

Marschak (DP, chap. 14) has begun the development of a theory of organization. It is assumed that an organization, called by Marschak a *team,* has a well-defined utility function. However, there are many individuals concerned, and among other costs are those of communication among them and of acquiring information. Of course, the whole situation applies to life problems only if there is intrinsic uncertainty in the environment with which the team deals. It is remarkable that even relatively simple formulations give rise to extremely complicated mathematical problems.

5.3. Adaptive Models of Multipersonal Behavior

In many different situations, a number of models have been suggested in which the behavior of individuals is changed in some adaptive way by the behavior of other individuals. Such models give rise, usually, to systems of differential equations. It may be observed that these models resemble the dynamic formulations of oligopoly and bargaining models, for example those of Zeuthen (1930) and Hicks (1932, chap. 7); for an excellent reinterpretation in modern terms, see Harsanyi (1956).

5.3.1. Among the most active students of such interaction models has been Nicolas Rashevsky.[15] Expositions of some of Rashevsky's models are

---

15. N. Rashevsky, *Mathematical Biology of Social Behavior,* Chicago: University of Chicago Press, 1951.

given by him (MP, chap. 2) and by James S. Coleman (MP, chap. 3). Some samples of his approach may be useful.

First, from neurophysiological considerations, Rashevsky postulates that the state of internal excitation, denoted by e, adjusts to an outside stimulus S in accordance with a differential equation, $de/dt = AS - ae$. That is, the internal state is supposed to adjust itself to the stimulus, but with a retardation factor which increases with the state of excitation already reached. The response, R, in turn depends on the state of internal excitation e. Imitative behavior is introduced into this system by assuming that the stimulus at any given moment is proportionate to the number of individuals displaying the appropriate response. This idea, together with some assumptions about the distribution of responses initially, leads to the simple system of differential equations in which it can be shown that the equilibrium position, where half the people display one response and half display the other, is unstable.

A rather sketchy model of the distribution of social status is developed from a similar idea. Status here may include wealth as well as any other index of ranking. It is assumed that individuals meet randomly, and that at each encounter there is a certain probability that the status of each individual will change. All the probabilities, of course, may depend on the social statuses of the individuals initially. This general model leads to a linear integro-differential equation. About its properties, however, little can be said.

5.3.2. In a rather similar approach, Simon (MP, chap. 8) has a mathematical version of the human interaction model due to Homans (1950).

Let T be the intensity of interaction among a group, I the amount of friendliness, W the amount of group activity, and F the amount of activity required of the group by its external environment. F is assumed to be determined exogenously. The other variables satisfy the following relations:

$$T = a_1 I + a_2 W,$$

$$\frac{dI}{dt} = b(T - \beta I),$$

$$\frac{dW}{dt} = c_1(I - \gamma W) + c_2(F - W).$$

"The first equation may be translated, roughly: interaction will be produced by friendliness and/or group activity. The second: friendliness will tend to increase or decrease as the amount of interaction is disproportionately large or disproportionately small, respectively, in relation to the existing level of friendliness. (The two variables will be in adjustment when $T = \beta I$). The third: group activity will tend to increase as the level of friendliness is high relative to the existing level of activity (the two being in equilibrium when $I = \gamma W$), and as the requirements of the external system are high relative to the existing level of activity, otherwise group activity will tend to decrease" (Simon, MP, pp. 408–409).

The second equation is essentially an adaptive learning process, while the first and third represent motivations. It might be possible to put this model in the form of a rational model where the variables are being adjusted to find a maximum, rather than reaching the maximizing point immediately. One might think of the utility function which is attached to friendship and to group survival, with a cost attached to acquiring friendship—the cost, however, decreasing as the opportunities increase.

5.3.3. Flood (DP, chap. 10) has considered the problem of playing a zero-sum two-person game where the payoffs are initially unknown to the players and can be learned only by observations on past performances. As a start, it might be assumed that the players learned in accordance with the Bush-Mosteller model discussed above (see Section 3.2.1). The resulting stochastic process is not easily amenable to analysis, so trial computations were run. The scanty empirical evidence suggested that against a fixed mixed strategy on the part of one player, a subject following the Bush-Mosteller model would learn essentially the best strategy within about 200 trials, but that a person proficient in game theory would be more successful in competition.

5.4. Experimental Studies

5.4.1. Since the theory of n-person games was designed as a model for multipersonal bargaining situations, it is reasonable to watch small-scale versions of these games under controlled experimental situations to obtain further insights into the large-scale situations which are interesting. An exceedingly interesting paper of this kind is that by Hoffman, Festinger, and Lawrence (DP, chap. 16). Their situation is essentially a three-person game in which the sole possibility of winning consists of forming a two-member coalition; the game is completely symmetric among all individuals. They test two hypotheses: (1) individuals tend to be motivated not by their absolute scores but by their scores relative to the scores of those other individuals whom they regard as comparable; and (2) the intensity of this motivation is increased, the more important the task is regarded. The experimental procedure for testing these hypotheses is extremely ingenious and confirms them. The first hypothesis in particular suggests that the utility of an outcome does not depend solely on an individual's own achievement but on his achievement or income relative to that of others. This form lends strength to the relative income hypothesis of consumption set forth by Duesenberry (1949) and by Dorothy Brady and Rose Friedman (1947).

5.4.2. Kalisch, Milnor, Nash, and Nering (DP, chap. 19) have studied the behavior of participants in a series of *n*-person games. In one group the games were constant-sum games with side payments permitted, as formulated by von Neumann and Morgenstern. Coalition formation was the only strategic element. A number of properties emerged from observation. (1) Members of a coalition tended to split evenly, regardless of the characteristic function. (2) Personality differences among the players were important in many contexts. (3) The geometric arrangement of the players around a table made a difference in the outcome. One might hazard the generalization that (1) suggests that ethical rules are used to economize on the computational and personal hardships of extremely accurate bargaining and that (3) corresponds to the role of communications in the establishment of economic relations. Some checks suggest that the outcomes were to a certain but not conclusive extent compatible with a rational model based on game-theoretical considerations. In particular, the average outcome to a player of a series of runs of the same game was not too far from the game value suggested by Shapley (1953). Other attempts were made to study games, with varying restrictions on the method of negotiation and side payments, but little was achieved in the way of conclusive results.

Both this study and the preceding one point up sharply the value of such experimental situations in providing an opportunity to test out some possibilities of rational behavior in circumstances which, in many respects, are more favorable for study than they are in the real world. Such indications as have been received suggest strongly that motivational and cognitive factors, which do not ordinarily enter into our economic theory, play a strong role, at least as far as the dynamics of the processes are concerned. It may be premature, however, to say that the equilibrium situation will also be affected. On the other hand, we know that in the *n*-person games we have yet to achieve a satisfactory theory of equilibrium. It may be, as shown especially by the paper by Hoffman, Lawrence, and Festinger, that the stability of coalitions is determined largely by the noneconomic factors.

References

Allais, M., "L'extension des théories de l'équilibre économique général et du rende-ment social au cas du risque," *Econometrica,* vol. 21 (1953), pp. 269–290.

Arrow, K. J., "Alternative Approaches to the Theory of Choice in Risk-Taking Situations," *Econometrica,* vol. 19 (1951a), pp. 404–437; Chapter 2 in this volume.

Arrow, K. J., *Social Choice and Individual Values,* New York: John Wiley & Sons, 1951b.

Arrow, K. J., "Le rôle des valeurs boursières pour la répartition la meilleure des risques," in *Fondements et applications de la théorie du risque en économetrie,* Paris, France: Centre National de la Recherche Scientifique, 1953; Chapter 3, Volume 2, of these *Collected Papers.*

Arrow, K. J., and G. Debreu, "Existence of Equilibrium for a Competitive Econ-omy," *Econometrica,* vol. 22 (1954), pp. 265–290; Chapter 4, Volume 2, of these *Collected Papers.*

Arrow, K. J., T. E. Harris, and J. Marschak, "Optimal Inventory Policy," *Econometrica,* vol. 19 (1951), pp. 250–272; to appear in a later volume of these *Collected Papers.*

Bellman, R., *An Introduction to the Theory of Dynamic Programming,* Santa Monica, California: RAND Corporation, 1953.

Bernoulli, D., "Specimen theoriae novae de mensura sortis," *Commentarii acade-miae scientiarum imperialis Petropolitanae,* vol. 5 (1738), pp. 175–192; trans-lated as "Exposition of a New Theory on the Measurement of Risk," *Econo-metrica,* vol. 22 (1954), pp. 23–26.

Brady, D., and R. Friedman, "Savings and the Income Distribution," *Studies in Income and Wealth,* vol. 10, New York: National Bureau of Economic Re-search, 1947, pp. 247–265.

Chernoff, H., "Rational Selection of Decision Functions," *Econometrica,* vol. 22 (1954), pp. 422–443.

Coombs, C. H., *A Theory of Psychological Scaling,* Ann Arbor, Michigan: Engineer-ing Research Institute, University of Michigan, 1952.

Davidson, D., P. Suppes, and S. Siegel, *Decision Making: An Experimental Ap-proach,* Stanford, California: Stanford University Press, 1957.

Debreu, G., "The Coefficient of Resource Utilization," *Econometrica,* vol. 19 (1951), pp. 273–292.

Duesenberry, J., *Income, Saving, and the Theory of Consumer Behavior,* Cam-bridge, Massachusetts: Harvard University Press, 1949.

Edwards, W., "The Theory of Decision-Making," *Psychological Bulletin,* vol. 51 (1954), pp. 380–417.

Festinger, L., "A Theory of Social Comparison Processes," reprinted in P. Hare, E. F. Borgatta, and R. F. Bales, *Small Groups: Studies in Social Interaction,* New York: A. A. Knopf, 1955.

de Finetti, B., "La prévision: ses lois logiques, ses sources subjectives," *Annales de l'Institute Henri Poincaré,* vol. 7 (1937), pp. 1–68.

de Finetti, B., "Recent Suggestions for the Reconciliation of Theories of Probabil-ity," in J. Neyman (ed.), *Proceedings of the Second Berkeley Symposium on*

Mathematical Statistics and Probability, Berkeley and Los Angeles: University of California Press, 1951, pp. 217–226.

Fisher, R. A., *Statistical Methods and Scientific Inference,* Edinburgh and New York: T. and A. Constable and Hafner Publishing Company, 1956.

Friedman, M., "Choice, Chance, and the Personal Distribution of Income," *Journal of Political Economy,* vol. 41 (1933), pp. 277–290.

Friedman, M., and L. J. Savage, "The Utility Analysis of Choices Involving Risk," *Journal of Political Economy,* vol. 56 (1948), pp. 279–304.

Georgescu-Roegen, N., "Choices, Expectations, and Measurability," *Quarterly Journal of Economics,* vol. 68 (1954), pp. 503–534.

Harsanyi, J. C., "Approaches to the Bargaining Problem before and after the Theory of Games: A Critical Discussion of Zeuthen's, Hicks', and Nash's Theories," *Econometrica,* vol. 24 (1956), pp. 144–157.

Hart, A. G., "Risk, Uncertainty, and the Unprofitability of Compounding Probabilities," in O. Lange, F. McIntyre, and T. O. Yntema (eds.), *Studies in Mathematical Economics and Econometrics,* Chicago: University of Chicago Press, 1942, pp. 110–118.

Hicks, J. R., "The Theory of Uncertainty and Profit," *Economica,* vol. 11 (1931), pp. 170–189.

Hicks, J. R., *The Theory of Wages,* London: The Macmillan Company, 1932.

Homans, G., *The Human Group,* New York: Harper, 1950.

Katona, G., *Psychological Analysis of Economic Behavior,* New York, Toronto, and London: McGraw-Hill Book Company, 1951.

Knight, F. H., *Risk, Uncertainty, and Profit,* New York: Houghton Mifflin Company, 1921.

Kuhn, H. W., and A. W. Tucker, "Nonlinear Programming," in J. Neyman (ed.), *Proceedings of the Second Berkeley Symposium on Mathematical Statistics and Probability,* Berkeley and Los Angeles: University of California Press, 1951, pp. 481–492.

Markowitz, H., "The Utility of Wealth," *Journal of Political Economy,* vol. 60 (1952), pp. 151–158.

Marschak, J., "Role of Liquidity with Complete and Incomplete Information," *American Economic Review, Papers and Proceedings,* vol. 39 (1949), pp. 182–195.

Massé, P., *Les réserves et la régulation de l'avenir dans la vie économique,* Paris: Hermann et Cie., 1946.

Moore, O. K., "Divination — A New Perspective," *American Anthropologist,* vol. 59 (1957), pp. 69–74.

Mosteller, F., and P. Nogee, "An Experimental Measurement of Utility," *Journal of Political Economy,* vol. 59 (1951), pp. 371–404.

Nash, J., "Equilibrium Points in *N*-Person Games," *Proceedings of the National Academy of Sciences,* vol. 36 (1950), pp. 48–49.

Nash, J., "Two-Person Cooperative Games," *Econometrica,* vol. 21 (1953), pp. 128–140.

von Neumann, J., and O. Morgenstern, *Theory of Games and Economic Behavior,* 2nd ed., Princeton, New Jersey: Princeton University Press, 1947.

Neyman, J., "Outline of a Theory of Statistical Estimation Based on the Classical

Theory of Probability," *Philosophical Transactions of the Royal Society,* series A, vol. 236 (1937), pp. 333–380.

Ramsey, F. P., "Truth and Probability," in *The Foundations of Mathematics and Other Logical Essays,* London: Kegan Paul, and New York: Harcourt, Brace & Co., 1931.

Savage, L. J., *The Foundations of Statistics,* New York: John Wiley & Sons, and London: Chapman & Hall, 1954.

Shapley, L., "A Value for *n*-Person Games," in H. W. Kuhn and A. W. Tucker (eds.), *Contributions to the Theory of Games, II,* Princeton, New Jersey: Princeton University Press, 1953, pp. 307–318.

Simon, H., *Models of Man: Social and Rational,* New York: John Wiley & Sons, and London: Chapman & Hall, 1957.

Wald, A., *Statistical Decision Functions,* New York: John Wiley & Sons, 1950.

Weldon, J. C., "On the Problem of Social Welfare Functions," *Canadian Journal of Economics and Political Science,* vol. 18 (1952), pp. 452–463.

Wold, H., and L. Jureen, *Demand Analysis,* New York: John Wiley & Sons, 1953.

Zeuthen, F., *Problems of Monopoly and Economic Warfare,* London: G. Routledge & Sons, 1930, chap. 4.

5   The Measurement of Price Changes

In the middle 1950s there was an increase in prices which, however small by the standards of the last fifteen years, gave rise to an intense fear of inflation. One manifestation was a study by the Joint Economic Committee of the United States Congress on price stability. There was a series of commissioned papers on various aspects. I was asked to write on problems of measurement. Although I had not and have not since done any research on index numbers, I have found the subject fascinating and have taught it from time to time. In particular, I was attracted by index numbers based on utility theory, since they alone seemed to make intrinsic sense. As a graduate student I had encountered the papers of Ragnar Frisch and of my professor, Abraham Wald, which developed the concept of functional index numbers. The invitation gave me a chance to propagandize for these index numbers, with, I suppose, very little success.

In this chapter I will be concerned almost exclusively with measurement of the cost of living, or the consumer price index. It is this field of price indexes to which economic theory has made the most important contributions directly. However, I am quite convinced that there are no great differences in principle as far as other price indexes, such as the wholesale

Reprinted from *The Relationship of Prices to Economic Stability and Growth,* Joint Economic Committee, U.S. Congress (Washington, D.C.: Government Printing Office, 1958), pp. 77–88.

price index, are concerned. All commodities in a sense are intended ultimately for consumption, and therefore all prices reflect indirectly the valuations placed on them by ultimate consumers (including, in many cases, investors).

Stress will be laid on the theoretical contributions. Recommendations as to sources of data and representativeness of sampling can hardly be done effectively by one outside the government agencies responsible.

Basic Considerations

A consumers' price index is a measure for one period of time, say 1, with respect to another period, say 0. It is generally defined as the ratio of the expenditures needed in time 1 to maintain a given standard of living, to the expenditures needed in time 0 for the same purpose. The standard of living for this purpose clearly cannot be identified with a fixed basket of commodities. Suppose, for example, that in the base period 0 the price of beef is high but that of lamb is low, while the reverse is true in period 1 due to, say, a change in supply conditions. We would expect that the consumer will purchase a great deal of lamb and relatively little beef in period 0, and the reverse in period 1. If we use as a fixed basket of goods that consumed in the base period, then we will find a rise in the cost of living because the lamb, which has appeared so strongly in period 0, has undergone a price rise. On the other hand, the reverse would be true if we started with period 1 as the base period.

There seems no recourse but to recognize frankly that a standard of living is not any fixed basket of goods, but a subjective level of satisfaction. In the example just given, it may well be that the consumer feels about as well off in one period as another since he has had a chance to compensate for the price changes by changes in the proportions in which different commodities are consumed. The government statistician, for obvious reasons, shies away from the notion of tying the seemingly objective price index to subjective concepts of utility or satisfaction, but in fact there is no escape from this proposition. Any attempt to explain the meaning of the cost-of-living index must eventually come to the notions just described unless we are to stop at banal tautologies analogous to "national income is that which is measured by national income statisticians."

It is, of course, perfectly true that we are not in the position now, and we may never be, to measure the subjective satisfactions of consumers directly. However, as the previous example already hints, economic theory argues that something, at least, can be learned by studying the overt behavior of the individual in the market. The reason is that the individual is motivated to secure for himself the highest utility consistent with his monetary resources. His utilities or satisfactions then are already reflected in market behavior, and thus it is not implausible that we may use this behavior to cast some light on his satisfactions and in particular on the cost-of-living index as defined previously. Unfortunately, as is well known, the inference from quantities and prices observed to the true cost-of-living index is by no means a simple one.

Let us consider the simplest inference, a very well known one. Suppose we wish to know the cost-of-living index defined as the minimum expenditure in period 1 needed to obtain the level of satisfaction of period 0 as a ratio to the expenditure in period 0. One way to make sure to achieve the same level of satisfaction in period 1 as in period 0 is to purchase the same goods. This will, in general, not be the cheapest way of achieving that level of satisfaction. Let p_0 and p_1 denote prices in periods 0 and 1, respectively, and let q_0 represent quantities in period 0. Then the above reasoning shows that $\Sigma p_1 q_0 / \Sigma p_0 q_0$ will be at least as great as and probably greater than the true cost-of-living index.

We thus see that price-quantity figures permit some inference as to the true cost-of-living index. In this case they set an upper bound, but we also see that a simple set of figures does not give a complete determination. In particular, the formula used is a base-year weighted price index (frequently referred to as Laspeyres' formula); that is, it is precisely the formula which is used in most ordinary statistical work. We see, then, that this formula tends to overstate the rise in the cost of living from any fixed base. It is indirectly the realization of this fact which causes the base to be revised as frequently as it is.

In the following sections the use of additional information other than that in the formula just given will be suggested to narrow down the limits which we can place on the true cost-of-living index by inference from price-quantity observations.

Use of Engel Curves for Price Indexes

The definition of the cost-of-living index number suggests immediately that it really should not be regarded as a single number. The cost-of-living index number corresponding to one level of satisfaction in a base period may be very different from that in another. This shows up conspicuously when the differences are large, as between poor and rich. The consumption pattern of the rich is quite different from that of the poor, and a shift in prices which increases the cost of living to one may decrease it to another. Thus, if servants' wages rise while the prices of manufactured goods fall, it may well be that the expenditure needed by a wealthy person to maintain his standard of living, that is, his level of satisfaction, will be going up, while that of the poor person is going down. This fact is implicitly recognized in index numbers which restrict their announced coverage to "middle-income families," but it argues that quite a bit more can be done along these lines. There should be a separate cost-of-living index number for each income level.

Empirical data on which any such index numbers are based are found in budget studies. For those, we have two years, 0 and 1, in which the budgets of individuals over a wide range of incomes have been made available. For each commodity, we can find the average consumption in each income class. The relation between consumption of a particular commodity and income is known as an Engel curve, after the German statistician of the last century who pioneered in this area. We assume, then, that we have an Engel curve for each commodity in each of the two years under consideration. We now construct two new curves which represent, at each income level, the purchases of commodities in one year evaluated at the prices of the other. Thus, if E_1 represents an expenditure level in year 1, take the average amounts consumed of each commodity by those with expenditure level E_1, and calculate what that bundle would have cost in the prices of year 0. In symbols, if $q_1(E_1)$ represents quantities purchased in year 1, when total expenditures are E_1, then in the notation previously used, we calculate

$$\Sigma p_0 q_1(E),$$

which will be designated as $E_{10}(E_1)$. A similar calculation can be made interchanging the roles of the years 0 and 1. Thus, we have a second curve $E_{01}(E_0)$. For any expenditure level E_0 in year 0, let $q_0(E_0)$ be the commodities purchased by individuals whose total expenditure was E_0. Then

$$E_{01}(E_0) = \Sigma p_1 q_0(E_0).$$

The two curves are plotted on Figure 5.1. The horizontal axis represents expenditures in year 0, the vertical axis those in year 1. The curve $E_{01}(E_0)$ will be plotted against the horizontal axis. The curve $E_{10}(E_1)$ will be plotted against the vertical axis.

The problem of finding the true cost of living is that of matching up expenditures E_0 and E_1 so that for each value E_0 we find the corresponding

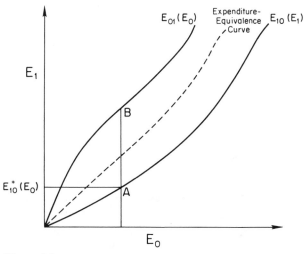

Figure 5.1

minimum expenditure E_1 which will yield the same level of satisfaction. We then want a curve relating the two variables. To read a cost-of-living index number for any given level of satisfaction on this curve, we may take a particular value of E_0 and find the corresponding value of E_1; the ratio of these two values is the cost-of-living index corresponding to an expenditure level of E_0 in the base period. The fact that the curve will not usually be a straight line to the origin shows that the cost-of-living index number will in general vary by income levels.

The question is the determination, or at least the approximation, of this expenditure-equivalence curve. The reasoning of the preceding section shows that for any E_0, $E_{01}(E_0)$ is an overstatement of the equivalent expenditure in year 1. Reversal of the argument shows that for any expenditure E_1 in year 1, the number $E_{10}(E_1)$ is an overstatement of the equivalent expenditure in year 0. Therefore we can say without any further discussion that the expenditure-equivalence curve must lie between the two curves $E_{01}(E_0)$ and $E_{10}(E_1)$. For a verbal reference, we will refer to the first of these as the current-year-weighted base-year expenditure curve and the base-year-weighted current-year expenditure curve.

It is already clear from this discussion how much more information is available about the cost-of-living index by the knowledge of the two sets of Engel curves than from simply knowing some kind of national average. The latter at best amounts to knowing one point on each of the two expenditure curves. Although there is some information contained in this statement, since the expenditure-equivalence curve would have to lie between the two points, it is clear that the restrictions on the location of the curve are not very severe.[1]

In many cases the two expenditure curves will be very close together so that the expenditure-equivalence curve will be determined quite accurately. An approximation formula was developed for the interpolation of an expenditure-equivalence curve by Abraham Wald.[2] If we refer to Figure 5.1, we can take any base-year expenditure E_0 and find from the curve $E_{10}(E_1)$ that expenditure in year 1 for which the base-year weighted expenditures are equal to E_0. In the figure this value is represented by $E_{10}^*(E_0)$. It is clear from the figure that this value is an underestimate of the equivalent expenditure in year 1. We have already noted that $E_{01}(E_0)$ is an overestimate of the equivalent expenditures; it is natural then to seek for a method of averaging the two. The particular average suggested by Wald is the following : Let a_{01} be the slope of the upper curve at point B, and let a_{10}^* be the slope of the lower curve at A. In both cases the slope is found with respect to the E_0-axis, that is, the way the curves are drawn now. Then Wald's formula is

$$\frac{\sqrt{a_{10}^*}E_{01}(E_0) + \sqrt{a_{01}}E_{10}^*(E_0)}{\sqrt{a_{10}^*} + \sqrt{a_{01}}}.$$

In the present state of theory this seems about as satisfactory a formula as can be found.

It will, of course, be objected that obtaining Engel curves from annual budget studies is an expensive operation. Here, as elsewhere, the rule that you don't get something for nothing is applicable: it seems clear that higher accuracy in the index numbers requires greater expenditure by the government. The value received in terms of ability to make better economic plans will unquestionably repay additional expenditures many times over. This is especially true in the present context, because annual budget studies have

---

1. The importance of Engel curves for a more accurate determination of price index numbers was first pointed out by Ragnar Frisch. For a very clear exposition at greater length, see his paper "Some Basic Principles of Price of Living Measurements," *Econometrica*, vol. 22, no. 4, October 1954, pp. 407–421.

2. Wald's results were first published in "A New Formula for the Index of Cost of Living," *Econometrica*, vol. 7, no. 4, October 1939, pp. 319–331. For a simpler exposition, see K. S. Banerjee, "Simplification of the Derivation of Wald's Formula for the Cost of Living Index," *Econometrica*, vol. 24, no. 4, July 1956, pp. 296–298.

many uses other than the improvement of index numbers. Changing consumption patterns will be detected at a much earlier stage and will find a great deal of use both in private industry and in many government policies, such as the prediction of revenues from excise taxes; the consumption weights used in national income calculations can be greatly improved.

I would further urge that if budget studies were put on an annual basis, provisions be made that a major proportion of the families be reinterviewed annually. The value of panel studies—that is, repeated studies on the same individuals—has been amply demonstrated in work on consumption patterns as well as on sociological phenomena. The effect of income changes and changing age and family composition on consumption can be studied in this way as in no other. The variability of income and expenditures over time will form an important tool in the study of income distributions. There are thus many side benefits to annual budget studies and their analysis in terms of Engel curves, so that one can easily justify the additional expenditure.

Multiple Time Comparisons

The preceding section has dealt with comparisons between two points of time, say two successive years. However, one of the main functions of an index number is to provide a time series for the cost of living. We would like to be able, in fact, to make all sorts of comparisons including, ideally, comparisons of the cost of living in periods quite remote in time. To begin, we will consider only the single comparisons based on national averages which are currently used, and abandon the Engel-curve approach of the last section.

It has been seen that the use of quantity weights as of a fixed time period tends to overstate the increase in the cost of living in a subsequent time period. Thus, if 1947 rates are used, the price index of 1955 will be higher with respect to 1947 than it should be. The same will be true of the price index of 1956. The indexes are also used to compare 1955 with 1956. Here it is not clear what the bias will be, but it is clear that the 1947 quantity rates may or may not be very useful ones for the 1955–56 comparison.

There is a considerable divergence of viewpoint here between the practice of statisticians of almost all governments and the views of index number theorists. In comparisons involving distant points of time, index number theorists generally take one of two positions: either they argue that the comparison between any two years should be based solely on the data for those two years and not on any others, or they advocate a chain index. In a chain index comparisons are made only for adjacent years directly. The resulting index numbers for pairs of years are then multiplied together in an obvious way to get index number comparisons between years which are not consecutive. Thus an index number for 1949 with respect to 1947 would be obtained by multiplying the index for 1948 with respect to 1947 by the index for 1949 with respect to 1948.

It is not possible to give a definitive argument on the relative merits of chain index numbers and the more conventional fixed weight index numbers, primarily because neither is a thoroughly accurate solution. Nevertheless, there are some considerations that suggest that between the two, the chain index number is preferable.

First, it is clear from the preceding discussion that the difficulty with index number comparisons arises because of the inadequate knowledge of the want structure of the individual. An increase in the number of observations made on market behavior would be expected to increase the possible accuracy of index numbers.[3] The upward bias in base-year-weighted index numbers illustrates the inevitable errors resulting from the use of a limited number of observations—in this case, a pair. A chain index number between two points of time separated, say, by five or six years makes use of all the intermediate observations.

Second, the difficulties and possible errors of index number comparisons are increased when the consumption patterns in the two periods being compared are farther apart. Economic magnitudes tend to change continuously. Comparisons of adjacent years, then, are comparisons between more nearly homogeneous universes. It is more legitimate to use various approximations such as averaging of quantity weights. Indeed, the weights based on quantities in two adjacent years will differ less than they will in years taken farther apart, as a rule. Therefore, each link in the chain index number will be more accurate than direct comparisons at some distance apart.

That these considerations play some role in practice is shown by the relatively frequent changes in base years employed in practice. If the base of an index number is changed relatively frequently, there is in effect a chain index number, calculated perhaps on a quinquennial rather than an annual

---

3. For a more extended discussion of the possibilities and limits of improving index number comparisons by increased observations, see Paul A. Samuelson, *Foundations of Economic Analysis,* Cambridge, Mass.: Harvard University Press, 1947 [enlarged ed., 1983], pp. 146–163.

basis. Once the need for changing bases is recognized, it becomes merely a question of discussing the optimal frequency. An attempt at a logical foundation for chain indexes has been given by François Divisia.[4] If we write down the statement that total expenditures equal the sum of expenditures on individual items, where expenditures on any one item are equal to the product in price and quantity, $E = \Sigma pq$, then during a small period of time the change in the rate of expenditures can be expressed approximately in the following way: $\Delta E = \Sigma p \Delta q + \Sigma q \Delta p$. Here the symbol Δ means "change in." This formula assumes that in a small period of time, prices and quantities can only change by small amounts. The first term represents that part of the change in expenditures attributable to a change in quantities evaluated at the original prices and can therefore be thought of as the change in a certain quantity index. Similarly, the second term can be thought of as attributable to the change in prices using quantities as weights. If we imagine that we have both a price index and a quantity index, it is natural to demand that their product be equal to total expenditures, $E = PQ$, and therefore a small change in expenditures will be approximately expressed by $\Delta E = P \Delta Q + Q \Delta P$. Comparison of the two formulas for ΔE suggests that the right-hand sides can be identified term for term. Carrying out in detail the reasoning suggested here shows that the price index is a chain index with quantity weights. In each length of the chain, if the links are sufficiently short, the base-year and current-year quantities will be very similar, so it makes little difference which is used. Ideally, the links should actually be very short in time indeed, but there are some difficulties with seasonal fluctuations which suggest that it is unwise to use periods shorter than one year.

Divisia's reasoning is plausible but is not closely tied to the definition of a cost-of-living index in terms of expenditures needed to maintain a given level of satisfaction. The connection between the two concepts has been investigated to a certain extent by Jean Ville.[5] In general he shows that the chain index does not give exactly the true cost-of-living index except in the

---

4. For a description of Divisia's viewpoint, see Erland von Hofsten, *Price Indexes and Quality Changes,* Stockholm: Bokförlaget Forum, and London: George Allen and Unwin, 1952, pp. 21–23.

5. See his paper, "Sur les conditions d'existence d'une ophélimité totale et d'un indice du niveau des prix," *Annales de l'Université de Lyon,* sec. A (3), vol. 9 (1946), pp. 32–39, particularly pp. 36–38; translated into English as "The Existence-Conditions of a Total Utility Function," *Review of Economic Studies,* vol. 19 (1951–52), pp. 123–128, particularly pp. 125–127.

special case where at any fixed set of prices an individual will divide his income among different commodities in the same proportions, regardless of the level of his income; that is, the Engel curves are straight lines through the origin. This case is, of course, unrealistic, although it may be approximately valid for relatively small changes in real income.

The reasons why the chain index falls short of perfection can be put in diffferent ways. One point is that if additional observations are designed to get a better knowledge of the want structure of the individual, then there is no reason to confine oneself to observations in temporal order. All information within a time period in which wants can be regarded as homogeneous should be equally relevant to a comparison between any two time periods. Another point is that if the level of satisfaction of the population is rising, as is usual, then the comparison between successive years referred to different levels of satisfactions. After a period of time, then, the chaining involves price changes which are irrelevant to different standards of living. The special case, which Ville discussed, is one in which the consumption pattern is the same at all levels of satisfaction and thus no ambiguity arises. One form in which these imperfections may show up is the following paradox. It can happen that prices vary over time in such a way that after a few years, let us say, they return to their initial values. Obviously in that case, any properly defined price index should be equal to 100 as between the beginning and end years. Yet it is possible for a chain index number to differ from 100, either above or below. If, for example, as is usual in seasonal fluctuations, prices tend to be high when quantities are low and vice versa, then in general the chain index will tend to give too high a value.[6] Too much should not be made, however, of paradoxes like this. Virtually any index number known can lead to similar difficulties in suitably unfavorable circumstances.

On balance, the case for chain index numbers as opposed to fixed weight aggregates seems strong in spite of the drawbacks just noted.[7] However, the case is considerably strengthened if we combine the chain index of this section with the Engel curve methods of the last. Since each pairwise Engel curve comparison gives us a complete set of equivalences between expenditures in one year and expenditures in the next, the chaining is quite straightforward. Given any expenditure level in, say, 1947, we can find an

---

6. This was pointed out by Ladislaus von Bortkiewicz; see von Hofsten, *Price Indexes,* pp. 14–15, 27.

7. This position is also taken by Frisch, "Basic Principles," p. 417, and Bruce D. Mudgett, *Index Numbers,* New York: John Wiley & Sons, and London: Chapman and Hall, 1951, pp. 70–79.

expenditure in 1948 which gives approximately the same level of satisfaction. Starting with expenditure levels for 1948, we can find the corresponding expenditure levels for 1949. By linking the two pieces of information we can find an equivalence between expenditure levels in 1947 and 1949. This is still a chain comparison subject to the disabilities noted earlier; it finds its primary justification in the assumption that neighboring comparisons are apt to be more accurate than those at a distance. In terms of Figure 5.1 the two bounding curves are apt to be much closer together than they are for comparisons of several years apart.

A more experimental approach to index numbers based on multiple comparisons of time has been originated in a paper by Lawrence R. Klein and Herman Rubin.[8] If we have observations for a number of years, we have some possibility of estimating the effect of price changes on the consumption of different commodities. One can hope, at least, to obtain demand functions which express the consumption of any commodity in terms of the prices of that commodity and competitive ones, and the income of the country or of the individual if we have observations on separate individuals. If the demand functions are accurately obtained, it is possible to infer the underlying want structure and therewith to make all desired cost-of-living comparisons. The problem resides in the difficulty of accurately determining statistical demand functions; nevertheless, a great deal of progress has been made on this. It would seem worthwhile to experiment with this approach in different ways and see how it compares with other, more traditional methods. In principle, it is certainly the most satisfactory since, for example, all observations are treated equally and thus more information is used.[9]

---

8. "A Constant-Utility Index of the Cost of Living," *Review of Economic Studies,* vol. 15, 1948, pp. 84–87.

9. Klein and Rubin have analyzed the particular case where the demand functions are such that the expenditure for any commodity is a linear function of prices and income. They obtain, therefore, a specific formula for the cost-of-living index number. Paul Samuelson has objected that the linear demand functions are not likely to be found in practice; see "Some Implications of Linearity," *Review of Economic Studies,* vol. 15, 1948, pp. 88–90. However, linear functions have been fitted to British data by J. R. N. Stone; see "Linear Expenditure Systems and Demand Analysis: An Application to the Pattern of British Demand," *Economic Journal,* vol. 64, no. 255, September 1954, pp. 511–527. For an excellent exposition, see Ragnar Frisch, "Linear Expenditure Functions," *Econometrica,* vol. 22, no. 4, October 1954, pp. 505–510. Klein and Rubin assumed that the demand functions needed for their index would be obtained statistically by fitting to aggregate data. If Engel curves were available for each year, the chances of reliable fits would be much improved. In any case, it should be made clear that any statistically derived demand functions which satisfy certain consistency conditions can be used to derive index numbers; they need not be of the linear form assumed by Klein and Rubin.

The Problem of Quality Changes

One of the greatest problems in any index number comparisons over time is that of changes in the quality of existing commodities or the introduction of new ones. A thorough theoretical analysis of the subject was made by Erland von Hofsten, who was in charge of the Swedish cost-of-living index.[10] We will discuss the problem here mainly from the Engel curve viewpoint.

It should be made clear that we are discussing this problem at a theoretical level where it is assumed that we have a price for every conceivable commodity, including every variety. We ignore here the question of sampling in groups of related goods at a representative price. The splicing method frequently used in discussing quality changes depends in part on a sampling concept as well as a purely theoretical one. The difficulties attached to the sampling process have been ably pointed out by von Hofsten.[11] At this level of abstraction there is no logical difference between a different variety of the same commodity and a different commodity. We will assume our classification to be as fine as called for by the circumstances so that, for example, two different models of Cadillacs are to be regarded as separate commodities.

Suppose then we observe, in comparing year 0 with year 1, that a commodity appears in year 1 which was not consumed at all in year 0. Actually, from the Engel curve point of view, the problem might arise at each expenditure level. We may find a commodity purchased only by upper-income people in year 0 which is now purchased in year 1 by lower-income individuals. We will postulate that the want structure of individuals is the same in the two situations in spite of the introduction of a new commodity. The absence of a commodity in the former period will be explained by the hypothesis that the price at which it could have been produced was so high that the demand for it would be 0. The problem comes in evaluating the lower boundary curve of Figure 5.1, $E_{10}(E_1)$. Some of the current year expenditures will be of the new commodity. When reevaluated at base-year prices, what price shall be assigned to it? The theoretically correct answer will be the lowest price which will keep every individual from purchasing the commodity. Unfortunately, this price, unlike the others that have been used to this point, is a hypothetical one, not an actual one, and its use introduces a hypothetical element into the calculations. However, I believe that any rule which will accomplish the end of accounting for quality

---

10. See von Hofsten, *Price Indexes.*
11. Ibid., pp. 53–58, 71–72.

changes in a price index must involve judgment somewhere, and it is deceptive to state an objective-sounding rule which is not based on a logical theoretical foundation.

It will be useful to distinguish between several situations. One is that in which a new commodity that is different from any now existing is being introduced — for example, automobiles around the turn of the century, or television sets more recently. In this situation there is apt to be a continuous rise in consumption. In the first year in which the commodity is introduced, the consumption is probably rather small. Therefore any error committed in attributing to the previous year a hypothetical price will not have a great effect on the base-year-weighted current-year expenditure curve. Here again we have an example of the value of a chain index. There is no point at which the introduction of a new commodity will produce great problems, provided the introduction is gradual. Once it has appeared as an item of expenditure, the successive future steps of its growth are accounted for in the price index, just as with any other commodity.

An even more favorable situation is that in which the newly introduced commodity is a close substitute for one previously existing, say an improved model. If both are available in the second period, then it is reasonable to postulate that the consumer would reject completely one or the other of the two goods if the price ratio differed very much from that which actually prevailed in year 1. Therefore, a hypothetical price for a newly introduced variety in year 0 is so chosen that the ratio of its price to the price of the variety in existence in both periods is slightly higher in year 0 than in year 1. This approach to the pricing of new varieties is very similar to the splicing method. However, it meets von Hofsten's strictures as long as all the varieties are counted each time. The difficulty encountered in the splicing method arises because the particular varieties selected may be unrepresentative.

A more difficult case is that in which one variety disappears and is in effect replaced by another. The most common instance of this is the change of models in many consumers' durable goods, notably automobiles. The principle is not altered. However, it is now necessary to have a hypothetical price in both situations. If model A was produced in year 0 and replaced by a more or less equivalent model B in year 1, the index maker must hypothesize a price for model B in year 0 just high enough so that none of it would have been consumed even if it were available. Similarly, he must hypothesize a price for model A in year 1 just high enough, again, to ensure that there would have been no consumption even if available. At this point, the index maker will probably start to resort to objective measures of quality of some kind, such as performance or durability characteristics of the object. He will, in effect, be postulating that the consumer would choose between two varieties if both were available, according to whether or not the price ratio exceeds the quality ratio. Of course, the only true measure of quality is the satisfaction yielded to the consumer, and the quality ratio used by the index maker must be related to his guess as to the consumer's tastes.

The entire argument to this point has been based on the assumption of an unchanged want structure between one period and the next. We have gone so far as to impute tastes for commodities not available in one time period or the other in order to preserve this theoretical foundation. However, as von Hofsten stresses, this point of view cannot be maintained for goods subject to style changes. As one can observe with regard to women's dresses, it is possible for styles to change from year to year and return to their starting point. If all prices had remained unchanged during this period, then the change in varieties could only be explained by the assumption of a change in tastes. There seems no simple way out of this problem except a judgment by the statistician that the new style performs an equivalent function in terms of satisfaction to the old one.

Concluding Remarks

Index numbers are, of course, desired for purposes other than to measure the cost of living. One obvious possibility is to consider some subset of cost-of-living items, such as food. The logic of the preceding argument goes through precisely provided we assume that the distribution of food expenditures in any period among different foods depends only on the total volume of food expenditures and is independent of the prices of other goods, for any given total volume of food expenditures. This does not deny substitution between foods and other commodities, but we assume that the total effect of this substitution is already reflected in the choice of a volume of food expenditures. In a broad way, similar considerations apply to the pricing of producers' goods, which should be interpreted as reflecting indirectly consumers' preferences. However, there is undoubtedly a good deal more in the detailed working out of the theory that has never been developed.

This leads to the final suggestion that considerable effort be put into pure research on the theoretical problems of index number construction. This has to be done, of course, in close context with practical problems and, therefore, through the existing statistical agencies. Either there should be provision for a research unit within existing statistical agencies, or arrangements should be made for contract research by universities under the supervision of the Bureau of Labor Statistics and similar agencies. For real progress, a good deal of freedom must be granted. The possibility of experimental construction of index numbers must be allowed a wide scope. In this research, issues of comparability with the past should not be allowed to dominate too strongly; the most important thing is the collection of the data necessary for price measurements. Even though such data were not available in the past, we should at least now plan for the future an adequate amount of information.

6   Rational Choice Functions and Orderings

The development of my work on social choice depended in part on an understanding of the relation between the choices from varying sets of alternatives and an underlying ordering of preferences. The ideas were indeed related to Paul Samuelson's concept of revealed preference, but unlike that work mine took an abstract view of the domains of choice instead of confining them to budget sets. This led to a different perspective and indeed to a different set of results. When only budget sets are considered, the weak axiom of revealed preference is not sufficient to imply the existence of an ordering; but it is sufficient when choice from all finite sets is considered. In general, this chapter and the very considerable literature following it represent a systematic comparison of alternative rationality concepts; an ordering is a consistency relation among choices from pairwise sets, and it is compared with other kinds of consistency relations.

The language of the theory of consumers' demand is still somewhat confused despite the great progress that has been made.[1] The basic purpose of the theory is to explain the demand vector $d(p,M)$ chosen by an individual when faced with a price vector p and an income M. Cournot, who introduced the concept of the demand function, and others simply postu-

---

1. For restatements of the theory, see Wold and Juréen (1953, pt. 2), and Hicks (1956).

Reprinted from *Economica*, n.s., 26 (1959):121–127.

lated some properties such as monotonic decrease of demand for any commodity with respect to its own price. The development of utility theory in the second half of the nineteenth century by Gossen, Jevons, Menger, and Walras and its subsequent reinterpretation on an ordinal basis by Pareto led to an alternative formulation in terms of an ordering of all conceivable commodity bundles. The demand vector for a particular p and M is that vector among all those compatible with the budget limitation which is most preferred.

The derivation of demand functions from orderings (expressed as indifference maps or utility functions) became standard, and its fruitfulness in yielding implications for demand functions was made evident by the work of Slutsky (1915), Hicks and Allen (1934), Hotelling (1935), and Roy (1942). Apart from the problems raised by the integrability question,[2] the first distinctly novel approach was the revealed preference approach of Samuelson (1938). Here again an assumption is made on the demand function (see Condition C5 below). From this assumption a number of properties of the demand function can be deduced, although so far not as many as from the assumption of an underlying ordering.

A good deal of effort has gone into finding assumptions on the demand function which would imply the existence of an ordering from which it could be derived. Samuelson's original assumption (now generally known as the Weak Axiom of Revealed Preference) is not sufficiently strong. Independently, Ville (1946) and Houthakker (1950) have shown that a modification of this axiom, referred to as the Strong Axiom of Revealed Preference (see C1 below) is sufficient to ensure the desired result.

Both demand functions and orderings can be regarded as special cases of choice functions. For any set of alternatives X let $C(X)$ be the set of alternatives chosen (we admit the possibility of multiple choices). The function $C(X)$ is, of course, not necessarily defined for all possible sets X. Let $\mathcal{B}$ be the class of sets for which $C(X)$ is defined. The revealed-preference and other demand-function approaches essentially deal with the case in which $\mathcal{B}$ is the class of sets defined by budget constraints of the form[3]

$$(6\text{-}1) \qquad \Sigma p_i x_i \leqq M, \qquad x_i \geqq 0.$$

2. Georgescu-Roegen (1936, pp. 567–568) conclusively showed that the real issue behind the integrability problem was the question of transitivity. In terms of this chapter, the integrability problem is a somewhat misleading way of putting the problem of the relation between assumptions on the demand functions and the existence of an ordering which generates them.

3. The budget constraint is here written in the form used by current theory, which stresses inequalities and nonnegativity constraints.

On the other hand, an ordering can be interpreted as a series of statements about choices from sets containing two elements. Choices from larger sets, including those defined by (6-1), are defined in terms of the binary choices. Thus the choice functions defined by an ordering are defined for a class $\mathcal{B}$ which includes not only sets of form (6-1) but many others, including in particular two-element sets and in fact all finite sets.

It is the suggestion of this chapter that the demand-function point of view would be greatly simplified if the range over which the choice functions are considered to be determined were broadened to include all finite sets. Indeed, as Georgescu-Roegen has remarked, the intuitive justification of assumptions such as the Weak Axiom of Revealed Preference has no relation to the special form of the budget constraint sets but is based rather on implicit consideration of two-element sets (see Georgescu-Roegen, 1954, p. 125n29).

Definitions

The investigation suggested in the previous section was begun in a significant paper by Uzawa (1956); his notation is followed here with minor modifications.

A binary relation R is said to be a *weak ordering* if

(R1)   for all x and y, $x\,R\,y$ or $y\,R\,x$;
(R2)   for all x, y, and z, $x\,R\,y$ and $y\,R\,z$ imply $x\,R\,z$.

A choice function $C(X)$ maps a nonnull set X into a nonnull subset. It is defined for all X in some class $\mathcal{B}$. We make the following assumption.

ASSUMPTION. *The domain of definition $\mathcal{B}$ of any choice function $C(X)$ contains all finite sets.*

DEFINITION 1. *For any binary relation R, we define*

$$C(X) = \{x | x \in X,\, x\,R\,y \quad \text{for all } y \in X\},$$

to be the choice function derived from R.

DEFINITION 2. *For any choice function $C(X)$, we define*

$$x\,R\,y = \text{df. } x \in C(\{x,y\})$$

to be the relation generated by $C(X)$.

Here $\{x,y\}$ is the set consisting of the two elements x and y. The motivation of these definitions is obvious.

We now wish to make assumptions about choice functions. Since these assumptions are those of rational behavior, we follow Uzawa in referring to choice functions satisfying them as *rational choice functions.* We give altogether five definitions of a rational choice function and study the relations of implication among them and to the existence of a weak ordering. First, we introduce two more relations defined by a given choice function.

DEFINITION 3.   *We say that x is revealed preferred to y (symbolized by x $\tilde{P}$ y) if, and only if, for some X, x ∈ C(X) and y ∈ X − C(X).*

DEFINITION 4.   *The element x is indirectly revealed preferred to y (x P* y) if, and only if, there exist x^i (i = 0, . . . , n) such that $x^0 = x$, $x^n = y$, and x^{i-1} $\tilde{P}$ x^i (i = 1, . . . , n).*

Uzawa has suggested the following two definitions for rational choice functions.

(C1)   For all x and y, if there exists an X for which $x \in C(X)$, $y \in C(X)$, then $x \overline{P^*} y$.

(The overbar denotes negation.)

(C2)   If $X \subset Y$, then $X - C(X) \subset Y - C(Y)$.

(By $X \subset Y$ is meant that every alternative in X also belongs to Y. By $A - B$ is meant the set of alternatives in A but not in B.) (C1) is a form of the Strong Axiom of Revealed Preference due to Ville and Houthakker. (C2), as will be seen below, is a weaker assumption; it asserts that any element not chosen from a set of alternatives X will not be chosen if the range of alternatives is widened.

It will be shown below that the following condition is equivalent to (C2).

(C3)   If $X \subset Y$, then $C(Y) \cap X \subset C(X)$.

(By $A \cap B$ is meant the set of alternatives in both A and B.)[4] Because (C2) and its equivalent (C3) are weak assumptions, a slight strengthening is called for.

---

4. (C3) is the same as postulated in Chernoff (1954, pp. 429–430).

(C4)   If $X \subset Y$ and $C(Y) \cap X$ is nonnull, then $C(X) = C(Y) \cap X$.

(C4) can be given the following intuitive interpretation. If some elements are chosen out of a set Y and then the range of alternatives is narrowed to X but still contains some previously chosen elements, no previously unchosen element becomes chosen and no previously chosen element becomes unchosen.[5]

Finally, we introduce the definition of rationality by the Weak Axiom of Revealed Preference.

(C5)   If $x \, \tilde{P} \, y$, then there exists no Y such that $x \in Y$, $y \in C(Y)$.

Interrelations among Definitions of Rational Choice Functions

We first establish relations of logical implication among the definitions of rational choice functions.

THEOREM 1. *Definition (C1) implies definitions (C2–C5); (C4) and (C5) are equivalent and imply (C2) and (C3); (C2) and (C3) are equivalent.*

It suffices to prove that (a) (C1) implies (C5); (b) (C4) and (C5) are equivalent; (c) (C4) implies (C3); and (d) (C2) and (C3) are equivalent.

(a) Suppose that (C1) holds and (C5) does not. Then we can choose x, y, Y so that $x \, \tilde{P} \, y$, $x \in Y$, $y \in C(Y)$. If $x \in Y - C(Y)$, then $y \, \tilde{P} \, x$; by Definition 4, $y \, P^* \, y$, which contradicts (C1). If $x \in C(Y)$, then again (C1) is contradicted, since $x \, \tilde{P} \, y$ implies $x \, P^* \, y$, while both x and y belong to $C(Y)$.

(b) First we prove that (C4) implies (C5). Suppose (C4) to be true and (C5) false. Then there exist x, y, X, Y, such that

(6-2) $x \in C(X)$,
(6-3) $y \in X - C(X)$,
(6-4) $x \in Y$,
(6-5) $y \in C(Y)$.

From (6-2)–(6-3), $\{x,y\} \subset X$, and $\{x,y\} \cap C(X)$ contains the single element x. From (C4),

(6-6) $C(\{x,y\}) = \{x\}$.

---

5. Definition (C4) was originally introduced in Arrow (1948, pp. 4–8), and the properties presented in this chapter were first proved there.

But from (6-4)–(6-5), $\{x,y\} \subset Y$, and from (6-5), $\{x,y\} \cap C(Y)$ is nonnull and contains y. By (C4), $y \in C(\{x,y\})$, which contradicts (6-6), unless $y = x$; but this last is impossible from (6-2) and (6-3).

Now suppose that (C5) and the hypothesis of (C4) hold but that $C(X) \neq C(Y) \cap X$. Then either (i) $C(X) - [C(Y) \cap X]$ is nonnull, or (ii) $[C(Y) \cap X] - C(X)$ is nonnull.

(i) Let $y \in C(X) - [C(Y) \cap X]$, $x \in C(Y) \cap X$. Then $x \in C(Y)$, $y \in Y$ (since $y \in C(X) \subset X \subset Y$), and $y \notin C(Y)$, so that $y \in Y - C(Y)$, and therefore $x \tilde{P} y$. But $y \in C(X)$, $x \in X$, a contradiction to (C5).

(ii) Let $x \in C(X)$, $y \in [C(Y) \cap X] - C(X)$. Then $x \in C(X)$, $y \in X - C(X)$, so that $x \tilde{P} y$. But $x \in C(X) \subset X \subset Y$, $y \in C(Y)$, which again contradicts (C5).

(c) If $C(Y) \cap X$ is nonnull, then clearly (C4) implies (C3). If $C(Y) \cap X$ is null, then (C3) holds in any case.

(d) Suppose $X \subset Y$. If (C2) holds, then $X - C(X)$ is disjoint from $C(Y)$, that is, $C(Y) \cap [X - C(X)]$ is null. This is equivalent to the statement that $[C(Y) \cap X] - C(X)$ is null, which in turn is equivalent to the conclusion of (C3). Conversely, if (C3) holds, then $[C(Y) \cap X] - C(X)$ is null, which is equivalent to saying that $C(Y) \cap [X - C(X)]$ is null, and therefore $X - C(X)$ is disjoint from $C(Y)$. But $X - C(X) \subset X \subset Y$, so the conclusion of (C2) follows.

We will see (corollary to Theorem 3) that a slightly stronger statement can be made than that contained in Theorem 1, namely that (C1), (C4), and (C5) are all equivalent.

Weak Orderings and Derived Choice Functions

THEOREM 2. *If R is a weak ordering, let C(X) be the choice function derived from it and R′ the relation generated by C(X). Then C(X) satisfies (C1)–(C5) and R′ is identical with R.*

Proof. That $C(X)$ satisfies (C1) is shown by Uzawa (1956, theorem 1). By Theorem 1, then, $C(X)$ satisfies (C2)–(C5). By Definition 2, $x R′ y$ if and only if $x \in C(\{x,y\})$ and, by Definition 1, if and only if both $x R x$ and $x R y$. But $x R x$ holds for all x, from (R1).

Theorem 2 is in the usual direction of implications from assumptions about orderings or indifference maps to properties of the demand functions, or the choice functions in a more generalized setting.

Rational Choice Functions and Relations Generated by Them

THEOREM 3. *If $C(X)$ satisfies (C1), (C4), or (C5), let R be the relation generated by $C(X)$ and $C'(X)$ the choice function derived from R. Then R is a weak ordering, and $C'(X) = C(X)$.*

Proof. It suffices to assume that $C(X)$ satisfies (C4) in view of Theorem 1.

Since $C(\{x,y\})$ is defined, either $x \in C(\{x,y\})$, or $y \in C(\{x,y\})$, that is, $x \mathrel{R} y$ or $y \mathrel{R} x$, so that (R1) holds.

Now suppose $x \mathrel{R} y$ and $y \mathrel{R} z$. If $y = z$ or if $x = y$, the conclusion $x \mathrel{R} z$ follows immediately. If $x = z$, then $x \mathrel{R} z$ is the same as $x \mathrel{R} x$, which follows from (R1), already established. Now suppose x, y, z to be distinct. Let X consist of the elements x, y, z and suppose $x \notin C(X)$. If $y \in C(X)$, $\{x,y\} \cap C(X)$ is nonnull so that $C(\{x,y\}) = \{x,y\} \cap C(X)$. Since $x \in C(\{x,y\})$ by assumption, $x \in C(X)$, a contradiction.

(6-7) $x \notin C(X)$ implies $y \notin C(X)$.

By exactly the same argument, $y \notin C(X)$ implies that $z \notin C(X)$. But with the aid of (6-7), $x \notin C(X)$ implies that $C(X)$ is null, which is contrary to the basic Assumption. Hence, $x \in C(X)$. Since $x \in \{x,z\} \cap C(X)$, $x \in C(\{x,z\})$, or $x \mathrel{R} z$. Therefore (R2) holds, and R is a weak ordering.

Let $x \in C(X)$, y be any element of X. Then $x \in \{x,y\} \cap C(X)$ and therefore $x \in C(\{x,y\})$, or $x \mathrel{R} y$. From Definition 1,

(6-8) $C(X) \subset C'(X)$.

Let $x \in C'(X)$, $y \in C(X)$. Then $\{x,y\} \cap C(X)$ is nonnull. Since $x \mathrel{R} y$, by Definition 1, $x \in C(\{x,y\}) = \{x,y\} \cap C(X) \subset C(X)$, so that $C'(X) \subset C(X)$. In conjunction with (6-8), the theorem is proved.

COROLLARY. *Definition (C1) is equivalent to Definitions (C4) and (C5).*

Proof. That (C1) implies (C4) and (C5) is already stated in Theorem 1. Suppose $C(X)$ satisfies (C4) or (C5). Then, by Theorem 3, $C(X) = C'(X)$, where $C'(X)$ is derived from a weak ordering R and therefore satisfies (C1), by Theorem 2.

Remark 1. Let P be the relation of preference derived from a weak ordering R, that is, $x \mathrel{P} y$ if and only if $x \mathrel{R} y$ and not $y \mathrel{R} x$. Then Uzawa has shown (1956, theorem 3) that under the Assumption $P = P^*$, so that under any of the definitions of a rational choice function (C1, C4, or C5) the relation of preference coincides with that of indirect revealed preference.

Remark 2. Conditions (C2) or (C3) are not sufficient for Theorem 3, as can easily be seen from the following example. Let R be an ordering, $C(X)$ the choice function derived from R, and $C'(X) = C(X)$ for all sets X other than those containing two elements, for which $C'(X) = X$. By Theorem 2, $C(X)$ satisfies (C2). On the other hand, if X has one or two elements, $X - C'(X)$ is the null set so that

(6-9)   if $X \subset Y$, then $X - C'(X) \subset Y - C'(Y)$,

whenever X has not more than two elements. If X has more than two elements, then Y must also, and (6-9) holds since then $C'(X) = C(X)$ and $C'(Y) = C(Y)$. As can be seen from (C3), the problem is that when passing from Y to a subset X, the choice set $C(X)$ may be relatively too big.

Uzawa (1956, theorem 4) has shown that if $C(X)$ contains only a single element for all X, then (C2) is a sufficient condition for the results of Theorem 3; however, the assumption that $C(X)$ contains only a single element rules out the possibility of indifference.

General Remark

The most interesting conclusion is the complete equivalence of the Weak Axiom of Revealed Preference with the existence of an ordering from which the choice function can be derived. This equivalence is demonstrable by very elementary means, provided we concede that choices should be definable from finite sets as well as budget-constraint sets. It is true that very interesting mathematical problems are bypassed by this point of view, but this should not perhaps be a compelling consideration.

It has already been argued that requiring the choice functions to be defined for finite sets is thoroughly consistent with the intuitive arguments underlying revealed preference. It should also be observed that any hope of using experimental methods for studying preference will require inferring from choices on finite sets to choices on infinite ones (see May, 1954; Papandreou, 1957; and for a somewhat different but parallel situation, Davidson and Suppes, 1956).

References

Arrow, Kenneth J., "The Possibility of a Universal Social Welfare Function," Project RAND, RAD(L)-289, 26 October 1948, Santa Monica, California (hectographed).

Chernoff, Herman, "Rational Selection of Decision Functions," *Econometrica,* 22 (1954):422–443.

Davidson, Donald, and Patrick Suppes, "A Finitistic Axiomatization of Subjective Probability and Utility," *Econometrica,* 24 (1956):264–275.

Georgescu-Roegen, Nicholas, "The Pure Theory of Consumer's Behavior," *Quarterly Journal of Economics,* 50 (1936):545–593.

Georgescu-Roegen, Nicholas, "Choice and Revealed Preference," *Southern Economic Journal,* 21 (1954):119–130.

Hicks, John R., *A Revision of Demand Theory.* Oxford: Clarendon Press, 1956.

Hicks, John R., and R. G. D. Allen, "A Reconsideration of the Theory of Value," *Economica,* n.s., 1 (1934):52–76, 196–219.

Hotelling, Harold, "Demand Functions with Limited Budgets," *Econometrica,* 3 (1935):66–78.

Houthakker, Hendrik S., "Revealed Preference and the Utility Function," *Economica,* n.s., 17 (1950):159–174.

May, Kenneth O., "Transitivity, Utility, and Aggregation in Preference Patterns," *Econometrica,* 22 (1954):1–13.

Papandreou, Andreas G., "A Test of a Stochastic Theory of Choice," *University of California Publications in Economics,* 16 (1957):1–18.

Roy, René, *De l'utilité. Actualités Scientifiques et Industrielles,* no. 930. Paris: Herman and Cie, 1942.

Samuelson, Paul A., "A Note on the Pure Theory of Consumer's Behavior," *Economica,* n.s., 5 (1938):61–71, 353–354.

Slutsky, Eugene, "Sulla teoria del bilancio del consumatore," *Giornale degli Economisti,* 51 (1915):1–26.

Uzawa, Hirofumi, "Note on Preference and Axioms of Choice," *Annals of the Institute of Statistical Mathematics,* 8 (1956):35–40.

Ville, Jean, "Sur les conditions d'existence d'une ophélimité totale et d'un indice du niveau des prix," *Annales de l'Université de Lyon,* 9 (1946): Section A(3), 32–39.

Wold, Herman, and Lars Juréen, *Demand Analysis.* New York: John Wiley and Sons, 1953.

7   Additive Logarithmic Demand Functions and the Slutsky Relations

My former colleague at Stanford, Hendrik Houthakker, has devoted a major part of his illustrious career to the estimation of consumer demand functions. On one occasion he was speaking to a seminar about his development of a class of functions which satisfied the budget constraint, were reasonably flexible, and were fairly simple to estimate. After developing his general class, he explained that he was considering only a subclass for simplicity. As I listened, it occurred to me that his original class was too large, for he had not considered the implications of the Slutsky conditions. I spent the rest of the seminar in quick calculations, confirmed later at leisure. Houthakker encouraged me to publish the results.

H. S. Houthakker (1959; see also 1960, especially the discussion of "indirect addilog" demand functions, pp. 252–253) has suggested the following ingenious form for demand functions to be fitted to price-quantity-income data:

$$(7\text{-}1) \qquad x_i = \mu f_i(p,\mu)/p_i \, F(p,\mu),$$

where x_i is demand for the ith commodity, p_i its price, p the vector of prices, μ is income, and

$$(7\text{-}2) \qquad F(p,\mu) = \sum_i f_i(p,\mu).$$

Reprinted from *Review of Economic Studies*, 28 (1961):176–181.

A similar idea, applied to the estimation of price elasticities from budget data, was proposed earlier by C. E. V. Leser (1941–42).

Form (7-1) is perfectly general in that any set of demand functions which satisfy the budget constraint (or "adding-up criterion"),

$$(7\text{-}3) \qquad \sum_i p_i x_i \equiv \mu,$$

can always be written in the form (7-1). For future reference we also write (7-3) in the form

$$(7\text{-}4) \qquad \sum_i y_i \equiv \mu,$$

where

$$(7\text{-}5) \qquad y_i = p_i x_i,$$

the expenditure on the ith commodity.

As is well known, it has not been easy to find simple functional forms for the demand functions x_i which satisfy the budget constraint and which also fit the data well. The double logarithmic form for demand as a function of income (at constant prices) fits well but does not satisfy (7-3). Leser and Houthakker note, in effect, that if $f_i(p,\mu)$ has a relatively simple form, then it is possible to estimate demand functions by fitting the function

$$x_i/x_j = p_j f_i(p,\mu)/p_i f_j(p,\mu),$$

a form which may be reasonably simple even though (7-1) may be too complicated to estimate directly.

In choosing appropriate functions, $f_i(p,\mu)$, we impose the condition, derived from consumers' demand theory, that the demand functions be homogeneous of degree zero in prices and income. This condition is automatically satisfied if the functions $f_i(p,\mu)$ are all homogeneous of the same degree.

Houthakker in particular considers the case where

$$(7\text{-}6) \qquad f_i(p,\mu) = a_i \mu^{b_i} \prod_j p_j^{c_{ij}}.$$

He raises the question as to the conditions under which demand functions defined by (7-1), (7-2), and (7-6) are derivable from a utility function. He shows in particular that this condition is satisfied if

$$(7\text{-}7) \qquad c_{ij} = -b_i \quad \text{for } i = j, \qquad c_{ij} = 0 \quad \text{for } i \neq j.$$

In this case, (7-6) becomes

$$f_i(p,\mu) = a_i(\mu/p_i)^{b_i}.$$

The method of Leser and Houthakker then leads to the relation

$$y_i/y_j = (a_i/a_j)(\mu/p_i)^{b_i}(\mu/p_j)^{-b_j},$$

or

$$\log(y_i/y_j) = \log(a_i/a_j) + b_i \log(\mu/p_i) - b_j \log(\mu/p_j).$$

This relation may be fitted to a budget study for any pair of commodities and supplies estimates of b_i and b_j. Thus, if fitted for a number of pairs of commodities such that every commodity is in at least one pair, estimates of the parameter b_i may be obtained for all commodities. These estimates have been obtained by Houthakker (1959).

Relation (7-6) is rich in parameters and flexible in the empirical relations to which it can be fitted, and (7-7) appears to be an excessive and arbitrary restriction on our freedom. All commodities enter in a relatively symmetric way into the formulation. Since the demand function is given by (7-1), and $F(p,\mu)$ depends, from (7-2), on all prices, it follows that the demand for any commodity will depend on all prices, as it must, but prices of other commodities enter only in the denominator, which is the same for all demand functions. There is no room for specialized relations of complementarity or substitution among particular pairs of commodities.

These observations suggested the possibility of generalizing (7-7). However, it does seem reasonable to require that the demand functions be derivable from a utility function. In this chapter we have sought the most general functions of type (7-6) satisfying this condition. Surprisingly, it turns out that Houthakker's form (7-7) is the most general possible.[1] Thus the requirement of integrability of the demand functions plus the restriction to the apparently very flexible forms (7-6) is sufficient to reduce the range of admissible demand functions to the restricted category (7-7), in which many nuances of specialized relations among commodities cannot be represented.

The method used (for an empirical application, see Stone, 1954) is that applied by Klein and Rubin (1947–48) to linear demand functions, namely,

---

1. My original result appeared to be slightly more general than Houthakker's. I am indebted to him for pointing out that the extra generality was in fact illusory.

writing down the Slutsky symmetry relations and deriving their consequences. The relations are

(7-8) $K_{ij} = K_{ji}(i \neq j)$,

where

(7-9) $K_{ij} = (\partial x_i/\partial p_j) + x_j(\partial x_i/\partial \mu)$.

For the present application, it will be more convenient to work with
elasticities. As usual, we define

(7-10) $Ex_i/Ep_j = (p_j/x_i)(\partial x_i/\partial p_j)$, $Ex_i/E\mu = (\mu/x_i)(\partial x_i/\partial \mu)$.

Let

(7-11) $L_{ij} = \mu p_i p_j K_{ij}$,

so that the Slutsky condition (7-8) can be written

(7-12) $L_{ij} = L_{ji}(i \neq j)$.

From (7-9)–(7-11), with some simplifications and use of (7-5),

(7-13) $L_{ij} = \mu y_i(Ex_i/Ep_j) + y_i y_j(Ex_i/E\mu)$.

Write (7-1) in the following two forms,

(7-14) $\log x_i = \log \mu + \log f_i - \log p_i - \log F$,

(where the logarithms are natural),

(7-15) $f_k/F = y_k/\mu$.

By differentiating (7-14) with respect to $\log p_j(j \neq i)$ and $\log \mu$, we find

(7-16) $Ex_i/Ep_j = (Ef_i/Ep_j) - (EF/Ep_j)(i \neq j)$,
(7-17) $Ex_i/E\mu = 1 + (Ef_i/E\mu) - EF/E\mu$.

From (7-2) and (7-10),

(7-18) $EF/Ep_j = (1/F)[\partial F/\partial(\log p_j)]$
            $= (1/F) \sum_k [\partial f_k/\partial(\log p_j)]$
            $= \sum_k (f_k/F)(Ef_k/Ep_j) = (1/\mu) \sum_k y_k(Ef_k/Ep_j)$,

the last following from (7-15). Similarly,

(7-19) $EF/E\mu = (1/\mu) \sum_k y_k(Ef_k/E\mu)$.

If we substitute from (7-16)–(7-19) into (7-13) and then into (7-12), we have a general form for Slutsky's relations. We now make use of the special form (7-6), in which

(7-20) $Ef_k/Ep_j = c_{kj}, \qquad Ef_k/E\mu = b_k.$

Substitute from (7-16)–(7-20) into (7-13):

(7-21) $L_{ij} = \mu y_i[c_{ij} - (1/\mu) \sum_k c_{kj} y_k] + y_i y_j[1 + b_i - (1/\mu) \sum_k b_k y_k].$

Define

(7-22) $M_{ij} = L_{ij} + [(1/\mu) \sum_k b_k y_k - 1] y_i y_j.$

The relations (7-12) become

(7-23) $M_{ij} = M_{ji} (i \neq j),$

while, from (7-4), (7-21), and (7-22),

(7-24) $M_{ij} = c_{ij} y_i \left(\sum_k y_k \right) - \sum_k c_{kj} y_i y_k + b_i y_i y_j.$

For any fixed i, j $(i \neq j)$, M_{ij} is a quadratic form in the y's, which may be written

(7-25) $M_{ij} = \sum_k \sum_l A_{kl}^{ij} y_k y_l,$

where the matrix A^{ij} is symmetric. Then we take (7-23) to be an identity in the y's (but see below for further comments), so that $A^{ij} = A^{ji}$, or

(7-26) $A_{kl}^{ij} = A_{kl}^{ji}$ for all k, l.

The relations (7-26) can be written

(7-27) $A_{kl}^{ij} = A_{kl}^{ji}$ for k, l distinct from i, j;
(7-28) $A_{ik}^{ij} = A_{ik}^{ji}$ for $k \neq i, j$;
(7-29) $A_{ij}^{ij} = A_{ij}^{ji};$
(7-30) $A_{ii}^{ij} = A_{ii}^{ji};$
(7-31) $A_{ki}^{ij} = A_{ki}^{ji}$ $(k \neq i, j);$
(7-32) $A_{ji}^{ij} = A_{ji}^{ji};$
(7-33) $A_{jk}^{ij} = A_{jk}^{ji}$ $(k \neq i, j);$
(7-34) $A_{kj}^{ij} = A_{kj}^{ji}$ $(k \neq i, j);$
(7-35) $A_{jj}^{ij} = A_{jj}^{ji}.$

These conditions are, however, not all independent as i, j range over all pairs $i \neq j$. Since A^{ij} and A^{ji} are symmetric matrices, (7-31), (7-32), and (7-34) follow from (7-28), (7-29), and (7-33), respectively. Further, (7-33) and (7-35) follow from (7-28) and (7-30), respectively, by interchanging i and j. Hence, we have only to evaluate the elements of Eqs. (7-27)–(7-30).

In (7-24), there are no terms of the form y_k, y_l, with k, l distinct from i, j. Hence, $A^{ij}_{kl} = 0$ for all k, l distinct from i, j; by interchanging i and j, $A^{ji}_{kl} = 0$, so that (7-27) is automatically satisfied.

Now suppose $k \neq i, j$. Then by inspection of (7-24),

(7-36) $A^{ij}_{ik} = (\tfrac{1}{2})(c_{ij} - c_{kj})$ for $k \neq i, j$.

(The factor $\tfrac{1}{2}$ comes from the symmetry of the matrix.) Also,

(7-37) $A^{ij}_{jk} = 0$ for $k \neq i, j$.

If we interchange i and j in (7-37), $A^{ji}_{ik} = 0$; from (7-36) and (7-28),

(7-38) $c_{ij} = c_{kj}$ for k, i, j distinct.

Next we observe that, from (7-24),

(7-39) $A^{ij}_{ij} = (\tfrac{1}{2})(c_{ij} - c_{jj} + b_i)$.

By symmetry, $A^{ij}_{ji} = (\tfrac{1}{2})(c_{ij} - c_{jj} + b_i)$; if we interchange i and j, we find that,

(7-40) $A^{ji}_{ij} = (\tfrac{1}{2})(c_{ji} - c_{ii} + b_j)$.

If we substitute (7-39)–(7-40) into (7-29), we have

(7-41) $c_{ij} - c_{jj} + b_i = c_{ji} - c_{ii} + b_j (i \neq j)$.

Finally, we observe again from (7-24) that

(7-42) $A^{ij}_{ii} = c_{ij} - c_{ij} = 0,$ $A^{ij}_{jj} = 0$.

From the second statement, by interchanging i and j, we have that $A^{ji}_{ii} = 0$, so that, from (7-42), (7-30) is automatically fulfilled.

We are left, therefore, with the conditions (7-38) and (7-41). Write (7-38) as

(7-43) $c_{ij} = d_j$ for $i \neq j$.

If we substitute from (7-43) into (7-41) and transpose, we find

$$c_{ii} - d_i + b_i = c_{jj} - d_j + b_j \quad \text{for } i \neq j,$$

which can be written

(7-44) $c_{ii} = d_i - b_i + a$ for all i,

where a is a constant independent of i and j.
    Substitute (7-43) and (7-44) into (7-6). Then

(7-45) $f_i(p,\mu) = a_i(\mu/p_i)^{b_i} p_i^a (\Pi p_j^{d_j})$.

    Let

(7-46) $g_i(p,\mu) = \left(\mu^{-a} \prod_j p_j^{-d_j} \right) f_i(p,\mu)$, $G(p,\mu) = \sum_i g_i(p,\mu)$.

Since the first factor in $g_i(p,\mu)$ is independent of i, we see immediately from (7-1) that

(7-47) $x_i = \mu f_i(p,\mu)/p_i F(p,\mu) = \mu g_i(p,\mu)/p_i G(p,\mu)$.

    But from (7-45) and (7-46),

(7-48) $g_i(p,\mu) = a_i \mu^{b_i-a} p_i^{a-b_i} = a_i(\mu/p_i)^{b_i'}$,

where $b_i' = b_i - a$. But (7-48) is precisely Houthakker's form as given in Eq. (12) of Houthakker (1960).
    We have assumed that the symmetry relation (7-23) must hold identically in the expenditures y_i. This presupposes that any expenditure vector y will be attained by suitable choice of prices and income, or, more precisely, that the set of such expenditure vectors fills out some n-dimensional set. This can only fail to be true if we assume some special relations among the c_{ij}'s. To see this, let $y_1 \ldots y_n$ be an arbitrary set of expenditures,

$$\mu = \sum_i y_i, \, z_i = \log (y_i/y_n)(i = 1, \ldots, n-1).$$

From (7-1), $z_i = \log f_i - \log f_n$. Hence, the problem is to choose prices so that

(7-49) $\sum_i (c_{ij} - c_{nj})p_j = z_i + (b_n - b_i) \log \mu$

$+ \log (a_n/a_i)(i = 1, \ldots, n-1)$.

These constitute $n-1$ equations in n unknowns. If they can be solved, there is no difficulty. If, however, the matrix $(c_{ij} - c_{nj})(i = 1, \ldots, n-1, j = 1, \ldots, n)$ has rank less than $n-1$, the equation can be solved only for special values of the z_i's and therefore of the y_i's. Then the relation (7-23) need hold only for those values of the y_i's. This possible exception does not seem very interesting.

References

Houthakker, Hendrik S., "The Influence of Prices and Incomes on Household Expenditure in Various Countries," Memorandum B-2, Stanford Project for Quantitative Research in Economic Development, Stanford University, April, 1959.

Houthakker, Hendrik S., "Additive Preferences," *Econometrica,* 28 (1960):244–257.

Klein, Lawrence R., and Herman Rubin, "A Constant-Utility Index of the Cost of Living," *Review of Economic Studies,* 15 (1947–48):84–87.

Leser, C. E. V., "Family Budget Data and Price Elasticities of Demand," *Review of Economic Studies,* 9 (1941–42):40–57.

Stone, Richard, "Linear Expenditure Systems and Demand Analysis: An Application to the Pattern of British Demand," *Economic Journal,* 64 (1954):511–527.

8 Utility and Expectation in Economic Behavior

Utility Theory of Economic Behavior

Choice under Static Conditions

Theory. Broadly speaking, utility theory is concerned with the problem of choice by an individual from a set of alternative possibilities available to him. The most usual economic context is that of choosing commodities. Suppose an individual has a given income. There are n commodities, each of which can be purchased in any quantity, but at a fixed price per unit. Then the individual is, in effect, permitted to choose only such amounts $x_1, \ldots, x_n$ of commodities $1, \ldots, n$, respectively, as do not exceed in cost the amount of income available to him. If $p_1, \ldots, p_n$ are the prices of commodities $1, \ldots, n$, respectively, then his total expenditures are $\Sigma_i^n p_i x_i$. If M is the individual's total income, then we are restricting the choice of commodities to those combinations which satisfy the condition $\Sigma_i^n p_i x_i \leqq M$. If M or any of the prices p_i changes, then the chosen amount $x_1, \ldots, x_n$ will change. Thus for each i, x_i is a function of $p_1, \ldots, p_n$ and M. This relation is known as a *demand function.*

The prices and income together limit the range of alternative commodity bundles among which the consumer may choose. They thus define what Pareto has called the "obstacles." The utility theory of choice states that the choice in any given situation depends on an interaction of the externally

Reprinted from *Psychology: A Study of a Science,* ed. S. Koch (New York: McGraw-Hill, 1963), vol. 6, pp. 724–752. Copyright ©1963 by McGraw-Hill Book Company. Used with the permission of McGraw-Hill Book Company.

given obstacles with the *tastes* of the individual, and that the obstacles and tastes can be thought of as independent variables. The utility theory asserts, more precisely, that the tastes can be represented by an ordering according to preference of all conceivable alternatives. In the usual theory of consumption it is imagined that the individual could be asked in advance for his preference between any pair of given bundles.[1] It is assumed that these pairwise comparisons taken together have the property of *transitivity*—that is, if bundle *A* is preferred to bundle *B* in a choice between those two, and *B* to *C* in a similar pairwise choice, then *A* would be preferred to *C* if those were the two alternatives.

Preference among commodity bundles is thus assumed to constitute an ordinal scale. For any given set of obstacles—that is, any range of alternatives available to the chooser—there will be, under certain mathematical conditions that need not be elaborated here, one alternative which is preferred to all others. This alternative to be chosen can be predicted from a knowledge of the obstacles, which are presumably objectively given, and the tastes, which in principle are determinable from a series of experiments of a different type.

In economics, a convenient representation of this choice process has been given by means of a *utility function.* This is a function assigning to every alternative—that is, every commodity bundle—a number, in such a way that the utility of one bundle is greater than the utility of another if and only if the first bundle is preferred to the second. Notice that this is simply a convenient mathematical way of describing an ordinal scale; it does not have any further significance at the present level of discussion. In particular, the utility function is unique only up to a monotone transformation. If we represent preference scales by utility functions, we can say that the demand functions are defined by maximizing the utility function, subject to the constraints implied by the restriction that total expenditures not exceed total income.

This theory of the formation of demand is not a very strong theory, but it is not a tautology either. In many respects, it is very close to the hedonistic

---

1. From the point of view of proper experimentation, the above statement is much too simple. What is really desired is the actual choice an individual would make if confronted with a pair of commodity bundles, not his verbal responses to a question. The relation between verbally expressed and behavioral preferences is one of considerable methodological interest. If conditions could be found under which they could be expected to coincide, experimentation could be considerably simplified.

position in psychology which currently seems to be undergoing a revival. However, psychological theory is usually much more explicit than pure economic theory about the nature of pleasures and pains.[2]

Time-Series Verification. Economists usually use two kinds of data to study consumption: budgets and time series of consumption of specific items. In the former, a sample of families at different income levels is taken and the consumption pattern of each family is found. Then, for any specific commodity — tea, for example — consumption can be related to income. Of course, other variables enter in. For the purpose of testing utility theory, this is not very satisfactory, since at any given moment in time, prices are the same for all families. Hence the only variation being studied is income.

The alternative is to take data on the total consumption of a commodity by years or by other time periods and relate it to prices of that and other commodities and to total national income. There is a somewhat illegitimate step here in that the theory relates to the consumption of the individual, while the data relates to the consumption of a national or other unit.

The utility theory implies that the demand function will satisfy certain conditions. One is that the demand function for any commodity is homogeneous of degree zero in prices and income — that is, if all prices and income were multiplied through by the same number, the demand would remain unchanged. (In effect, a change in all prices and in income is the same as a change in the name of the monetary unit and therefore should be of no consequence.) Virtually all time-series analysis presupposes homogeneity, and, since it is usual to get relations which fit very well, this may be taken as a confirmation of the homogeneity implication of the utility theory.

A more severe test is posed by the so-called Slutsky relation. Let $f_i(p_1, \ldots, p_n, M)$ be the demand for commodity i as a function of prices

---

2. I cannot help being struck by the parallelism between the economists' concepts of tastes and obstacles and Freud's pleasure principle and reality principle. The former, the phase of the "omnipotence of wishes," seems to correspond to a pure expression of tastes, while the reality principle corresponds to recognition that tastes can only be satisfied insofar as they are compatible with the obstacles presented by the external world, including other individuals.

Freud's use of the term *economic* in his discussions of metapsychology is remarkably precise. He is referring to the allocation of the scarce resources of the libido among competing uses, just as the individual allocates his scarce income among competing commodities. It might be interesting for the historian of thought to see what, if any, influence the thought of economists had in Freud's development. Vienna in the 1870s and 1880s was the center of a great school of economists who were very much interested in the utility theory — indeed, this group was one of its originators.

and income; there is one such demand function for every commodity. Then the utility theory has the following implication:

$$\frac{\partial f_i}{\partial p_j} + f_j \frac{\partial f_i}{\partial M} = \frac{\partial f_j}{\partial p_i} + f_i \frac{\partial f_j}{\partial M}.$$

There have been a few attempts made to verify this relationship. One is due to Wold and Juréen (1953, pp. 300–302). By regression analysis on data from 1921 to 1939 for Sweden, they estimated the demands for animal foods and vegetable foods as functions of the two prices and income. The estimated coefficients do not contradict the Slutsky relation, although they can hardly be said to support it very strongly. A similar conclusion was reached in a study of British data by Stone (1954).

Experimental Verification. Studies such as those by Wold and Juréen and by Stone suffer, of course, from the uncontrolled nature of the underlying conditions. Many other properties of the economic system have changed during the period studied; thus it is not surprising that it is difficult to get any clear-cut results. It is this which has led some economists and psychologists to investigate the transitivity of preference and similar problems by experimental methods. Perhaps the earliest was the study of L. L. Thurstone (1931). He considered three commodities—hats, shoes, and overcoats—and assumed that the utility function had the form

$$\sum_{i=1}^{3} k_i \log x_i.$$

Under these conditions, one may also consider the utility function for any two commodities, obtained simply by ignoring the third term. Thurstone first took a fixed bundle x_1^0, x_2^0 of the first two commodities; by repeated questions, he found which pairs x_1, x_2 were preferred to x_1^0, x_2^0 and which pairs were found inferior. Verbal responses were used. By interpolation an indifference curve could be found, which gave for each x_1 a value of x_2 such that x_1, x_2 was indifferent to x_1^0, x_2^0. For the particular utility function assumed, this indifference curve should have the form

$$k_1 \log x_1 + k_2 \log x_2 = \text{constant}.$$

The best-fitting such curve was found (note that only the ratio k_2/k_1 is of consequence). This operation was repeated for alternative fixed bundles x_1^0, x_2^0. Since k_1 and k_2 are assumed to be independent of the fixed bundle, a pooled estimate of these parameters was obtained.

By a similar procedure, estimates of k_2 and k_3 were obtained. Since these estimates are defined only up to proportional changes in k_2 and k_3, they can be normalized, so that the two estimates of k_2 are the same. Under the assumptions made, the preference as between two bundles of commodities 1 and 3 is determined by the relative values of

$$k_1 \log x_1 + k_3 \log x_3.$$

Actual preference statements as between pairs x_1, x_3 were tested against those predicted. From a graphic representation, it can be seen that the prediction is good, but not perfect. No tests of significance were used.

It should be made clear that in Thurstone's work, as in all subsequent work, the hypothesis of strict transitivity in a deterministic sense is not being seriously entertained; it is clearly rejected by the data. What is really being tested is some concept of stochastic transitivity. In the studies reviewed in this section, the stochastic element is not analyzed in great detail but is added on to a deterministic hypothesis, much in the way residual terms are added to a deterministic relation in the usual application of regression analysis to hypothesis testing. More recent attempts at a theory which encompasses probabilistic choices in its structure are discussed later in the chapter (see the section on probabilistic choices).

Several rather ingenious studies have been devised to test the transitivity hypothesis. P. H. Benson (1955) asked individuals to rank separately appetizers, entrées, and desserts from a specified list. Prices were given for the various items, and the subjects were asked to choose a meal within a fixed budget constraint. He scaled the three separate rankings according to a modified form of the methods of paired comparisons and assumed that the utility of the meal was the sum of the utilities of the appetizer, entrée, and dessert, utility being assumed equal to scale found. It has been discovered that the choice of the meal could be very well explained by the assumption of utility maximization subject to the given prices and incomes. The assumption that the utilities are additive for the given scale is rather arbitrary; it is perhaps then even more surprising that agreement is so good.

In addition, there have been two very carefully controlled experiments which tend to confirm the transitivity hypothesis. One was developed by Andreas G. Papandreou (1957). Individuals were asked to choose between pairs of combinations of tickets for different recreational events, for example, to choose between two opera and two ballet tickets, or one opera and three ballet tickets. It was not assumed that the choice made between a given pair of alternatives would remain the same on repeated trials; instead, it was hypothesized that the difference between the utilities of any two alternatives was a random variable, the alternative with the higher utility being chosen on any particular trial. This hypothesis was tested against the alternatives of any probabilities of choosing among alternatives. The evidence was overwhelming that the transitivity hypothesis was satisfied.

A similar result was obtained by Arnold M. Rose (1957), who asked opinions about the relative seriousness of different criminal offenses. The questionnaire consisted of pairwise comparisons and was repeated after two months. It was considered that observed circularities (intransitivities) could result from random choices between alternatives that are really very close, carelessness, or "true" intransitivity. No explicit model of the alternative hypothesis was formulated, but a number of observations which tended to minimize the possibility of true intransitivity were made. Three of the 74 subjects had no circularities on either test, and 47 did not repeat on the second test any circularity which occurred on the first. Less than 10 percent of all circularities were repeated. It appears that most circularities could be attributed to carelessness. Of the repeated circularities, most were made on close alternatives (closeness being measured by the Thurstone scale based on paired comparisons for all subjects) and thus could be attributed to forcing a decision between alternatives that are virtually indifferent. It was concluded that "true" intransitivity was rare.

On the other hand, Kenneth O. May (1954) found a considerable degree of intransitivity in choices by college students as to the qualities of three hypothetical marriage partners. Each potential wife was described in terms of intelligence, looks, and wealth, and the three possible partners were so chosen that if ranking was done by considering a majority of the three qualities, the result was circular. The subjects made pairwise choices among the three partners, who were given different designations but the same descriptions in the different choices. Seventeen out of 62 subjects had the circular preference pattern defined by a majority of the qualities; the remainder, close to three-fourths of the whole, had different transitive preference patterns.

The evidence seems mostly to be on the side of verifying the transitivity postulate, but obviously the data are far from conclusive. In particular, it would be useful to run experiments in which the individual could actually get some of the rewards, so that the choice would be behavioristic rather than merely verbal.

Utilities and Reference Groups. Among other choices made by an individual with a given income, one is dividing that income between consumption and savings. Although this division leads into dynamic problems, to be discussed in the section on choice in dynamic situations, it can be thought of first in the same way as a choice among commodities. In this context, there has been one line of thought which relates decisions about savings to the behavior of others in the community.

Dorothy Brady and Rose Friedman (1947) studied budget data for different parts of the country and found that the relation between savings and income was different by geographic areas. However, it could be shown that the ratio of savings to income could be explained in terms of the individual's *relative* position on the income scale of his particular geographic area. Thus an individual whose income was the median for the South would save the same proportion of his income as one who was at the median income position for the Northeast, even though those two median levels were very different.

This line of investigation was continued by James S. Duesenberry (1949). He argued that the utility derived by an individual for a given bundle, particularly a given level of consumption, was not absolute but relative to the general consumption level of those whom he regarded as his peers. Thus there is a theory of changes in the individual's preference system. At any given moment — that is, at any given level of consumption by the community at large — the preference ranking of an individual for different amounts of consumption is well defined, but the ranking will change with changes in the community's consumption level.

This hypothesis has the advantage of explaining an apparent contradiction between time-series and budget data. If one takes a given point in time and relates savings of families to incomes, the savings-income ratio tends to increase with income. On the other hand, time-series data such as those of Simon Kuznets (1942) show that the percentage saved by the community as a whole has been roughly constant since 1879. These two observations are apparently incompatible because, if the first relation held, a rise in income of the average member of the community would result in a higher savings-income ratio. Duesenberry's hypothesis would reconcile this paradox by arguing that individual preference rankings have shifted over time with the growth in real income and therefore of consumption. He found further support for this view in studies such as those of Richard Centers and Hadley Cantril (1946), which showed that the income to which an individual aspired tended to be related to differences between social status and economic status, in other words, to peer-group influences.

A common general hypothesis in social psychology is that the desirability of alternatives is related to the standard set by the group of which the individual considers himself a member. An experiment which bears closely on the economic issues is that of Paul Hoffman, Leon Festinger, and Douglas Lawrence (1954). The subjects engage in a three-person game. The game is completely symmetric among all individuals, and therefore the individual's only chance of winning is by forming a two-member coalition.

One of the hypotheses tested is that individuals are motivated by their scores relative to the scores of others whom they regard as comparable, not by their absolute scores. This hypothesis was tested by an ingenious experimental procedure. In each group of three, there was one instructed participant (unknown to the other two). It was arranged that he would command an initial lead. The other two formed coalitions with each other to an extent significantly greater than chance, indicating a preference for reducing the instructed participant's lead rather than achieving a greater score.

On the other hand, a study of savings data from some highly selected groups by James Tobin (1951) seems to show that savings depend on absolute income rather than relative income. However, this interpretation of the data has been challenged (Friedman, 1957, pp. 169–182).

Choice in Dynamic Situations

Theory. Obviously, much choice behavior is forward-looking. Decisions made today have repercussions for the future and are themselves conditioned by what has happened in the past. In the field of consumption, the most obvious example is that of durable consumers' goods. The purchase of a refrigerator or an automobile is made with a view toward the stream of benefits to be received over a future period. To put it another way, the decision to purchase durable consumers' goods will be influenced by the stock of such goods which have accumulated in the past.

A satisfactory theory which will logically account for consumption choices interrelated in time requires a modification — or more precisely, a reinterpretation — of the static model described earlier. Each individual is really choosing conceptually a set of commodities not only for the present, but also for each future instant of time. His choice is constrained, then, not merely by the current income that he receives and the prices that he pays, but also by prices and incomes of all future times.

Let us formulate the theory of choice and dynamic conditions more precisely, following the exposition of John R. Hicks (1946). Let x_{it} be the amount of commodity i consumed in time period t, and let p_{it} be the price to be paid for a unit of commodity i in time period t. We will assume that the consumer plans for T periods ahead. Then his expenditures at time t will be

$$(8\text{-}1) \qquad \sum_{i=1}^{n} p_{it} x_{it},$$

and his total expenditures for T periods are given by

$$(8\text{-}2) \qquad \sum_{t=1}^{T} \sum_{i=1}^{n} p_{it} x_{it}.$$

Let M_t be the income to be received at time period t.

We will now make an important assumption to simplify the exposition. It will be assumed at the present moment that the individual can borrow or lend money without interest, subject only to the condition that he have no indebtedness at the end of the period. This means that his expenditures and income do not have to balance in each time period separately, but only over the entire planning horizon of T periods.[3] This implies that, in making decisions in the initial period, the individual has available the total income which he has received during the entire period, that is,

$$(8\text{-}3) \qquad \sum_{t=1}^{T} M_t,$$

which we will designate by M.

The choice between consumption and savings is now a part of the above analysis. In any particular time period, expenditures may fall short of income or may exceed them. If the individual is to go through a normal life cycle, we may expect him to save during the early and the middle years of his life and to dissave at the end. It is therefore implied that, in the year under consideration, the amounts consumed and the amounts saved are certain functions of the total or permanent income M, not of the income of a given year.

The situation is now formally analogous to the static case. The individual chooses among commodity bundles which are enlarged to be extended in

---

3. The assumption that the lending and borrowing are without interest is not, of course, realistic; it is made here solely for simplification. In Hicks's presentation, interest is accounted for. The analysis above is not changed essentially, but the interpretation of future prices is somewhat different.

time. A single bundle is described by the coordinates $x_{11}, \ldots, x_{1T}, \ldots,$ $x_{n1}, \ldots, x_{nT}$. His preference ranking may then be described by a utility function $U(x_{11}, \ldots, x_{1T}, \ldots, x_{n1}, \ldots, x_{nT})$. He maximizes the utility function, subject to the restraint that the total expenditure over the period does not exceed the total income, that is,

$$(8\text{-}4) \qquad \sum_{t=1}^{T} \sum_{i=1}^{n} p_{it} x_{it} \leqq M = \sum_{t=1}^{T} M_t.$$

In the problem as formulated, the obstacles now involve future prices and future income. This is not meaningful, of course, because the future is unknown. Although the assumption of perfect foresight sometimes made by economists is not quite as absurd as it sounds, for various reasons that will not be discussed here, there is no doubt that it gives an inadequate picture of reality. One approach is to assume that the individual forms expectations of future prices and incomes and acts as if he knew with certainty that his expectations were correct.[4] A more complicated assumption is that the individual is aware that he cannot know the future and anticipates it in the form of a range of possibilities, possibly a probability distribution.

The first form is, of course, more easily studied. In this form, the objection sometimes made to utility analysis — that it does not permit genuine decision making — is not valid. Decision making now comes in choosing the correct expectations. The utility theory does say that if expectations are the same in two situations, the choice of consumption and saving will be the same. Hence there is no contradiction between the hypothesis that choice is governed by utility maximization and the fact that an individual can change his mind in the light of new information. New information is incorporated in revised expectations of the future. However, it must be admitted that this formulation, while saving the utility theory, does so at the expense of putting most of its content into the expectations. Utility theory here serves mainly the method of suggesting which variables enter into the analysis and something about the way in which they affect current decisions.

Empirical Evidence. The main conclusion that we seem to have drawn from utility theory thus far is that consumption of commodities will be determined by the individual's permanent or lifetime income rather than by his current income. A number of writers have studied this question in different ways. George Katona (1951, pp. 155–160), in an important

---

4. For a very complete discussion of the incorporation of expectation into the theory of economic behavior, see Modigliani and Cohen (1961).

pioneer study, showed that income increases resulted in a much greater increase in consumption when the individual expected the income change to be permanent rather than temporary. This study was based on questionnaire data. This result, of course, is compatible with the permanent-income hypothesis; an increase in income, accompanied by the expectation of its continuance, obviously results in the expectation of a much larger permanent income than does an income increase which is accompanied by the expectation that it will last for one period only. Similar results were found by Lawrence R. Klein (1954, pp. 215–216).

The permanent-income hypothesis was stated explicitly and studied most extensively by Milton Friedman (1957) and by Franco Modigliani and Richard Brumberg (1954). It is not possible to pursue the line of argument and the variety of empirical evidence here, but both conclude, mainly on the basis of studies of budget data, that the ratio of savings to permanent income tends to be quite constant.[5]

Until there is a more thorough understanding of the formation of expectations, the permanent-income hypothesis, when true, remains only a partial contribution to the understanding of consumption behavior.

Choice under Conditions of Uncertainty

Theory. Suppose an individual has to make a decision, the consequences of which he regards as uncertain. In a strict sense, of course, there is no decision which does not have this characteristic. For example, an individual who is contemplating the purchase of a house will be uncertain as to the future course of house prices. He might, for example, gain by postponing the purchase for a while. He will also be uncertain about the future income he will receive and about the length of time he will occupy the house. Each alternative is, of course, really a range of consequences. Which consequence will come true will depend on a whole series of other events, which are sometimes termed "the state of the world."

A classic treatment of the subject in theory originates with Daniel Bernoulli (1738). Let there be m states of the world, and let their probabilities be $p_1, \ldots, p_m$, respectively. For any alternative x, let $U_i(x)$ be the utility of x

---

5. The definition of savings is somewhat different from the commonsense one because of the treatment of durable consumers' goods. The purchase of a durable consumers' good is considered to be an act of saving, not consumption, but the use of previously existing durable consumers' goods is added to consumption.

if state *i* occurs. Then the utility to be attached to the alternative *x*, which is essentially a gamble or uncertainty, is the expected utility, that is,

$$\sum_{i=1}^{n} p_i U_i(x).$$

The alternatives are then ranked according to the expected utility associated with them, and in any given situation that one of the available alternatives which maximizes the expected utility is chosen. The maximization-of-expected-utility hypothesis has the virtue of being capable of explaining certain real-world phenomena. For example, insurance is typically actuarially unfair—that is, the expected money returned to the insured is negative. However, if we assume that the utility of different money outcomes is typically of a form showing decreasing increments to unit increases in money, the policy of taking out insurance may have a higher expected utility than the policy of not taking out insurance, even though the expected money income is lower for the first policy.

Although to this day there has been no serious rival to the Bernoulli hypothesis, it has been subject to much reinterpretation. A new line of development was initiated by Frank P. Ramsey (1931, chap. 7). Instead of postulating that individuals maximize expected utility, a series of assumptions was made about behavior in the presence of uncertainty. These assumptions presumably defined how a "rational" man would behave.[6] While there are a number of assumptions involved, the basic one may be illustrated in the following special case. Let G_1, G_2, G_3, and G_4 be four possible options—that is, the choice of any one implies a probability distribution over the possible outcomes. Now let us consider two compound gambles or options: H_1, H_2. H_1 is a two-stage gamble in which first a choice is made between G_1 and G_2, G_1 being chosen with probability p, G_2 with probability $1 - p$. Similarly, let H_2 involve a preliminary stage where G_3 is chosen with probability p and G_4 with probability $1 - p$. After the initial random choice has been made, then the actual outcome is governed by the appropriate G_1, G_2, G_3, or G_4, as the case may be.

H_1 and H_2 have been defined as two-stage gambles, but they are clearly equivalent to a single-stage gamble, which we can find by using the laws of compound probability. For example, if there is an outcome *O* which would

---

6. A similar point of view was developed later independently by John von Neumann and Oskar Morgenstern (1947, appendix).

be obtained under G_1 with probability r_1, and under G_2 with probability r_2, then under H_1, the probability of outcome O is $pr_1 + (1 - p)r_2$. The probability under H_1 for any possible outcome under either G_1 or G_2 can be found similarly.

With these preliminaries, we now state the basic assumption. Suppose that G_1 would be preferred by an individual to G_3, and that G_2 would be preferred to G_4. Then it is assumed that the compound gamble H_1 would be preferred to the compound gamble H_2. The intuitive appeal of this assumption is obvious, especially if we think of rational decisions. It is surprisingly powerful in its implications; it implies that numerical values may be assigned to the different possible outcomes so that an individual's preference among options involving uncertainty can be described as the maximization of the expected numerical values. These numerical values may, in a natural way, be referred to as "utilities." Thus the Bernoulli expected-utility hypothesis can be derived from more primitive and intuitively plausible assumptions about the behavior of individuals in the face of uncertainty.[7]

So far, the analysis has assumed that the different possible outcomes can be assigned probabilities. This may be satisfactory for the analysis of gambling or certain insurance situations, in which the probabilities of events have been found by theory or empirical observations. However, an individual facing uncertainty—for example, a consumer purchasing a second-hand car which may break down—frequently does not have available to him any set of objective probabilities. The question of rational behavior under these conditions was also studied by Ramsey and Bruno de Finetti (1937). A synthesis of these viewpoints has been made in a remarkable book by Leonard J. Savage (1954). This analysis brings us to the following conclusion: An individual acts as if he assigns probabilities to all possible events and utilities to all possible outcomes. Then he chooses among the available outcomes the one which maximizes his expected utility,[8] in very much the same way he would choose in a case where probabilities were known.

Other views of decision making under uncertainty have been developed, but usually with a reference to normative rather than descriptive application, particularly to serve as foundations for statistical method. One such

---

7. For an excellent exposition of the axiomatic approach to utility theory under uncertainty, see R. Duncan Luce and Howard Raiffa (1957, pp. 19–34).

8. Excellent expositions of this and related theories are given in Luce and Raiffa (1957, chap. 13), and by Jacob Marschak (in Lazarsfeld, 1954, chap. 4).

theory, however, has been developed with reference to economic behavior by G. L. S. Shackle (1949).[9]

Experimental Verification. The expected-utility hypothesis in any of its forms gives rise to a utility function which is a ratio scale rather than an ordinal scale, as in the case of choice under conditions of certainty. The greater power of this theory has been a strong incentive to experimental work. The earliest such study was done by Frederick Mosteller and Philip Nogee (1951). The subjects were supplied with gambling situations in which the probabilities were known. By varying the rewards in money terms, it was possible to measure a utility curve for money — that is, a function of money such that the individual's choice of a bet is governed by a utility-maximization hypothesis. If the individual is indifferent between taking and not taking a gamble with a stake of 5 cents and a probability p of winning an amount A, then

$$pU(A) + (1 - p)U(-5 \text{ cents}) = U(0).$$

If we let $U(-5 \text{ cents}) = -1$, $U(0) = 0$ (as we may, since origin and unit are arbitrary), we can solve for $U(A)$. This can be done for each A by varying p until the subject is indifferent between the two alternatives.

In one part of the experiment, utility curves were used to predict outcomes in more complicated gambles than those from which the curve was derived. The measure of agreement was fair but not overwhelming.

The Mosteller-Nogee experiment had the difficulty — from the point of underlying theory — that it assumed that individuals act subjectively in accordance with the objective probabilities. A much more careful series of experiments, which sought to control the subjective probabilities among other problems, was carried out by Donald Davidson, Patrick Suppes, and Sidney Siegel (1957). Their experimental procedure was first to isolate an event whose subjective probability is one-half. This can be determined, according to the theory, by finding an event E such that the individual is indifferent between the following two options: (1) receiving an amount of money a when E occurs and an amount b when E does not occur; and (2) receiving the amount b when E occurs and a when E does not occur. Here a and b are differing amounts of money — it being supposed, of course, that an individual always prefers a greater amount of money to a lesser. If an event E is such that options 1 and 2 are indifferent for some particular a and b, then,

---

9. For a general survey of theories of uncertainty and risk with special reference to economic applications, see Arrow (1951).

under the expected-utility hypothesis, the two options should be indifferent for all other values of a and b for which $a < b$. This implication was confirmed for all subjects.

Once E is determined, its subjective probability being one-half, the preferences between gambles on the occurrence of E can be established. For example, if one option is that an individual will receive x if E occurs and y if E does not occur, and if a second option is that an individual will receive u if E occurs and v if it does not, then, according to the expected-utility hypothesis, a preference for the first option over the second is equivalent to the statement

$$\tfrac{1}{2}U(x) + \tfrac{1}{2}U(y) > \tfrac{1}{2}U(u) + \tfrac{1}{2}U(v).$$

The utility function for money can then be traced out with a limited number of observations, and prediction to other choices can be made. For example, let a and b, $a < b$, be two fixed amounts of money. By varying c, we can find one value such that the option c if E occurs, b if E does not occur, is just indifferent to the certainty of a. Similarly, d is found such that the option d if E occurs, a if E does not occur, is indifferent to the certainty of b. Then the expected-utility hypothesis implies that the option d if E occurs, c if E does not, is indifferent to the option b if E occurs, a if E does not. The verification of the predictions is a verification of the expected-utility hypothesis. This was found to hold very well for 15 out of 19 subjects.

The question of the formation of subjective probabilities is not completely taken care of by this study, since only subjective probabilities of one-half entered. A second experiment tested some of the implications of the Ramsey theory for existence of subjective probabilities. For any event E and any amounts of money x, y, z, under Ramsey's theory, there should be a unique amount of money w, such that the options x if E, y if not E, and z if E, w if not E, are indifferent. Then the subjective probability of E would be

$$\frac{U(w) - U(y)}{U(x) - U(y) - U(z) + U(w)}$$

and, for given E, this magnitude should be independent of the amounts $x, y,$ and z. Again there was confirmation, but one puzzling feature is that the subjective probability was lower than the objective probability. The situation was one of such complete symmetry that it is hard to believe there will not be inconsistencies with other experiments which involve more complicated gambles.

A study by Paul M. Hurst and Sidney Siegel (1956) also confirmed the expected-utility hypothesis. The subjects were given a series of choices among pairs of options at even odds. Under the expected-utility hypothesis, the outcomes of any set of choices imposed constraints on the possible utility functions; in general, in fact, the results on a subset of the choices were sufficient to imply enough about the utility function to predict the remaining choices. The options concerned a numerical variable so that the expected value of each option was meaningful. It was found that the predictions made from the expected-utility hypothesis were significantly better than those made from the hypothesis that the individual always made a choice which maximized expected value. Additional results of the study relate to the experimental problem of determining indifference. As a rule, the experimental situation requires the individual to choose among alternatives, and if the individual is actually indifferent, there is clearly danger of introducing errors into the analysis. Hurst and Siegel found that the latency time for the cases where the expected-utility hypothesis failed was considerably greater than that where it succeeded. This suggests that the theory appears to fail only because of the difficulty of observing indifference.[10]

"Commonsense" Empirical Observations. The whole axiomatic approach can be thought of as crystallizing everyday or introspective observations. A very interesting use of casual empirical observation was made in a paper by Milton Friedman and Leonard J. Savage (1948). They observed that some individuals gamble, others take out insurance, some do both, and finally that lottery owners find it profitable to offer several prizes instead of one large one. It turns out that all of these phenomena can be explained on the expected-utility hypothesis provided the utility function of money is supposed to have first a segment in which the derivative (in economic terms, the marginal utility) is decreasing, then a segment in which it increases, and finally a segment in which it decreases again. A modification of this theory designed to explain some further phenomena was introduced by Harry Markowitz (1952). The main innovation was that the utility should be thought of as a function of departures from the present situation rather than as a function of income. This hypothesis weakens very considerably the force of the original version and should be accepted, it appears to me, only with caution. It would be difficult to bring experimental evidence to bear on

10. From the point of view of scaling theory, it is perhaps important to remark that although the expected-utility hypothesis theoretically gives rise to a ratio scale, it does so only when an infinite number of observations can be made. A finite number of observations give rise to something closer to an ordered metric scale; see Sidney Siegel (1956).

this question because it would be necessary to make a fairly large change in the individual's initial income to test the Markowitz hypothesis.

Mention should be made of a very severe criticism of the expected-utility theory due to Maurice Allais (1953). The argument in part consists of examples which are designed to show the counterintuitive character of some implications of the expected-utility hypothesis. Consider the following four gambles:

1. Certainty of receiving $1 million.
2. $5 million with probability 0.1; $1 million with probability 0.89; 0 with probability .01.
3. $1 million with probability 0.11; 0 with probability 0.89.
4. $5 million with probability 0.1; 0 with probability 0.90.

It can easily be seen that under the expected-utility hypothesis, an individual who prefers 1 to 2 must necessarily prefer 3 to 4. But, Allais argues, most people, especially if rather conservative in their attitude to uncertainty, would prefer 1 to 2 but 4 to 3. Similar arguments have been developed by Pierre Massé and Georges Morlat (1953).

Probabilistic Choices

The theory of choice as formulated up to this point, whether for conditions of certainty or uncertainty, is stated in the form that for any two alternatives A and B, one of the two will be chosen and will be chosen every time the two alternatives are offered under the same conditions, except in the special case where the two are indifferent. This assumption implies a kind of perfect ability to discriminate, which, of course, goes counter to the trend of virtually all psychological experiments. In fact, as we have seen, all the experiments on transitivity described earlier have had to introduce ad hoc theories which permit the choice to be something less than perfectly invariable. A more general formulation is suggested: For any pair of alternatives A and B there is a certain probability, depending on the two alternatives, that A will be chosen over B. The classical theory then becomes a special case where this probability takes on only the values one, zero, and possibly one-half, the last to account for indifference. Some of the classical methods of psychophysics, such as Thurstone's law of comparative judgment, are special formulations of such a probabilistic theory of choice. Though a number of writers — R. Duncan Luce and Jacob Marschak, in particular — have raised the question in one form or another in connection with preference theory, no thoroughly satisfactory alternative has developed. They try to exhibit a utility function which has the property that the probability of preferring a to b depends monotonically on the distance between the two—that is, on $U(a) - U(b)$. It seems quite difficult, however, to arrive at an appropriate set of assumptions which will not have very undesirable consequences;[11] in particular, difficulties arise when some, but not all, choices can be perfectly discriminated.

An attempt has been made by Richard E. Quandt to reformulate the theory of consumer behavior under certainty so as to admit a probabilistic element in choice (1956). He suggests two sources of random behavior. One is that the individual orders his preferences among commodity bundles in accordance with a set of basic characteristics of the commodities; however, in any given comparison he may consider only some of the relevant characteristics, with the particular characteristics on which the choice is based being chosen according to some random process.[12] Second, the individual may be in error in regard to his *own* preference scale. This theory, however, has not been very much elaborated or subjected to any empirical tests.

Omar K. Moore (1957) has suggested that the widespread use of divination methods can be regarded as a deliberate use of randomization in controlling behavior. Indeed, there seems to be evidence that most gambling originated as a form of divination. For example, Moore suggests as an interpretation that in hunting game, primitive tribes implicitly hit upon a method of deriving a mixed strategy in the sense of game theory.

Utility Theory and Motivation Theory

Economists' utility theory of behavior has many points of affinity with at least some studies of motivation and conflict in psychology. The pairwise comparisons of the utility theory are, in psychological terms, approach-approach conflicts. The consumer who has to choose among all commodity bundles which he can afford is in a multiple-approach situation, with a continuum of alternatives. Mathilda Holzman (1958) has shown that much

---

11. See, for example, Luce and Raiffa (1957, appendix 1); Luce (1959); Jacob Marschak (1955, 1960); Donald Davidson and Jacob Marschak (1959).

12. There is a similarity between this concept and the associationist theory of learning due to William K. Estes, described later in the chapter.

of the apparent difference between economists' and psychologists' approaches to choice situations is due not to any fundamental difference in assumptions about behavior but to the different range of alternatives allowed. Choice tends to look much more like conflict when only two alternatives are permitted.

It should also be noted that there is no real distinction in economic terminology between approach-approach and avoidance-avoidance situations. Utility being an ordinal — or at most an interval scale — there is no natural zero. This difference between economic and psychological theories is probably more semantic than anything else. In most psychological experiments there is some available alternative of complete inaction, which can be ascribed a zero utility. Then positive utilities correspond to approach situations, negative utilities to avoidance situations.

To illustrate the relation between utility and motivation theories, we may look at the interesting papers of Neal Miller (1955, 1959).[13] Miller is concerned with an approach-avoidance situation. At the same spot, there is a pleasurable stimulus (for example, food) and an unpleasant one (for example, electric shock). A rat decides, in effect, how close he shall come to the spot in question. Miller's model may be formulated in economic terminology: Let x be the distance at which the rat stops; $U_f(x)$ the utility derived from proximity to the food, and $U_s(x)$ the (negative) utility derived from proximity to the shock situation. U_f is a decreasing function of x; that is, the larger is x — and therefore the greater the distance from the stimulus — the less the satisfaction derived from the food. On the other hand, U_s is an increasing function of x. Miller's theory is that the rat chooses x so as to maximize $U_f(x) + U_s(x)$. The condition of maximization is that the first derivative of this utility function be zero and that the second derivative be negative. In symbols, $U_f' + U_s' = 0$, $U_f'' + U_s'' < 0$. In Miller's terminology, the first states that the avoidance and approach gradients are equal, the second that the avoidance gradient is steeper than the approach gradient.

The difference between the economic and the psychological formulations is not that they are contradictory in any way, but rather that they deal with different matters. The economist would usually be interested in saying simply that the rat has a utility function associated with distance, whereas the psychologist attempts to go into the structure of that utility function more carefully. The interesting implication of the deeper analysis is that the

13. I am indebted to Daniel Berlyne for very helpful comments on Miller's work, though he may well not agree completely with the following interpretation.

rewards and punishments which are strictly localized objectively neverthe-less are generalized in space, which may be taken as a paradigm for stimulus generalization along many dimensions of perception.

The role of stimulus generalization in economics is almost completely unexplored. The economic analogue would be perhaps a case where new opportunities for consumption or for business arose. The economic agent would tend to respond by attributing to the new modes of behavior utilities related to their distance from the old and previously rewarded modes. Failures in economic development may be in some part related to this failure to evaluate new situations in terms different from the older ones.

Dynamic Aspects of Behavior

Although, as we have already seen, utility theory of behavior by no means excludes dynamic aspects completely, there are many phenomena which are not encompassed by that theory, at least in its present form. We have seen in discussing choice in dynamic situations that expectations of the future are relevant. There have been a number of studies in recent years which cast some light on the role of expectations, both their impact on behavior and the process of their formation. The formation of expectations about the future is, of course, closely related to learning in a classical sense, and we will explore some of the relations between learning theory and economic theory.

The Influence of Expectations on Behavior

As far as consumers are concerned, the evidence of influence of expectations on behavior is at best fragmentary. The most complete study seems to be that of George Katona and Eva Mueller (1953). Interviews were used to get opinions as to the short-term and long-term business outlook, expectations of changes in individual income, subjective evaluation of changes in the financial situation, and expectations of price changes. These variables were related chiefly to opinions about the favorableness of buying conditions. The associations of the expectation variables to the intentions to purchase are in the expected direction. For example, expectation of better times was related to a more favorable opinion toward buying durable goods. However, the associations on the whole were quite weak. Also, of course, it would be more desirable to have a study on actual purchases rather than opinions of buying conditions.[14]

An elaborate study of expectations of business firms was made by Franco Modigliani and Owen Sauerlender (1955). The data were derived from three sources: (1) forecasts of shipments made to railroads by shippers; (2) forecasts made for *Fortune* by a number of top executives, and (3) an interview survey of business expectations conducted by Dun and Bradstreet. By means of a rather elaborate statistical analysis, it was shown that the expectations are relevant to the firm's actual behavior — in the sense that, to some extent at least, changes in inventory and production policy can be predicted from changes in expectations.

From a practical point of view, the extent to which anticipations data can be used for short-term forecasting is very important, of course, but from the point of view of psychological theory it may be said that studies on the influence of expectations on behavior have at the moment methodological rather than substantive interest. In the case of any decision having consequences to be worked out in the future — for example, an investment by a firm in plant and equipment — we may reasonably postulate the existence of expectations or something equivalent as an intervening variable. Then the point of studies such as those of Katona and Mueller and of Modigliani and Sauerlender is rather to relate the expectation qua an intervening variable to verbally expressed expectations. If a relationship between the two can be established, then verbalized expectations may be used as an additional source of data in further research.

The Formation of Expectations

Evidence from Time Series. One theory which is frequently plausible is that the expectations about any variable are extrapolations of some type of the previous behavior of that variable. Though this general point of view has usually been accepted by economic theorists, very little has been done to make it specific. An attractive hypothesis was advanced, however, by Phillip Cagan (1956). Suppose, for example, we are considering expectations by an individual of the price of a commodity. He suggests that there is a continu-

---

14. There was a relation studied between evaluation of change in financial situation and purchases of durable goods during the preceding twelve months. Again this was in the expected direction, but the association was by no means strong.

ous adjustment in such a way that each expectation is compared with the reality when it is observed, and the expectation for the following period is obtained by revising the previous expectation in the direction of the actual figure. Thus, let $\bar{p}_t$ represent the anticipation held at time $t - 1$ of the price to prevail at time t, and let p_t be the actual price at time t. Then Cagan's hypothesis can be stated as follows:

$$\bar{p}_{t+1} - \bar{p}_t = a(p_t - \bar{p}_t),$$

where a is a number between zero and one. This theory may be termed that of *adaptive expectations*. It is analogous to the corrective mechanism used in firing a gun, where the accuracy is improved in successive rounds by adjusting toward the target and away from the previous aim. To give the theory another interpretation, it follows from the previous formula that

$$\bar{p}_t = a \sum_{u=1}^{\infty} (1 - a)^{u-1} p_{t-u},$$

that is, the expectation of current price is a weighted average of all previous prices, with the weights decreasing as the price becomes more remote.

Cagan was particularly interested in studying the demand for holding cash balances under hyperinflationary conditions, such as those prevailing in Germany after World War I. The demand for cash balances ordinarily depends on a number of variables, but in hyperinflations it is reasonable to suppose that the expected rate of change of prices is the dominant one. The particular formula suggested by Cagan as the explanatory variable for cash balances turned out to predict very well under a wide variety of hyperinflationary situations.

Another application of the same hypothesis was made by Marc Nerlove (1956; 1958, chap. 2, sec. 1; chap. 8, secs. 1, 2). A farmer, when deciding how much acreage to plant, cannot know the price at which the product will be sold, since this lies some months in the future. It is to be presumed that he acts in accordance with expectation of that price. The simple hypothesis that the price expected to prevail at the time of harvest is the same as the price at the time of planting has not been successful. Nerlove showed that the hypothesis of adaptive expectations yields an excellent explanation for the supply of corn and wheat in the United States.

The hypothesis has been used in a different form by Milton Friedman (1957) in developing the theory of consumption as a function of permanent income described earlier. Since permanent income is really expected income, the hypothesis would imply that consumption in any year depends on an exponentially weighted average of past and present income. Friedman finds that this hypothesis applied to aggregate time-series data yields a better explanation than rival ones.

Experimental Evidence.   Experimental evidence on the formation of expectations has been reported by Rotter (1954, pp. 165–183). The results are partially in accord with the theory of adaptive expectations but partially different. In repeated trials, the subjects were asked for their expectancy, measured either as an expected score or as an amount they were willing to bet on success in the next trial. Without going into details, the basic result seems to be that expectations are indeed revised regularly to bring them into line with observations, but in a repetition of similar situations the extent of revision tends to be inversely proportional to the number of trials already undertaken. This difference in results is presumably related to the degree to which the subject regards the situations as being really similar. In an economic context, an individual may feel that the world is steadily changing and therefore that any new observation is not simply one more made under circumstances identical to those in the past.

Inferences from Surveys of Expectations.   A new source of data that became available in the postwar period is a survey of predictions by entrepreneurs conducted by the IFO–Institut für Wirtschaftsforschung in Munich. In the survey, each entrepreneur is asked about the direction of change of a large number of variables such as production, buying and selling prices, demand conditions, and so forth. The answers are qualitative — that is, the only three answers are "Increase," "Decrease," or "No change." These have been analyzed from a number of points of view. In the present context, the most relevant studies are two papers by Oskar Anderson, Jr., and collaborators at the IFO–Institut für Wirtschaftsforschung (1955, 1956) and a paper by Henri Theil and J. S. Cramer (1954; see also Theil, 1958, chap. 6, sec. 3).

The studies by Anderson and his associates relate primarily to prediction of variables that are, in whole or in part, under the control of the firm, such as production and prices. These are really to be thought of as plans of the firm rather than expectations about events outside its control. Let x stand for the set of variables over which the firm has no control, and let y be its planned production, for example. Then if x were known, y would be a known function $f(x)$. At the time when the firm is asked for its expectations for the next month or two, it does not actually know the value of x and therefore uses an expectation x. The expectation of the controlled variables, then, is $\hat{y} = f(\hat{x})$.[15] When the firm finds out the actual value of x, it would like to change y from $\hat{y}$ to $f(x)$. It may not succeed in carrying through the change completely, since some commitments will have already been made, but the change will be in the direction suggested by the change from $\hat{x}$ to x. Thus if $f(x)$ is an increasing function of x, for example, production is an increasing function of price, the firm will have an actual production which is higher than its planned production if the actual price is higher than the planned price, and vice versa. These hypotheses are fully confirmed by the data.

The hypotheses cast, of course, only an indirect light on the whole question of expectations. They do, however, suggest that the verbal expectations held by businessmen bear at least some relation to the hypothetical expectations which govern their behavior in economic planning. They also suggest that the expectations about the variables over which the firm has no control are of the adaptive type suggested in the last section. Similar results were obtained in the work of Irwin Friend and Jean Bronfenbrenner (Crockett) (1955), based on American postwar data of intentions to invest. Analysis of the departures between actual and planned investment showed that they could be partially explained by changes from expectations of the variables over which the firm had no control.

Theil and Cramer, in addition to other work, did a direct analysis of expectations of variables not under the control of the firm, buying prices in particular. They found that the expectation of a buying price was indeed related to its own past behavior; it was also related to the behavior of other prices that might be expected to influence it. Thus expectations about the price of leather correlated not only with the past prices of leather but also with the past prices of hides. This suggests that the entrepreneur uses a multiplicity of cues in forming his expectations for the future, as indeed he should if he has any degree of rationality.

Statistical Learning Theory and Economics

The formation of expectations as a result of past experience is, of course, a learning process, and it might be instructive to consider some developments in statistical learning theory for their economic implications. As representative, we take the study of William Estes (1954, 1959). Individuals are asked

---

15. Strictly speaking, $\hat{y}$ need not be the same function of $\hat{x}$ that y is of x if the firm recognizes that the expectation is, in fact, uncertain. However, there will be a general similarity in the two relations.

simply to predict occurrence or nonoccurrence of an event (rather than a continuous variable, as is more usual in economics). In fact, the event occurs randomly with a constant probability π, although this fact is not, of course, known to the subjects. Let p_n be the probability that the individual will predict that the event will occur at time $n + 1$. It is assumed that an observed success increases the probability of the individual's predicting the occurrence of the event and a failure decreases that probability, and that these two effects are symmetric. Then

$$p_{n+1} = p_n + \theta(1 - p_n)$$

if there was a success on the nth trial, and

$$p_{n+1} = p_n - \theta p_n$$

otherwise. These formulas bear a distinct similarity to the adaptive expectations discussed earlier. Under the experimental conditions assumed, it can be shown that the average of p_n over many individuals will approach π in a large number of trials. This theoretical implication has been confirmed experimentally.

If we assume that the aim of an individual is to maximize the expected number of successes—that is, that the expected-utility hypothesis holds with the number of successes as the utility function—then the individual's optimal behavior can easily be seen to predict success all the time if π is greater than one-half, and failure all the time if π is less than one-half. It is true that he will not adopt this behavior immediately if the value of π is unknown, but after a sufficient number of trials to "learn" the true value, he will—under the assumed conditions—behave as indicated. We have here a seeming contradiction between two theories of behavior.

There have been attempted reconciliations by Merrill M. Flood (1954) and Siegel (1961). Flood has suggested two explanations. One is that the utility function is not simply the number of successes. There is disproportionately high utility attached to getting a perfect score, or—to put it another way—high utilities attached to guessing the less frequent event. The second is that the subject, not being aware that success and failure are generated by a random mechanism, may believe that there is a nonstationary process at work. His strategy, then, is in part a method of guarding against this possibility.

The first explanation in particular suggests that varying the reward attached to successes would alter the outcome. If the reward for a successful prediction and the penalty for an unsuccessful prediction were sufficiently high, one might expect a closer convergence to the economist's ideal. Experiments in which the reward was varied have been performed by Ward Edwards (1956) and Siegel (1961). Both found that increased rewards increased the probability of choosing the more frequent response over the probability suggested by the probability-matching rule.

Siegel has advanced as explanations both an additional utility for predicting the less frequent event and a disutility for repeatedly making the same prediction. If the probability π is in fact known to the subject—as it presumably will be after repeated trials—and p is the proportion of times the more frequent event is predicted by the subject, then the utility of correct prediction is

$$ap\pi + b(1 - p)(1 - \pi),$$

where a and b are positive constants, and the utility of variability may be taken as

$$cp(1 - p),$$

this being a function with a maximum at $p = \frac{1}{2}$, the point of greatest variability in prediction. An experiment was performed in which the subject was given 5 cents for a successful prediction and penalized 5 cents for an unsuccessful one. It was assumed that under these conditions $a = b$, so that only the utility of variability remains as a factor. An individual who seeks to maximize his total utility would choose

$$p = (a/c)(\pi - \tfrac{1}{2}) + \tfrac{1}{2}.$$

By running the experiment for a particular value of π and measuring p, an estimate of a/c was obtained. Since this ratio is, under the hypothesis, independent of π, the hypothesis can be tested by repeating the experiment with a different value of π and comparing the predicted value of p from the above formula with the actual value. A very close confirmation was obtained. The general model, including both effects, has not been tested.

Hints of a Utility Theory of Learning

So far in this discussion, the theory of expectations has been treated as something to be added to a utility theory involving choice over time. However, some methods of forming expectations seem more rational than others, and, at least formally, one can treat the learning process itself as a process of successive choices by the individual. His domain of choice now is a *strategy*—that is, in each stage he finds his next step as a function of all the information available to him up to the present time.

Some beginnings of a theory of this type have been made, though most often in a normative context. The most important development has been that of sequential analysis of statistical data by Abraham Wald (1947). Statistical observations are assumed to be collected one after another. After each observation one of two decisions must be made: to terminate the observations and draw whatever inference is called for, or to draw at least one more observation. The observations bear some kind of cost, but this incentive to stop must be weighed against the value of the additional information obtained. There is a close analogy to learning experiments which consist of a series of trials in which the subject's choices are sometimes rewarded and sometimes not. The individual, after making many choices, eventually begins to discriminate between the proper response and the improper one. At some point, presumably, he could terminate the experiment, at least in the sense of disregarding further observations and making the same choice each time.

Wald has developed the optimal rules for making sequential decisions, at least under simple conditions. Sequential analysis differs from standard learning experiments primarily in that there are no rewards for decisions made during the course of the observations; there is only a terminal decision. Attempts to incorporate the former have been made; they lead to great mathematical complexities, as shown in the important work of M. A. Girshick, Samuel Karlin, and Halsey L. Royden (1957), for example.

Some modification must, of course, be made in the above theories in order to fit the experimental facts, such as those found by Estes and others. The chief trouble is that most optimal statistical procedures would eventually lead toward a convergence of choice on one or the other of two alternatives. Estes' hypothesis introduces the concept of a limited cognition of the stimulus elements at each stage in the learning process. This could be incorporated in a more complicated model of rational learning by introducing a cost to a complete scanning of the field of relevant information at each stage. Such developments, if at all appropriate, await future work.

References

Allais, M. Fondements d'une théorie positive des choix comportant un risque et critique des postulats et axiomes de l'école Américaine. In *Économetrie*, XL, *Colloques Internationaux du Centre National de la Recherche Scientifique.* Paris: Centre National de la Recherche Scientifique, 1953. Pp. 257–332.

Anderson, O., Jr., Bauer, R. K., Führer, H., and Petersen, J. P. Short-term entrepreneurial reaction patterns. IFO–Institut für Wirtschaftsforschung, Munich, 1955. (Mimeographed.)

Anderson, O., Jr., Furst, H., and Schulte, W. Zur Analyse der unternehmerischen Reaktionsweise. *IFO–Studien,* 1956, vol. 2.

Arrow, K. J. Alternative approaches to the theory of choice in risk-taking situations. *Econometrica,* 1951, vol. 19, 404–437.

Benson, P. H. A model for the analysis of consumer preference and an exploratory test. *J. Appl. Psychol.,* 1955, vol. 39, 375–381.

Bernoulli, D. Specimen theoriae novae de mensura sortis. *Commentarii Academiae Scientiarum Imperialis Petropolitanae,* 1738, vol. 5, 175–192. Translated as Exposition of a new theory on the measurement of risk, *Econometrica,* 1954, vol. 22, 23–26.

Brady, Dorothy, and Friedman, Rose. Savings and the income distribution. In *Studies in income and wealth,* vol. 10. New York: National Bureau of Economic Research, 1947. Pp. 250–266.

Cagan, P. The monetary dynamics of hyperinflation. In M. Friedman (ed.), *Studies in the quantity theory of money.* Chicago: University of Chicago Press, 1956. Pp. 25–117.

Centers, R., and Cantril, H. Income satisfaction and income aspiration. *J. Abnorm. Soc. Psychol.,* 1946, vol. 41, 64–69.

Davidson, D., and Marschak, J. Experimental tests of stochastic decision theory. In C. W. Churchman and P. Ratoosh (eds.), *Measurement: Definitions and theories.* New York: Wiley, 1959. Pp. 233–269.

Davidson, D., Suppes, P., and Siegel, S. *Decision-making: An experimental approach.* Stanford, Calif.: Stanford University Press, 1957.

de Finetti, B. La prévision: Ses lois logiques, ses sources subjectives. *Ann. Inst. Henri Poincaré,* 1937, vol. 7, 1–68.

Duesenberry, J. S. *Income, saving, and the theory of consumer behavior.* Cambridge, Mass.: Harvard University Press, 1949.

Edwards, W. Reward probability, amount, and information as determiners of sequential two-alternative decisions. *J. Exp. Psychol.,* 1956, vol. 52, 177–188.

Estes, W. K. Individual behavior in uncertain situations: An interpretation in terms of statistical association theory. In R. M. Thrall, C. H. Coombs, and R. L. Davis (eds.), *Decision processes.* New York: Wiley, 1954. Pp. 127–138.

Estes, W. K. The statistical approach to learning theory. In S. Koch (ed.), *Psychology: A study of a science,* vol. 2. New York: McGraw-Hill, 1959. Pp. 380–491.

Flood, M. M. Environmental non-stationarity in a sequential decision-making experiment. In R. M. Thrall, C. H. Coombs, and R. L. Davis (eds.), *Decision processes.* New York: Wiley, 1954. Pp. 287–300.

Friedman, M. *A theory of the consumption function.* Princeton, N.J.: Princeton University Press, 1957.

Friedman, M., and Savage, L. J. The utility analysis of choices involving risk. *J. Polit. Econ.,* 1948, vol. 56, 279–304.

Friend, I., and Bronfenbrenner (Crockett), J. Plant and equipment programs and their realization. In *Studies in income and wealth,* vol. 17, *Short-term economic forecasting.* Princeton, N.J.: Princeton University Press, 1955. Pp. 53–98.

Girshick, M. A., Karlin, S., and Royden, H. L. Multistage statistical decision procedures. *Ann. Math. Stat.,* 1957, vol. 28, 111–125.

Hicks, J. R. *Value and capital* (2nd ed.). New York: Oxford, 1946.

Hoffman, P., Festinger, L., and Lawrence, D. Tendencies toward group comparability in competitive bargaining. In R. M. Thrall, C. H. Coombs, and R. L. Davis (eds.), *Decision processes.* New York: Wiley, 1954. Pp. 231–254.

Holzman, M. Theories of choice and conflict in psychology and economics. *J. Conflict Resolution,* 1958, vol. 2, 310–320.

Hurst, P. M., and Siegel, S. Prediction of decisions from a higher ordered metric scale of utilities. *J. Exp. Psychol.,* 1956, vol. 52, 138–144.

Katona, G. *Psychological analysis of economic behavior.* New York: McGraw-Hill, 1951.

Katona, G., and Mueller, E. *Consumer attitudes and demand, 1950–1952.* Ann Arbor, Mich.: University of Michigan Press, 1953. Chap. 4.

Klein, L. R. Statistical estimation of economic relations from survey data. In L. R. Klein (ed.), *Contributions of survey methods to economics.* New York: Columbia University Press, 1954.

Kuznets, S. *Uses of national income in peace and war.* New York: National Bureau of Economic Research, 1942. (Occasional paper no. 6.)

Lazarsfeld, P. F. (ed.). *Mathematical thinking in the social sciences.* Glencoe, Ill.: Free Press, 1954.

Luce, R. D. *Individual choice behavior.* New York: Wiley, 1959.

Luce, R. D., and Raiffa, H. *Games and decisions.* New York: Wiley, 1957.

Markowitz, H. The utility of wealth. *J. Polit. Econ.,* 1952, vol. 60, 151–158.

Marschak, J. Norms and habits of decision-making under certainty. In *Mathematical models of human behavior.* Stamford, Conn.: Dunlap and Associates, 1955. Pp. 45–53.

Marschak, J. Binary-choice constraints and random utility indicators. In K. J. Arrow, S. Karlin, and P. Suppes (eds.), *Mathematical methods in the social sciences, 1959.* Stanford, Calif.: Stanford University Press, 1960. Pp. 312–329.

Massé, P., and Morlat, G. Sur le classement économique des perspectives aléatoires. In *Économetrie,* 15, *Colloques Internationaux du Centre National de la Recherche Scientifique.* Paris: Centre National de la Recherche Scientifique, 1953. Pp. 165–193.

May, K. O. Transitivity, utility, and aggregation in preference patterns. *Econometrica,* 1954, vol. 22, 1–14.

Miller, N. E. Development and extension of conflict theory. In D. C. McClelland (ed.), *Studies in motivation.* New York: Appleton-Century-Crofts, 1955. Pp. 507–516.

Miller, N. E. Liberalization of basic S-R concepts: Extensions to conflict behavior, motivation, and social learning. In S. Koch (ed.), *Psychology: A study of a science,* vol. 2. New York: McGraw-Hill, 1959. Pp. 196–292.

Modigliani, F., and Brumberg, R. Utility analysis and the consumption function: An interpretation of cross-section data. In K. Kurihara (ed.), *Post Keynesian economics.* New Brunswick, N.J.: Rutgers University Press, 1954. Pp. 388–436.

Modigliani, F., and Cohen, K. J. *The role of anticipations and plans in economic behavior and their use in economic analysis and forecasting.* Urbana, Ill.: University of Illinois, Bur. Econ. Bus. Res., 1961.

Modigliani, F., and Sauerlender, O. Economic expectations and plans of firms in relation to short-term forecasting. In *Studies in income and wealth,* vol. 17, *Short-term economic forecasting.* Princeton, N.J.: Princeton University Press, 1955. Pp. 261–351.

Moore, O. K. Divination – a new perspective. *Amer. Anthrop.,* 1957, vol. 59, 69–74.

Mosteller, F., and Nogee, P. An experimental measurement of utility. *J. Polit. Econ.,* 1951, vol. 59, 371–404.

Nerlove, M. Estimates of the elasticities of supply of selected agricultural commodities. *J. Farm Econ.,* 1956, vol. 38, 496–509.

Nerlove, M. *The dynamics of supply.* Baltimore, Md.: Johns Hopkins Press, 1958.

Papandreou, A. G. A test of a stochastic theory of choice. *Univer. Calif. Publ. Econ.,* 1957, vol. 16, 1–18.

Quandt, R. E. A probabilistic theory of consumer behavior. *Quart. J. Econ.,* 1956, vol. 70, 507–536.

Ramsey, F. P. *The foundations of mathematics and other logical essays.* London: Routledge, 1931.

Rose, A. M. A study of irrational judgments. *J. Polit. Econ.,* 1957, vol. 65, 394–402.

Rotter, J. B. *Social learning and clinical psychology.* Englewood Cliffs, N.J.: Prentice-Hall, 1954.

Savage, L. J. *The foundations of statistics.* New York: Wiley, 1954.

Shackle, G. L. S. *Expectations in economics.* New York: Cambridge University Press, 1949.

Siegel, S. A method for obtaining an ordered metric scale. *Psychometrika,* 1956, vol. 21, 207–216.

Siegel, S. Decision making and learning under varying conditions of reinforcement. *Ann. N.Y. Acad. Sci.,* 1961, vol. 89, 766–783.

Stone, R. The linear expenditure systems and demand analysis: An application to the pattern of British demand. *Economic J.,* 1954, vol. 64, 511–527.

Theil, H. *Economic forecasts and policy.* Amsterdam: North-Holland, 1958.

Theil, H., and Cramer, J. S. *On the utilization of a new source of economic information.* The Netherlands, The Hague, Central Planning Office, 1954. (Mimeographed.)

Thurstone, L. L. The indifference function. *J. Soc. Psychol.,* 1931, vol. 2, 139–167.

Tobin, J. Relative income, absolute income, and saving. In *Money, trade and economic growth.* New York: Macmillan, 1951. Pp. 135–156.

von Neumann, J., and Morgenstern, O. *Theory of games and economic behavior* (2nd ed.). Princeton, N.J.: Princeton University Press, 1947.

Wald, A. *Sequential analysis.* New York: Wiley, 1947.

Wold, H., and L. Juréen. *Demand analysis.* New York: Wiley, 1953.

9   The Theory of Risk Aversion

In 1962 I gave a course in the economics of uncertainty during which I discussed James Tobin's paper, which had become an immediate classic, deriving liquidity preference from risk aversion (see note 6). It seemed to me that the results could be presented more systematically. I was especially concerned with deriving the comparative statics for demand for risky assets, analogous to the usual developments in ordinary consumer demand theory. It was in studying the wealth effects that I realized that the much-used quadratic utility function implied that risky assets were inferior goods, an empirically dubious proposition. This led to the general formulation of the two measures of risk aversion studied in this chapter, which were developed independently by John Pratt.

Shortly thereafter I received an invitation to deliver the first of the Yrjö Jahnsson lectures in Helsinki. I decided to present the work on risk aversion, together with an exposition of the axiomatics of expected utility (to be found in an expanded form in Chapter 10 of this volume) and an introduction to the concepts of moral hazard and adverse selection (Chapter 6, Volume 4). They were delivered in December 1963.

From the time of Bernoulli on, it has been common to argue that (1) individuals tend to display aversion to the taking of risks, and (2) that risk

Reprinted from K. J. Arrow, *Aspects of the Theory of Risk-Bearing* (Helsinki: Yrjö Jahnssonin säätiö, 1965), lecture 2.

aversion in turn is an explanation for many observed phenomena in the economic world. In this chapter I wish to discuss more specifically the measures of risk aversion and to show how, in conjunction with the expected-utility hypothesis, they can be used to derive quantitative rather than merely qualitative results in economic theory.

A risk averter is defined as one who, starting from a position of certainty, is unwilling to take a bet which is actuarially fair (a fortiori, he is unwilling to take a bet which is actuarially unfair to him). The proposition that risk aversion is the prevalent phenomenon has been defended from personal introspection, from a consideration of the St. Petersburg paradox, discussed in Chapter 10, and from its success in explaining the economic phenomena to be mentioned below. There is, however, one common observation which tells against the prevalence of risk aversion, namely, that people gamble. Organized gambling is typically actuarially unfair to the individual gambler; indeed, it is precisely the departure of the expected value from zero which is the profit of the gambling establishment, without which it would not exist. I will not dwell on this point extensively, emulating rather the preacher who, expounding a subtle theological point to his congregation, frankly stated: "Brethren, here there is a great difficulty; let us face it firmly and pass on." Let me just consider two ways by which gambling is reconcilable with a general predominance of risk aversion. First, it has been shown by Friedman and Savage[1] that it is compatible with the expected-utility hypothesis for an individual to show risk aversion with respect to some risks but not with respect to others. In particular, it follows from their model that risk aversion will rule when sufficiently large amounts are at risk. Second, it may be argued that the gambler is one who believes the odds are more favorable to him than they really are; according to his *subjective* probabilities, the bet is favorable to him, but there is, for one reason or another, a divergence between the subjective and objective probabilities.[2] Then gambling can still be consistent with risk aversion, where the risks are understood subjectively.

The risk-aversion hypothesis owes its durability, in spite of the difficulty just mentioned, to its success in giving a qualitative explanation of otherwise puzzling examples of economic behavior. The most obvious example is insurance, which hardly needs elaboration. Common stocks with limited liability to the stockholders find a market because of risk aversion. The

---

1. M. Friedman and L. J. Savage, "The Utility Analysis of Choices Involving Risks," *Journal of Political Economy,* 56, 1948, pp. 279–304.

2. Any reader of Dostoevsky's *The Gambler* will have noted that the characters (and surely the author himself) had no doubt that the odds were favorable to them, if they could only find the capital to play the proper system at roulette.

cost-plus and other forms of risk-sharing contracts are again explicable only on the same hypothesis. Finally, and very importantly in the workings of the economic system, the holding of money depends in part at least on the motive of avoiding risks. Money, according to Aristotle, is barren; why then do individuals hold cash balances (including in this term, demand deposits) if they could instead buy interest-bearing securities or make other investments with a positive return? Economic theory gives two answers; one, with which we shall not be concerned, is the fact that time and trouble must be taken to obtain money when needed for a transaction (for example, by selling securities); the other is that all forms of investment are risky, and the desire for risk aversion may be satisfied only by holding some part of wealth in unprofitable but safe form. I shall return to this problem in the latter part of this chapter.

Let us now proceed to a more detailed characterization of risk aversion, based on the expected-utility hypothesis of Bernoulli. Let

$$Y = \text{wealth},$$
$$U(Y) = \text{total utility of wealth } Y.$$

Confronted with a choice of two policies, each of which determines Y as a random variable, the individual is supposed to choose that policy which makes $E[U(Y)]$ the larger, where E is expected value in the sense of probability theory. Recall further that $U(Y)$ is taken to be a bounded function; as will be shown in Chapter 10, such an assumption is needed to avoid paradox.

For simplicity, we here take wealth to be a single commodity and disregard the difficulties of aggregation over many commodities. For most purposes, Y is taken to be the money value of commodity holdings (including holdings of money itself) at market prices. There is no loss of generality under perfect competition as long as prices remain constant.

We assume that the utility of wealth is a differentiable function, indeed, twice differentiable; this is probably harmless. Let primes denote differentiation; thus,

$$U'(Y) = \text{marginal utility of wealth},$$
$$U''(Y) = \text{rate of change of marginal utility with respect to wealth}$$
$$\text{(second derivative of total utility)}.$$

We can always assume that wealth is desirable;

(9-1) $U'(Y) > 0.$

Then $U(Y)$ is a strictly increasing function of Y; the statement that it is bounded can then be written,

(9-2) $\lim_{Y \to 0} U(Y)$ and $\lim_{Y \to +\infty} U(Y)$ exist and are finite.

Consider now an individual with wealth Y_0 who is offered a chance to win or lose an amount h at fair odds. His choice is then between income Y_0 with probability 1 and a random income taking on the values $Y_0 - h$ and $Y_0 + h$ with probabilities 0.5 each. A risk averter by definition prefers the certain income; by the expected-utility hypothesis,

$$U(Y_0) > (\tfrac{1}{2})U(Y_0 - h) + (\tfrac{1}{2})U(Y_0 + h),$$

or, with a little rewriting,

$$U(Y_0) - U(Y_0 - h) > U(Y_0 + h) - U(Y_0).$$

The utility differences corresponding to equal changes in wealth are decreasing as the wealth increases; thus, as is well known and easily proved, the utility function of a risk averter is characterized by the condition

(9-3) $U'(Y)$ is strictly decreasing as Y increases.

It may be useful to note at this point that the boundedness of the utility function implies that any individual must be predominantly a risk averter. Suppose that, for some positive number ϵ, the total length of all the intervals on which $U'(Y) \geqq \epsilon$ is infinite; then, since $U(Y)$ is in any case increasing even on the remaining intervals, $U(Y)$ would have to tend to infinity as Y approaches infinity, a contradiction to (9-2). Hence, for any positive number ϵ, no matter how small, we must have $U'(Y) < \epsilon$ for all but a set of intervals whose total length is finite. One might then say that the marginal utility essentially tends to zero, and this means that, with relatively rare exceptions, $U'(Y)$ must be decreasing. Hence, pure theory joins with economic observation to imply the predominance of risk aversion over risk preference.

Although the mere existence of risk aversion can be used as an explanation of the existence of insurance, equities, and the other economic institutions noted earlier, we will need a suitable measure for risk aversion to arrive at quantitative theories. The ultimate justification for any particular measure is its usefulness in theories of specific forms of economic behavior under uncertainty; indeed, it was in considering the demand for money, discussed below, that I was led to the specific measures to be discussed. But it is useful to begin with some formal considerations.

In view of (9-3), which is a necessary and sufficient condition for risk aversion, one may be tempted to use the rate of change of $U'(Y)$, that is, $U''(Y)$, as a measure. But this suffers from one very severe formal defect. The utility function is, after all, a way of representing a preference ordering; it is only the latter, and not the former, which has behavioral significance. But the utility function is defined only up to positive linear transformations; multiplying the utility function by a positive constant or adding a constant to it does not change the preference ordering represented. Adding a constant to $U(Y)$ does not, of course, alter $U'(Y)$ and a fortiori leaves $U''(Y)$ invariant. But multiplying $U(Y)$ by a positive constant multiplies $U''(Y)$ by the same constant; thus the numerical value of $U''(Y)$ has in itself no significance.

We thus seek a measure which is based on $U''(Y)$ but which is modified so as to remain invariant under positive linear transformations of the utility function. It can easily be shown that if the measure is to have these properties and is not to depend on derivatives higher than the second, then it must be determined by the ratio $U''(Y)/U'(Y)$ and possibly by Y. Two simple measures of this type are

(9-4) $R_A(Y) = -U''(Y)/U'(Y) =$ absolute risk aversion,
(9-5) $R_R(Y) = -YU''(Y)/U'(Y) =$ relative risk aversion.

Notice first that a positive linear transformation of $U(Y)$ multiplies $U''(Y)$ and $U'(Y)$ by the same positive constant and so leaves their ratio unchanged. Second, in view of (9-1), both measures are positive when there is risk aversion, that is, when $U''(Y) < 0$. The relative risk aversion is the elasticity of the marginal utility of wealth; it is invariant not only with respect to changes in the units of utility but also with respect to changes in the units of wealth. It will be seen that both measures are useful in different contexts, though the relative risk aversion appears to be the more useful of the two.

The two measures have simple behavioral interpretations. Consider an individual with wealth Y who is offered a bet which involves winning or losing an amount h with probabilities p and $1 - p$, respectively. The individual will be willing to accept the bet for values of p sufficiently large (certainly for $p = 1$) and will refuse it if p is small (certainly for $p = 0$; a risk averter will refuse the bet if $p = \frac{1}{2}$ or less). The willingness to accept or reject a given bet will in general also depend on his present wealth Y. Given the amount of the bet h and the wealth Y, there will, by continuity, be a probability $p(Y,h)$ such that the individual is just indifferent between accepting and rejecting the bet. If attention is restricted to small values of h, the function $p(Y,h)$ can, for fixed Y, be approximated by a linear function of h, which turns out to be

(9-6) $p(Y,h) = (\frac{1}{2}) + \dfrac{R_A(Y)}{4} h + \text{terms of higher order in } h.$

(See section [1] in the Appendix to this chapter.) The absolute risk aversion directly measures the insistence of an individual for more-than-fair odds, at least when the bets are small.

If we measure the bets not in absolute terms but in proportion to Y, the absolute risk aversion is replaced by the relative risk aversion. Denote the amount of the bet by nY, where n is the fraction of wealth at stake; if we let $h = nY$ in (9-6) and use the definitions (9-4) and (9-5), we have

(9-7) $p(Y,nY) = (\frac{1}{2}) + \dfrac{R_R(Y)}{4} n + \text{terms of higher order in } n.$

Another similar interpretation of the risk-aversion measures has been developed independently by John W. Pratt.[3] Consider an individual faced with a random income Y and offered the alternative of a certain income, Y_0. A risk averter would be willing to accept a value of Y_0 less than the mean value, $E(Y)$, of the random income; the difference may be thought of as an insurance premium. In particular, choose Y_0 so that the individual is just indifferent between Y_0 and the random income Y, and let

$\pi = E(Y) - Y_0.$

Then, if the distribution is sufficiently concentrated (technically, if the third absolute central moment is sufficiently small compared with the variance), Pratt shows that

$\pi = (\frac{1}{2})\sigma^2 R_A(Y_0) + \text{terms of higher order,}$

where σ^2 is the variance of Y. A similar interpretation can be offered for the relative risk aversion.

Both risk-aversion measures are in general functions of Y, though they can, in particular, be constants. The behavior of these measures as Y changes is of the greatest importance for prediction of economic reactions in the presence of uncertainty. Two hypotheses are propounded here.

---

3. J. W. Pratt, "Risk Aversion in the Small and in the Large," *Econometrica*, vol. 32, 1964, pp. 122–136.

INCREASING RELATIVE RISK AVERSION.   *The relative risk aversion $R_R(Y)$ is an increasing function of Y.*

DECREASING ABSOLUTE RISK AVERSION.   *The absolute risk aversion $R_A(Y)$ is a decreasing function of Y.*

The second hypothesis certainly seems supported by everyday observation. From the interpretation (9-6), it amounts to saying that the willingness to engage in small bets of fixed size increases with wealth, in the sense that the odds demanded diminish. If absolute risk aversion increased with wealth, it would follow that as an individual became wealthier, he would actually decrease the amount of risky assets held.

One simple utility function that has been much employed in the literature is the quadratic

$$U(Y) = a + bY + cY^2.$$

The condition of risk aversion requires that $c < 0$. However, the quadratic is unacceptable since it violates the principle of decreasing absolute risk aversion; as can easily be calculated,

$$R_A(Y) = \frac{1}{d - Y},$$

where

$$d = -b/2c > 0.$$

Note that $U(Y)$ attains its maximum at $Y = d$; we are only interested in values of Y below d, since beyond d, wealth has negative marginal utility, and it would be better to throw some away. Within the range from 0 to d, $R_A(Y)$ increases and becomes infinite at $Y = d$. Indeed, at that point, the maximum possible utility, any gamble, no matter what the odds, would yield a loss in utility. As Y approaches d, the willingness to gamble for a bet of fixed size will necessarily decrease, a result which shows the absurdity of the quadratic assumption.[4]

The hypothesis of increasing relative risk aversion is not so easily confrontable with intuitive evidence. The assertion is that if both wealth and the size of the bet are increased in the same proportion, the willingness to accept the bet (as measured by the odds demanded) should decrease. The hypoth-

---

4. This paradoxical implication of a quadratic utility function has already been noted by J. R. Hicks, "Liquidity," *Economic Journal*, vol. 72, 1962, pp. 787–802, esp. p. 802.

esis will be defended partly by its consistency with general theoretical principles and partly by its success in explaining economic behavior. The theoretical argument will be taken up here; the empirical defense will emerge in the discussion of the demand for money below.

The important theoretical point is that the variation of the relative risk aversion with changing wealth is intimately connected with the boundedness of the utility function. It can be shown as a mathematical proposition that if the utility function is to remain bounded as wealth becomes infinite, then the relative risk aversion cannot tend to a limit below one; similarly, for the utility function to be bounded (from below) as wealth approaches zero, the relative risk aversion cannot approach a limit above one as wealth tends to zero. (See section [2] in the Appendix.)

Thus, broadly speaking, the relative risk aversion must hover around one, being, if anything, somewhat less for low wealths and somewhat higher for high wealths. Two conclusions emerge: (1) it is broadly permissible to assume that relative risk aversion increases with wealth, though theory does not exclude some fluctuations; (2) if, for simplicity, we wish to assume a constant relative risk aversion, then the appropriate value is one. As can easily be seen, this implies that the utility of wealth equals its logarithm, a relation already suggested by Bernoulli. To be sure, the logarithm is not bounded at either end, but it may still be regarded as an approximation to a bounded utility function, for if the relative risk aversion were ever so slightly greater than one at the high end of the wealth scale and ever so slightly less than one at the lower end, the utility function would be bounded at both ends and yet essentially logarithmic throughout the greater part of the range.

We now apply these concepts to a specific model of choice between risky and secure assets. It will be simplest to think of the secure asset as being money, with no risk and no return. More generally, we could interpret the secure asset as government bonds, with no risk but a positive return; the model to be presented would then require some reinterpretation, as will be noted.

We suppose then a risky asset, by which we mean one whose rate of return is a random variable. An individual can buy as much of this asset as he wishes; it is assumed that what might be termed *stochastic constant returns to scale* prevail. By this is meant that the distribution of the rate of return is independent of the amount invested. An individual with given initial wealth invests part of it in the risky asset and the rest in the secure asset, say cash balances. The wealth at the end of the period is then a random variable, since it depends in part on the return realized on the risky asset. In symbols, let

X = rate of return on risky asset (a random variable),
A = initial wealth,
a = amount invested in risky asset,
m = amount invested in secure asset = $A - a$,
Y = final wealth.

It follows from the definition that

(9-8) $\qquad Y = A + aX.$

The decision of the individual is to choose a, the amount invested in the risky asset, so as to maximize

(9-9) $\qquad E[U(Y)] = E[U(A + aX)] = W(a),$

say, where a is restricted to lie between 0 and A.

(If the secure asset bears a positive rate of return, the model is essentially the same, except that X is now interpreted as the difference between the rates of return on the risky and secure assets and, in (9-8), A is replaced by

$$A' = A(1 + \rho),$$

where ρ is the rate of return on the secure asset.)

The first two derivatives of (9-9) with respect to a are

(9-10) $\qquad W'(a) = E[U'(Y)X], \qquad W''(A) = E[U''(Y)X^2].$

Since we are assuming risk aversion, $U''(Y) < 0$ for all Y and therefore $W''(a) < 0$ for all a. Since $W'(a)$ is therefore always decreasing, the graph of $W(a)$ must have one of the three following shapes.

In Figure 9.1, $W(a)$ has its maximum at $a = 0$; a necessary and sufficient condition is that

$$W'(0) \leq 0,$$

since $W'(a)$ must then be negative for $a > 0$. But if $a = 0$, $Y = A$, and $U'(Y) = U'(A)$, which is a positive constant; hence,

$$W'(0) = U'(A)E(X),$$

and therefore,

(9-11) $\qquad a = 0 \quad$ if and only if $\quad E(X) \leq 0.$

Thus, a risk averter takes no part of an unfavorable or barely fair gamble; on the other hand *he always takes some part of a favorable gamble,* for (9-11)

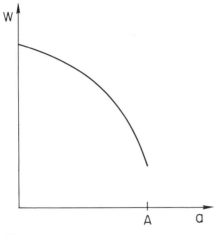

Figure 9.1

can be written in the equivalent form

(9-12) $a > 0$ if and only if $E(X) > 0$.

Intuitively the argument is that the risk can be reduced to arbitrarily small proportions by making the amount purchased of the risky asset small, while the expected profit per unit investment is positive and constant. Hence, for sufficiently small amounts at risk, the positive expectation outweighs the risk. Another way of putting it is to note that for small amounts at risk, the utility function is approximately linear, and risk aversion disappears.

The case of Figure 9.3, where the individual invests all his wealth in risky assets, is less interesting; the condition is that

$$W'(A) \geq 0,$$

or

(9-13) $E[U'(A + AX)X] \geq 0$.

(See section [3] in the Appendix.)

Now suppose that neither (9-11) nor (9-13) hold; then, as in Figure 9.2, there is an interior maximum at which $W'(a) = 0$, or

(9-14) $E[U'(Y)X] = 0$,

where Y, of course, depends on the amount at risk, a, according to (9-8). The individuals for whom (9-14) holds invest some but not all of their wealth in

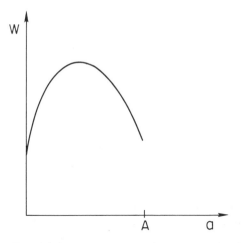

Figure 9.2

risky assets. Since X is the (random) value increment to an additional unit invested in the risky asset, $U'(Y)X$ is the random utility increment to an additional unit investment in the risky asset, and investment there is pushed to the point where the expected increment of utility becomes zero.

There are a number of economically interesting questions one could address to a result such as (9-14). Primarily, we are interested in the variation

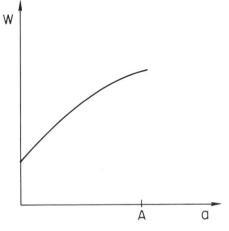

Figure 9.3

of the optimal solution, a, with respect to various parameters. Apart from the utility function, the basic parameters are the initial wealth, A, and the probability distribution of the rate of return, X. We will first concentrate, however, on the effects of shifts in A on a, that is, the wealth effects (analogous to the income effects of consumer's demand theory).

First, suppose we had assumed a quadratic utility function; then (9-14) would, on some simplification, imply

$$a = \frac{(d - A)E(X)}{E(X^2)};$$

since we must have $E(X) > 0$ (otherwise the solution would call for $a = 0$), we see clearly that investment in risky assets would decrease as initial wealth, A, increases, becoming zero when A approaches d. This is clearly implausible, confirming our previous remarks.

More generally, to see the dependence of a on A, we can differentiate (9-14) with respect to a, and derive the result,

(9-15) $$\frac{da}{dA} = -\frac{E[U''(Y)X]}{E[U''(Y)X^2]}.$$

The denominator has already been seen to be negative; hence, the sign of da/dA is the same as that of the numerator. It can be shown that decreasing absolute risk aversion implies that the numerator is positive and hence that the amount of risky investment increases with wealth, as would be expected. In other words, risky investment is not an inferior good. (See section [4] in the Appendix.)

This result is not very deep. A more profound analysis is obtained by considering the wealth elasticity of the demand for cash balances (investment in the secure asset). Recall that cash balances are simply the portion of initial wealth not invested in the risky asset, that is, $m = A - a$. Then, if we let Em/EA be the elasticity in question, it can be seen, after some manipulation, that

(9-16) $$\frac{Em}{EA} = 1 + \frac{E[U''(Y)XY]}{mE[U''(Y)X^2]}.$$

The denominator of the fraction in (9-16) being again negative, we see that

$$Em/EA \geqq 1 \quad \text{if and only if} \quad E[U''(Y)XY] \leqq 0.$$

With some further analysis, it can be shown that increasing relative risk aversion implies the second inequality, and therefore *it follows from the hypothesis of increasing relative risk aversion that the wealth elasticity of demand for cash balances is at least one.* In usual economic terms, cash balances and, more generally, security are luxury goods or, at any rate, not necessities. (See section [5] in the Appendix.)

Of course the demand for cash balances is not, in the real world, completely determined by risk aversion; transaction costs also enter. But the conclusion is in striking accord with statistical studies of United States time series. Studies of the movements of cash balance holdings, wealth, and income (taken as a measure of wealth) by Selden, Friedman, Latané, and Meltzer, by different methods and under different assumptions, agree in finding a wealth elasticity of demand for cash balances of at least 1 (Friedman's estimate, the highest, is actually 1.8).[5] It should be noted, moreover, that it is hard to imagine any alternative explanation for the observed secular constancy or rise in the ratio of money held to income or wealth. Transaction costs should, if anything, matter less in the decision to hold cash as the wealth of individuals increases relative to transaction costs. Further, technological and institutional improvements in efficiency in the banking system and the money markets lead to falling transaction costs and again, therefore, to less holding of cash. Thus, the notion that security, in the particular form of cash balances, has a wealth elasticity of at least one seems to be the only remaining explanation of the historical course of money holdings.

Now let us consider shifts in the distribution of X. Such a shift can be represented as a transformation of the original random variable X. It is convenient to think of a family of such transformations, each member being characterized by the value of a shift parameter, h. Thus a simple movement of the distribution to the right or left can be written as $X(h) = X + h$. Similarly a simple expansion of the distribution about a center, X^*, can be written as $X(h) = X^* + (1 + h)(X - X^*)$. We choose the parametrization so that $X(0) = X$.

Write then the equation (9-14) as

$$E\{U'[Y(h)]X(h)\} = 0,$$

---

5. R. T. Selden, "Monetary Velocity in the United States," in *Studies in the Quantity Theory of Money,* M. Friedman, ed. Chicago: University of Chicago Press, 1956, pp. 179–257. M. Friedman, "The Demand for Money: Some Theoretical and Empirical Results," *Journal of Political Economy,* vol. 67, 1959, pp. 327–351. H. Latané, "Income Velocity and Interest Rates: A Pragmatic Approach," *Review of Economics and Statistics,* vol. 42, 1960, pp. 445–449. A. H. Meltzer, "The Demand for Money: The Evidence from Time Series," *Journal of Political Economy,* vol. 71, 1963, pp. 219–246, esp. p. 225.

where $Y(h) = A + aX(h)$. Now a will depend on h, as well as on A, which we are now holding constant. Then $dY/dh = a(dX/dh) + X(h)(da/dh)$. Differentiation with respect to h yields

$$E\{U''(Y)[a(dX/dh) + X(h)(da/dh)]X(h) + U'(Y)(dX/dh)\} = 0,$$

or

(9-17) $$E\{[aU''(Y)X(h) + U'(Y)](dX/dh)\} + (da/dh)E\{U''(Y)[X(h)]^2\} = 0.$$

The coefficient of da/dh is certainly negative. Hence,

(9-18) da/dh has the same sign as
$$E\{[aU''(Y)X(h) + U'(Y)](dX/dh)\}.$$

We will consider several possible types of shifts abstractly and then illustrate with several economic applications. Consider first the additive shift, $X(h) = X + h$. Then $dX/dh = 1$. Certainly $E[U'(Y)] > 0$. But $E[aU''(Y)X]$ has the sign of $E[U''(Y)X]$, since $a > 0$, and therefore, by (9-15), the sign of da/dA. Therefore,

(9-19)   For an additive shift in the probability distribution of rates of return, $X(h) = X + h$, the demand for risky assets increases with the shift parameter if the demand for risky assets increases with wealth.

We have seen before that the assumption $da/dA > 0$ is certainly reasonable and is also a consequence of decreasing absolute risk aversion. Now suppose there is a multiplicative shift around the origin, $X = 0$. That is, $X(h) = (1 + h)X$. Here, $dX/dh = X$. From (9-18), da/dh has the same sign as

$$E[aU''(Y)X^2] + E[U'(Y)X].$$

But the second term is zero at an optimal portfolio choice, by (9-14), while the first term is certainly negative, so that da/dh is negative. But in fact a much stronger statement can be made, as was first shown by Tobin.[6] Let $a(h)$ be the optimum investment in risky assets when the return is $X(h)$, and let $a = a(0)$. Then

$$E\{U'[Y(h)](1 + h)X\} = 0, \qquad E[U'(Y)X] = 0.$$

6. J. Tobin, "Liquidity Preference as Behavior Towards Risk," *Review of Economic Studies,* vol. 25, 1957–58, pp. 65–86.

Let $a' = a(h)(1 + h)$, $Y' = A + a'X$. Then $Y' = A + a(h)X(h) = Y(h)$, so that $E[U'(Y')(1 + h)X] = 0$. But by factoring out $1 + h$, we see that

$$E[U'(Y')X] = 0,$$

which implies that a' is optimal when the return variable is X. That is, $a' = a$, so that $a(h) = a/(1 + h)$.

(9-20)   (Tobin)   If a is the demand for investment goods when the return is a random variable X, then $a/(1 + h)$ is the demand when the return is the variable $(1 + h)X$.

Finally, we consider a multiplicative shift about an arbitrary center X^*. Then

$$X(h) = X^* + (1 + h)(X - X^*) = (1 + h)X - hX^*.$$

This can be regarded as a multiplicative shift about the origin, followed by a downward additive shift hX^*. For $X^* \geq 0$, the second shift reinforces the first, from (9-19) and (9-20).

(9-21)   A multiplicative shift about a nonnegative center diminishes the demand for risky assets in even greater proportion than the shift itself.

On the other hand, for $X^* < 0$, the demand for risky assets decreases in smaller proportion and might even increase.

A particular application of (9-21) is that in which $X^* = E(X)$. In that case, the shift preserves the mean but increases the spread about it. It may therefore be regarded as a pure increase in uncertainty. Since we are assuming an interior maximum, $E(X) > 0$, so that (9-21) applies; a pure uncertainty-increasing spread decreases the demand for risky assets in even greater proportion.

We now turn to some applications. Tobin has shown that the Keynesian theory of liquidity preference can be expressed in such terms.[7] Consider the risky asset to be bonds; for simplicity, assume them to be perpetuities. The risk is the possibility of capital gains or losses. Let r be their current yield, so that their current price is proportional to $1/r$. The return from a dollar's investment, assuming that the bond is to be sold at tomorrow's price after collecting one period's interest, is

(9-22) $X = rp + r - 1.$

---

7. Ibid.

Suppose that tomorrow's price is a random variable p. More specifically, assume that the elasticity of expectation is, in a stochastic sense, equal to one, by which is meant here that the ratio of tomorrow's price to today's, that is, rp, is a random variable distributed independently of today's price and hence of r. Then (9-22) tells us that the effect of an increase in r is a simple upward additive shift in the distribution of X. By (9-19),

(9-23)   In the choice between perpetuities and a secure asset, if the ratio of tomorrow's price to today's is distributed independently of today's price and if the demand for risky assets increases with initial wealth, then the demand for the risky assets is an increasing function of the current rate of return on the perpetuity and therefore the demand for the secure asset is a decreasing function of that rate.

If the expectations of future prices of the perpetuity are inelastic in a stochastic sense, the story is somewhat different. Now we assume that the distribution of p is independent of r. Consider a shift from r to $(1 + h)r$. Then, from (9-22),

(9-24) $X(h) = (1 + h)r(p + 1) - 1 = (1 + h)(X + 1) - 1 = (1 + h)X + h.$

This is a multiplicative shift around the origin followed by an upward additive shift. From (9-19) and (9-20), the two shifts have opposite effects, and the signs of the changes in a and therefore in $m = A - a$ cannot be stated a priori.

It has been implicitly assumed that the rate of return on the secure asset is zero; suppose instead that it is p. As has been observed earlier, the whole analysis applies, except that X has to be reinterpreted as the difference between the rates of return on the risky and secure assets. Then (9-22) is altered to

(9-25) $X = rp + r - (p + 1).$

But the argument leading to (9-23) is unaltered; (9-24) becomes

$$X(h) = (1 + h)X + h(1 + p),$$

and again the sign of the effect is ambiguous.

It is also obvious that an increase in the rate of return on the secure asset amounts to a downward shift in X and therefore to a decrease in the demand for the risky asset and an increase in that for the secure asset.

We may conclude by another simple application, the demand for shares in a firm. Suppose that a firm's activities are such as to yield a value V per share, where V is a random variable. Let p be the current price of a share. Then the return to a dollar invested is $X = (V/p) - 1$. Suppose p changes to $p/(1 + h)$; then

$$X(h) = (1 + h)(V/p) - 1 = (1 + h)(X + 1) - 1 = (1 + h)X + h.$$

Let $D(p)$ be the demand for shares, while $a(h)$ is the number of dollars invested. Then $a(h) = [p/(1 + h)]D[p/(1 + h)]$, $a = pD(p)$, so that

$$D[p/(1 + h)] = [a(h)/a](1 + h)D(p).$$

The shift in $X(h)$ is a multiplicative shift about the origin followed by an additive shift. The first would, by itself, decrease $a(h)$ in the proportion $1/(1 + h)$, but the second increases $a(h)$ so that $a(h) > a/(1 + h)$, and therefore $D[p/(1 + h)] > D(p)$ for $h > 0$.

(9-26)   The demand for a fixed fraction of a random variable is a decreasing function of its price.

Again, in justifying (9-26), it has been assumed that the secure asset yielded a return of 0. If instead the secure asset has a return ρ, then $X = (V/p) - 1 - \rho$, and $X(h) = (1 + h)X + h(1 + \rho)$. Hence the argument leading to (9-26) remains valid. But it can also be noted that the larger is ρ, the larger is the difference $a(h) - [a/(1 + h)]$ and therefore the larger is the difference $D[p/(1 + h)] - D(p)$. Let $D(p,\rho)$ be the demand for shares considered as a function of p and ρ. Then we can conclude, by letting h approach 0, that

(9-27) $\partial^2 D(p,\rho)/\partial p \partial \rho < 0$.

Appendix

[1] Since the individual is indifferent between the certainty of Y and the gamble of winning h with probability $p(Y,h)$ and losing h with probability $1 - p(Y,h)$, the expected utility theory implies

$$U(Y) = p(Y,h)U(Y + h) + [1 - p(Y,h)]U(Y - h).$$

Expand $U(Y + h)$ in powers of h; then

$$U(Y + h) = U(Y) + hU'(Y) + (h^2/2)U''(Y) + R_1,$$

where R_1/h^2 approaches zero with h. Similarly,

$$U(Y - h) = U(Y) - hU'(Y) + (h^2/2)U''(Y) + R_2,$$
$$R_2/h^2 \to 0 \text{ with } h.$$

By substitution and simplification,

$$U(Y) = U(Y) + (2p - 1)hU'(Y) + (h^2/2)U''(Y) + R,$$

where $R = pR_1 + (1 - p)R_2$, and therefore R/h^2 approaches zero with h. If we solve for p, we find

$$p(Y,h) = (\tfrac{1}{2}) + (h/4)[-U''(Y)/U'(Y)] - [R/2hU''(Y)].$$

[2] Let R be a number such that

(A-1) $R_R(Y) \leq R$ for all $Y \geq Y_0$,

for some Y_0. If we use the definition of $R_R(Y)$ and multiply both sides of the inequality by $-1/Y$, we find

$$U''(Y)/U'(Y) \geq -R/Y.$$

Integration from Y_0 to Y yields

$$\log U'(Y) - \log U'(Y_0) \geq -R(\log Y - \log Y_0),$$

or

(A-2) $U'(Y) \geq U'(Y_0)Y_0^R Y^{-R}$ for $Y \geq Y_0$,

a result which will also be used extensively in later sections of this Appendix. Observe that if either inequality in (A-1) is reversed, then so is the first inequality in (A-2); if both inequalities in (A-1) are reversed, then the first inequality in (A-2) still holds.

In (A-2), let $C = U'(Y_0)Y_0^R > 0$, and integrate both sides from Y_0 to Y.

$$\begin{aligned} U(Y) &\geq U(Y_0) + [C/(1 - R)](Y^{1-R} - Y_0^{1-R}) \quad \text{if } R \neq 1, \\ &\geq U(Y_0) + C(\log Y - \log Y_0) \quad \text{if } R = 1. \end{aligned}$$

Clearly if $R = 1$ or if $R < 1$, the right-hand side approaches $+\infty$, so that $U(Y)$ would be unbounded, contrary to assumption. Hence, we cannot have $R_R(Y) \leq 1$ throughout some neighborhood of infinity (a set of the form $Y \geq Y_0$); that is, $R_R(Y) > 1$ for arbitrarily large Y-values. In particular, $R_R(Y)$ cannot converge to a limit less than 1.

By a parallel argument, $R_R(Y)$ must be less than 1 for values of Y arbitrarily close to 0.

[3] This section discusses in detail some conditions under which this corner maximum will or will not occur; that is, conditions under which the

demand for the secure asset is or is not 0. An important role is played by the following function, which is determined by the probability distribution of return, X:

(A-3) $\qquad G(R) = E[X(1 + X)^{-R}].$

Assume for simplicity that the distribution of X is determined by a continuous density function, $\phi(x)$. Then (A-3) can be written

$$G(R) = \int_{-1}^{+\infty} x(1 + x)^{-R} \phi(x) \, dx.$$

It is convenient also to consider this integral over smaller intervals. Let

(A-4) $\qquad G(R;a,b) = \int_{a}^{b} x(1 + x)^{-R} \phi(x) \, dx.$

Note that if $b \leq 0$, then $G(R;a,b) \leq 0$, while if $a \geq 0$, $G(R;a,b) \geq 0$. Also, $G(0) = E(X)$, which we will assume to be positive (if not, we know that the entire wealth will be invested in the secure asset). By differentiation we see that

$$G'(R;a,b) = -\int_{a}^{b} (1 + x)^{-R} x \log (1 + x) \phi(x) \, dx.$$

Since x and $\log (1 + x)$ always have the same sign, $G'(R;a,b) < 0$.

(A-5) $\qquad G(R;a,b)$ is strictly decreasing in R.

If $P(X \geq 0) = 1$ (certainty of no loss), then $G(R) = G(R;0,+\infty) \geq 0$. Otherwise, there is some $X_0 < 0$ such that $P(X \leq X_0) > 0$.

$$G(R) = G(R;-1,X_0) + G(R;X_0,0) + G(R;0,+\infty).$$

From previous remarks, including (A-5),

$$G(R;X_0,0) \leq 0, \qquad G(R;0,+\infty) \leq G(0;0,+\infty).$$

Since $(1 + x)^{-R} \geq (1 + X_0)^{-R}$ for $x \leq X_0$, and $X_0 < 0$, $x(1 + x)^{-R} \leq x(1 + X_0)^{-R}$ for $x \leq X_0$, so that

$$G(R;-1,X_0) \leq (1 + X_0)^{-R} G(0;-1,X_0),$$

and therefore,

$$G(R) \leq (1 + X_0)^{-R} G(0;-1,X_0) + G(0;0,+\infty).$$

Since $G(0;-1,X_0) < 0$ and $(1 + X_0)^{-R}$ approaches $+\infty$ as R approaches $+\infty$, it follows that $G(R) < 0$ for all R sufficiently large. The equation $G(R) = 0$ has then a unique solution, R^*, which will be referred to as the *critical risk aversion;* note that R^* is a property of the probability distribution of X alone, not of the risktaker's preferences.

(A-6)   There exists R^* such that $G(R) > 0$ for $R < R^*$, $G(R) < 0$ for $R > R^*$.

Also define $H(A) = W'(A) = E[U'(A + AX)X]$. We are seeking conditions for determining the sign of $H(A)$. Let

$$H(A;a,b) = \int_a^b U'(A + Ax)x \, \phi(x) \, dx.$$

Suppose $R_R(Y) \leq R^*$, all Y. Let $Y = A + AX$, so that $Y \geq A$ if and only if $X \geq 0$. By (A-2),

$$U'(A + AX) \geq U'(A)A^{R*}(A + AX)^{-R*} = U'(A)(1 + X)^{-R*}$$

for $X \geq 0$, so that

$$U'(A + AX)X \geq U'(A)(1 + X)^{-R*}X \quad \text{for } X \geq 0.$$

It is easy to see that the same holds for $X \leq 0$ since there are two offsetting sign reversals. By integration, we see that $H(A) \geq U'(A)G(R^*) = 0$.

(A-7)   If the relative risk aversion never exceeds the critical level, then the demand for the secure asset is 0 for all levels of initial wealth.

In exactly parallel manner, it can be seen that

(A-8)   If the relative risk aversion exceeds the critical level for all incomes, then the demand for the secure asset is positive for all levels of initial wealth.

We now turn to conditions which determine the existence of demand for the secure asset for values of A sufficiently small or sufficiently large. We assume that $R_R(Y)$ converges as Y approaches 0 and as Y approaches $+\infty$; we designate these limits as $R_R(0)$ and $R_R(\infty)$, respectively.

Suppose $R_R(0) < R^*$; then $G[R_R(0)] > 0$. It follows then that it is possible to choose $\overline{X}$ sufficiently large so that

$$G[R_R(0);-1,\overline{X}] > 0.$$

For any A, let $\overline{Y} = A + A\overline{X}$, and define $\underline{R} = \inf\limits_{Y \leq \overline{Y}} R_R(Y)$, $\overline{R} = \sup\limits_{Y \leq \overline{Y}} R_R(Y)$.

Then for $X \leq \overline{X}$,

$$U'(\overline{Y})\overline{Y}^{\overline{R}}(A + AX)^{-\overline{R}} \geq U'(A + AX)$$
$$\geq U'(\overline{Y})\overline{Y}^{\underline{R}}(A + AX)^{-\underline{R}},$$

or, since $\overline{Y} = A + A\overline{X}$,

$$U'(\overline{Y})(1 + \overline{X})^{\overline{R}}(1 + X)^{-\overline{R}} \geq U'(A + AX)$$
$$\geq U'(\overline{Y})(1 + \overline{X})^{\underline{R}}(1 + X)^{-\underline{R}}.$$

Multiply the second inequality through by $X \geq 0$ and integrate from 0 to $\overline{X}$:

$$H(A;0,\overline{X}) \geq U'(\overline{Y})(1 + \overline{X})^{\underline{R}}G(\underline{R};0,\overline{X}).$$

By a similar argument,

$$H(A;-1,0) \geq U'(\overline{Y})(1 + \overline{X})^{\overline{R}}G(\overline{R};-1,0).$$

Since $H(A;\overline{X},+\infty) \geq 0$,

$$H(A) \geq U'(\overline{Y})[(1 + \overline{X})^{\underline{R}}G(\underline{R};0,\overline{X})$$
$$+ (1 + \overline{X})^{\overline{R}}G(\overline{R};-1,0)].$$

The expression in brackets is a continuous function of $\underline{R}$ and $\overline{R}$. As A approaches 0, $\overline{Y}$ also approaches 0, and therefore $\underline{R}$ and $\overline{R}$ both approach $R_R(0)$. The expression in brackets then approaches

$$(1 + \overline{X})^{R_R(0)}G[R_R(0);-1,\overline{X}],$$

which is positive. Hence, $H(A) > 0$ for A sufficiently small.

(A-9)　　If the relative risk aversion approaches a limit less than the critical level as Y approaches 0, then the demand for the secure asset approaches 0 as initial wealth approaches 0.

The case where $R_R(0) > R^*$ is handled similarly but not identically. Since $G[R_R(0)] < 0$, we now choose $\overline{X}$ sufficiently large that

$$G[R_R(0);-1,\overline{X}] + G[0;\overline{X},+\infty] < 0.$$

Since U' is decreasing, $U'(A + AX) \leq U'(A + A\overline{X}) = U'(\overline{Y})$ for $X \geq \overline{X}$. Then by arguments like those used above,

$$H(A) \leq U'(\overline{Y})[(1 + \overline{X})^{\overline{R}}G(\overline{R};0,\overline{X})$$
$$+ (1 + \overline{X})^{\underline{R}}G(\underline{R};-1,0) + G(0;\overline{X},+\infty)],$$

and the expression in brackets is negative for A sufficiently small.

(A-10)   If the relative risk aversion approaches a limit above the critical level as Y approaches 0, then the demand for the secure asset is positive for A sufficiently small.

In particular, suppose that $U'(0)$ is finite, a not-too-plausible case. This cannot occur if $R_R(0) > 0$. Therefore $R_R(0) = 0$ and certainly $R_R(0) < R^*$, and the demand for the secure asset is 0 for sufficiently small A, by (A-9).

As has been observed, the boundedness hypothesis implies that $R_R(0) \leqq 1$. Hence, $R^* \geqq 1$ certainly implies zero demand for the secure asset. But $R^* \geqq 1$ is equivalent to the statement $G(1) \geqq 0$; by definition,

$$G(1) = E[X(1 + X)^{-1}] = 1 - E[1/(1 + X)].$$

Since $1/(1 + X)$ may be interpreted as the realized rate of discount on the risky investment, we may assert:

(A-11)   If the expected discount rate on the risky investment does not exceed 1, then the demand for the secure asset is 0 for A sufficiently small.

We now turn to conditions for the existence of demand for the secure asset for large A. We assume as before that $P(X < 0) > 0$. First, suppose that relative risk aversion becomes indefinitely large for large incomes, that is, $R_R(\infty) = +\infty$. Again choose $X_0 < 0$ so that $P(X \leqq X_0) > 0$. Then

$$H(A;-1,X_0) \leqq U'(A + AX_0)G(0;-1,X_0),$$
$$H(A;X_0,0) \leqq 0,$$
$$H(A;0,+\infty) \leqq U'(A)G(0;0,+\infty).$$

For arbitrary R, $R_R(Y) \geqq R$ for Y sufficiently large and therefore $R_R(Y) \geqq R$ for $Y \geqq A + AX_0$, A sufficiently large. Then,

$$U'(A) \leqq U'(A + AX_0)(A + AX_0)^R A^{-R}$$
$$= U'(A + AX_0)(1 + X_0)^R,$$

so that

$$H(A) \leqq U'(A + AX_0)[G(0;-1,X_0)$$
$$+ (1 + X_0)^R G(0;0,+\infty)].$$

Since $1 + X_0 < 1$, $(1 + X_0)^R$ can be made arbitrarily small. Since $G(0;-1,X_0) < 0$, $H(A) < 0$ for A sufficiently large.

(A-12)   If the relative risk aversion approaches infinity with large wealth, then the demand for the secure asset will be positive for sufficiently large initial wealth.

Such an extreme degree of risk aversion seems implausible even in the limit. Assume now that $R_R(\infty)$ is finite. We need to distinguish two cases, according to whether total ruin, that is, $X = -1$, is or is not possible. Formally, we consider two alternative assumptions: (a) $\phi(-1) > 0$, and (b) for some $\underline{X} > -1$, $P(X < \underline{X}) = 0$. Strictly speaking, these two cases are not exhaustive; we could, for example, have a density which is 0 at $X = -1$ but positive for all $X > -1$. However, the two cases studied will indicate the range of possibilities.

First, suppose $\phi(-1) > 0$. We assume further that $R_R(\infty) > 1$. Note that boundedness implies $R_R(\infty) \geq 1$ in any case; further, if $R_R(Y)$ is monotonic increasing, then $R_R(\infty) = 1$ implies $R_R(Y) \leq 1$, all Y, and therefore the unboundedness of the utility function.

Choose $\overline{Y}$ and R so that $R > 1$, $R_R(Y) \geq R$ for $Y \geq \overline{Y}$. Choose $Y < \overline{Y}$, and define $X = (Y - A)/A$ so that $X \to -1$ as $A \to +\infty$.

$$U'(Y) \leq U'(\overline{Y})\overline{Y}^R Y^{-R} \quad \text{for } Y \geq \overline{Y}.$$

For $A \geq \overline{Y}$, $A + AX \geq \overline{Y}$ for $X \geq 0$. Therefore, with $Y = A + AX$,

$$H(A;0,+\infty) \leq U'(\overline{Y})\overline{Y}^R A^{-R} G(R;0,+\infty).$$

Clearly,

$$H(A;X,0) \leq 0, \qquad H(A;-1,X) \leq U'(Y)G(0;-1,X),$$

so that

$$A^R H(A) \leq U'(Y)Y^R G(R;0,+\infty)$$
$$+ A^{R-1} U'(Y)AG(0;-1,X).$$

Clearly, $G(0;-1,X) < 0$; since $R > 1$, it suffices, in order to show that $H(A) < 0$ for A large, that $AG(0;-1,X)$ is bounded away from 0 for large A. But

$$AG(0;-1,X) = A(1 + X)\left[\int_{-1}^{X} x\phi(x)\,dx/(1 + X)\right]$$
$$\to -Y\phi(-1) < 0,$$

since $A(1 + X) = Y$.

(A-13)   If the density of the rate of return is positive at -1 and if the relative risk aversion approaches a limit greater than 1 as wealth approaches $+\infty$, then the demand for the secure asset is positive for sufficiently large initial wealth.

Finally, we consider the case where $P(X < \underline{X}) = 0$ for some $\underline{X} > -1$, so that total ruin is impossible. But now $A + AX$ is arbitrarily large for A large. Then, since $X \geq \underline{X}$ with probability 1, $A + AX \geq Y_0$ with probability 1 for any arbitrary Y_0, if A is sufficiently large. We can then use results (A-7) and (A-8). For if $R_R(\infty) < R^*$, then $R_R(Y) < R^*$ for all Y sufficiently large. But then, for A sufficiently large, $R_R(A + AX) < R^*$ with probability 1, and so, by (A-7), the demand for the secure asset will be 0. The case $R_R(\infty) > R^*$ can be argued similarly.

(A-14)   If for some $\underline{X} > -1$, $P(X < \underline{X}) = 0$, then if relative risk aversion is less than the critical level for all wealth sufficiently large, the demand for the secure asset is 0 for all sufficiently large initial wealth, while if the relative risk aversion is above the critical level for large final wealth, the demand for the secure asset is positive for all sufficiently large initial wealth.

[4] If absolute risk aversion is monotone decreasing, then $R_A(A + aX) \leq R_A(A)$ for $X \geq 0$. From the definition of R_A,

$$U''(A + aX) \geq -R_A(A)U'(A + aX) \quad \text{for } X \geq 0.$$

Multiply both sides of this inequality by X:

$$U''(A + aX)X \geq -R_A(A)U'(A + aX)X$$

for $X \geq 0$. However, it can easily be seen that the same inequality holds for $X \leq 0$. Take the expectation of both sides.

$$E[U''(A + aX)X] \geq -R_A(A)E[U'(A + aX)X] = 0,$$

from (9-14). Hence, from (9-15), $da/dA \geq 0$, as was to be shown.

If absolute risk aversion were increasing, it would follow that risky investment is an inferior good, a most implausible conclusion.

[5] We first derive (9-16) and then show that indeed increasing relative risk aversion implies that $E[U''(Y)XY] \leq 0$, where $Y = A + aX$. From the definitions of elasticity and of m, we see that

$$\frac{Em}{EA} - 1 = \frac{A}{m}\frac{dm}{dA} - 1 = \frac{A}{m}\left(1 - \frac{da}{dA}\right) - 1$$

$$= \frac{(A - m) - A(da/dA)}{m}$$

$$= \frac{(A - m)E[U''(Y)X^2] + AE[U''(Y)X]}{mE[U''(Y)X^2]}$$

(from Eq. 9-15)

$$= \frac{E[U''(Y)(aX^2 + AX)]}{mE[U''(Y)X^2]} = \frac{E[U''(Y)X(a + AX)]}{mE[U''(Y)X^2]},$$

which is (9-16), since $Y = A + aX$.

Since $R_R(Y)$ is increasing, $R_R(A + aX) \leqq R_R(A)$ for $X \leqq 0$. By the definition of R_R,

$$U''(Y)Y \geqq -R_R(A)U'(Y) \quad \text{for } X \leqq 0.$$

Multiply both sides of this inequality by X. Then

$$U''(Y)XY \leqq -R_R(A)U'(Y)X$$

for $X \leqq 0$. The same must be true for $X \geqq 0$. Take the expectation of both sides.

$$E[U''(Y)XY] \leqq -R_R(A)E[U'(Y)X] = 0,$$

by (9-14).

10   Exposition of the Theory of Choice under Uncertainty

Structure of a Theory of Behavior under Uncertainty

The basic need for a special theory to explain behavior under conditions of uncertainty arises from two considerations: (1) subjective feelings of imperfect knowledge when certain types of choices, typically involving commitments over time, are made; (2) the existence of certain observed phenomena, of which insurance is the most conspicuous example, which cannot be explained on the assumption that individuals act with subjective certainty.

A theory of choice is a set of propositions about choice rules, rules which indicate for each set of available actions that action which will in fact be chosen. It is assumed in general that certain consistency relations hold among the choices from different sets of possible actions and also that these sets belong to some restricted class; from these assumptions, which may be stronger or weaker, it is possible to deduce some propositions about the observable behavior of the individual agents. In the case of the theory of consumer's demand under certainty, for example, an action is the choice of a consumption bundle; the set of possible actions, for any given income and set of prices, is the set of consumption bundles satisfying the budget constraint; and the choice rule is maximization in accordance with the ordering expressing the individual's preference pattern. This theory, though certainly not very strong, implies the well-known Slutsky relations, which are state-

Reprinted from *Decision and Organization,* ed. C. B. McGuire and R. Radner (Amsterdam: North-Holland, 1971), pp. 19–55.

ments about the functional relation between the action taken and the price-income parameters defining the set of possible actions.

The immediate basis for a special theory of behavior under uncertainty is the subjective sensation that an *action* may not uniquely determine the consequences to the agent. It follows that a structure of choices among sets of consequences is not sufficient to determine choices among actions, unlike the situation under (subjective) certainty where actions imply unique consequences, and therefore choices among consequences imply choices among actions.

To formalize the theory of choice under uncertainty, it is convenient to introduce the concept of the *state of the world,* a description of the world so complete that, if true and known, the consequences of every action would be known. In what follows, the symbol s will stand for a state of the world, and a for an action.

The meaning of uncertainty is that the agent does not know the state of the world. By definition, the consequences would be known if both the action and the state of the world were known; that is, there is a function mapping ordered pairs (a,s) of actions and states of the world into consequences. We will understand that in the description of a consequence is included all that the agent values, so that he will be indifferent between two actions which yield the same consequence for each state of the world.

From this description it is clear that any choice function for actions must be synthesized out of two components, the valuation of the consequences and the relative strength of belief in the occurrence of the different states of the world. Just as in the theory of consumers' demand, choice is subjective; in choice among actions, both the values and the beliefs are subjective in the sense that only the values and the beliefs of the economic agent are relevant to explaining his choice, regardless of how these might differ from values or beliefs "objectively" given in some sense.

But it is of the utmost importance to observe that the subjectivity of beliefs does not exclude their being influenced by experience. Let us define an *event* as some set of the states of the world. Beliefs about different events are necessarily interrelated if only because of the logical relations among them; hence, knowledge that some event has occurred, that is, that the states of the world are now known to lie in some restricted range, will lead to a revaluation of beliefs about the remaining possible states of the world. When beliefs are represented by probabilities, then the observation of an event causes the agent to act in accordance with the conditional probabilities given that event rather than with the probabilities held before the observation.

The influence of experience on beliefs is of the utmost importance for a rational theory of behavior under uncertainty, and failure to account for it must be taken as a strong objection to theories such as Shackle's (1952).

A Set of Postulates

Events are statements about states of the world, or, in a different language, they are sets of states of the world (that is, an event consists of all states of the world which satisfy some given condition). It is not feasible, in general, to consider all sets of states of the world if we wish to assign probabilities to those events which satisfy the usual assumptions of probability theory. We do assume as usual that various sets derived from other events are also events. Thus, if E_1 and E_2 are events, the *union* of the two events, denoted by $E_1 \cup E_2$ and defined to be the set of all states of the world in either E_1 or E_2 or both, is also an event. More generally, let $\{E_i\}(i = 1, \ldots, \infty)$ be an infinite sequence of events; the union, here denoted by $\cup_{i=1}^{\infty} E_i$, is the set of all states of the world in at least one of the events E_i; again we assume the union of a sequence of events to be an event. For any event E, the *complement,* denoted by $\tilde{E}$ and defined to be the set of all states of the world not in E, is assumed to be an event. Finally, the set of all possible states of the world is assumed to be an event. In technical terms, the set of events is assumed to be σ-algebra.[1]

In the present case, it will also be assumed that sets consisting of a single state of the world are events. As a matter of notation we will let s denote, where appropriate, the event consisting of the single state s; the ambiguity of notation whereby s sometimes represents a state of the world and sometimes the event which consists only of that state will occasion no difficulty.

We now specify in more detail a set of assumptions designed to characterize reasonable behavior under conditions of uncertainty. The history of these assumptions is long, dating back indeed, in some respects, to the classic paper of Daniel Bernoulli (1738) but owing special debt to Frank Ramsey (1926), Bruno de Finetti (1937), John von Neumann and Oskar Morgenstern (1944; detailed proofs in 1953), and Leonard J. Savage (1954).

The most primitive assumption is that which is basic to the theory of rationality in consumer demand.

---

1. In the text, the concept "states of the world" is assumed to be primitive and events described in terms of them. It is alternatively possible and perhaps more elegant to start with the concept "event" as primitive; see Villegas (1964, pp. 1787–88).

Ordering. The individual's choice among actions can be represented by an ordering.

By this is meant the following two statements: (1) Given any two actions, the agent prefers one to the other or else regards them as indifferent; this property is termed *connectedness;* (2) given three actions, a^1, a^2, and a^3, if the agent prefers a^1 to a^2 or is indifferent between them and if the same holds as between a^2 and a^3, then he must prefer a^1 to a^3 or be indifferent between them; this property is termed *transitivity.* An ordering is usually taken to be a hallmark of rationality; in the absence of connectedness, no choice at all may be possible; in the absence of transitivity, choice may whirl about in circles.

The expressions $a^1 > a^2, a^1 \gtrsim a^2, a^1 \sim a^2$ will denote the statements "a^1 is preferred to a^2," "a^1 is preferred or indifferent to a^2," and "a^1 is indifferent to a^2," respectively.

The second assumption is also a simple analogue of one used, often unthinkingly, in consumers' demand theory. We assume continuity of preferences in the sense that if one action is preferred to another, then any action sufficiently close to the first is also preferred to the second and, similarly, the first action is preferred to any action sufficiently close to the first. However, the concept "sufficiently close" has not been formally defined with respect to actions.

A complete formalization of the concept of closeness will not be attempted. Rather, a condition which is intuitively sufficient for closeness is formalized, and it is asserted only that preferences are not altered by changes from one action to another which satisfy this condition for closeness. Consider a *monotone decreasing* sequence of events $\{E_i\}$, that is, a sequence for which $E_{i+1} \subset E_i$ (in words, every state of the world in E_{i+1} is also in E_i). A monotone decreasing sequence of events such that there is no state of the world common to all members of the sequence will be termed a *vanishing sequence.* Clearly, an event which is far out on a vanishing sequence is "small" by any reasonable standard. If one action is derived from another by altering the consequences for states of the world on an event which is sufficiently small in this sense, the preference relation of that action with respect to any other given action should be unaltered.

Monotone Continuity.[2] Given a and b, where $a > b$, a consequence c, and a vanishing sequence $\{E^i\}$, suppose the sequences of actions $\{a^i\}$, $\{b^i\}$

---

2. This axiom was first proposed by Villegas (1964, p. 1789) for the restricted class of actions to be called *bets* in a later section.

satisfy the conditions that (a^i,s) yield the same consequences as (a,s) for all s in $\tilde{E}_i$ and the consequence c for all s in E_i, while (b^i,s) yields the same consequences as (b,s) for all s in $\tilde{E}_i$ and the consequence c for all s in E_i. Then, for all i sufficiently large, $a^i > b$ and $a^i > b^i$.

The assumption of Monotone Continuity seems, I believe correctly, to be the harmless simplification that is almost inevitable in the formalization of any real-life problem. It is sometimes held that certain possible consequences, such as death, are incommensurably greater than others, such as receiving one cent. Let action a^1 involve receiving one cent with no risk of life, a^2 receiving nothing with no risk of life, and a^3 receiving one cent with an exceedingly small probability of death. Clearly, a^1 is preferred to a^2. Continuity would demand that a^3 be preferred to a^2 if the probability of death under a^3 is sufficiently small. This may sound outrageous at first, but I think a little reflection will demonstrate the reasonableness of the result. The probability in question may be 10^{-6} or 10^{-10}, inconceivably small magnitudes. Also, if in this example one cent were replaced by one billion dollars, one would hardly raise the same argument, and yet to go from one cent to one billion dollars certainly involves no discontinuity, however big the difference in scale may be. "Every journey, no matter how long, begins with a single step."

Blaise Pascal indeed suggested that the salvation of the soul or the avoidance of eternal damnation might be of infinitely greater value than any earthly regard; but the humble economist may be excused for regarding such choices as beyond the scope of his theories.

The assumptions of Ordering and Monotone Continuity made so far are, in spirit, common to theories of choice in a wide range of circumstances. The first assumption special to the theory of choice under uncertainty may be put this way: what might have happened under conditions that we know will not prevail should have no influence on our choice of actions. Suppose, that is, we are given the information that certain states of nature are impossible. We reform our beliefs about the remaining states of nature, and on the basis of these new beliefs we form a new ordering of the actions. The principle of Conditional Preference, which will now be introduced, asserts that the ordering will depend only on the consequences of the actions for those states of the world not ruled out by the information.

Conditional Preference. For any given event E, there is defined an ordering over actions satisfying also the condition of Monotone Continuity such that any two actions which have the same consequences for all states of the world in E will be indifferent given E. Preference of a^1 over a^2, given E, will be denoted by $a^1 > a^2|E$, and similarly for the relations of indifference and preference-or-indifference.

Given the concept of conditional preference, it is now possible to introduce a very strong and yet highly acceptable postulate, relating conditional to unconditional preference. Two definitions are needed. A *null event* is an event E such that the conditional ordering given its complement $\tilde{E}$ is the same as the unconditional ordering. The intended interpretation is that null events are those deemed impossible to begin with, so that the unconditional preferences would not be altered upon being informed that $\tilde{E}$ held, that is, that E was in fact not true. A *partition* is defined as a finite or infinite collection of events which are mutually exclusive and collectively exhaustive, that is, every state of the world belongs to one and only one event in the partition.

Dominance. Let P be a partition. Given two actions, a^1 and a^2, if, for every event E in the partition P, $a^1 \gtrsim a^2|E$, then $a^1 \gtrsim a^2$; and if in addition there exists a collection P' of events in P whose union is not a null event and such that $a^1 > a^2|E$ for all events E in P', then $a^1 > a^2$.

A third assumption expresses the condition that for a given state of the world actions are effectively valued solely by their consequences, together with an additional hypothesis which permits conceptually the attainment of any consequence in any state.

Valuation of Actions by Consequences. (a) If a^1, a^2, b^1, b^2 are actions, and s_1, s_2 states of the world, such that (a^1,s_1) and (a^2,s_2) yield the same consequence and similarly with (b^1,s_1) and (b^2,s_2), then $a^1 > b^1|s_1$ if and only if $a^2 > b^2|s_2$. (b) If $a(s)$ is any function which assigns to each state s a consequence, then there is an action a such that (a,s) yields the consequence $a(s)$ for all s.

If, first of all, we set $s_1 = s_2 = s$ and $b^1 = b^2 = a^1$, then $a^1 \sim a^1|s$ if and only if $a^1 \sim a^2|s$. But by Conditional Preference, certainly $a^1 \sim a^1|s$, so that any two actions which yield the same consequence in state s are indifferent, and this is true for any s. Further, by (b), all consequences are yielded by some action in s. Hence, all consequences are ordered for a given state s, and by (a) the ordering is the same for all s. Thus, we may speak unequivocally of an ordering of consequences, and we will use the same notation as for ordering actions.

It is natural and, from these assumptions, proper to identify a consequence with an action which yields that consequence for all s; such actions always exist by (b). Let a^1 yield consequence c_1 for all s, and let $\mathbf{a}^2$ yield c_2. If $c_1 > c_2$, then $a^1 > a^2 | s$ for all s. By Dominance, $\mathbf{a}^1 > \mathbf{a}^2$ since the states of the world form a partition. Similar results hold if $c_1 \sim c_2$ or $c_1 < c_2$; hence, $a^1 > a^2$ if and only if $c_1 > c_2$, so that the ordering of consequences is indeed the same as that of actions which yield constant consequences.

Any action $\mathbf{a}$ defines a function, $a(s)$, mapping states of the world into consequences. If two actions define the same such function, they are indifferent given any s and therefore are indifferent unconditionally, by Dominance; hence, it will be harmless to identify action $\mathbf{a}$ with the function $a(s)$. For any given action $\mathbf{a}$, and given consequence c, we will be considering such sets of states of the world as $\{s | a(s) \sim c\}$ or $\{s | a(s) > c\}$. It is clearly convenient to restrict the set of actions to be considered to those for which these sets are events, and this will be assumed in what follows.

The following simple consequence of these axioms will be used repeatedly in the sequel.

LEMMA 1. *If $a(s) \gtrsim$ (respectively, $>$) $b(s)$ for all s in E, where E is nonnull, then $\mathbf{a} \gtrsim$ (respectively, $>$)$\mathbf{b} | E$.*

Proof. Let $\mathbf{a}^*$ be an action for which $a^*(s) = a(s)$ for s in E, $a^*(s) = b(s)$ for s in $\tilde{E}$. From the last we conclude by conditional preference

$$a^* \sim b | \tilde{E}.$$

If $a(s) = a^*(s) \gtrsim b(s)$, all $s \in E$, then, by Dominance, $\mathbf{a}^* \gtrsim \mathbf{b}$. But if $\mathbf{a}^* < \mathbf{b} | E$, it would follow, again by Dominance, that $\mathbf{a}^* < \mathbf{b}$, a contradiction; hence, $\mathbf{a}^* \gtrsim \mathbf{b} | E$. But by Conditional Preference $\mathbf{a} \sim \mathbf{a}^* | E$; hence, $\mathbf{a} \gtrsim \mathbf{b} | E$. A similar argument holds when strict preference obtains.

Finally, we need an assumption about the structure of beliefs. Provisionally, the strong assumption will be made that beliefs are expressed by a probability distribution over the states of the world. Later in this chapter it will be shown, following Ramsey, de Finetti, Savage, and Villegas, that it is possible to derive this conclusion from more intuitive and basic assumptions.

Since an action determines consequences as a function of the state of the world, a given action defines the probability distribution of consequences for any given probability distribution over the states of the world. It will be assumed that there are no "indivisible" events; specifically, a probability distribution is said to be *atomless* if any event E with probability greater than zero can be partitioned into two events, each with probability greater than zero. This will certainly hold if there is some indefinitely repeatable occurrence more or less independent of the rest of the state of the world, for example, a coin tossing. Imagine the coin tossed indefinitely, with independence from trial to trial, and a positive probability of heads and also of tails. If E is an event with positive probability, the statements defining E can refer only to finitely many tosses of the coin (otherwise the probability of E would be zero). Hence, E can be divided into two events, each of positive probability, by considering the alternative outcomes of a coin toss not included in the definition of E. To say that beliefs are expressed by these probabilities has the following meaning in terms of choices among actions.

Probabilistic Beliefs. The probability distribution of states of the world is atomless. If the probability distribution of consequences is the same for two actions, they are indifferent.

Remark. In the sequel, the assumption of Probabilistic Beliefs will be applied only to actions which take on only a finite number of consequences.

The Expected-Utility Theorem

With these assumptions, it can be shown that choice among actions can be represented in a remarkably simple way. It is possible to attach numbers called *utilities* to consequences in such a way that the expected value of utility measures the preference for an action. In more detail, consider any way of attaching utility numbers to consequences. For a given action, the utility then becomes a random variable. If the probability distribution of utility satisfies some additional hypotheses, for example, if utility is confined to a bounded set with probability one, then utility has a well-defined expected value or average. The proposition then is that by choosing properly the utility numbers assigned to different consequences, it will be true that one action will be preferred to another if and only if the expected value of the utility of its consequences is greater.

It is still more fruitful and general to consider utility as attached to an action; since a consequence can, as previously remarked, always be thought of as a particular form of action—namely, one that yields the same consequence regardless of the state of nature—the utility of consequences is defined as a special case of the utility of actions. The utility for actions must have the usual properties of any utility, specifically that preferences are expressed by higher utility values. We now state formally the following theorem.

EXPECTED-UTILITY THEOREM. *It is possible to define a real-valued utility function over actions, with the following properties:* (1) $a^1 > a^2$ *if and only if* $U(a^1) > U(a^2)$; (2) $U(a) = E\{U[a(s)]\}$.

A utility function with these properties will be referred to as a *Bernoulli utility indicator*.

Remark. Because of (2), the utility function has the following continuity property if the range of the function is bounded with probability 1 (as will be shown to be true): Let $\{a^i\}$ be a sequence of actions, a a particular action; suppose that, for any set C of consequences for which the sets $\{s|a^i(s) \in C\}$, $\{s|a(s) \in C\}$ are all measurable, $P[a^i(s) \in C]$ converges to $P[a(s) \in C]$ uniformly in C; then $U(a^i)$ approaches $U(a)$.

I want to attempt a somewhat novel presentation of the proof by relating it to the economic concept of independent goods. Suppose an individual is asked for his preferences among different combinations of amounts of two commodities. He may state that he cannot answer without knowing what he will have of some third commodity; the choice between bread and cereal may depend on how much butter is available. But it can happen that his preferences among combinations of the two commodities are in fact independent of the amounts of any third commodity; and this may be true of any pair of commodities.

More generally, if there are more than three commodities, it can happen that preferences among bundles, for which the components in any given set of commodities are constant, are independent of the levels at which they are constant. In that case, there is a well-known theorem that it is possible to represent these preferences by a utility function which adds up utilities from the different commodities; in symbols,

$$(10\text{-}1) \qquad U(x_1, \ldots, x_n) = U_1(x_1) + U_2(x_2) + \ldots + U_n(x_n),$$

where $U(x_1, \ldots, x_n)$ is the utility of a bundle containing x_1 of the first commodity, and so forth.[3] This choice of utility function is also known to be unique up to positive linear transformations; that is, if there are two utility

---

3. See, for example, Samuelson (1947, pp. 174–180). For a more general approach, see Debreu (1960). Similar theorems arise in mathematical psychology; for a survey of recent literature on additive utility theory see Fishburn (1966).

indicators of the form of (10-1), either can be obtained from the other by adding a constant and multiplying through by a positive constant.

With this remark we proceed to the proof proper. Because of the assumption of Probabilistic Beliefs we can speak indifferently of ordering actions and of ordering probability distributions of consequences. For the time being we will confine attention to actions which yield consequences in a fixed finite set. We will start off with what seems to be a remarkably special problem, but in fact is very general: attaching utilities to probability distributions of probability distributions. More precisely, let $E_1, \ldots, E_n$ constitute a partition, with each event E_j having probability $1/n$. Let $\pi_1, \ldots, \pi_n$ be probability distributions over consequences in the given set. We will consider actions for which the conditional distribution of consequences, given E_j, is π_j, where the distributions π_j are considered as variables which can range over all possible distributions over the fixed finite set of consequences. Any such action will be denoted by $(\pi_1, \ldots, \pi_n)$. For such an action, the unconditional probability distribution of consequences is simply the average, $\Sigma_{j=1}^{n}\pi_j/n$; according to our assumptions, all such distributions can be ordered, and we therefore have an ordering of the sets of n probability distributions, $(\pi_1, \ldots, \pi_n)$. Such an ordering is precisely analogous to the ordering of sets of n commodities with which we are familiar from demand theory, and we will apply to it the theory of independent goods sketched above.

First, it is established that the ordering of these probability distributions of consequences has the continuity properties usually assumed for finite-dimensional commodity spaces; specifically, that for any given distribution π^0 the sets $\{\pi|\pi > \pi^0\}$ and $\{\pi|\pi^0 > \pi\}$ are open sets.

Let π^* and π_* be two distributions over the fixed finite set of consequences, and suppose $\pi^* > \pi_*$. Let $\{\pi^i\}$ be a sequence of probability distributions over these consequences converging to π^*. Since there are only finitely many consequences, the probability distributions are finite-dimensional vectors, and the usual definition of convergence applies. It will be shown that $\pi^i > \pi_*$ for i sufficiently large. By a parallel argument, it can be shown that if $\pi^i \rightarrow \pi_*$, then $\pi^* > \pi^i$ for i sufficiently large.

Choose a vanishing sequence $\{F_k\}$ such that $P(F_k) > 0$ for all k, where $P(F)$ is the probability of the event F; such a sequence exists by the assumed atomlessness of the probability distribution of states of the world. Let a^* be an action such that

$$P[a^*(s) = c|\tilde{F}_1] = \pi^*(c) \quad \text{for all } c,$$

and also

$$P[a^*(s) = c | F_k - F_{k+1}] = \pi^*(c) \quad \text{for all } c \text{ and } k,$$

where $F_k - F_{k+1}$ consists of all s in F_k but not F_{k+1}. Since the sets $\tilde{F}_1$, $F_k - F_{k+1}$ constitute a partition, it follows that $P[a^*(s) = c] = \pi^*(c)$ for all c. That a^* can be constructed as indicated follows again from the atomlessness of the probability distribution of states. Also choose an action a_* with probability distribution π_* over consequences. Then the statement $\pi^* > \pi_*$ is equivalent to the statement $a^* > a_*$.

Let $\underline{c}$ be the least preferred of all the consequences considered. Then by Monotone Continuity it is possible to choose F_k so that the action a^{**}, defined by

$$a^{**}(s) = \begin{cases} a^*(s) & \text{if } s \in \tilde{F}_k, \\ \underline{c} & \text{if } s \in F_k, \end{cases}$$

is preferred to a_*.

By construction, $P(\tilde{F}_k) = 1 - P(F_k) < 1$. Since $\pi^i(c)$ approaches $\pi^*(c)$, $\pi^i(c) \geq \pi^*(c) P(\tilde{F}_k)$ for i sufficiently large if $\pi^*(c) > 0$, and the inequality certainly holds if $\pi^*(c) = 0$. Since there are only finitely many c, the inequality holds for all c for i sufficiently large. Define

$$\bar{\pi}(c) = [\pi^i(c) - \pi^*(c) P(\tilde{F}_k)] / P(F_k);$$

then $\bar{\pi}$ is a probability distribution. Define the action $\bar{a}$ to coincide with a^* on $\tilde{F}_k$ and such that the conditional probability distribution of $\bar{a}$, given F_k, is $\bar{\pi}$. From construction, the conditional distribution of a^*, given $\tilde{F}_k$, is π^* for any k; hence, an easy calculation shows that the distribution of $\bar{a}$ is π^i.

We wish to show that $\bar{a} > a_*$; this is equivalent to saying that $\pi^i > \pi_*$. But $\bar{a}$ coincides with a^{**} on $\tilde{F}_k$, and hence $\bar{a} \sim a^{**} | \tilde{F}_k$. Since $\underline{c}$ is the least preferred consequence, it follows from Lemma 1 that $\bar{\pi} \geq \underline{c}$, and therefore $\bar{a} \geq a^{**} | F_k$. By Dominance again, $\bar{a} \geq a^{**} > a_*$, as was to be proved.

Let E be the event of either E_1 or E_2, that is, it contains all states of the world in either of these two events. By the assumption of Conditional Preference, all actions can be ordered given E, and the ordering depends only on the outcomes for states of the world in E. Together with the assumption of Probabilistic Beliefs this implies that there is a well-defined ordering of the pairs (π_1, π_2). Now consider two sets of n probability distributions, $(\pi_1, \pi_2, \pi_3, \ldots, \pi_n)$ and $(\pi'_1, \pi'_2, \pi_3, \ldots, \pi_n)$, which yield the same conditional probability distributions of consequences in states $E_3, \ldots,$

E_n. By virtue of the Dominance axiom, then, $(\pi_1, \pi_2, \pi_3, \ldots, \pi_n) >$ $(\pi'_1, \pi'_2, \pi_3, \ldots, \pi_n)$ if and only if $(\pi_1, \pi_2) > (\pi'_1, \pi'_2) | E$; to see this, we must take our partition to be the sets E, E_3, $\ldots$, E_n. The choice is thus independent of $\pi_3, \ldots, \pi_n$. Any pair or, more generally, any collection of events could have been substituted for E_1 and E_2 in this argument; thus, the preferences for varying any set of conditional probability distributions holding all others constant are in fact independent of the levels at which the others are held constant. It follows that the conditional probability distributions act as independent goods, and by the theorem of Debreu (1960) we can express the preferences among sets of probability distributions $(\pi_1, \ldots, \pi_n)$ by a continuous additive utility function,

(10-2) $$V_n(\pi_1, \ldots, \pi_n) = \sum_{j=1}^{n} W_{jn}(\pi_j).$$

The subscript n is designed to remind us that we have so far considered a partition into a fixed number of events.

The assumption of Probabilistic Beliefs also assures that interchanging any pair of conditional probability distributions leads to a new action which is indifferent to the first, since only the resulting unconditional probability distribution, $\sum_{j=1}^{n} \pi_j / n$, matters as far as preference is concerned. Hence, the function $W_{jn}(\pi_j)$ must be the same for all j, and the subscript j can be deleted.

(10-3) $$V_n(\pi_1, \ldots, \pi_n) = \sum_{j=1}^{n} W_n(\pi_j).$$

The next step is to relate the utility functions for different values of n, that is, different numbers of equiprobable events. For this purpose we define

(10-4) $$U_n(\pi) = n W_n(\pi),$$

and (10-3) becomes

(10-5) $$V_n(\pi_1, \ldots, \pi_n) = \sum_{j=1}^{n} (1/n) U_n(\pi_j).$$

Notice that, since the probability of E_j is $1/n$ for each j, the right-hand side is the expected value of a utility function. We will show that $U_n(\pi)$ is in fact the same function for all n.

Since (10-5) holds for any n, it holds in particular for mn, where m is any positive integer. When there are mn equally probable events, it will be convenient to label them with pairs of subscripts; thus, E_{jk}, with j running from 1 to n and k from 1 to m. Then (10-5) becomes

(10-6) $V_{mn}(\pi_{11}, \ldots, \pi_{mn}) = \sum_{j=1}^{n} \sum_{k=1}^{m} (1/mn)U_{mn}(\pi_{jk}).$

In particular, now let us suppose that for any given index j the conditional probability distribution is the same for all events E_{jk}; in symbols, $\pi_{jk} = \pi_j$ for $k = 1, \ldots, m$. Then

$$\sum_{k=1}^{m} (1/mn)U_{mn}(\pi_{jk})$$

is a sum of m terms, each of which is the same, $(1/mn)U_{mn}(\pi_j)$, and therefore equals $(1/n)U_{mn}(\pi_j)$. Further, the unconditional distribution of consequences is $\sum_{j=1}^{n}\sum_{k=1}^{n}\pi_{jk}/mn = \sum_{j=1}^{n}\pi_j/n$, so that the expression (10-6) defines an ordering on the sets of n conditional probability distributions $(\pi_1, \ldots, \pi_n)$. Since we have

$$V_{mn}(\pi_{11}, \ldots, \pi_{mn}) = \sum_{j=1}^{n} (1/n)U_{mn}(\pi_j),$$

when $\pi_{jk} = \pi_j$, we see that V_{mn} constitutes an additive utility function for sets of n conditional probability distributions. But additive utility functions are unique up to positive linear transformations; it follows that $U_{mn}(\pi)$ is essentially the same as $U_n(\pi)$. As $U_m(\pi)$ is also the same as $U_{mn}(\pi)$, it follows that $U_n(\pi)$ is essentially the same as $U_m(\pi)$ for any pair of integers m, n, and therefore we may drop the subscript n. Thus,

(10-7) $V_n(\pi_1, \ldots, \pi_n) = \sum_{j=1}^{n} (1/n)U(\pi_j).$

Note that this expression can also be regarded as the utility attached to the unconditional distribution, so that

(10-8) $V\left(\sum_{j=1}^{n} \pi_j/n\right) = \sum_{j=1}^{n} (1/n)U(\pi_j).$

Suppose in particular that all π_j's are the same: $\pi_j = \pi$. Then $\sum_{i=1}^{n}\pi_j/n = \pi$, and

$$\sum_{j=1}^{n} (1/n)U(\pi_j) = \sum_{j=1}^{n} (1/n)U(\pi) = U(\pi),$$

so that $U(\pi) = V(\pi)$. If we now substitute in (10-8), we find that

(10-9) $\quad U\left(\sum_{j=1}^{n} \pi_j/n\right) = \sum_{j=1}^{n} (1/n)U(\pi_j);$

in words, the utility of an average of probability distributions is the average of their utilities.

We have now defined a utility function, unique up to positive linear transformations, for all probability distributions with finitely many consequences, and have shown that it has the property that the utility of a random choice among any finite number of equally probable conditional probability distributions is the expected utility of the conditional probability distribution.

Next we wish to relax the condition that the partition consists of equally probable events. Suppose now we have n events with probabilities which are rational numbers: we can put all these probabilities over a common denominator, say N. Then

$$P(E_j) = m_j/N.$$

For each j, let us partition E_j into m_j equally probable events, E_{jk}, $k = 1, \ldots, m_j$, so that $P(E_{jk}) = 1/N$. The events E_{jk} then constitute a partition into equally probable events, and we can apply (10-9). In particular, let π_{jk}, the conditional probability distribution given event E_{jk}, be π_j independent of k. The unconditional distribution then is clearly

$$\sum_{j=1}^{n} \sum_{k=1}^{m_j} \pi_j/N = \sum_{j=1}^{n} (m_j/N)\pi_j = \sum_{j=1}^{n} P(E_j)\pi_j.$$

The right-hand side of (10-9) becomes

$$\sum_{j=1}^{n} \sum_{k=1}^{m_j} (1/N)U(\pi_{jk}) = \sum_{j=1}^{n} (m_j/N)U(\pi_j) = \sum_{j=1}^{n} P(E_j)U(\pi_j),$$

so that (10-9) generalizes to

(10-10) $\quad U\left(\sum_{j=1}^{n} P(E_j)\pi_j\right) = \sum_{j=1}^{n} P(E_j)U(\pi_j);$

in words, the utility of a weighted mixture of probability distributions is the weighted average of their utilities.

This has been proved so far only for rational probabilities. Now suppose one or more of the probabilities $P(E_j)$ is not a rational number. We can always choose rational numbers, p_j, so that

$$p_j < P(E_j),$$

and indeed as close as we wish. Let E_j' be a subset of E_j such that

(10-11) $P(E_j') = p_j$ $(j = 1, \ldots, n)$.

Let E_j'' consist of all the elements of E_j not in E_j'. Without loss of generality, we renumber the events so that π_1 is the least preferred among the probability distributions π_j (or a least preferred distribution if there is a tie), and similarly π_n is a most preferred distribution among the π_j's. Let a^1, a^2, a^3 be three actions for which the conditional probability distributions of consequences given the events E_j', E_j'' are as follows:

a^1: conditional distribution given E_j' is π_j;
  conditional distribution given E_j'' is π_j.
a^2: conditional distribution given E_j' is π_j;
  conditional distribution given E_j'' is π_1.
a^3: conditional distribution given E_j' is π_j;
  conditional distribution given E_j'' is π_n.

The events E_j', E_j'' constitute a partition. The conditional distribution given E_j' is the same for all three actions and so, by the postulate of Conditional Preference, the three actions are indifferent given E_j' for each j. However, by construction, π_n is preferred or indifferent to π_j and the latter to π_1; hence $a^3 \succsim a^1 \,|\, E_j''$ and $a^1 \succsim a^2 \,|\, E_j''$ for each j. By the postulate of Dominance, $a^3 \succsim a^1 \succsim a^2$, so that

$$U(a^3) \geqq U(a^1) \geqq U(a^2).$$

Now write E_{n+1}' for the set of states of the world not in any of the events $E_1', \ldots, E_n'$, or equivalently for the set of states of the world in one of the events $E_1'', \ldots, E_n''$. Note first that

$$P(E_{n+1}') = 1 - \sum_{j=1}^{n} P(E_j') = 1 - \sum_{j=1}^{n} p_j$$

is a rational number. For the action a^2, the conditional distribution given E_j'' is the same for each j, namely, π_1. Therefore, the conditional distribution given E_{n+1}' must also be π_1. We can now apply (10-10) since the probabilities of the events $E'_1, \ldots, E'_n, E'_{n+1}$ are all rational:

$$U(a^2) = \sum_{j=1}^{n} P(E'_j)U(\pi_j) + P(E'_{n+1})U(\pi_1).$$

Similarly,

$$U(a^3) = \sum_{j=1}^{n} p_j U(\pi_j) + \left(1 - \sum_{j=1}^{n} p_j\right) U(\pi_n).$$

Now let the numbers p_j approach $P(E_j)$ for each j. Then $1 - \Sigma_{j=1}^{n} p_j$ approaches zero. Both $U(a^2)$ and $U(a^3)$ converge to

$$\sum_{j=1}^{n} P(E_j)U(\pi_j),$$

which is therefore equal to $U(a^1)$. But a^1 is so defined that the conditional distribution given either E'_j or E''_j is π_j. Hence the conditional distribution given E_j is also π_j since E_j is simply divided into E'_j and E''_j. Thus, the unconditional distribution for a^1 is simply $\Sigma_{j=1}^{n} P(E_j)\pi_j$, and it has now been demonstrated that (10-10) also holds when the probabilities $P(E_j)$ are irrational.

Before going on, let us interpret (10-10) in terms of utilities of consequences. Consider any action which yields the finitely many different possible consequences $c_1, \ldots, c_n$. Let E_i be the event that c_i occurs, and let π_i be the distribution under which c_i occurs with probability 1. Then $U(\pi_i)$ may very reasonably be interpreted as the utility of the consequence c_i, and we will use the notation $U(c_i)$. The mixed probability distribution, $\Sigma_{i=1}^{n} P(E_i)\pi_i$, is now just the probability distribution of the consequence. Then (10-10) states that the utility of any action which has only a finite number of consequences is the expected utility of the consequence.

So far, attention has been confined to utility comparisons of actions which yield consequences in a fixed finite set, say K. Provisionally, this restriction may be symbolized by writing the utility function as $U(a|K)$, defined for all actions a for which $a(s) \in K$, all s. But if $K_1 \subset K_2$, the set of actions a for which $a(s) \in K_1$, all s, is a subset of that for which $a(s) \in K_2$, all s. Hence, $U(a|K_2)$ defines a utility indicator of the former class of actions, and this indicator satisfies (10-10). Therefore, the function $U(a|K_2)$ is, up to a positive linear transformation, identical with the function $U(a|K_1)$ for actions with consequences in K_1. It follows that the utility function is essentially the same for all K; for if a^1 and a^2 are any two actions with finitely many consequences, we need only choose K to be any finite set of consequences such that both $a^1(s) \in K$ and $a^2(s) \in K$ for all s; then $a^1 > a^2$ if and only if $U(a^1|K) > U(a^2|K)$, and the function U satisfies (10-10).

Thus, a Bernoulli utility indicator has been defined, with finite values, for all actions with finitely many consequences. The final step is to drop the restriction that the number of different possible consequences is finite. For most practical purposes it is easier to consider random variables which are continuous and therefore take on an infinite number of values. This last step is, however, not quite straightforward and turns out, somewhat surprisingly, to imply that the utility function must be bounded; we cannot have utilities which are indefinitely large in either the positive or the negative direction.

The argument depends, interestingly, on the very problem that originally gave rise to Daniel Bernoulli's original paper (1738) and which has been given the name "St. Petersburg paradox" after the place where Bernoulli wrote. In its original form, a gambling game was considered in which a prize of 2^n was given with a probability of $(\frac{1}{2})^n$ for $n = 1, \ldots,$ *ad infinitum*. The expected value in money terms was infinite, yet it is obvious to common sense that no one would pay any very large fee for the right to play the game. Bernoulli suggested that maximizing expected utility instead of expected money income was the proper criterion of action and if, for example, the utility of a quantity of money were equal to its logarithm, one could easily compute that the maximum entrance fee which an individual would be willing to pay was finite and in fact reasonably small.

But this solution is in fact incomplete. If the utility function is unbounded, one can always construct an action with an infinite utility, as was first observed by the mathematician Karl Menger (1934). To see this, suppose the utility function is unbounded above. Then we can find a consequence with a utility as large as we wish. In particular, choose consequence c_i so that

$$U(c_i) \geqq 2^i \quad \text{and also} \quad U(c_i) > U(c_{i-1}),$$

for each i. Let $\{E_i\}(i = 1, \ldots,$ *ad. inf.*) be a partition, with $P(E_i) = (\frac{1}{2})^i$. Let a^1 be the action which gives rise to consequence c_i when event E_i occurs. Fix a positive integer N, and let a^2 be the action which gives rise to consequence c_i when E_i occurs, for $i \leqq N$, and to c_{N+1} when E_i occurs for any $i > N$. The action a^2 has only a finite number of possible consequences, and so (10-10) is valid. Note that the probability of c_{N+1} under action a^2 is $1 - \Sigma_{i=1}^{N} P(E_i)$.

$$U(a^2) = \sum_{i=1}^{N} P(E_i)U(c_i) + \left[1 - \sum_{i=1}^{N} P(E_i)\right] U(c_{n+1})$$

$$\geqq \sum_{i=1}^{N} (\tfrac{1}{2})^i U(c_i) \geqq \sum_{i=1}^{N} (\tfrac{1}{2})^i 2^i = N.$$

On the other hand, a^1 coincides with a^2 on $E_i(i = 1, \ldots, N+1)$, while on $E_i(i > N+1)$ it yields c_i, which is preferred to c_{N+1}, the outcome of a^2. By Lemma 1, $a^1 > a^2$. Now let a be any action with finitely many consequences; choose N integer, $N > U(a)$. Then $U(a^2) > U(a)$, so that $a^2 > a$, and therefore $a^1 > a$. It has thus been shown that, if the utility function is unbounded above, then a^1 is preferred to any action with finitely many consequences.

But this leads to a contradiction. Let $\{\bar{c}_i\}$ be a sequence of consequences such that $\bar{c}_i > c_i$, each i, and let a^3 be the action defined by $a^3(s) = \bar{c}_i$ for $s \in E_i$. Then, by Dominance, $a^3 > a^1$. Let $F_j = \bigcup_{i=j}^{\infty} E_i$; then $\{F_j\}$ is certainly a vanishing sequence. Let c be any arbitrary consequence. By Monotone Continuity it is possible to choose j so that the action a^4 defined by

$$a^4(s) = \begin{cases} a^3(s) & \text{for } s \in \tilde{F}_j, \\ c & \text{for } s \in F_j, \end{cases}$$

is preferred to a^1. By definition of F_j, $a^4(s) = \bar{c}_i$ for $s \in E_i, i < j, a^4(s) = c$ for $s \in F_j$. Then a^4 has finitely many consequences and is preferred to a^1, a contradiction.

By a similar argument the utility function must be bounded from below. It is now possible to establish the Expected-Utility Theorem for any probability distribution of consequences. Since the utility function is bounded in both directions, let $\underline{u} = \inf U(c)$, $\bar{u} = \sup U(c)$. First let us assume that these bounds are actually attained, that there are consequences $\underline{c}, \bar{c}$ such that $\underline{c} \leq c \leq \bar{c}$ for all consequences c, and therefore $\underline{c} \leq a(s) \leq \bar{c}$ for all actions a and all states of the world s. Note that $\underline{u} = U(\underline{c})$, $\bar{u} = U(\bar{c})$.

Divide the interval from $\underline{u}$ to $\bar{u}$ into a finite number of intervals; let the boundary points in increasing order be $u_i(i = 0, \ldots, n)$, with $u_0 = \underline{u}$ and $u_n = \bar{u}$. Given any action a, the utility of the consequence, $U[a(s)]$, is a random variable with a known distribution. Let $E_i = \{s | u_i \leq U[a(s)] < u_{i+1}\}$ $(i = 0, \ldots, n-1)$, $E_n = \{s | U[a(s)] = u_n\}$. Let a^{1n} be an action with finitely many consequences for which $E\{U[a^{1n}(s)]|E_i\} = u_i (i = 0, \ldots, n)$, a^{2n} an action with finitely many consequences for which $E\{U[a^{2n}(s)]|E_i\} = u_{i+1}$ $(i = 0, \ldots, n-1)$, $E\{U[a^{2n}(s)]|E_n\} = u_n$. Such actions can always be found; for example, let a^{1n} take on only the two values $\underline{c}, \bar{c}$, and be so defined that the conditional probability distribution of $a^{1n}(s)$ given E_i satisfies the conditions:

$$P[a^{1n}(s) = \bar{c}|E_i]\bar{u} + P[a^{1n}(s) = \underline{c}|E_i]\underline{u} = u_i,$$
$$P[a^{1n}(s) = \bar{c}|E_i] + P[a^{1n}(s) = \underline{c}|E_i] = 1.$$

To prove that $a \succsim a^{1n}|E_i$ and $a^{2n} \succsim a|E_i$, the following lemma is established.

LEMMA 2. *If E is nonnull, $a(s) \succsim b|E$ for all s in E, and b has finitely many consequences, then $a \succsim b|E$.*

Note that in the hypothesis the *consequence* $a(s)$ is being compared with the *action* b, for any given s.

Proof. The action b defines a conditional probability distribution over finitely many consequences, given E; this distribution then has a utility, which we may denote by $U(b|E)$. For any given s' in E, define $b_{s'}$, which coincides with b on E, with $b_{s'}(s) = a(s')$ on $\tilde{E}$. On the one hand, $U(b_{s'}) = U(b|E)P(E) + U[a(s')]P(\tilde{E})$; on the other, $a(s') \succsim b_{s'}|E$, and $a(s') = b_{s'}|\tilde{E}$, so that $a(s') \succsim b_{s'}$, and therefore $U[a(s')] \geqq U(b_{s'})$, from which it follows that $U[a(s')] \geqq U(b|E)$ for all s' in E. Let

$$u_* = \inf_{s \in E} U[a(s)] \geqq U(b|E).$$

There are two possibilities: either the infimum is assumed or it is not. In the first case, let s_* be such that $U[a(s_*)] = u_*$, and define actions a^*, b^* to coincide with a, b respectively, on E, with $a^*(s) = b^*(s) = a(s_*)$ for $s \in \tilde{E}$. Then, by construction, $a^*(s) \succsim a(s_*)$ for all s, so that $a^* \succsim a(s_*)$. Also, $a(s_*) \succsim b^*|E$, by hypothesis, and $a(s_*) = b^*|\tilde{E}$, so that $a(s_*) \succsim b^*$. Hence, $a^* \succsim b^*$. Since $a^* = b^*|\tilde{E}$, it follows from Dominance that $a^* \succsim b^*|E$; but since a^*, b^* coincide with a, b, respectively, on E, $a \succsim b|E$, as was to be shown.

In the second case, $U[a(s)] > u_*$ for all s in E. Let s_i be a sequence of states of the world in E, such that $U[a(s_i)]$ decreases to u_*. Let $E_i = \{s|a(s_i) > a(s), s \in E\}$; then $\{E_i\}$ is a vanishing sequence. Define a^i so that $a^i(s) = a(s)$ for $s \in E - E_i$, $a^i(s) = a(s_i)$ for $s \in E_i$, $a^i(s) = a(s_i)$ for $s \in \tilde{E}$. Define b^i so that $b^i(s) = b(s)$ for $s \in E$, $b^i(s) = a(s_i)$ for $s \in \tilde{E}$. Then clearly $a^i(s) \succsim a(s_i)$, all s, so that $a^i \succsim a(s_i)$. By hypothesis, $a(s_i) \succsim b^i|E$; by construction, $a(s_i) = b^i|\tilde{E}$, so that $a(s_i) \succsim b^i$, and hence $a^i \succsim b^i$. Since $a^i = b^i|\tilde{E}$, it follows by the usual argument that $a^i \succsim b^i|E$, and therefore $a^i \succsim b|E$.

Now take any fixed consequence, c, and let $\underline{a}^i$, $\underline{a}$, $\underline{b}$ be actions which coincide with a^i, a, b, respectively, on E and yield c on $\tilde{E}$. Then by the usual Dominance argument, $\underline{a}^i \gtrsim \underline{b}$. But a^i differs from $\underline{a}$ only on a vanishing sequence; hence, $\underline{a} \gtrsim \underline{b}$. Finally, since $\underline{a} = \underline{b}|\tilde{E}$, $\underline{a} \gtrsim \underline{b}|E$, or $a \gtrsim b|E$, as was to be proved.

We now return to the proof of the Expected-Utility Theorem. By Lemma 2, $a \gtrsim a^{1n}|E_i$ for any nonnull E_i and, by a similar argument, $a^{2n} \gtrsim a|E_i$. Since these statements hold for all nonnull E_i, we can say that $a^{2n} \gtrsim a \gtrsim a^{1n}$. But from (10-10),

$$U(a^{1n}) = \sum_{i=0}^{n} P(E_i)u_i, \quad U(a^{2n}) = \sum_{i=0}^{n-1} P(E_i)U_{i+1} + P(E_n)u_n.$$

Now let the subdivision become finer so that n increases and the distance between successive u_i's becomes smaller. From general theorems on Lebesgue integration, it follows that $U(a^{1n})$ and $U(a^{2n})$ approach a common limit, which is the expected value of the utility, $E\{U[a(s)]\} = u^*$, say. Since $\bar{u} \geq u^* \geq u$, we can construct an action a^* which yields only the two consequences $\underline{c}$, $\bar{c}$, such that $U(a^*) = u^*$. It will be shown that $a \sim a^*$.

Suppose a were preferred to a^*. We will construct a^{**}, an action with finitely many consequences, such that $a > a^{**} > a^*$. This leads to a contradiction. For $U(a^{**}) > U(a^*)$; since $U(a^{2n}) \rightarrow U(a^*)$, $U(a^{2n}) < U(a^{**})$ for n large, and therefore $a^{**} > a^{2n}$, contrary to the constructions which ensure $a^{2n} \gtrsim a > a^{**}$.

It remains to construct a^{**}. Suppose that $P[a^*(s) = \bar{c}] = 1$. Then by Dominance, $a^* \gtrsim a$, contrary to assumption. Thus, $P[a^*(s) = \underline{c}] > 0$. Let $E_1 = \{s|a^*(s) = \underline{c}\}$, $\{E_i\}$ be a vanishing sequence with $P(E_i) > 0$. Then, by Monotone Continuity, if $a > a^*$, we can find i and a^{**}, with $a^{**}(s) = a^*(s)$ for $s \in \tilde{E}_i$, $a^{**}(s) = \bar{c}$ for $s \in E_i$, $a > a^{**}$. Since $E_i \subset E_1$, $a^{**}(s) = \bar{c} > \underline{c} = a^*(s)$ for $s \in E_i$, and therefore by Dominance $a^{**} > a^*$.

Thus, it is impossible that $a > a^*$ and similarly impossible that $a^* > a$. Then a is indifferent to an action a^* whose utility is $E\{U[a(s)]\}$. From this the Expected-Utility Theorem has been shown to hold if there exist a best and a worst consequence.

Now drop the assumption that maximal and minimal consequences exist. For any fixed pair of consequences, $\underline{c}$, $\bar{c}$, with $\underline{c} \lesssim \bar{c}$, consider the class of actions, $K(\underline{c},\bar{c})$, for which $\underline{c} \lesssim a(s) \lesssim \bar{c}$. Within any such class, the Expected-Utility Theorem holds. Define an action a to be *bounded below* if, for some consequence $\underline{c}$, $P[a(s) \gtrsim \underline{c}] = 1$; define *bounded above* similarly, and say an action is *bounded* if it is bounded both above and below. By modifying the consequences of a bounded action, $\boldsymbol{a}$, on a set of probability zero, we can obtain a second action, $\boldsymbol{a}'$, such that $\boldsymbol{a} \sim \boldsymbol{a}'$, $\boldsymbol{a}' \in K(\underline{c},\bar{c})$ for some $\underline{c}$, $\bar{c}$, and $E\{U[a(s)]\} = E\{U[a'(s)]\}$. If $\boldsymbol{a}$ and $\boldsymbol{b}$ are two bounded actions, then we can choose $\underline{c}$, $\bar{c}$ so that both $\boldsymbol{a}$ and $\boldsymbol{a}'$ belong to $K(\underline{c},\bar{c})$; then $\boldsymbol{a} > \boldsymbol{b}$ if and only if $E\{U[a(s)]\} > E\{U[b(s)]\}$.

Now let $\boldsymbol{a}$ be any action bounded below but not necessarily above. We construct a vanishing sequence $\{E_i\}$ and a sequence of actions, $\{a^i\}$, such that

$$(10\text{-}12) \qquad a^i(s) = \begin{cases} c & \text{for } s \in E_i, \text{ for some } c, \\ a(s) & \text{for } s \in \tilde{E}_i; \end{cases}$$

$$(10\text{-}13) \qquad \boldsymbol{a}^i \text{ bounded};$$

$$(10\text{-}14) \qquad \boldsymbol{a} > \boldsymbol{a}^i;$$

$$(10\text{-}15) \qquad E\{U[a(s)]\} > E\{U[a^i(s)]\}.$$

If $\boldsymbol{a}$ is unbounded above, for any consequence c, $P[a(s) > c] > 0$, and therefore $U[a(s)] > U(c)$ with positive probability. Let $\{c_i\}$ be a sequence of consequences, with $c_{i+1} > c_i$ and $\lim U(c_i) = \bar{u}$, let $E_i = \{s | a(s) > c_i\}$, and define $a^i(s) = c_1$ for $s \in E_i$, $a^i(s) = a(s)$ for $s \in \tilde{E}_i$. Then $a^i(s) \leq c_i$, all s, so that (10-12) and (10-13) are satisfied; (10-14) follows immediately from Dominance, and (10-15) by obvious integration.

If, on the other hand, $\boldsymbol{a}$ is bounded above, let $\{E_i\}$ be any vanishing sequence for which $P(E_i) > 0$, and let $c = \underline{c}$ in (10-12), where $\underline{c}$ is a lower bound for the action $\boldsymbol{a}$. Then again (10-12)–(10-15) are easily seen to hold.

Now let $\boldsymbol{a}$ and $\boldsymbol{b}$ be any two actions bounded below but not necessarily above, and let $\{a^i\}$ and $\{b^j\}$ be corresponding sequences satisfying (10-12)–(10-15). Suppose $\boldsymbol{a} > \boldsymbol{b}$. From (10-12) and Monotone Continuity, with i sufficiently large, $\boldsymbol{a}^i > \boldsymbol{b}$; but $\boldsymbol{b} > \boldsymbol{b}^j$, by (10-14), so that $\boldsymbol{a}^i > \boldsymbol{b}^j$, all j. Since $\boldsymbol{a}^i$ and $\boldsymbol{b}^j$ are bounded,

$$E\{U[a^i(s)]\} > E\{U[b^j(s)]\}, \quad \text{all } j.$$

Let j approach infinity; then $E\{U[a^i(s)]\} \geq E\{U[b(s)]\}$; from (10-15), $E\{U[a(s)]\} > E\{U[b(s)]\}$.

Conversely, suppose $E\{U[a(s)]\} > E\{U[b(s)]\}$. Then for i sufficiently large,

$$E\{U[a^i(s)]\} > E\{U[b(s)]\},$$

and by (10-15),

$$E\{U[a^i(s)]\} > E\{U[b^j(s)]\}.$$

Since a^i and b^j are bounded actions, and the Expected-Utility Theorem has been shown to hold for such actions, $a^i > b^j$. By Monotone Continuity, $a^i \gtrsim b$; by (10-14), $a > b$.

The Expected-Utility Theorem has thus been shown to hold for all actions bounded below. By an exactly parallel argument, its range of applicability can be extended to all pairs of actions.

Not only have we proved the existence of an expected utility function, but we have shown the following theorem.

UTILITY BOUNDEDNESS THEOREM. *Any utility function which satisfies the conditions of the Expected-Utility Theorem must be bounded both from above and from below.*

Personal Probability

A particular class of actions of interest are those which yield only two possible consequences. Such an action is uniquely defined by specifying the more preferred of the two consequences, c^*, the less preferred, c_*, and the event E for which the action yields the consequence c^*; it yields c_* on $\tilde{E}$. An action of this form may, for obvious reasons, be termed a *bet* on E, with *prizes* c^*, c_*. (It is assumed that the two consequences are not indifferent to each other; if they were, the action so defined would also be indifferent to both of the consequences, by Dominance, and preference statements about the action would be independent of the set E.) To avoid a trivial case we assume that not all consequences are indifferent.

The ordering of all actions implies in particular an ordering of bets. It is reasonable to assert, in particular, that the ordering of bets with given consequences is determined exclusively by beliefs concerning the occurrence of the events bet on. If it is preferable to bet on one event rather than another with given prizes for winning and losing, then the same preference should manifest itself if the prizes are altered, as long as the prize for winning is preferred to that for losing. This conclusion is an obvious implication of the Expected-Utility Theorem, for a bet on E_1, with prizes c^*, c_*, is preferred to a bet of E_2 with the same prizes if and only if

$$P(E_1)U(c^*) + [1 - P(E_1)]U(c_*) > P(E_2)U(c^*) + [1 - P(E_2)]U(c_*),$$

which is obviously equivalent to the statement $P(E_1) > P(E_2)$, provided $U(c^*) > U(c_*)$. Changing the prizes does not alter the ordering among bets.

Following Ramsey (1926) and later writers, we drop the assumption of

Probabilistic Beliefs and seek to show that it can in fact be derived merely from the assumption that preferences among bets are independent of the prizes plus a more technical assumption. The argument used here is a paraphrase of Villegas (1964), who first showed that the probability distributions obtained are countably and not merely finitely additive.

Ordering of Events. If E_1 and E_2 are events, and c^*, c_*, $\underline{c}^*$, $\bar{c}_*$ are consequences for which $c^* > c_*$, $\bar{c}^* > \underline{c}_*$, then the bet on E_1 with prizes c^*, c_* is preferred to the bet on E_2 with the same prizes if and only if the bet on E_1 with prizes $\bar{c}^*$, $\underline{c}_*$ is preferred to the bet on E_2 with the same prizes.

In view of this assumption, preferences among bets are statements only about the events involved. It is meaningful then to speak of preference or indifference among events, and we use the obvious notation: thus, $E_1 > E_2$ means that a bet on E_1 is preferred to one on E_2 with the same prizes. (The statement $E_1 > E_2$ might be read "E_1 is more probable than E_2," but for sake of uniformity the language of preference rather than that of probability judgment will be used here.)

The assumptions of Dominance and of Monotone Continuity yield interesting implications for the ordering of events. We will have occasion to single out the *universal event,* consisting of all possible states of the world and denoted by V, and the *empty event,* consisting of no state of the world and denoted by Λ. If c^* and c_* are the winning and losing prizes, a bet on V is simply c^* and a bet on Λ is c_*; since $c^* > c_*$,

(10-16) $V > \Lambda$.

Recall that E is termed a null event if, for all actions a^1 and a^2, $a^1 > a^2$ if and only if $a^1 > a^2|\tilde{E}$. This holds trivially if $E = \Lambda$. A bet on any event E loses, and therefore coincides with a bet on Λ if $\tilde{E}$ holds; hence, $E \sim \Lambda|\tilde{E}$ for any event E. If, in particular, E is a null event, then $E \sim \Lambda$.

(10-17)   A null event is indifferent to the empty event.

(The converse of this statement is also true; see Corollary 5 below.)

Dominance implies an important monotony property for preferences among events.

LEMMA 3 (MONOTONY). *If E_1 is disjoint from E_2, and F_1 from F_2, $E_1 < F_1$ (respectively, $E_1 \lesssim F_1$), and $E_2 \lesssim F_2$, then $E_1 \cup E_2 < F_1 \cup F_2$ (respectively, $E_1 \cup E_2 \lesssim F_1 \cup F_2$).*

Proof. First assume $E_2 = F_2$. Then E_1 and F_1 are both disjoint from F_2; if F_2 occurs, both lose. Then $E_1 = F_1|F_2$, and therefore $E_1 \sim F_1|F_2$. If $E_1 < F_1$, suppose $E_1 \gtrsim F_1|\tilde{F}_2$; by Dominance, $E_1 \gtrsim F_1$, contrary to hypothesis. Hence, $E_1 < F_1|F_2$. Further, if $\tilde{F}_2$ were a null event, we would have $E_1 \sim F_1$, again contrary to hypothesis, so that $\tilde{F}_2$ is nonnull. If, on the other hand, it is hypothesized that $E_1 \lesssim F_1$, suppose $E_1 > F_1|\tilde{F}_2$; then, by Dominance, either $E_1 > F_1$, contrary to hypothesis, or $\tilde{F}_2$ is a null event. Hence, $E_1 \lesssim F_1|\tilde{F}_2$ unless $\tilde{F}_2$ is a null event. Since $E_2 = F_2$ is disjoint from $\tilde{F}_2$, we have trivially $E_1 = E_1 \cup E_2|\tilde{F}_2$, $F_1 = F_1 \cup F_2|\tilde{F}_2$. Then $E_1 \cup E_2 < F_1 \cup F_2|\tilde{F}_2$ if $E_1 < F_1$, while either $E_1 \cup E_2 \lesssim F_1 \cup F_2|\tilde{F}_2$ or $\tilde{F}_2$ is null if $E_1 \lesssim F_1$. Finally, E_2 and F_2 win on F_2, and therefore certainly $E_1 \cup E_2$ and $F_1 \cup F_2$ both win on F_2. Then $E_1 \cup E_2 = F_1 \cup F_2|F_2$. By Dominance, then, $E_1 \cup E_2 < F_1 \cup F_2$ if $E_1 < F_1$. If $E_1 \lesssim F_1$ and $\tilde{F}_2$ is nonnull, Dominance yields that $E_1 \cup E_2 \lesssim F_1 \cup F_2$; if $\tilde{F}_2$ is null, the last holds trivially.

Now remove the hypothesis that $E_2 = F_2$. Let

$$E_2' = E_2 - F_1, \qquad F_1' = F_1 - E_2, \qquad G = E_2 \cap F_1,$$

where $E - F = \{s | s \in E, s \notin F\}$. Then $E_2' \cap F_1 = \Lambda$, $F_1' \cap E_2 = \Lambda$, $E_2' \cup G = E_2$, $F_1' \cup G = F_1$; also, $E_2' \subset E_2$ and thus $E_2' \cap E_1 = \Lambda$, $F_1' \subset F_1$ and thus $F_1' \cap F_2 = \Lambda$, $G \subset E_2$ and therefore $E_1 \cap G = \Lambda$, $G \subset F_1$ and therefore $G \cap F_2 = \Lambda$. By construction, $E_2' \cap G = F_1' \cap G = \Lambda$. Then by use of the lemma for the special case, $E_2 = F_2$, already established,

$$E_1 \cup E_2' < F_1 \cup E_2' = F_1' \cup G \cup E_2' = F_1' \cup E_2 \lesssim F_1' \cup F_2$$
$$\text{if} \quad E_1 < F_1, \qquad E_1 \cup E_2' \lesssim F_1' \cup F_2 \quad \text{if} \quad E_1 \lesssim F_1.$$

But

$$(E_1 \cup E_2') \cap G = (E_1 \cap G) \cup (E_2' \cap G) = \Lambda,$$
$$(F_1' \cup F_2) \cap G = \Lambda,$$

so that

$$E_1 \cup E_2 = E_1 \cup E_2' \cup G < F_1' \cup F_2 \cup G$$
$$= (F_1' \cup G) \cup F_2 = F_1 \cup F_2 \quad \text{if} \quad E_1 < F_1,$$
$$E_1 \cup E_2 \lesssim F_1 \cup F_2 \quad \text{if} \quad E_1 \lesssim F_1.$$

COROLLARY 1 (SUBTRACTION). *If E_1 is disjoint from E_2 and F_1 from F_2, $E_1 \sim F_1$ and $E_1 \cup E_2 \sim F_1 \cup F_2$, then $E_2 \sim F_2$.*

Proof. Suppose $E_2 < F_2$. Then, by Lemma 3 (with subscripts 1 and 2 interchanged), $E_1 \cup E_2 < F_1 \cup F_2$, contrary to hypothesis. Similarly, $E_2 > F_2$ leads to a contradiction.

COROLLARY 2. *If $E \subset F$, then $E \precsim F$.*

Proof. Let $E_1 = F_1 = E$, $E_2 = \Lambda$, $F_2 = F - E$. By Dominance, $\Lambda \precsim F - E$; by Lemma 3, $E = E \cup \Lambda = E_1 \cup E_2 \precsim F_1 \cup F_2 = E \cup (F - E) = F$.

A sequence of events $\{E_i\}$ is said to be *monotone increasing (decreasing)* if $E_i \subset E_{i+1}$, all i ($E_{i+1} \subset E_i$, all i). A sequence is said to be *monotone* if it is either monotone increasing or monotone decreasing. For a monotone increasing sequence, define

$$\lim E_i = \bigcup_{i=1}^{\infty} E_i,$$

and for a monotone decreasing sequence, define

$$\lim E_i = \bigcap_{i=1}^{\infty} E_i.$$

In brief, the statement $\lim E_i = E$ means that either (a) $E_i \subset E$, all i, $\{E - E_i\}$ is a vanishing sequence, or (b) $E \subset E_i$, all i, $\{E_i - E\}$ is a vanishing sequence. In either case, a bet on E_i is an action which differs from a bet on E only on an element of a vanishing sequence. The assumption of Monotone Continuity then immediately yields a specialization to the case of events.

LEMMA 4 (MONOTONE CONTINUITY FOR EVENTS). *If $\lim E_i = E$, then $E > F$ implies that $E_i > F$ for i sufficiently large and $F > E$ implies that $F > E_i$ for i sufficiently large.*

COROLLARY 3. *If $\lim E_i = E$, $\lim F_i = F$, and $E_i \precsim F_i$, for all i, then $E \precsim F$.*

Proof. Suppose $E > F$. By Lemma 4, $E_i > F$ for all $i > I$, for suitably chosen I. For any given $i > I$, it again follows from Lemma 4 that $E_i > F_j$ for $j > J_i$. A contradiction to the hypothesis is achieved if $E_k > F_k$, some k. First suppose $\{E_i\}$ monotone increasing. Choose j so that $E_i > F_j$, $i < j$. But by Corollary 2, $E_j \succsim E_i$ when $\{E_i\}$ is monotone increasing so that we can choose $k = j$. By a parallel argument, the contradiction can also be found if $\{F_i\}$ is monotone decreasing. Suppose now $\{E_i\}$ monotone decreasing, $\{F_i\}$ monotone increasing. Let $k = \min(i,j)$. Then Corollary 2 assures that $E_k \succsim E_i$, $F_j \succsim F_k$; then from $E_i > F_j$, some i and j, follows $E_k > F_k$, a contradiction to the hypothesis.

A particularly interesting type of monotone decreasing sequence is that for which the successor, E_{i+1}, to any given member of the sequence, E_i, is obtained by partitioning E_i into two subevents and choosing for E_{i+1} one subevent which is not preferred to the other. As might be expected, the limit of such a sequence is indifferent to the empty event.

COROLLARY 4. *If $\{E_i\}$ is monotone decreasing, and $E_{i+1} \lesssim E_i - E_{i+1}$ for all i, then lim $E_i \sim \Lambda$.*

Proof.

$$\lim E_i = \bigcap_i E_i \subset E_{j+1} \lesssim E_j - E_{j+1} \subset \bigcup_{i=j}^{\infty} (E_i - E_{i+1}),$$

for any j. Since $E \subset F$ implies $E \lesssim F$ by Corollary 2,

(10-18) $\lim E_i \lesssim \bigcup_{i=j}^{\infty} (E_i - E_{i+1})$ for all j.

But since the events $E_i - E_{i+1}$ are disjoint, the right-hand expression in (10-18) is a vanishing sequence. If $\lim E_i > \Lambda$, (10-18) could not hold for j sufficiently large.

The theorem sought for is one which assigns numbers to events so as to be an indicator of preferences and also to satisfy the assumptions of probability theory. A (countably additive) *probability measure* is a real-valued function of events, $P(E)$, with the following properties:

(10-19) $P(E) \geq 0$,   all E; $P(V) = 1$;

(10-20)   If the events in the sequence $\{E_i\}$ are mutually disjoint, then

$$P\left(\bigcup_{i=1}^{\infty} E_i\right) = \sum_{i=1}^{\infty} P(E_i).$$

If $E_i = \Lambda$ for all i, then $\bigcup_{i=1}^{\infty} E_i = \Lambda$, so that (10-20) implies

$$P(\Lambda) = \sum_{i=1}^{\infty} P(\Lambda),$$

which is possible only if $P(\Lambda) = 0$. Now if we set $E_i = \Lambda$ for $i > 2$ in (10-19), $\bigcup_{i=1}^{\infty} E_i = E_1 \cup E_2$, and $P(E_i) = 0$ for $i > 2$, so that (10-20) implies the property of finite additivity,

(10-21)   If E_1 and E_2 are disjoint, then $P(E_1 \cup E_2) = P(E_1) + P(E_2)$.

A real-valued function on events satisfying (10-19) and (10-21) is termed a *finitely additive probability measure*. Since $\Lambda = \Lambda \cup \Lambda$, $P(\Lambda) = P(\Lambda) + P(\Lambda)$ or $P(\Lambda) = 0$. Also, for any event E, $V = E \cup \tilde{E}$, so that $1 = P(V) = P(E \cup \tilde{E}) = P(E) + P(\tilde{E})$, $P(E) \geq 0$, from (10-21) and (10-19).

(10-22)   If P is a finitely-additive probability measure, $1 \geq P(E)$ for all events E, and $P(\Lambda) = 0$.

A finitely- or countably-additive probability measure will be said to *agree* with a given ordering of events if $E > F$ if and only if $P(E) > P(F)$. Under the assumptions already made, particularly that of Monotone Continuity, we can show the following lemma.

LEMMA 5.   *A finitely-additive probability measure which agrees with the ordering of events is countably additive.*

Proof. By induction, (10-21) implies that if the events $E_i (i = 1, \ldots, n)$ are mutually disjoint, then

$$P\left(\bigcup_{i=1}^{n} E_i \right) = \sum_{i=1}^{n} P(E_i).$$

Now let the events in the infinite sequence $\{E_i\}$ be mutually disjoint. We can write

$$\bigcup_{i=1}^{\infty} E_i = \bigcup_{i=1}^{j} E_i \cup \bigcup_{i=j+1}^{\infty} E_i.$$

The right-hand side is a finite union of mutually disjoint events, so that

(10-23) $$P\left(\bigcup_{i=1}^{\infty} E_i \right) = \sum_{i=1}^{j} P(E_i) + P\left(\bigcup_{i=j+1}^{\infty} E_i \right).$$

From (10-22) and (10-19),

$$P\left(\bigcup_{i=1}^{\infty} E_i \right) \leq 1, \qquad P\left(\bigcup_{i=j+1}^{\infty} E_i \right) \geq 0.$$

so that, from (10-23),

$$\sum_{i=1}^{j} P(E_i) \leq 1, \quad \text{all } j.$$

Since $P(E_i) \geqq 0$, all i, $\Sigma_{i=1}^{j} P(E_i)$ converges as j approaches infinity, and therefore $P(E_i) \rightarrow 0$ or, for any ϵ, $P(E_i) < \epsilon$ for all i sufficiently large. There are two possibilities: (a) $0 < P(E_k) < \epsilon$ for some k, or (b) $P(E_i) = 0$ for all i sufficiently large.

(a) Since the probability measure P agrees with the ordering, $E_k > \Lambda$. The sequence $\{\cup_{i=j+1}^{\infty} E_i\}$ is a vanishing sequence (that is, approaching Λ), so that, for all j sufficiently large, $E_k > \cup_{i=j+1}^{\infty} E_i$, and therefore

$$ P\left(\bigcup_{i=j+1}^{\infty} E_i \right) < P(E_k) < \epsilon. $$

Countable additivity (10-20) follows by letting j approach infinity in (10-23).

(b) Choose j so that $P(E_i) = 0$ for all $i > j$. Then $E_i \sim \Lambda$ for $i > j$. By Corollary 3, $\cup_{i=j+1}^{\infty} E_i \sim \cup_{i=j+1}^{\infty} \Lambda = \Lambda$, so that

$$ P\left(\bigcup_{i=j+1}^{\infty} E_i \right) = P(\Lambda) = 0 = \sum_{i=j+1}^{\infty} P(E_i), $$

and countable additivity again follows from (10-23).

In view of Lemma 5, it suffices to establish the existence of a finitely-additive probability measure agreeing with the ordering.

In the assumption of Probabilistic Beliefs, it was postulated that the probability measure be atomless. An assumption will now be introduced on the ordering of events which has the same effect but does not presuppose the existence of a probability measure.

Atomlessness. If $E > \Lambda$, then there is a subset E_1 of E such that $E > E_1 > \Lambda$.

To clarify the exposition, a stronger assumption will be made in this section.

Equidivisibility. Any event E can be partitioned into disjoint subevents E_1, E_2, where $E_1 \cup E_2 = E$ and $E_1 \sim E_2$.

To see that Equidivisibility implies Atomlessness, suppose $E > \Lambda$. Since $\Lambda \subset E_1 \subset E$, $E \geq E_1 \geq \Lambda$. Suppose $E_1 \sim \Lambda$. Then $E_2 \sim \Lambda$ and, by Lemma 3, $E = E_1 \cup E_2 \sim \Lambda \cup \Lambda = \Lambda$, a contradiction. Clearly, $E = E_1|E_1$ since $E_1 \subset E$, and $E = E_1|\tilde{E}$ since both lose there; also, $E > E_1|E_2$ since E wins and E_1 loses. By Dominance, $E > E_1$ unless E_2 is a null event, and therefore indifferent to Λ by (10-17). But then $E_1 \sim \Lambda$, which has already been seen to lead to a contradiction. Hence, $E > E_1 > \Lambda$. The converse implication, that Atomlessness implies Equidivisibility, requires relatively advanced tools, and its proof is deferred to the last section of this chapter.

By Equidivisibility, the universal event can be divided into two mutually indifferent disjoint events, each of them can be similarly subdivided, and so forth. Thus, there is a sequence of partitions of the universal event, where the nth partition, say P_n, consists of 2^n mutually indifferent events, and P_{n+1} is derived from P_n by splitting each member of the latter into two mutually indifferent events. Intuitively, it is reasonable to ascribe the probability $1/2^n$ to any members of P_n and therefore the probability $m/2^n$ to any union of m members of P_n and the same probability to any event indifferent to a union of m members of P_n. Any event not assigned a probability by this process can be assigned one as the limit of a suitable sequence of approximations.

More formally, note that it can be deduced from Lemma 3, by induction, that all unions of m members of P_n are indifferent to each other. For any event E, let $m_n(E)$ be the largest m such that E is preferred or indifferent to a union of m members of P_n. Let S_n be a union of m_n members of P_n. It is also a union of $2m_n$ members of P_{n+1} so that, by definition of m_{n+1}, $m_{n+1} \geq 2m_n$, and therefore $m_{n+1}/2^{n+1} \geq m_n/2^n$. Since also $m_n \leq 2^n$, all n, the sequence $\{m_n/2^n\}$ is monotone increasing and bounded from above. Define

$$(10\text{-}24) \qquad P(E) = \lim_{n \to \infty} m_n(E)/2^n.$$

It is to be shown that $P(E)$ is a finitely additive probability measure and agrees with the given ordering of events; it will then be a probability measure by Lemma 5.

Since V is the union of all members of P_n, $m_n(V) = 2^n$, all n, and therefore $P(V) = 1$; thus, (10-19) holds.

Let $E = E_1 \cup E_2$, where E_1 and E_2 are disjoint. Suppose $m_n(E_1) + m_n(E_2) \geq 2^n$. Let $m'_n = 2^n - m_n(E_1)$; then $m'_n \leq m_n(E_2)$. Let S_n be a union of $m_n(E_1)$ members of P_n; $\tilde{S}_n$ is the union of m'_n members of P_n. Then $E_1 \succsim S_n$ and $E_2 \succsim \tilde{S}_n$, so that, by Lemma 3, $E \succsim V$. Obviously, then, $E \sim V$, which is possible only if $E_1 \sim S_n$ and $E_2 \sim \tilde{S}_n$. In this case, $P(E_1) = m_n(E_1)/2^n$, $P(E_2) = m'_n/2^n = m_n(E_2)/2^n$, and $P(E) = 1 = P(E_1) + P(E_2)$, so that (10-20) holds.

Now suppose that $m_n(E_1) + m_n(E_2) < 2^n$. Let $S_n(E_1)$, $S_n(E_2)$ be unions of $m_n(E_1)$, $m_n(E_2)$ members of P_n, respectively, so chosen that $S_n(E_1) \cap S_n(E_2) = \Lambda$. Then, by Lemma 3, $E \succsim S_n(E_1) \cup S_n(E_2)$, so that $m_n(E) \geq$

$m_n(E_1) + m_n(E_2)$. Suppose

(10-25) $m_n(E) \geqq m_n(E_1) + m_n(E_2) + 2$.

Let $T_n(E_1)$ be a union of $m_n(E_1) + 1$ members of P_n, $T_n(E_2)$ a union of $m_n(E_2) + 1$ members of P_n, so chosen that $T_n(E_1) \cap T_n(E_2) = \Lambda$. Then $T_n(E_1) \cup T_n(E_2)$ has $m_n(E_1) + m_n(E_2) + 2$ members, so that from the definition of $m_n(E)$ and the assumed inequality (10-25), $E \gtrsim T_n(E_1) \cup T_n(E_2)$. On the other hand, from the definitions of $m_n(E_1)$, $m_n(E_2)$, we must have $T_n(E_1) > E_1$, $T_n(E_2) > E_2$ and, by Lemma 3, $T_n(E_1) \cup T_n(E_2) > E_1 \cup E_2 = E$. The inequality (10-25) leads to a contradiction.

$$m_n(E_1) + m_n(E_2) \leqq m_n(E) \leqq m_n(E_1) + m_n(E_2) + 1.$$

If all terms in this inequality are divided by 2^n and we let n approach infinity, (10-21) is deduced.

It remains then to show that $P(E)$ agrees with the ordering. If $P(E_1) > P(E_2)$, then $m_n(E_1) > m_n(E_2)$ for some n. If S is the union of $m_n(E_1)$ members of the partition P_n, then $E_1 \gtrsim S > E_2$, by definition of m_n. It remains to establish the converse implication: that $P(E_1) = P(E_2)$ implies $E_1 \sim E_2$. First consider the special case where $E_2 = \Lambda$; then we seek to show that $P(E) = 0$ implies $E \sim \Lambda$. In this case, $m_n = 0$ for all n. If E_n is any member of P_n, $E_n > E$. We can choose E_{n+1} to be one of the two mutually indifferent subevents of E_n in P_{n+1}. Then $E_{n+1} \subset E_n$, and $E_{n+1} \sim E_n - E_{n+1}$. By Corollary 4, $\lim E_n \sim \Lambda$. By Corollary 3, $\lim E_n \gtrsim E$; hence, $E \sim \Lambda$.

Now consider the general case where $P(E_1) = P(E_2)$. Assme $E_1 \lesssim E_2$. Then $m_n(E_2) \geqq m_n(E_1)$, all n. Let S_n be a union of $m_n(E_1)$ members of P_n, T_n a union of $m_n(E_2) + 1$ members of P_n. Then $S_n \lesssim E_1, E_2 < T_n$. Further, we can choose S_n, T_n, so that $\{S_n\}$ is an increasing sequence, $\{T_n\}$ a decreasing sequence, and $S_n \subset T_n$ for all n. To see this, suppose it has already been carried out up to stage n. $T_n - S_n$ is the union of one or more members of P_n. Also, T_n is the union of $2[m_n(E_2) + 1]$ members of P_{n+1}; then $m_{n+1}(E_2) < 2[m_n(E_2) + 1]$, so that $m_{n+1}(E_2) = 2m_n(E_2)$ or $= 2m_n(E_2) + 1$. In the latter case, let $T_{n+1} = T_n$; in the former, subtract from T_n one member of P_{n+1} entirely contained in $T_n - S_n$. In either case, $T_{n+1} - S_n$ is the union of one or more members of P_{n+1}. Similarly, $m_{n+1}(E_1) = 2m_n(E_1)$ or $= 2m_n(E_1) + 1$. In the first case, let $S_{n+1} = S_n$; in the second, add to S_n one member of P_{n+1} entirely contained in $T_{n+1} - S_n$.

The sequences $\{S_n\}$ and $\{T_n\}$ converge to limits S and T respectively, with

$S \subset T$. Since $S_n \lesssim E_1$, $S \lesssim E_1$; similarly, $E_2 \lesssim T$. Also

$$P(S_n) = m_n(E_1)/2^n.$$

Since $S_n \subset S_{n+1}$, $S_{n+1} = S_n \cup (S_{n+1} - S_n)$, with the latter two sets disjoint;

$$P(S_{n+1} - S_n) = P(S_{n+1}) - P(S_n).$$

$S = \cup_{i=1}^{\infty} S_i = S_1 \cup \cup_{i=1}^{\infty} (S_{i+1} - S_i) = S_1 \cup \cup_{i=1}^{j} (S_{i+1} - S_i)$
$\cup \cup_{i=j+1}^{\infty} (S_{i+1} - S_i)$ so that, by finite additivity,

$$P(S) = P(S_1) + \sum_{i=1}^{j} P(S_{i+1} - S_i) + P\left[\bigcup_{i=j+1}^{\infty} (S_{i+1} - S_i) \right]$$

$$\geq P(S_1) + \sum_{i=1}^{j} [P(S_{i+1}) - P(S_i)]$$

$$= P(S_{j+1}),$$

and, since $\{P(S_{j+1})\}$ is a monotone increasing, bounded sequence of real numbers,

$$P(S) \geq \lim P(S_n) = P(E_1).$$

Similarly, since $P(T_n) = [m_n(E_2) + 1]/2^n$ and $V - T = \cup_{i=1}^{\infty} (V - T_i)$, it can be deduced that $P(V - T) \geq \lim P(V - T_n)$, and therefore $P(T) \leq \lim P(T_n) = P(E_2)$. Since $S \subset T$, $0 \leq P(T - S) = P(T) - P(S) \leq \lim P(T_n) - \lim P(S_n) = P(E_2) - P(E_1) = 0$ by assumption. Then, as just shown, $T - S \sim \Lambda$. Since $S \lesssim E_1$, $T = S \cup (T - S) \lesssim E_1 \cup \Lambda = E_1$. Since $T \gtrsim E_2 \gtrsim E_1$, it must be that $E_1 \sim E_2$.

PERSONAL PROBABILITY THEOREM. *Under the assumptions of Ordering, Monotone Continuity, Conditional Preference, Ordering of Events, and Equidivisibility, there is a probability measure, $P(E)$, defined over events such that for any two events, E_1 and E_2, a bet on E_1 is preferred to a bet on E_2 with the same prizes if and only if $P(E_1) > P(E_2)$.*

COROLLARY 5. *An event is null if and only if its probability is zero.*

Proof. For any event E, it follows by definition and the Ordering of Events that $E = \Lambda | \tilde{E}$, $E > \Lambda | E$; by Dominance, if E is nonnull, then $E > \Lambda$, and therefore $E \sim \Lambda$ implies E null. The converse has already been stated as (10-17) above. But by the theorem, $E \sim \Lambda$ if and only if $P(E) = P(\Lambda) = 0$.

Probabilistic Beliefs

It remains to prove that the probabilities which reproduce the ordering of events also suffice to permit the representation of the ordering of actions in general (not merely bets) by expected utilities. In view of the analysis of the third section, it suffices to show that the assumption of Probabilistic Beliefs follows from the assumptions used in the hypothesis of the Personal Probability Theorem; in fact, from the Remark following the assumption of Probabilistic Beliefs, it suffices to prove the following theorem.

THEOREM OF PROBABILISTIC BELIEFS. *If* a *and* b *are actions which yield as possible consequences* $c_i(i = 1, \ldots, n)$ *and if* $P[a(s) = c_i] = P[b(s) = c_i]$ *(i = 1, \ldots, n) then* $a \sim b$.

Proof. We will establish the following apparently more general theorem.

(10-26)   If $c_i(i = 1, \ldots, n)$ are all the consequences yielded by a or b for $s \in E$, and $P[a(s) = c_i|E] = P[b(s) = c_i|E]$ for all i, then $a \sim b|E$, provided $P(E) > 0$.

First, note that if the theorem holds for any n, then (10-26) holds for that n. Suppose a, b have the properties hypothesized in (10-26). Define actions a^*, b^* as follows: $a^*(s) = a(s), b^*(s) = b(s)$ for $s \in E; a^*(s) = b^*(s) = c_1$ for $s \in \tilde{E}$. Then the conclusion, $a \sim b|E$, is equivalent to the statement, $a^* \sim b^*|E$, by Conditional Preference, and it suffices to establish the latter. Since $P(E) > 0$, E is nonnull by Corollary 5. Since $a^* = b^*|\tilde{E}$, $a^* > b^*|E$ would imply $a^* > b^*$, and similarly $a^* < b^*|E$ would imply $a^* < b^*$. Therefore, $a^* \sim b^*$ implies that $a^* \sim b^*|E$. But

$$P[a^*(s) = c_i] = P[a^*(s) = c_i|E]P(E) + P[a^*(s) = c_i|\tilde{E}]P(\tilde{E}).$$

$P[a^*(s) = c_i|E] = P[a(s) = c_i|E]; P[a^*(s) = c_1|\tilde{E}] = 1, P[a^*(s) = c_i|\tilde{E}] = 0$ for $i > 1$. Similar remarks apply to b^* and b. Then, clearly

$$P[a^*(s) = c_i] = P[b^*(s) = c_i] \quad (i = 1, \ldots, n),$$

so that

(10-27)   If the theorem holds for any n, so does (10-26).

Next observe that the Personal Probability Theorem implies the Theorem of Probabilistic Beliefs for the case $n = 2$; for if $c_1 \sim c_2$, the conclusion holds by Dominance, while if c_1 is not indifferent to c_2 and c^* is the more preferred of the two, actions a and b are bets on the sets $\{s|a(s) = c^*\}$ and $\{s|b(s) = c^*\}$, respectively; since these are equally probable by hypothesis, the actions are indifferent by the Personal Probability Theorem.

Assume, then, the theorem, and therefore (10-26) valid for 2 and $n - 1$ consequences. Let

$$F = \{s | a(s) \neq c_n, b(s) = c_n\}, \qquad G = \{s | a(s) = c_n, b(s) \neq c_n\},$$
$$F_i = \{s | a(s) = c_i, b(s) = c_n\}.$$

Note that the sets F_i are disjoint and $F = \bigcup_{i=1}^{n-1} F_i$.

$$\{s | a(s) = c_n\} = G \cup \{s | a(s) = c_n, b(s) = c_n\},$$
$$\{s | b(s) = c_n\} = F \cup \{s | a(s) = c_n, b(s) = c_n\}.$$

The right-hand sides of these two expressions are unions of disjoint events, while the left-hand sides have the same probabilities, by hypothesis. Then

$$P(G) + P[a(s) = c_n, b(s) = c_n] = P(F) + P[a(s) = c_n, b(s) = c_n],$$

or

$$P(G) = P(F) = \sum_{i=1}^{n-1} P(F_i).$$

Then we can partition G into mutually disjoint subevents, $G_i (i = 1, \ldots, n - 1)$, such that $P(G_i) = P(F_i)$ $(i = 1, \ldots, n - 1)$. To see this, apply Equidivisibility m successive times to G so that G is expressed as the sum of 2^m equally probable events. For any fixed i, choose p_{im} as the largest integer p for which $p/2^m \leq P(F_i)/P(F)$. Let S_{im} be the union of p_{im} events in this partition; choose them in particular so that the different unions, S_{im}, for fixed m, are disjoint and also so that $S_{im} \subset S_{im+1}$. Let $G_i = \lim_{m \to \infty} S_{im}$; then, clearly $G_i \subset G$, $P(G_i) = P(F_i)$. The union of the events G_i can then differ from G by at most a set of probability zero, and this can be added to one of the G_i's.

Now define a finite sequence of actions, $a^i (i = 1, \ldots, n)$, as follows:

$$a^1 = a$$

$$(10\text{-}28) \qquad a^{i+1}(s) = \begin{cases} c_n & \text{for } s \in F_i \\ c_i & \text{for } s \in G_i, \\ a^i(s) & \text{for all other } s. \end{cases}$$

Since G and F are disjoint by definition, G_i and F_j are disjoint for all $i, j \leq n - 1$. By induction, it is easily seen that

$$(10\text{-}29) \qquad a^i(s) = \begin{cases} c_j & \text{for } s \in F_j \quad (\text{all } j \geq i), \\ c_n & \text{for } s \in G_j \quad (\text{all } j \geq i). \end{cases}$$

We need to prove that

(10-30) $a^i \sim a^{i+1}$.

From (10-28), $a^{i+1}(s) = a^i(s)$ for $s \notin G_i \cup F_i$. If $G_i \cup F_i$ is null, then (10-30) holds. Otherwise, to prove (10-30) it suffices to show that

(10-31) $a^i \sim a^{i+1}|G_i \cup F_i$.

But from (10-28) and (10-29) with $j = i$, both a^i and a^{i+1} take on only the two values c_i and c_n on $F_i \cup G_i$; further, since $P(F_i) = P(G_i)$ and $P(G_i \cup F_i) > 0$ by Corollary 5, $P(F_i|F_i \cup G_i) = P(G_i|F_i \cup G_i)$ so that $P[a^{i+1}(s) = c_i|F_i \cup G_i] = P[a^i(s) = c_i|F_i \cup G_i]$ and $P[a^{i+1}(s) = c_n|F_i \cup G_i] = P[a^i(s) = c_n|F_i \cup G_i]$. Since (10-26) holds with $n = 2$, (10-31) holds, and therefore (10-30).

The same calculations also show immediately that

(10-32) $P[a^{i+1}(s) = c_j] = P[a^i(s) = c_j]$,   all j.

From (10-30), it follows by induction that $a^1 \sim a^n$; since $a^1 = a$, it remains to show that $a^n \sim b$, in which case the theorem has been shown to hold for n consequences.

From (10-32), it follows by induction that

$$P[a^1(s) = c_j] = P[a^n(s) = c_j],   \text{all } j.$$

Since $a^1 = a$, it follows from the hypothesis that a and b yield the same probability distribution of consequences that

(10-33) $P[a^n(s) = c_j] = P[b(s) = c_j]$,   all j.

From (10-28), it follows by induction that $a^i(s) = c_n$ if and only if either $a(s) = b(s) = c_n$ or

$$s \in \bigcup_{j=1}^{i-1} F_j \cup \bigcup_{j=i}^{n-1} G_j.$$

In particular, let $i = n$; then $a^n(s) = c_n$ if and only if either $a(s) = b(s) = c_n$ or $s \in \bigcup_{j=1}^{n-1} F_j = F$. From the definition of F,

(10-34) $a^n(s) = c_n$ if and only if $b(s) = c_n$.

If $b(s) = c_n$ with probability 1, then the set $\{s|b(s) \neq c_n\}$ is a null set, and $a^n \sim b$, trivially. Otherwise, it follows immediately from (10-33) and (10-34) that

$$P[a^n(s) = c_j|b(s) \neq c_n] = P[b(s) = c_j|b(s) \neq c_n],   \text{all } j < n.$$

But from (10-34), actions a^n and b take only the $n-1$ consequences $c_j(j < n)$ on the set $\{s|b(s) \neq c_n\}$; by (10-26), for $n-1$ consequences, $a^n \sim b|b(s) \neq c_n$. Since $a^n = b|b(s) = c_n$ by (10-34), $a^n \sim b$ by Dominance, and the theorem has been demonstrated.

Atomlessness Implies Equidivisibility

It will now be shown that the assumption of Atomlessness implies that of Equidivisibility in the presence of the other assumptions.[4] The proof is essentially that of Villegas (1964). First, two implications of Atomlessness are developed.

LEMMA 6. *If $E > \Lambda$, there is a monotone decreasing sequence $\{E_i\}$ such that $E_i \subset E$, $E_i > \Lambda$, for all i, lim $E_i \sim \Lambda$.*

Proof. Let $E_1 = E$. If E_i has been defined and $E_i > \Lambda$, Atomlessness permits us to choose E'_{i+1} so that $E'_{i+1} \subset E_i$, $E_i > E'_{i+1} > \Lambda$. If $E_i - E'_{i+1} \sim \Lambda$, then $E_i \sim E'_{i+1}$ by Monotony, a contradiction; hence $E_i - E'_{i+1} > \Lambda$. Let $E_{i+1} = E'_{i+1}$ if $E'_{i+1} \lesssim E_i - E'_{i+1}$ and $E_{i+1} = E_i - E'_{i+1}$ otherwise. Then $E_{i+1} > \Lambda$, $E_{i+1} \lesssim E_i - E_{i+1}$. By Corollary 4, lim $E_i \sim \Lambda$.

LEMMA 7. *Any family of mutually disjoint events, each preferred to the empty event, must be finite or denumerably infinite.*

Proof. Let $E = V$ in Lemma 6, and construct the sequence $\{E_i\}$, with $E_i > \Lambda$, all i, lim $E_i \sim \Lambda$. If any event is preferred to Λ, then it is preferred to E_i for i sufficiently large (Lemma 4). Hence, it suffices for the proof of the lemma to show that for any given E_i there are at most finitely many events in the given family which are preferred to E_i.

Suppose not. Then for some i there is a sequence $\{F_j\}$ such that $F_j > E_i$, all j, and the sets F_j are disjoint. Let $G_n = \cup_{j=n}^{\infty} F_j$; then $F_j \subset G_j$ so that $G_j > E_i$, all j. But the sequence $\{G_n\}$ is vanishing. By Lemma 4, if $E_i > \Lambda$, then $G_j < E_i$, some j, a contradiction.

To prove that Atomlessness implies Equidivisibility, it appears necessary to appeal to one of a group of theorems in set theory closely related to the axiom of choice; typical examples are the Hausdorff maximal principle, Zorn's lemma, or the proposition that every set can be well ordered. For an excellent brief exposition, see Kelley (1955, pp. 31–36). The particular theorem which seems simplest to use here is a lemma due to Tukey. A family

---

4. I am indebted to H. L. Royden for a very helpful discussion relative to this section.

of sets is said to be of *finite character* if a necessary and sufficient condition for a set to belong to the family is that every finite subset belongs to the family. A set is said to be *maximal* in a family if it belongs to the family and is not a proper subset of any member of the family.

TUKEY'S LEMMA. *Each family of finite character has a maximal set.*

In what follows, we start with a fixed event E, where $E > \Lambda$. We seek to construct $E_1 \subset E$ so that $E_1 \sim E - E_1$. All events to be considered are subevents of E. An event F will be termed *minor* if $F \lesssim E - F$. Tukey's lemma will be applied to a family of collections of events. Specifically, the family consists of all collections of events such that (a) each event is preferred to the null event; (b) the events in the collection are mutually disjoint; and (c) the union of all the events in any finite subcollection is a minor event. This family is obviously of finite character, so there is a maximal collection K in the family.

Since K satisfies (a) and (b), it can have at most denumerably many members by Lemma 7. Let the events in K then be represented as the sequence $\{F_i\}$. Then by (c),

$$\bigcup_{i=1}^{n} F_i \lesssim E - \bigcup_{i=1}^{n} F_i, \quad \text{all } n.$$

The left-hand side is a monotone increasing sequence, the right-hand side monotone decreasing; by Corollary 3,

(10-34) $\quad E_1 \lesssim E - E_1,$

where E_1 is the union of all events in K.

From (10-34), $E - E_1 > \Lambda$ (otherwise $E \sim \Lambda$). By Lemma 6, there is a sequence $\{G_i\}$, with $G_i \subset E - E_1$, $G_i > \Lambda$, $\lim G_i \sim \Lambda$. Then G_i is disjoint from any event in K. Let K_i be the collection of events consisting of G_i and all members of K. Then K_i properly includes K and satisfies conditions (a) and (b) above. Since K is maximal in the family defined by (a), (b), and (c), K_i must violate (c). There is a finite subcollection of K_i whose union is preferred to its complement with respect to E. But the union of all events in K_i certainly includes the union of any finite subcollection, and the complement of the larger set is included in the complement of the smaller, so that the union of events in K_i is preferred to its complement. The union of events in K_i is clearly $E_1 \cup G_i$.

$$E_1 \cup G_i > E - (E_1 \cup G_i), \quad \text{all } i.$$

The sequences on the two sides are both monotone; by taking limits we have

$$E_1 \gtrsim E - E_1,$$

which, together with (10-34), establishes Equidivisibility, as desired.

References

Bernoulli, D. (1738), "Specimen Theoriae Novae de Mensura Sortis," *Commentarii Academiae Scientiarum Imperialis Petropolitanae 5*, 175–192. English translation by L. Sommer (1954), "Exposition of a New Theory on the Measurement of Risk," *Econometrica, 22*, 23–26.

Debreu, G. (1960), "Topological Methods in Cardinal Utility Theory," chap. 2 in K. J. Arrow, S. Karlin, and P. Suppes (eds.), *Mathematical Methods in the Social Sciences*, Stanford University Press, Stanford, pp. 16–26.

De Finetti, B. (1937), "La prévision: ses lois logiques, ses sources subjectives," *Annales de l'Institut Henri Poincaré 7*, 1–68. English translation by H. E. Kyburg (1964), in Kyburg and Smokler (eds.), *Studies in Subjective Probability*, Wiley, New York, pp. 95–158.

Fishburn, P. C. (1966), "A Note on Recent Developments in Additive Utility Theories for Multiple-Factor Situations," *Operations Research, 14*, 1143–1148.

Kelley, J. L. (1955), *General Topology*, Van Nostrand, New York.

Menger, K. (1934), "Das Unsicherheitsmoment in der Wertlehre, Betrachtungen im Anschluss an das sogenannte Petersburger Spiel," *Zeitschrift für Nationalökonomie, 5*, 459–485.

Ramsey, F. P. (1926), "Truth and Probability," chap. 7 in F. P. Ramsey (1950), *The Foundations of Mathematics and Other Logical Essays*, The Humanities Press, New York, pp. 156–198.

Samuelson, P. A. (1947), *Foundations of Economic Analysis*, Harvard University Press, Cambridge [enlarged ed., 1983].

Savage, L. J. (1954), *The Foundations of Statistics*, Wiley, New York.

Shackle, G. L. S. (1952), *Expectation in Economics* (2nd ed.), Cambridge University Press, Cambridge.

Villegas, C. (1964), "On Quantitative Probability σ-Algebras," *Annals of Mathematical Statistics, 35*, 1787–1796.

von Neumann, J., and O. Morgenstern (1944), *Theory of Games and Economic Behavior* (1st ed.), Princeton University Press, Princeton (see also 3rd ed., 1953).

11 The Use of Unbounded Utility Functions in Expected-Utility Maximization: Response

Karl Menger noted that if expected utility is to discriminate among all possible alternative probability distributions of returns, the utility function must be bounded.[1] This proposition has been restated several times since (see Terence Ryan's note for two of the references),[2] but clearly meets with a good deal of resistance. Ryan has introduced a new element into the discussion: If the range of probability distributions is restricted, the range of utility functions that permit discrimination among them is correspondingly increased.

This brief comment makes two points. (1) Although Ryan's results permit a relaxation of the requirement that utility be bounded *above,* no corresponding relaxation of the lower boundedness of the utility function is made or seems possible along the lines of his approach; and, indeed, stronger assumptions than usual are made about the derivatives of the utility function at zero wealth. (2) In the case where the utility function is assumed concave (displaying risk aversion) and monotone increasing, Ryan's theorem is applicable only in the case $n = 1$, but then the result holds under more general conditions; specifically, the finiteness of the marginal utility at the origin is not needed.

1. K. Menger, "Das Unsicherheitsmoment in der Wertlehre," *Zeitschrift für National-ökonomie,* 5 (1934), 459–485.
2. T. M. Ryan, "The Use of Unbounded Utility Functions in Expected-Utility Maximization," *Quarterly Journal of Economics,* 88 (Feb. 1974), 133–135.

Reprinted from *Quarterly Journal of Economics,* 88 (1974):136–138, by permission of John Wiley and Sons.

1. Ryan clearly assumes the finiteness of the first n derivatives everywhere, in particular at the origin. Indeed, the latter assumption is used explicitly in the first equation in his proof. It follows that utility is bounded below except in the unlikely case that $U(x)$ approaches $-\infty$ as x approaches $+\infty$, which implies that for *every* wealth level x, there is a *larger* value x', which is regarded as inferior. Income would indeed have to be a burden for this to hold.

I thought that perhaps Ryan's assumptions could be weakened to assume finiteness of utility and its first $n-1$ derivatives only for $x > 0$. Clearly, his proof would be equally valid if $U(x)$ were expanded in a Taylor series about some $x_0 > 0$. But if the nth derivative is uniformly bounded for $x > 0$, it is easy to prove, by downward induction, that $U^{(r)}(x)$ is bounded above and below by polynomials of degree $n-r$ on the interval $(0, x_0)(r \leqq n)$. Hence, $U^{(r)}(0)$ must be bounded for each such r. Therefore, there is no generalization of the results along these lines.

2. In the case of risk aversion, we assume that $U(x)$ is concave and also monotone increasing. Then $U'(x)$ is monotone decreasing but bounded from below by zero. Since, as noted, it is assumed that $U'(0)$ is finite, it follows without further assumptions that $U'(x)$ is uniformly bounded, between $U'(0)$ and 0. Ryan's theorem 2 for the case $n = 1$ then implies the following proposition.

PROPOSITION. *If $U(x)$ is concave and monotone increasing, $U'(0)$ is finite, and $E(x)$ is finite, then expected utility is finite.*

It might be thought from Ryan's theorem with $n > 1$ that even if $E(x)$ is not finite, there may be cases when expected utility exists. But this cannot happen; specifically, if the nth moment is finite for any n, $E(x)$ must be finite. To see this, note that

$$E(x^n) = \int_0^{+\infty} x^n \phi(x)\, dx = \lim_{\substack{a \to 0 \\ b \to +\infty}} \int_a^b x^n \phi(x)\, dx$$

$$= \lim_{b \to +\infty} \int_1^b x^n \phi(x)\, dx + \lim_{a \to 0} \int_a^1 x^n \phi(x)\, dx.$$

Since $x^n \phi(x)$ is nonnegative, the terms

$$\int_1^b x^n \phi(x)\, dx \quad \text{and} \quad \int_a^1 x^n \phi(x)\, dx$$

are monotone increasing in b and monotone decreasing in a, respectively. Hence, their limits exist if and only if they are bounded above.

For $x \geq 1$, $x \leq x^n$, so that

$$\int_1^b x\phi(x)\,dx \leq \int_1^b x^n\phi(x)\,dx \leq \int_1^{+\infty} x^n\phi(x)\,dx,$$

and the last expression is finite by hypothesis. Also, for $x \leq 1$,

$$\int_a^1 x\phi(x)\,dx \leq \int_a^1 \phi(x)\,dx \leq \int_0^1 \phi(x)\,dx,$$

and the last expression is finite, being the probability that $x \leq 1$. Hence, the existence of $E(x^n)$ for $n > 1$ entails the existence of $E(x)$, and the proposition given above is the most general that can be deduced from Ryan's theorem for the case of risk aversion.

However, by a slightly different argument, it can be shown that the hypothesis of a finite marginal utility of wealth at 0 can be dropped completely. If $U(x)$ is constant, the finiteness of expected utility is trivial, so let us assume that utility is monotone increasing but not constant. Then $U'(x_0) > 0$ for some $x_0 > 0$. By a well-known property of concave functions,

$$U(x) \leq U(x_0) + U'(x_0)(x - x_0),$$

so that

(11-1) $U(x) - U(0) \leq U'(x_0)x + A,$

where

$$A = U(x_0) - U(0) - U'(x_0)x_0$$

is a constant. Since $U(x)$ is monotone increasing, $[U(x) - U(0)]\phi(x)$ is nonnegative, and therefore

(11-2) $\int_a^b [U(x) - U(0)]\phi(x)\,dx$

is monotone increasing in b and monotone decreasing in a. The existence of $E[U(x)]$ is equivalent to that of $E[U(x) - U(0)]$ and therefore to the boundedness of (11-2). But from (11-1),

$$\int_a^b [U(x) - U(0)]\phi(x)\,dx \leq U'(x_0)\int_a^b x\phi(x)\,dx + A\int_a^b \phi(x)\,dx$$

$$\leq U'(x_0)E(x) + A.$$

THEOREM. *If $U(x)$ is concave and monotone increasing with $U(0)$ finite, and if $E(x)$ is finite, then expected utility is finite.*

12　Optimal Insurance and Generalized Deductibles

In a paper on the economics of medical care (Arrow, 1963), I developed an explanation of deductibles in insurance policies as an optimal response to administrative costs. The assumptions were, however, restrictive; it was assumed that any illness (or other loss) was equivalent to a monetary loss. In this chapter I came back to the subject with a view that the utility function might itself be differently shaped under different illnesses.

This study is intended as a contribution to the theory of demand for insurance. In many circumstances it appears that, given a range of alternative possible insurance policies, the insured would prefer a policy offering complete coverage beyond a deductible. In an earlier paper (Arrow, 1963) this argument was developed for the case where the risk being insured against was, effectively, loss of income. Ehrlich and Becker (1972) have extended these results considerably, as well as analyzing other responses of the insured to the price of insurance, responses beyond the scope of this chapter. For some other related work, see Pashigian, Schkade, and Menefee (1966), Smith (1968), and Gould (1969). However, income is not the only uncertainty, especially in the context of health insurance, and only under special and unrealistic circumstances can it be held that the other uncertainties have income equivalents. Put loosely, the marginal utility of income will

Reprinted from *Scandinavian Actuarial Journal* (1974):1–42. I would like to thank Robert Shishko of the RAND Corporation for his comments, which were useful in improving the exposition.

in general depend not only on the amount of income but also on the state of the individual or, more generally, on the state of the world.

The insurance policies considered here specify a cash payment for each possible state of the world. Therefore, they do not include exactly the typical health insurance policy, which provides for reimbursement of actual expenses in whole or in part. There is a twofold difference between the cash payment contingent on a state of the world and the reimbursement policy: (1) the payment in the latter case depends on a decision of the patient and the physician and not only on the objective state of affairs; in particular, it ignores the price elasticity of demand for medical services;[1] and (2) the reimbursement policy is a payment in kind, not in fungible cash, so that the satisfaction derived by the insured from an insurance payment may be lower than that from an equal cash payment.[2]

The choice of insurance policies is constrained in two ways: (1) the insurer is assumed to be risk-neutral, so that premiums depend only on the expected insurance payment, but because of administrative or other expenses, the premium may exceed the actuarial value; and (2) insurance payments are nonnegative. The latter assumption not only conforms to everyday observation but is virtually necessitated by moral hazard; in general, it may be difficult to collect from an insured even in a state whose outcome is favorable to him.

---

1. It is well known that contingent cash payment policies are more efficient means of resource allocation than alternatives, such as reimbursement policies. I believe the latter exist because of an informational inequality between insurer and insured. The insured (and his agents, such as his physicians) knows the extent of his illness in much more detail than the insurer. Indeed, the insurer usually has no independent source of information and could create one only at considerable cost both to himself and to the insured. Hence, the policy cannot be written as a schedule of cash payments for the different states because the insurer and the insured do not have equal access to this information. The payments themselves, or some related magnitudes, such as quantities of different kinds of medical care, on the other hand, are statements about the world that are verifiable by both parties to the transaction. I intend to develop this theme in subsequent work.

2. Fire and other forms of casualty insurance typically pay money for the occurrence of certain states, without restricting the subsequent expenditures of the individual; if my house burns down, the insurance payment is not contingent on my rebuilding it. Medical insurance, however, invariably is only a payment for medical expenses; I cannot choose to make a claim on the grounds of illness and then spend the money on a vacation. The difference is important only if the constraint is in fact binding. That is, if, given the illness and the payment of insurance, I would in fact choose to use the entire payment and perhaps even more for medical expenses even if I were free to divert the payment to other uses, then the medical insurance is simply an alteration of income. The effectiveness of the expenditure constraint in practice is worthy of some investigation.

More explicitly, it is assumed that the insured is given the probabilities of different states, his initial (preinsurance) income in each, a utility function for income in each state, which may vary from state to state (see Section 1), and a given ratio of expected benefits to premiums (not exceeding 1). Then he can freely choose a premium and a system of nonnegative insurance payment for all the states so as to maximize his expected utility.

In the case where the utility function for income is the same for all states (Section 2) the optimal policy has a simple form; a critical income level is selected, and the insurance payment is equal to the extent to which actual income falls short of the critical level. The distribution of a given volume of insurance among states is independent of the individual's utility function, though the total amount demanded does depend on it.

When utility of income is state-dependent (see Section 3), the policy is characterized by a critical marginal utility of income, with payments being made so as to bring the marginal utility down to the critical level in those states where this is needed. An algorithm is found for determining the optimal policy (see also Section 6).

If the expected benefits or the premium shift in any way, the optimal postinsurance incomes in those states with positive insurance all shift in the same direction, the changes being proportional to a magnitude known as the risk tolerance (Section 4). It can also be shown that if we hold expected benefits constant, then the critical marginal utility increases with the premium (and therefore postinsurance incomes in all insured states decrease); on the other hand, for constant premium, the critical marginal utility falls as expected benefits rise.

These partial results can be combined to give a full characterization of the optimal policy, to determine both the optimal premium and the optimal critical marginal utility. With some modifications, the policy is characterized by two relations: a budget constraint, that the ratio of expected benefits to premium be the specified benefit-premium ratio; and the condition that the ratio of the expected to the maximum marginal utility of postinsurance income equal this benefit-premium ratio (see Sections 5 and 7). In the actuarially fair case, when the benefit-premium ratio is 1, all states are insured; otherwise, the probability that an insured state occurs is less than the benefit-premium ratio.

The comparative statics of the optimal policy will be examined with respect to shifts in the various parameters. As the benefit-premium ratio increases, the critical marginal utility falls; the premium rises in general, but there may be exceptions. The effects of changes in the probabilities of different states are rather complicated to describe (see Theorem 7 in Section 9). Finally (Section 10), it will be shown that an increase in preinsurance income in any state decreases the critical marginal utility and therefore increases the postinsurance income in any insured state. The effect on the premium paid depends on whether the state for which preinsurance income rose was insured or not; in the first case, the premium decreases; in the second, it increases.

1. The Dependence of Utility on the State of the World

In the now-customary formulation of decision making under uncertainty, there is assumed to be a fixed set of possible states of the world. For present purposes it suffices to assume that the set is finite. The states will be indexed by $s = 1, \ldots, n$. The probability of state s will be denoted by p_s. In the usual formulation of the expected-utility hypothesis, the decision maker is assumed to be confronted with a set of alternative specifications of consequences in each state of nature, say x_s, where x_s is a consequence if state s occurs. Then it is hypothesized that among alternative specifications of sets of consequences, the individual will choose the one that maximizes

$$(12\text{-}1) \qquad \sum_s p_s U(x_s),$$

for some *utility function* $U(x)$. In this formulation the utility function does not depend on s. The hypothesis is that originally formulated by Daniel Bernoulli in 1738, with particular stress on the case where x_s is simply income in state s; the point of view is that of an individual whom the alternative states affect only through his income. In more modern discussions, from Ramsey (1931) on down, it is shown that hypothesis (12-1) can be deduced from some apparently convincing assumptions on rational behavior in the presence of uncertainty.

Nevertheless, in many applications it seems more reasonable to have the utility function depend on s. This is likely to be the case where health is involved. The health of an individual clearly affects the utility of other consequences (for example, money income). If recovery from an illness depends on the availability of medical care, then the marginal utility of income in a state of illness will typically be higher than in a state of health. This is true in a perfectly operational and ordinalist sense, with no illegitimate comparisons of marginal utility; starting from a situation in which income is the same in the states of health and illness, the individual would choose to buy an actuarially fair insurance policy to be paid in event of illness, so that at his preferred point, disposable income would be less in the healthy state than in the ill state.[3]

In an earlier paper (Arrow, 1963) I took this partially into account by supposing that an illness is equivalent to a reduction of income. That is, for each state s, there is a cash equivalent, $\bar{x}_s$, say, so that if x_s is the income in state s resulting from some of the possible decisions, the individual maximizes

$$\sum_s p_s U(x_s - \bar{x}_s).$$

However, this now appears to be inadequately general although sometimes appropriate. It is indeed true that the marginal utility of income will be raised in the presence of illness. But there are two limitations. (1) There is, after all, no reason why the *shape* of the utility function under illness should be the same as that in good health at a lower level of income. More specifically, the risk aversion will in general be different in the two cases; it might be expected to be greater under illness if a minimum degree of medical care is essential, but more medical care has rapidly diminishing usefulness. (2) The simple cash-equivalent model implies that states of the world that are utility-reducing are also marginal-utility-increasing. But in the case of illness, this is clearly not necessarily so. There are many states of invalidism in which medical care is of little use and the possibility of deriving satisfaction from consumption is small. Thus the marginal utility of income will be low rather than high in these states, even though they are very unsatisfactory and yield low utilities.

---

3. The theory of risk bearing under uncertainty uses as a basic concept the *state of the world,* a complete description of the economically relevant aspects of the entire world. The illustrations of the last paragraph, on the other hand, refer only to the *state of the individual;* and indeed insurance, as we ordinarily understand it, is a schedule of payments contingent on events relating to the individual alone. As a general proposition, insurance policies contingent on the state of the individual alone are not optimal and may not even be feasible. Even though the insured cares only about his personal state, the insurer has to be concerned with the prospect of payments to other insured, which depend on their states; thus, it would clearly be possible to introduce a life insurance policy more favorable ex ante to both parties if the payment made for any one death were lower when a great many other individuals died. Nevertheless, in the common situation where the risks to different insured individuals are independent, and there are many such, it is possible to write policies depending only on the state of the insured without loss of efficiency, for then the state of the world, except insofar as it concerns the insured, is a statistical certainty. Hence, in the rest of this study, the "states" can be interpreted indifferently as states of the world and states of the insured.

For these reasons, it seems to be more satisfactory to state the criterion for choice as the maximization of

(12-2) $\qquad \sum_s p_s U_s(x_s).$

As far as I know, such an expression was first used by Eisner and Strotz (1961) in the context of life insurance. Clearly, being dead is rather different from being alive. An individual who takes out life insurance has some utility for money for his family after his death, but the shape of the utility function in that case might well be different from its shape when he is alive. The expression (12-2) has also been defended by Hirshleifer (1970, pp. 218, 220–221).

For those accustomed to the axiomatic treatment of Ramsey and his followers, there may be a bit of a puzzle here. Those axioms, which seem compelling enough, lead to (12-1), not to (12-2); that is, to a utility function that does not depend on the state of nature. Properly understood, there is no contradiction. The simplest way to look at it is to consider that (12-1) holds, provided that x_s is interpreted to include *all* the effects on the individual of being in state s. From the viewpoint of economic analysis, however, only *some* of these effects are relevant. More specifically, insurance can relate only to some but not to all components of the consequence vector. Thus, the fact of having fallen ill is not in itself something the economic system can affect; it can only alter the medical services and other purchasable commodities a person receives. If we assume that prices are unaffected by the state of the world, then all economic effects can be subsumed into changes in income. The illness itself must be regarded as unalterable by economic activity. Hence, the full consequences x_s can be written as a pair, (y_s, z_s), where y_s is income in state s, and z_s is an unalterable characteristic of the state. Then (12-1) asserts that the individual strives to maximize

$$\sum_s p_s U(y_s, z_s),$$

but the only variables under his control are the y_s's. We can therefore write

$$U(x_s) = U(y_s, z_s) = U_s(y_s),$$

and then (12-1) is equivalent to the maximization of

(12-3) $\qquad \sum_s p_s U_s(y_s),$

which is an operational equivalent of (12-2), with only the economic variables displayed.[4]

2. Optimal Choice of Insurance Policy of Given Expected Value and Premium: The Case of State-independent Utility

The choice of insurance policies by the insured can be assumed to be made as follows. For any given premium, the insurer specifies an expected value; the insured can then choose any policy with that expected value of payments. The premium is assumed, of course, to be at least equal to the expected value; the excess is a loading due to administrative costs and safety considerations for the insurer. The premium is assumed to be proportional to the expected value. The decision of the insured can then be analyzed into two steps. (1) For any given premium and given expected value, what is the optimal policy—that is, the optimal choice of insurance payments—in each state of nature? (2) Given a proportionality relation between premium and expected value, what is the optimal scale of the policy? We assume further that insurance payments are always nonnegative.

In symbols, let

a_s = income in state s before the policy is chosen,
y_s = income in state s after policy is chosen,
$U_s(y_s)$ = utility of income in state s,
p_s = probability of state s,

---

4. Instead of reinterpreting the results of the usual axiom system, it would be possible to challenge it and derive (12-2) or (12-3) from an altered system. The guilty axiom is one that asserts a consequence possible under any one state of the world is possible under any other. Although the word "possible" here does not mean "feasible", it might be argued that some consequences are not only infeasible but inconceivable under some states of the world; if one is ill, one cannot be well. If this axiom is dropped, then only the weaker form (12-2) emerges.

It might be remarked here that the more general formulation (12-2) or (12-3) does offer some problems for the behavioral interpretation of probability. The expected-utility theorem or hypothesis, especially in conjunction with the Bayesian concept of subjective probability, implies the meaningful separability of tastes (as represented by the utility function) from beliefs (as represented by probabilities). But in the form (12-3), this separation is no longer operational. If we multiply any one function U_s by a positive constant, divide the corresponding probability p_s by the same amount, and then renormalize all the probabilities so that they still add up to one, the observed behavior of the individual is unchanged. Hence, no set of observations can distinguish the probabilities from the utilities. This point was made by Herman Rubin about 1964 in an axiomatization of behavior under uncertainty leading to a result of the form (12-2), presented to the Joint Berkeley-Stanford Mathematical Economic Seminar but unpublished.

i_s = insurance payment if state s occurs,
P = premium,
E = expected value of insurance payments,
$\alpha = E/P$ = benefit-premium ratio.

From these definitions,

(12-4) $y_s = a_s + i_s - P,$

(12-5) $E = \sum_s p_s i_s,$

and

(12-6) $E = \alpha P,$

where

(12-7) $0 \leqq \alpha \leqq 1.$

The nonnegativity of insurance payments is written

(12-8) $i_s \geqq 0.$

Then the optimal insurance policy is obtained by choosing i_s, E, and P to maximize (12-3),

$$\sum_s p_s U_s(y_s),$$

subject to (12-4), (12-5), (12-6), and (12-8).

As usual, we postulate the existence of risk aversion, which is to say that the functions $U_s(y_s)$ are all strictly concave and twice differentiable functions, although hereafter "strictly" will be understood.

(12-9) $U''(y_s) < 0,$ all s and all y_s.

As noted, we can break up the problem into two parts: first, the maximization of (12-3) with respect to i_s subject to (12-4), (12-5), and (12-8), with E and P given, and second, the choice of an optimal E and P subject to (12-6). In this and the following section the first problem is considered. In this section an additional assumption is made:

(12-10) $U_s(y_s) = U(y_s),$

that utility is in fact independent of the state.

The problem of this section can then be written as follows. Maximize

$$\sum_s p_s U(a_s - P + i_s)$$

subject to (12-5) and (12-8). In view of (12-9), the Kuhn-Tucker theorem (see, for example, Zangwill, 1969, pp. 40–44) assures us that the optimum is characterized by the conditions

(12-11a) $p_s U'(a_s - P + i_s) \leqq \lambda p_s,$

(12-11b) $p_s U'(a_s - P + i_s) < \lambda p_s$ implies $i_s = 0,$

(12-11c) $\sum_s p_s i_s = E,$

where λ is the marginal utility of income.

These conditions can be stated more simply by defining

$$S = \{s | U'(a_s - P + i_s) = \lambda\}.$$

Then the optimum is characterized by the existence of a number λ and a set S such that

(12-12a) $U'(a_s - P + i_s) = \lambda$ for $s \in S,$

(12-12b) $i_s = 0$ for $s \notin S,$

(12-12c) $U'(a_s - P) < \lambda$ for $s \notin S,$

(12-12d) $\sum_{s \in S} p_s i_s = E,$

as can be seen by dividing through by p_s in (12-11a) and (12-11b).

But the function $U(y)$ was assumed concave, so that U' is strictly decreasing and hence has a unique inverse, $(U')^{-1}(\lambda)$. If we write

$$V(\lambda) = (U')^{-1}(\lambda) + P,$$

then the conditions for an optimum can be written

(12-13a) $a_s + i_s = V(\lambda)$ for $s \in S,$

(12-13b) $i_s = 0$ for $s \notin S,$

(12-13c) $a_s > V(\lambda)$ for $s \notin S,$

(12-13d) $\sum_{s \in S} p_s i_s = E.$

The probability of the set of states, S, is given by

(12-14) $p(S) = \sum_{s \in S} p_s.$

Multiply through in (12-13a) by p_s, sum over $s \in S$, and substitute from (12-13d) and (12-14):

$$\sum_{s \in S} p_s a_s + E = V(\lambda)p(S).$$

If we solve this last equation for $V(\lambda)$ and substitute into (12-13a) and (12-13c), we have

(12-15a) $a_s + i_s = \left(\sum_{s \in S} p_s a_s + E \right)/p(S)$ for $s \in S,$

(12-15b) $a_s > \left(\sum_{s \in S} p_s a_s + E \right)/p(S)$ for $s \notin S.$

Note several remarkable implications of this characterization of the optimal solution. Neither the premium, P, nor the utility function appears in it. The optimal distribution of protection is completely known once the expected value of the policy is known. Let

(12-16) $\bar{a} = \left(\sum_{s \in S} p_s a_s + E \right)/p(S).$

Then, since $i_s \geq 0$, it follows from (12-15a) that $a_s \leq \bar{a}$ for $s \in S$, and from (12-15b), only for such s. Thus, as already argued (Arrow, 1963), the optimal policy is defined as full protection beyond a deductible $\bar{a}$, in the sense that whenever the income falls below $\bar{a}$, the insurance payments just suffice to restore it to that level, whereas if income is above $\bar{a}$, insurance payments are zero. Of course, income in both insured and uninsured states is reduced by the premium P.

The optimal policy is then completely characterized by $\bar{a}$. As has just been seen, S is determined by $\bar{a}$; more specifically,

(12-17) $S = \{s | a_s \leq \bar{a}\},$

and then,

$$i_s = \bar{a} - a_s \quad \text{if } s \in S,$$
$$= 0 \qquad \text{if } s \notin S.$$

If S is defined in terms of $\bar{a}$ by (12-17), then (12-16) becomes an equation for $\bar{a}$. Multiply both sides by $p(S)$, use its definition (12-14), and transpose. Then,

$$(12\text{-}18) \quad F(\bar{a}) \equiv \left(\sum_{s \in S} p_s \right) \bar{a} - \sum_{s \in S} p_s a_s = E.$$

In Appendix A at the end of this section, note that the function $F(\bar{a})$, the left-hand side of (12-18), is a strictly increasing continuous function, with $F(0) = 0$, $F(+\infty) = +\infty$. It follows that Eq. (12-18) has a unique solution in $\bar{a}$ for any given level of expected value E.

THEOREM 1. *Suppose that utility depends only on income, and the individual can choose any insurance policy with nonnegative payments of a specified expected value, the premium being specified also. Then the policy has the form of specifying a critical income level $\bar{a}$ (gross of premium) and paying out an amount necessary to bring gross income up to that level if it falls short. The critical income level is just such as to make the expected payments have the specified value and is independent of the utility function and of the premium.*

Remark. One difficulty that has been evaded above is that it is in no way guaranteed that postinsurance income be nonnegative; if the premium P is high enough, then y_s can indeed be negative, even though $i_s \geq 0$. For the time being, we will avoid this issue by assuming both in this and in the following two sections that

$$(12\text{-}19) \quad a_s \geq P, \text{ all } s.$$

Then (12-4) and (12-8) guarantee that $y_s \geq 0$, all s, for any feasible policy. In Section 7 this assumption will be relaxed.

Appendix A

To show that $F(\bar{a})$, as defined in (12-18) above, is strictly increasing and continuous, order the states s in increasing order of a_s, so that $a_1 < a_2 < \ldots < a_n$. Then S consists of the states $1, \ldots, r$ if and only if $a_r \leq \bar{a} < a_{r+1}$; S contains all states if $\bar{a} \geq a_n$ and no states (that is, there is no insurance) if $\bar{a} < a_1$. Therefore $F(\bar{a}) = 0$ if $\bar{a} < a_1$; if $\bar{a} > a_n$,

$$F(\bar{a}) = \left(\sum_{s=1}^{n} p_s \right) \bar{a} - \sum_{s=1}^{n} p_s a_s = \bar{a} - \sum_{s=1}^{n} p_s a_s,$$

which certainly approaches infinity as $\bar{a}$ approaches infinity. For $a_r \leq \bar{a} < a_{r+1}$,

$$(12\text{-}20) \quad F(\bar{a}) = \left(\sum_{s=1}^{r} p_s\right)\bar{a} - \sum_{s=1}^{r} p_s a_s,$$

which is a linear function with a positive slope; hence, $F(\bar{a})$ is strictly increasing and continuous as $\bar{a}$ increases within any of the intervals (a_r, a_{r+1}). It remains only to show that $F(\bar{a})$ is continuous at any point a_r. As $\bar{a}$ approaches a_{r+1} from below, (12-20) holds, so that $F(\bar{a})$ approaches

$$(12\text{-}21) \quad \left(\sum_{s=1}^{r} p_s\right)a_{r+1} - \sum_{s=1}^{r} p_s a.$$

As $\bar{a}$ approaches a_{r+1} from above, (12-20) holds with r replaced by $r + 1$, so that

$$\begin{aligned}
F(\bar{a}) &= \left(\sum_{s=1}^{r+1} p_s\right)\bar{a} - \sum_{s=1}^{r+1} p_s a_s \\
&= \left(\sum_{s=1}^{r} p_s\right) - \sum_{s=1}^{r} \bar{a}p_s a_s + p_{r+1}(\bar{a} - a_{r+1});
\end{aligned}$$

thus as $\bar{a}$ approaches a_{r+1} from above, $F(\bar{a})$ again approaches (12-21). Hence, $F(\bar{a})$ is continuous and increasing everywhere.

3. Optimal Choice of Insurance Policy of Given Expected Value and Premium: The Case of State-dependent Utility

Utility is now permitted to vary with the state of nature, along the lines discussed in Section 1. Following the general formulation given at the beginning of Section 2, when E and P are specified and the choice is only that of i_s, maximize (12-3) subject to (12-4), (12-5), and (12-8). The problem can then be stated as that of maximizing

$$\sum_s p_s U_s(a_s - P + i_s)$$

subject to

$$(12\text{-}5) \quad \sum_s p_s i_s = E,$$

$$(12\text{-}8) \quad i_s \geq 0.$$

In view of (12-9), the concavity of the functions U_s, the Kuhn-Tucker theorem permits characterization of the optimal insurance policy by

(12-22a) $\quad p_s U_s'(y_s) \leq \lambda p_s$,

(12-22b) $\quad p_s U_s'(y_s) < \lambda p_s \quad$ implies $i_s = 0$,

and (12-5) above, where $y_s = a_s - P + i_s$, from (12-4). Divide through in (12-22a)–(12-22b) by p_s, and let

(12-23) $\quad S = \{s | U_s'(y_s) = \lambda\}$.

Then (12-22a)–(12-22b) assert

(12-24) $\quad U_s'(y_s) < \lambda \quad$ and $i_s = 0 \quad$ for $s \notin S$.

Note that λ is the maximum marginal utility of postinsurance income.
   For simplicity of exposition, make a further assumption usually made in this context, which will be relaxed in Section 6.

(12-25) $\quad U_s'(0) = +\infty; \; U_s'(+\infty) = 0$.

Since U_s' is strictly decreasing and twice differentiable, it has a well-defined inverse, $(U_s')^{-1}(\lambda)$, for each s; this inverse is also strictly decreasing and, by (12-25), defined for all $\lambda \geq 0$. Then from (12-23) and (12-24),

$$y_s = (U_s')^{-1}(\lambda) \quad \text{for } s \in S$$

$$y_s > (U_s')^{-1}(\lambda) \quad \text{for } s \notin S.$$

Since $y_s = a_s - P + i_s$ for all s, $y_s = a_s - P$ for $s \notin S$, by (12-24). Write

(12-26) $\quad V_s(\lambda, P) = (U_s')^{-1}(\lambda) + P$.

Then the optimal insurance policy satisfies the conditions

(12-27a) $\quad a_s + i_s = V_s(\lambda, P) \quad$ for $s \in S$,

(12-27b) $\quad a_s > V_s(\lambda, P) \quad$ for $s \notin S$.

Since $i_s \geq 0$, $a_s \leq V_s(\lambda, P)$ for $s \in S$, from (12-27a). Hence, from (12-27b), we can characterize S by

(12-28) $\quad S = \{s | a_s \leq V_s(\lambda, P)\}$.

Thus, for a given P, the optimal policy is determined by the *critical marginal utility,* λ; this determines S by (12-28), and then, by (12-27a) and (12-24),

(12-29a) $i_s = V_s(\lambda,P) - a_s$ for $s \in S$,

(12-29b) $= 0$ for $s \notin S$.

Because of the definition of S in (12-28), the condition $i_s \geqq 0$ will be satisfied.

Thus, the quantity V_s can be interpreted as the *deductible limit* for the state s. Whereas in the case of state-independent utility there was a single deductible limit, now the limit should vary from state to state according to the schedule relating utility to income. As (12-28) and (12-29) show, the insurance is paid in those states for which income falls below the corresponding deductible limit.

It might be objected that this interpretation says very little, since both income and deductible limit vary from state to state, and the insurance payments are jointly determined by the optimization procedure. However, some further considerations show that V_s is indeed meaningfully regarded as a deductible limit. For one thing, suppose that there are several states in which the utility function is the same but in which incomes may differ. Thus there may be two states in which medical care is equally efficacious and other commodities equally enjoyable, but in one of which income is high and the other of which it is low. Then V_s will be the same in all such states, and the insurance payments will be just those needed to bring the income up to the deductible limit if it falls below.

For another thing, consider two different situations in which the list of the states and the utility function in each state are the same but the preinsurance incomes differ; let them be a_s and a'_s in the two situations, respectively. Let the optimal policy in the first situation with an expected value E be defined by a critical marginal utility of income, λ, so that the insurance payments are defined by (12-29). Now in the second situation consider the insurance policy defined by the same deductible limits, V_s, and therefore by the same critical marginal utility, λ. This policy will be optimal if it satisfies the new budget constraint—that is, if the expected value of the policy changes to E', which will permit the new insurance policy to be bought. More specifically, if we define

$$S' = \{s|a'_s \leqq V_s(\lambda,P)\},$$

$$a'_s + i'_s = V_s(\lambda,P) \quad \text{for } s \in S',$$

$$i'_s = 0 \quad \text{for } s \notin S',$$

and if we choose E' so that

$$E' = \sum_s p_s i_s',$$

then the payments i_s' will be optimal if the expected value of the policy changes in the income-compensating manner from E to E'. Hence, given compensating changes in income, the original policy as defined by deductible limits remains optimal.

Note briefly how the critical marginal utility of income, λ, can be determined from the budget constraint (12-5). Since $i_s = 0$ for $s \notin S$, this can be written

$$\sum_{s \in S} p_s i_s = E.$$

Multiply through in (12-29a) by p_s and sum over $s \in S$.

$$(12\text{-}30) \quad E = \sum_{s \in S} p_s V_s(\lambda, P) - \sum_{s \in S} p_s a_s = \Phi(\lambda, P)$$

The existence of a unique solution to this equation is argued in Appendix B.

THEOREM 2. *Suppose that utility of income depends on the state of the world and that the individual can choose any insurance policy with nonnegative payments of a specified expected value, the premium being specified also. Suppose also that (1) the specified premium does not exceed preinsurance income for any state, and (2) the marginal utility of income in any state decreases from $+\infty$ to 0 as income increases from 0 to $+\infty$. Then the policy has the form of stating a critical marginal utility of income and paying out an amount sufficient to bring the marginal utility of income down to that level if the marginal utility of postpremium preinsurance income were higher. The critical marginal utility is just such as to make the expected payments have the specified value.*

Appendix B

For each s, the function V_s is strictly decreasing in λ. Hence, the equation

$$V_s(\lambda, P) = a_s$$

has a unique solution $\lambda = \lambda_s$ for a given P, namely, $\lambda_s = U_s'(a_s - P)$. This number is well defined since we are assuming $a_s \geq P$, by (12-19); however, it will be $+\infty$ if the equality holds. Number the states so that $\lambda_1 > \lambda_2 > \ldots > \lambda_n$. Then if $\lambda_r \geq \lambda > \lambda_{r+1}$, S consists of the states $1, \ldots, r$, which remain unchanged so long as λ remains in that interval. Since V_s is strictly decreasing in λ for all $s \in S$, Φ is strictly decreasing in such an interval. As λ approaches λ_r from below, Φ approaches

$$\Phi(\lambda_r,P) = \sum_{s=1}^{r} p_s V_s(\lambda_r,P) - \sum_{s=1}^{r} p_s a_s$$

$$= \sum_{s=1}^{r-1} p_s V_s(\lambda_r,P) - \sum_{s=1}^{r-1} p_s a_s + p_r[V_r(\lambda_r,P) - a_r]$$

$$= \sum_{s=1}^{r-1} p_s V_s(\lambda_r,P) - \sum_{s=1}^{r-1} p_s a_s$$

from the definition of λ_r. If λ is slightly greater than λ_r, S consists of the states $1, \ldots, r-1$, so that

$$\Phi(\lambda,P) = \sum_{s=1}^{r-1} p_s V_s(\lambda,P) - \sum_{s=1}^{r-1} p_s a_s;$$

as λ approaches λ_r from above, this expression approaches

$$\sum_{s=1}^{r-1} p_s V_s(\lambda_r,P) - \sum_{s=1}^{r-1} p_s a_s = \Phi(\lambda_r,P),$$

which is also the limit from below, as we have seen. Hence, $\Phi(\lambda,P)$ is continuous at each of the points λ_r, while it is obviously continuous between these points. Since Φ is decreasing on all the intermediate intervals, it is decreasing everywhere in the interval $\lambda_1 \geq \lambda \geq \lambda_n$. If $\lambda > \lambda_1$, then S is an empty set of states, and therefore $\Phi(\lambda,P) = 0$.

If $a_s = P$, then $\lambda_s = +\infty$, and therefore we would have to let $\lambda_1 = +\infty$. In this case, we can, of course, have no $\lambda > \lambda_1$. But for λ very large, S consists of the single state 1, and therefore,

$$\Phi(\lambda,P) = p_1[V_1(\lambda,P) - a_1] = p_1[(U_s')^{-1}(\lambda) + P - a_1] = p_1(U_s')^{-1}(\lambda),$$

which approaches 0 as λ approaches $+\infty = \lambda_1$. Hence it remains true that $\Phi(\lambda_1,P) = 0$. If $\lambda \leq \lambda_n$, then again $\Phi(\lambda,P)$ is a linear combination of strictly decreasing functions and therefore is strictly decreasing. Further, as λ approaches 0, $(U_s')^{-1}(\lambda)$ approaches $+\infty$ from (12-25), so that $V_s(\lambda,P)$ approaches $+\infty$, and hence $\Phi(\lambda,P)$ approaches $+\infty$. Therefore, Φ ranges from 0 to $+\infty$ as λ decreases from λ_1 to 0, and so the equation (12-30) has a unique solution in λ for any given E.

4. Effects of Varying Premium, Expected Value, and Other Parameters

So far we have taken E and P as given. In the next section, the optimal choice of these variables will be discussed. As a preliminary, we discuss the effects of changes in several magnitudes taken as parametric in the preceding section, in particular E and P.

Broadly speaking, we can assume S constant. That is, the changes considered may be regarded as leaving the set of insured states unchanged; if the changes are sufficiently small, S will in fact not change, and therefore derivatives can be calculated on that assumption. Further, it is easy to demonstrate that the derivatives so calculated are continuous across the boundaries at which the set of insured states, S, does change.

Note that the policy is completely characterized by the critical marginal utility, λ. Thus, if any change does take place, it is comparatively easy to compute the effects on postinsurance income in the insured states, since this is determined by the equation $U'_s(y_s) = \lambda$, so that

(12-31) $dy_s/d\lambda = 1/U''_s(y_s) = (1/\lambda)U'_s(y_s)/U''_s(y)$.

Now the ratio $-U''_s(y_s)/U'_s(y_s)$ has been introduced into the theory of risk bearing under the name *absolute risk aversion*. Its reciprocal has been named *risk tolerance*.

(12-32) $T_s = -U'_s(y_s)/U''_s(y_s)$.

A closely related concept is the *relative* or *proportionate risk aversion*,

(12-33) $R_{Rs} = -y_s U''_s(y_s)/U'_s(y_s) = y_s/T_s$

(Pratt, 1964; Arrow, 1965, lecture 2, reprinted as Chapter 9 of this volume; Wilson, 1968, p. 120). From (12-31) and (12-32), we note:

(12-34)   The changes in postinsurance income in insured states due to some parameter shift are proportional to the risk tolerances.

This can be restated using (12-33):

(12-35)   The proportionate changes in postinsurance incomes in insured states due to some parameter shift are inversely proportional to the relative risk aversions.

Since the shifts in postinsurance incomes in insured states are completely determined by λ, it is useful to consider the variation in λ with respect to different parameters. First we consider the effect of changing P (E remaining fixed). For simplicity of notation, define

$$\partial V_s / \partial \lambda = V'_s.$$

Note that from (12-26), V'_s is independent of P and indeed $V_s = y_s + P$, so that, from (12-31) and (12-32),

(12-36) $V'_s = -T_s/\lambda.$

Differentiate the basic equation (12-30), which determines λ, with respect to P:

$$\sum_{s \in S} p_s \left[\frac{\partial V_s}{\partial \lambda} \frac{d\lambda}{dP} + 1 \right] = 0,$$

so that, from (12-36),

$$d\lambda/dP = \lambda p(S) / \sum_{s \in S} p_s T_s,$$

where $p(S) = \Sigma_{s \in S} p_s$, as defined in (12-14). For any $s \in S$, $p_s/p(S)$ is the conditional probability of the state s, given that one of the states in S has occurred. Hence, if numerator and denominator are both divided by $p(S)$,

(12-37) $d\lambda/dP = \lambda/E(T_s|S) > 0,$

where $E(T_s|S)$ means the conditional expectation of T_s, given that one of the insured states has occurred. Strictly speaking, this formula has been derived only when S is constant for sufficiently small variations in P, which is to say at any point for which λ differs from all of the λ_s's. But by continuity (easily demonstrated, as was done earlier), (12-37) also holds at the juncture points λ_s.

Equations (12-31) and (12-37) together show the variation of y_s as P rises, E remaining fixed, for $s \in S$. Clearly, y_s must fall for all s. Since $i_s = y_s + P - a_s$, we can also infer the behavior of the insurance payments. As P increases, it can happen that one or more of the i_s's decreases and eventually becomes 0; for still larger P, that state s ceases to be insured. On the other hand, it is possible for some previously uninsured state (state not in S) to enter S as P becomes larger.

It may be worth noting that, on the average, desired insurance payments are not altered by changes in the premium. This can be seen by differentiating the budget constraint

$$\sum_{s \in S} p_s i_s = E$$

with respect to P, yielding

$$\sum_{s \in S} p_s (di_s/dP) = 0.$$

If we divide through by $p(S)$, we can say that $E(di_s/dP|S) = 0$. Thus an increase in premium, as long as S does not change, simply reallocates insurance payments to those states with low risk tolerances.

For the analysis of the next section, we will need to know the effects of a change in P on the maximum expected utility attainable by the individual. Then, let $W(E,P)$ be the expected utility attainable by following the optimal insurance policy for a given E and P:

$$(12\text{-}38) \qquad W(E,P) = \sum_{s=1}^{n} p_s U_s(y_s),$$

where

$$(12\text{-}39) \qquad y_s = a_s + i_s - P \quad \text{is optimal for given } E \text{ and } P.$$

Then we can calculate $\partial W/\partial P$ easily by using Samuelson's envelope theorem (1947, p. 34): The marginal effect on W of changing a parameter is the same whether the policy variables are optimally adjusted to the change or remain unchanged. Hence, we can compute $\partial W/\partial P$ by calculating the effect of a change in P, holding i_s constant. Since $\partial y_s/\partial P = -1$,

$$(12\text{-}40) \qquad \partial W/\partial P = - \sum_{s=1}^{n} p_s U_s'(y_s) = - E[U_s'(y_s)].$$

We now turn to a similar calculation of the effects on policy and welfare of changing E, the expected value of insurance payments, with constant P. Again differentiate (12-30), now with respect to E, in order to find the effect on λ.

$$\sum_{s \in S} p_s \frac{\partial V_s}{\partial \lambda} \frac{d\lambda}{dE} = 1,$$

so that

$$(12\text{-}41) \qquad d\lambda/dE = - \lambda \Big/ \Big(\sum_{s \in S} p_s T_s \Big) = - \lambda/p(S) E(T_s|S) < 0.$$

Thus an increase in E (in effect, in income) increases postinsurance income and the amount of insurance bought in every insured state, but more in those for which the risk tolerance is greatest. Clearly, as E increases, the insurance in any insured state never becomes zero, but previously uninsured states may become insured. To see the latter point, notice that $\lambda - U_s'(y_s) > 0$ for an uninsured state, with $y_s = a_s - P$. As E increases, y_s is constant and therefore so is $U_s(y_s)$, while λ decreases in accordance with (12-41). If the difference becomes zero, s passes over into the class S of insured states.

The effect of a change in E on W is easily derived by noting that W is the result of maximization under a budget constraint, with E as the magnitude of the constraint. Then (see, for example, Zangwill, 1969, pp. 66–68) the rate of change of the maximand with respect to the magnitude of the constraint is simply the Lagrange multiplier.

(12-42) $\partial W/\partial E = \lambda.$

For later reference, it will also be useful to consider the effects of changes in the initial incomes, a_s. Consider any one of them, say a_t. Following now-familiar lines, differentiate (12-30) with respect to a_t.

$$\sum_{s \in S} p_s V_s'(\partial \lambda/\partial a_t) - \sum_{s \in S} p_s(\partial a_s/\partial a_t) = 0.$$

But $\partial a_s/\partial a_t = 1$ if $s = t$ and 0 otherwise, so that

$$\sum_{s \in S} p_s(\partial a_s/\partial a_t) = p_t \quad \text{if } t \in S,$$

$$= 0 \quad \text{if } t \notin S,$$

and therefore,

(12-43) $\partial \lambda/\partial a_t = p_t / \left(\sum_{s \in S} p_s V_s' \right) = -\lambda p_t / \left(\sum_{s \in S} p_s T_s \right) \quad \text{if } t \in S,$

$$= 0 \quad \text{if } t \notin S.$$

Expression (12-43) can be given a slightly more unified appearance if we introduce the conditional probability $p(t|S)$. Note that $p(t|S) = p(t)/p(S)$ if $t \in S, = 0$ if $t \notin S$. If we divide numerator and denominator of the right-hand side of (12-43) for the case $t \in S$ through by $p(S)$, we have

(12-44) $\partial \lambda/\partial a_t = -\lambda p(t|S)/E(T_s|S),$

which is also valid for the case $t \notin S$.

Finally, the effect of a change in a_t on W can be found by the use of the envelope theorem. Since $y_s = a_s + i_s - P$,

(12-45) $\partial W / \partial a_t = p_t U'_t(y_t)$.

5. Choice of the Optimum Scale of an Insurance Policy

We now consider the individual to be able to choose the scale E of his policy as well as the allocation of payments to states for a given scale. Of course, he can increase E only at the cost of increasing premium P. We will assume a proportional relation,

(12-46) $E = \alpha P$.

Thus α is the (expected) *benefit-premium ratio*.

For any given E and P, we are assuming the insurance payments i_s optimally determined. Hence, E and P should be chosen to maximize $W(E,P)$ subject to (12-46). Note that $W(E,P)$ is a concave function; for the maximand, $\Sigma_{s=1}^n p_s U_s(a_s + i_s - P)$, is jointly concave in the variables i_s, P.[5] Hence, the first-order conditions for maximization are both necessary and sufficient. We select P as our independent variable and assume E determined by (12-46).

---

5. The general theorem is the following:

Let $f(x_1, \ldots, x_n, y_1, \ldots, y_m)$, $g_j(x_1, \ldots, x_n, y_1, \ldots, y_m)$ $(j = 1, \ldots, r)$ be each jointly concave in the decision variables $x_1, \ldots, x_n$ and the parameters $y_1, \ldots, y_m$. For any fixed set of values of $y_1, \ldots, y_m$, let $F(y_1, \ldots, y_m)$ be the maximum of $f(x_1, \ldots, x_n, y_1, \ldots, y_m)$ among all values of $x_1, \ldots, x_n$ satisfying the constraints $g_j(x_1, \ldots, x_n, y_1, \ldots, y_m) \geq 0$. Then $F(y_1, \ldots, y_m)$ is a concave function.

Proof. Let x, y be the vectors with components $(x_1, \ldots, x_n)$ and $(y_1, \ldots, y_m)$, respectively. Let x^k $(k = 0, 1)$ maximize $f(x, y^k)$ subject to $g_j(x, y^k) \geq 0$ $(j = 1, \ldots, r)$. For any λ, $0 \leq \lambda \leq 1$, let $y = (1 - \lambda)y^0 + \lambda y^1$, $x = (1 - \lambda)x^0 + \lambda x^1$. Then, from concavity of g_j, $g_j(x,y) \geq (1 - \lambda) g_j(x^0,y^0) + \lambda g_j(x^1,y^1) \geq 0$, since x^k satisfies the constraints when $y = y^k$. Hence, x satisfies the constraints $g_j(x,y) \geq 0$ $(j = 1, \ldots, r)$. By definition of F and concavity of f, $F(y) \geq f(x,y) \geq (1 - \lambda)f(x^0,y^0) + \lambda f(x^1,y^1) = (1 - \lambda) F(y^0) + \lambda F(y^1)$, that is, F is concave.

In the present application, the decision variables are $i_s (s = 1, \ldots, n)$, the parameters are E and P, the function being maximized is

$$\sum_{s=1}^n p_s U_s(a_s + i_s - P),$$

and the single constraint is (12-5), which can be written as

$$E - \sum_{s=1}^n p_s i_s \geq 0.$$

(12-47) $dW/dP = \alpha(\partial W/\partial E) + (\partial W/\partial P) = \alpha\lambda - E[U_s''(y_s)],$

from (12-40) and (12-42).

We will continue to maintain the assumptions (12-21), that $a_s \geq P$, all s, and (12-25), that U_s' decreases from infinity to zero. Since P is a variable here, the first of these assumptions will be taken to hold at the optimal insurance policy. Both of these assumptions will be relaxed in the following sections.

First, what is the condition that there be no insurance? This is achieved when $dW/dP \leq 0$ at $P = 0$. Of course, when $P = 0$, $E = 0$, by (12-46), and therefore $i_s = 0$, all s, so that $y_s = a_s$, all s. Also, in general,

$$\lambda = \max_s U_s'(y_s).$$

If we set $y_s = a_s$ in (12-47), we see that the condition that no insurance be taken out is that

(12-48) $\alpha \leq E[U_s'(a_s)]/\max_s U_s'(a_s).$

In words, no insurance at all is taken out if the benefit-premium ratio does not exceed the ratio of expected to maximum marginal utility of preinsurance income.

Now suppose some insurance is taken out, so that the maximum of W occurs at an interior point, where $dW/dP = 0$.

(12-49) $\alpha\lambda = E[U_s'(y_s)].$

Then the optimum insurance can be determined as follows. For any given P, E is determined by (12-46), then λ from (12-30), and therefore i_s by (12-29). By substitution into (12-49), the optimum P is determined.

Will there be insurance in all states? In that case, $U_s'(y_s) = \lambda$ in all states; (12-49) becomes $\alpha\lambda = \lambda$, or $\alpha = 1$. Thus, there will be some uninsured states unless the policy is actuarially fair. Conversely, if the policy is actuarially fair, optimal choice will in general call for insurance in all states. To see this, first note that there must be some insurance if in the preinsurance state the marginal utility varies from state to state (if it were initially constant, then, of course, insurance would be superfluous), for then the right-hand side of (12-48) is less than one, and therefore (12-48) cannot hold when $\alpha = 1$. There must then be an interior maximum, so that (12-49) holds. At the optimum, $U_s'(y_s) \leq \lambda$, all s, so that $E[U_s'(y_s)] \leq \lambda$, and the inequality is strict unless $U_s''(y_s) = \lambda$ for all s. Thus for $\alpha = 1$, (12-49) implies that S must consist of all states.

The value of y_s for each s is determined by the condition $U_s''(y_s) = \lambda$. We can find the appropriate value of λ by solving (12-30). Here S consists of all states, and $E = P$. Since $V_s(\lambda,p) = (U_s')^{-1}(\lambda) + P$, by (12-26), Eq. (12-30) reduces to

(12-50) $\sum_s p_s[(U_s')^{-1}(\lambda) - a_s] = 0.$

The left-hand side is a strictly decreasing function of λ; further, since U_s' has been assumed to decrease from infinity to zero, it follows that $(U_s')^{-1}(\lambda)$ decreases from infinity to zero as λ increases from zero to infinity. Hence, the left-hand side of (12-30) decreases from infinity to $-\sum_s p_s a_s < 0$, so that (12-50) always has a unique positive solution.

There is a trivial nonuniqueness in the choice of optimal policy in the actuarially fair case. Let i_s be an optimal policy with premium P, and let $i_s' = i_s + h$, $P' = P + h$, $h \geq 0$. Under the assumption of actuarial fairness, the new policy is feasible. If y_s and y_s' are the net incomes in state s under the original and new policies, we see that $y_s' = a_s + i_s' - P' = a_s + i_s - P = y_s$, all s, so the new policy is also optimal. Indeed, it is possible to choose $h < 0$, as long as the condition $i_s' \geq 0$ is satisfied. That is, for any optimal policy,

(12-51) $P \geq \max_s [a_s - (U_s')^{-1}(\lambda)],$

and we can choose indifferently any such P. The condition we are imposing, that $a_s \geq P$, all s, can be satisfied provided

(12-52) $\min_s a_s \geq \max_s [a_s - (U_s')^{-1}(\lambda)].$

In the actuarially unfair case, $\alpha < 1$, the probability of being in a state covered by insurance is less than 1. In fact, (12-49) implies a simple inequality, if it is recalled that $U_s''(y_s) = \lambda$ for $s \in S$, that $U_s''(y_s) > 0$, all s, and that there is at least one state not in S.

$$a\lambda = \sum_s p_s U_s''(y_s) = \sum_{s \in S} p_s U_s''(y_s) + \sum_{s \notin S} p_s U_s''(y_s) > \lambda \sum_{s \in S} p_s = \lambda p(S),$$

so that

(12-53) $p(S) < \alpha$ if $\alpha < 1.$

It will be recalled that we have assumed that the optimal solutions found satisfy condition (12-19), that $a_s \geq P$, all s. To complete the analysis, we wish to show when this condition holds. Let $\bar{P} = \min_s a_s$; then (12-19) is equivalent to the statement $P \leqq \bar{P}$. For any such P, there is a corresponding choice of λ that satisfies (12-30). Then an optimal policy is defined by that $P \leqq \bar{P}$ for which $dW/dP = 0$. Since W is concave, dW/dP is decreasing. If (12-48) does not hold, then $dW/dP > 0$ for $P = 0$; hence, $dW/dP = 0$ for some $P \leqq \bar{P}$ if and only if $dW/dP \leqq 0$ for $P = \bar{P}$. In view of (12-46), this can be stated as follows: Define $\bar{\lambda}$ to satisfy the equation

(12-54) $\Phi(\bar{\lambda}, \bar{P}) = \alpha\bar{P}$;

then there is an optimal policy with $P \leqq \bar{P}$ if, and only if,

(12-55) $\alpha\bar{\lambda} \leqq E[U'_s(\bar{y}_s)]$,

where

(12-56) $\bar{y}_s = a_s + \bar{i}_s - \bar{P}, \bar{i}_s$ is optimal insurance when $P = \bar{P}, E = \alpha\bar{P}$.

The last condition reduces to (12-52) in the case $\alpha = 1$.

As noted earlier, following (12-24), in the optimal policy for given P, with $E = \alpha P$, the maximum marginal utility of postinsurance income is λ. If $y_s(P)$ is the postinsurance income for the optimal policy for given P, then (12-48), (12-49), and (12-55) can all be stated in terms of the ratio of expected to maximum marginal utility of postinsurance income — that is,

$$R(P) = E[U'_s(y_s(P))]/\max_s U'_s(y_s(P)).$$

The condition (12-48) for no insurance becomes $\alpha \leqq R(0)$; if any insurance is purchased, the amount is defined by (12-49), $R(P) = \alpha$; and the condition for a solution with $a_s \geqq P$, all s, becomes $\alpha \leqq R(\bar{P})$.

THEOREM 3. *Suppose that the utility of income depends on the state of the world and that the individual can choose any insurance policy with nonnegative payments with a given ratio, $\alpha \leqq 1$, of expected benefits to premium. Assume further that the marginal utility of income in any state decreases from $+\infty$ to 0 as income increases from 0 to $+\infty$. Let $\bar{P} = \min_s a_s$. For any $P \leqq \bar{P}$, let $R(P)$ be the ratio of expected to maximum marginal utility of postinsurance income according to the optimal policy specified in Theorem 2 for premium P and expected benefits αP.*

(a) No insurance is taken out if and only if the expected benefit-premium ratio does not exceed the ratio of expected to maximum marginal utility of preinsurance income — that is, $\alpha \leqq R(0)$.

(b) If $R(0) < \alpha \leqq R(\bar{P})$, then there is an optimal policy with premium

$P \leq \overline{P}$, *which is optimal in the sense of Theorem 2 for that premium and expected benefits αP, and which satisfies the condition R(P) = α.*

(c) *If the offering is not actuarially fair, so that α < 1, then the probability of being in a state covered by the optimal policy is less than α.*

(d) *If the offering is actuarially fair (α = 1), then the policy of equalizing the marginal utility of postinsurance income in all states at a level just insuring actuarial fairness (expected value of preinsurance income equals expected value of postinsurance income) is optimal.*

Remark. Strictly speaking, part (d) has been proved only under the additional condition (12-52) that the minimum preinsurance income is at least equal to the maximum decrease from preinsurance to postinsurance income. But, as will be shown in Section 7, the condition is in fact superfluous.

6. The Optimum Insurance Policy without Restrictions on the Range of Marginal Utilities

It would be desirable to remove two restrictions in the previous analysis. The first, to be discussed in this section, is that the marginal utility of income in each state varies from $+\infty$ down to 0; the second, to be covered in the following section, is that the choice of optimum premium has so far been restricted so that it does not exceed minimum preinsurance income.

The first is probably of less consequence, since the assumption being removed is usually reasonable. The condition that the marginal utility approach zero as income approaches infinity is, of course, implied if one assumes that utility functions are bounded, as some assert (see Chapter 11 of this volume). Even apart from this argument, which is strongly contested by some, the idea that the marginal utility approaches a positive rather than a zero limit seems unreasonable: it would imply that the individual would be essentially risk-neutral with respect to fluctuations at high income levels. But this would imply that wealthy individuals hold no safe assets; indeed, they would hold only the riskiest assets with the highest expected values.

The assumption at the other end, that marginal utility becomes infinite as income approaches zero, is more disputable in certain contexts. Consider the case where one of the states is death. In other words, we are imagining a policy that includes life insurance as one aspect. Income still has utility if the individual has the desire to leave a bequest. But if the intended heir has other wealth, human or material, the marginal utility of the bequest at zero should not be infinite. Since, however, the restrictions on the range of the marginal utilities can be removed completely, without excessive complications to the analysis, we will do so here.

Since $U_s'(y_s)$ is strictly decreasing, its range is in general bounded above by $\bar{\lambda}_s = \lim_{y_s \to 0} U_s'(y_s)$ and below by $\underline{\lambda}_s = \lim_{y_s \to +\infty} U_s'(y_s)$, where $\bar{\lambda}_s$ is either $+\infty$ or a finite positive number $\bar{\lambda}_s \geq 0$. Then $(U_s')^{-1}(\lambda)$ is defined only for $\bar{\lambda}_s \geq \lambda \geq \underline{\lambda}_s$; at the lower limit, the "definition" is somewhat metaphorical, since $(U_s')^{-1}(\underline{\lambda}_s) = +\infty$.

Let us first review the reasoning of Section 4, that is, we seek the optimal policy for given premium and expected benefits. The analysis through (12-24) remains unchanged. Since $U_s'(y_s) < \lambda$ for $s \notin S, \lambda > \underline{\lambda}_s$. However, for any given λ, it is possible that $\lambda > \bar{\lambda}_s$, so that $(U_s')^{-1}(\lambda)$ would be undefined. Then, for $s \notin S$, we have

$$\text{either} \quad y_s > (U_s')^{-1}(\lambda) \quad \text{or} \quad \lambda > \bar{\lambda}_s.$$

In either case, $i_s = 0$, so that $y_s = a_s - P$. We are assuming $a_s \geq P$. Hence, if we extend (12-26) by defining

$$V_s(\lambda, P) = (U_s')^{-1}(\lambda) + P \quad \text{if } \underline{\lambda}_s \leq \lambda \leq \bar{\lambda}_s,$$
$$= P \quad \text{if } \lambda > \bar{\lambda}_s,$$

we can conclude $a_s \geq V_s(\lambda, P)$ with the strict inequality if either $a_s > P$ or $\lambda \leq \bar{\lambda}_s$. Thus the characterization of S in (12-28) should be slightly altered, to exclude the case where both $a_s = P$ and $\lambda > \bar{\lambda}_s$; however, this alteration is unimportant for defining the optimal policy, since we would have $i_s = 0$, according to (12-29a), even if we had included that state in S.

The existence of a unique solution to (12-30) remains valid but requires some alteration in the algorithm. Since $(U_s')^{-1}(\underline{\lambda}_s) = +\infty$, we must have $\lambda > \underline{\lambda}_s$ for all the states in S, or, equivalently,

$$\lambda > \max_{s \in S} \underline{\lambda}_s.$$

We define $\lambda_s = U_s'(a_s - P)$ as before; if, in particular, there is a state for which $a_s = P$, then $\lambda_s = \bar{\lambda}_s$. In any case, $\bar{\lambda}_s \geq \lambda_s \geq \underline{\lambda}_s$, all s. As before we number the states in decreasing order of λ_s. Now define $\tilde{\lambda}_s$ to be the largest of the numbers $\underline{\lambda}_1, \ldots, \underline{\lambda}_s$. Note that

$$\tilde{\lambda}_s = \max (\tilde{\lambda}_{s-1}, \underline{\lambda}_s).$$

Let p be the smallest number s, if any, for which $\tilde{\lambda}_s \geq \lambda_{s+1}$.

First we note that

(12-57) $\lambda_p > \tilde{\lambda}_p \geq \lambda_{p+1}.$

To see this, first suppose $p = 1$. But certainly $\lambda_1 > \underline{\lambda}_1 = \tilde{\lambda}_1$, by definition. Now suppose $p > 1$. Then by construction $\lambda_p > \tilde{\lambda}_{p-1}$. Since $\tilde{\lambda}_p = \max (\tilde{\lambda}_{p-1}, \underline{\lambda}_p)$ and $\underline{\lambda}_p < \lambda_p, \tilde{\lambda}_p < \lambda_p$. The second inequality in (12-57) is immediate from the definition of p.

Now let λ decrease from λ_r to λ_{r+1}, with $r < p$. Then $\lambda_{r+1} \geqq \lambda_p > \tilde{\lambda}_p$, so that $\lambda > \underline{\lambda}_s, s = 1, \ldots , p$, and, in particular, $s = 1, \ldots , r$. Since $\lambda \leqq \lambda_r \leqq \lambda_s \leqq \tilde{\lambda}_s(s = 1, \ldots , r), \underline{\lambda}_s < \lambda \leqq \tilde{\lambda}_s(s = 1, \ldots , r)$, so that $(U'_s)^{-1}(\lambda)$ is defined for $s = 1, \ldots , r$, and therefore $\Phi(\lambda, P)$ is well defined and increases as λ decreases. However, $\tilde{\lambda}_p = \underline{\lambda}_s$ for some $s \leqq p$. Hence, as λ decreases from λ_p to $\tilde{\lambda}_p$, it must be true that $(U'_s)^{-1}(\lambda)$ approaches infinity for at least one $s \leqq p$, and hence $\Phi(\lambda, P)$ approaches infinity as λ approaches $\tilde{\lambda}_p$ from above.

If p is not defined, then $\lambda_{s+1} > \tilde{\lambda}_s(s = 1, \ldots , n - 1)$. If we set $s = n - 1$, we have $\lambda_n > \tilde{\lambda}_{n-1}$, and therefore, by an argument just used, $\lambda_n > \tilde{\lambda}_n$. Then as λ decreases from λ_n to $\tilde{\lambda}_n$, $\Phi(\lambda, P)$ approaches $+\infty$. Thus $\Phi(\lambda, P)$ is strictly decreasing in λ, approaches $+\infty$ as λ approaches $\tilde{\lambda}_p$ or $\tilde{\lambda}_n$ (according to whether p is defined or not), and approaches 0 as λ approaches λ_1, as before. Thus (12-30) always has a solution.

It follows that Theorem 2 remains valid when the hypothesis (b) there is deleted. However, the algorithm for finding the optimal policy has to be modified as indicated.

(In the situation studied in Section 2, where the utility function is independent of the state of the world, no use was made of the hypothesis that marginal utility declined from infinity to zero, and therefore Theorem 1 remains valid. This can also be seen from the just preceding reasoning. For then $\tilde{\lambda}_s$ and $\underline{\lambda}_s$ are independent of s, say equal to $\tilde{\lambda}$ and $\underline{\lambda}$, respectively; then $\tilde{\lambda}_s$ is also equal to $\underline{\lambda}$ for all s. It can then be seen that $\lambda_s > \underline{\lambda} = \tilde{\lambda}_n$, so that the algorithm of Section 3 remains valid; but for the special case of identical utility functions in all states, this is the same as the algorithm of Section 2.)

The steps leading from Theorem 2 to Theorem 3 did not make any use of the range of the marginal utilities, and therefore Theorem 3 also remains valid with no hypothesis on the range of the marginal utilities.

7. Optimum Insurance Policies with Premium Waivers Needed

We now reconsider the optimum policy but remove the requirement (12-19) that the premium never exceed preinsurance income. Clearly if (12-19) fails to hold, we must be prepared for the possibility that in some states the insured could not afford to pay his premium without insurance. He therefore must have an insurance payment in such states simply to meet his premium obligations. We might refer to such payments as constituting *premium waivers,* to stretch an ordinary insurance term somewhat. That is, to the constraint that insurance payments be nonnegative, we add the constraint that the postinsurance income be nonnegative, $y_s \geq 0$. Since $y_s = a_s + i_s - P$, this condition can be written, for given P, as

$$i_s \geq P - a_s.$$

Since we also require $i_s \geq 0$, we can write

(12-58) $i_s \geq \max (P - a_s, 0).$

We can then reconsider the problem of Section 3, the choice of an optimum policy for given P and E, with the nonnegativity constraint (12-8) replaced by (12-58): we seek to maximize

$$\sum_s p_s U_s'(y_s)$$

subject to (12-58) and the budget constraint

(12-5) $\sum_s p_s i_s = E.$

The simplest procedure turns out to be a reinterpretation of the variables to permit the direct application of Theorem 2. Let

(12-59) $b_s = a_s + \max (P - a_s, 0),$

(12-60) $j_s = i_s - \max (P - a_s, 0).$

Note that

(12-61) $y_s = a_s + i_s - P = b_s + j_s - P,$

and that the constraint (12-58) can be written

(12-62) $j_s \geq 0.$

Finally, from (12-5) and (12-60), the budget constraint can be written

(12-63) $\sum_s p_s j_s = F,$

where

(12-64) $F = E - \sum_s p_s \max (P - a_s, 0).$

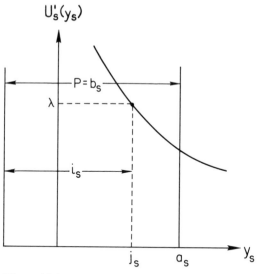

Figure 12.1

We have to assume that $F \geq 0$ for the problem to be feasible. Then the optimization problem is identical to that of Section 3 for given E and P, with the parameters a_s being replaced by b_s and the variables i_s by j_s. (See Figure 12.1 for the case $a_s > P$.) We can thus, as before, find an optimal policy defined by a critical marginal utility of income. Certain interpretive remarks can be made.

1. The set S is now the set of states for which $j_s > 0$. From (12-60), we see that the total insurance payment can be written as the sum of a *premium waiver*, max $(P - a_s, 0)$, and a *discretionary insurance payment*, j_s. If we write

(12-65) $Q = \{s | a_s < P\}$,

we see that Q is the set of states in which premium waivers are paid, while S is the set of states in which discretionary insurance payments are made. In general, there is no necessary relation between these two sets. The set of states for which some insurance payment is made is the *union* of these two sets, denoted by $S \cup Q$, namely the set of states that are in at least one of S and Q.

2. However, if we assume $U_s''(0) = +\infty$ for all s, then Q must be a subset of

S. For if $s \in Q$ but $s \notin S$, then $b_s = a_s + (P - a_s) = P$, while $j_s = 0$, so that $y_s = 0$. For any s, $U_s'(y_s) \leq \lambda$, which is impossible if $y_s = 0$ and $U_s'(0) = +\infty$.

THEOREM 4. *Suppose that utility of income depends on the state of the world and that the individual can choose any insurance policy with nonnegative payments of a specified expected value, the premium being specified also. Let the premium waiver for any state be the difference between premium and preinsurance income if positive, and zero otherwise. Suppose further that the expected benefits are at least equal to the expected premium waiver. Then the optimal policy has the form of stating a critical marginal utility of income and paying (a) exactly the premium waiver if preinsurance income falls short of the premium and the marginal utility at zero income does not exceed the critical marginal utility, (b) the amount needed to be added to postpremium preinsurance income to bring the marginal utility to the critical level if the marginal utility at zero is greater than the critical level and if the postpremium preinsurance income is either negative or has a marginal utility higher than the critical level, and (c) nothing in other states. The critical marginal utility is just such as to make the expected payments have the specified value.*

If the marginal utility of zero income is always infinite, then possibility (a) is ruled out for all states.

In the special case where the utility functions in all states of the world are the same, it can be seen that (a) cannot occur. For if $U_s'(0) \leq \lambda$ for some s, the same holds for all s when utility is independent of state. In that case, $U'(y_s) < \lambda$ when $y_s > 0$, which would mean that no insurance is paid at all, other than premium waivers. If expected benefits exceed expected premium waivers, this could hardly be optimal. Hence, Theorem 1 remains valid as stated.

Now we consider the full problem of optimization, with premium variable and expected benefits a prescribed fraction, α, of the premium. As before, we approach this through the intermediate problem of studying the effects of varying E and P. The transformed problem is slightly more complicated than before, because a change in P has not only the direct effect studied before but also has effects through the fact that in part it determines the values of b_s and of F, as can be seen from (12-59) and (12-64). Let the maximum utility obtained in the transformed problem with parameters F, P, b_1, . . . , b_n be denoted by $\overline{W}(F,P,b_1, \ldots ,b_n)$, while the maximum utility can also be expressed in terms of the original parameters as $W(E,P)$, so that

(12-66) $W(E,P) = \overline{W}(F,P,b_1, \ldots ,b_n).$

In view of (12-65), we can write (12-59) and (12-64) as

$$b_s = P \quad \text{if } s \in Q$$
$$= a_s \quad \text{if } s \notin Q,$$

$$F = E - \sum_{s \in Q} p_s(P - a_s) = E + \sum_{s \in Q} p_s a_s - Pp(Q),$$

and therefore

(12-67) $db_s/dP = 1 \quad \text{if } s \in Q$
$$= 0 \quad \text{if } s \notin Q,$$

(12-68) $\partial F/\partial P = -p(Q), \qquad \partial F/\partial E = 1.$

It should be noted, though, that db_s/dP and $\partial F/\partial P$ are not continuous functions of P. Specifically, as P increases through a value a_s, for some s, both of these magnitudes change discontinuously, the first changing from 0 to 1, the second decreasing by p_s when P passes beyond a_s, so that s is added to Q.

A change in E operates only through a change in F; hence from (12-66) and the second half of (12-68),

(12-69) $\partial W/\partial E = (\partial \overline{W}/\partial F)(\partial F/\partial E) = \partial \overline{W}/\partial F = \lambda$

by (12-42) applied to the transformed problem.
    From (12-66),

$$\partial W/\partial P = (\partial \overline{W}/\partial F)(\partial F/\partial P) + (\partial \overline{W}/\partial P) + \sum_s (\partial \overline{W}/\partial b_s)(db_s/dP).$$

But from (12-40) and (12-45), applied to the transformed problem,

$$\partial \overline{W}/\partial P = - \sum_s p_s U_s'(y_s), \qquad \partial \overline{W}/\partial b_s = p_s U_s'(y_s).$$

Hence, with the aid of (12-67) through (12-69),

$$\partial W/\partial P = -\lambda p(Q) - \sum_s p_s U_s'(y_s) + \sum_{s \in Q} p_s U_s'(y_s)$$

$$= -\lambda p(Q) - \sum_{s \notin Q} p_s U_s'(y_s).$$

Among the states not in Q, consider separately those in S and those not in S. Let

(12-70) $M = S \cup Q,$

that is, those states in either S or Q. For all states in S, and in particular those in $S \sim Q$ (that is, those in S but not in Q), $U'_s(y_s) = \lambda$. Those states in neither S nor Q are precisely those not in M.

$$\sum_{s \notin Q} p_s U'_s(y_s) = \lambda p(S \sim Q) + \sum_{s \notin M} p_s U'_s(y_s).$$

Hence,

$$\partial W/\partial P = -\lambda[p(Q) + p(S \sim Q)] - \sum_{s \notin M} p_s U'_s(y_s).$$

Since the sets Q and $S \sim Q$ are disjoint and their union is M, $p(Q) + p(S \sim Q) = p(M)$.

(12-71) $\partial W/\partial P = -\lambda p(M) - \sum_{s \notin M} p_s U'_s(y_s).$

It is easy to see that, as before, W is a concave function of E and P. Hence, if we vary P with $E = \alpha P$, the total derivative is nonincreasing. From (12-69) and (12-71),

(12-72) $dW/dP = [\alpha - p(M)]\lambda - \sum_{s \notin M} p_s U'_s(y_s).$

We now parallel the discussion in Section 5. For P sufficiently small, specifically when $P < \min_s a_s$, the set Q of waiver states is empty. The condition that there be no insurance at all therefore remains the same as before, as given by (12-48).

Can there be insurance in all states? Note that M is the set of insured states, whether through waivers or through discretionary insurance or both. Hence, the question is whether, at an optimum, M consists of all states. If it did, the second term in (12-72) vanishes, while $p(M) = 1$. Clearly if $\alpha < 1$, then $dW/dP < 0$ at such a point, implying that it is not optimal. Therefore, as before, complete coverage is not optimal if the offering is actuarially unfair. The converse is also true, as can be seen rather trivially by raising all payments and the premium by the same amount, preserving postinsurance incomes. Then every state can be made into a waiver state. This is possible because the budget constraint for the actuarially fair case,

(12-73) $\sum_s p_s i_s = P,$

will remain valid under the simultaneous and equal increase of insurance payments and premium. The optimal policy in the actuarially fair case is determined in a somewhat more general way than described in Section 5, since we are no longer assuming that $U_s''(0) = +\infty$. What we do is choose y_s to maximize

$$\sum_s p_s U_s(y_s),$$

subject to $y_s \geq 0$, and

$$\sum_s p_s y_s = \sum_s p_s a_s.$$

Then choose i_s, P so that $i_s = P - a_s + y_s$, the desired postinsurance incomes are achieved, and P is sufficiently large so that $i_s \geq 0$, all s. The budget constraint (12-73) will then automatically be satisfied.

When $\alpha < 1$, there will be an interior maximum. In general, this will occur when $dW/dP = 0$, but since dW/dP is not continuous at values of P equal to some a_s, we have only the weaker condition that $dW/dP \geq 0$ for P slightly smaller, $dW/dP \leq 0$ for P slightly larger. If we define

$$(12\text{-}74) \qquad R_1(P) = p(M) + \left[\sum_{s \notin M} p_s U_s''(y_s)/\lambda \right],$$

we can say that optimal P is determined by the condition

$$R_1(P) = \alpha$$

at any point of continuity of $R_1(P)$, and

$$R_1(P - 0) \leq \alpha \leq R_1(P + 0)$$

at a point of discontinuity, where $R_1(P - 0)$ means the limit of R_1 as P is approached from the left, and $R_1(P + 0)$ the limit as P is approached from the right.

A point of discontinuity of $R_1(P)$ can occur only when M changes. However, a change in M without a change in Q occurs at a point P not equal to any of the initial incomes a_s; there must therefore be a change in S. If a state s is added to S, then $p(M)$ is increased by p_s, while the term in brackets is reduced by $p_s U_s''(y_s)/\lambda$. But when a state not in S for smaller P enters into S, it must be true, by continuity, that $U_s''(y_s) = \lambda$, and we have an increase of p_s balanced by an equal decrease, and therefore no discontinuity. Hence, a discontinuity in $R_1(P)$ can occur only at a point of change in Q, that is, when P reaches one of the values a_t. But even in this case, if $t \in S$ at $P = a_t$, there would be no discontinuity. The only discontinuities possible occur at points a_t for which $t \notin S$—that is, for which $U_s''(y_t) < \lambda$. Clearly, by continuity, if $t \notin S$ at $P = a_t$, $t \notin S$ in a neighborhood of a_t. Also, by the definition of Q,

(12-65), $t \notin Q$ for $P \leq a_t$, $t \in Q$ for $P > a_t$. Hence, $t \notin M$ for $P \leq a_t$, $t \in M$ for $P > a_t$. Therefore, for all possible discontinuities,

$$R_1(P-0) = p(M) + [p_t U_t''(y_t)/\lambda] + \left[\sum_{\substack{s\notin M \\ s\notin t}} p_s U_s''(y_s)/\lambda\right] = R_1(P),$$

$$R_1(P+0) = p(M) + p_t + \left[\sum_{\substack{s\notin M \\ s\notin t}} p_s U_s''(y_s)/\lambda\right].$$

(In these formulas, the set M is understood to be that at $P = a_t$.)

Thus the premium level P is optimal if one of the following two conditions holds:

(12-75) $R_1(P) = \alpha$,

$$R_1(P) \leq \alpha \leq p(M) + p_t + \left[\sum_{\substack{s\notin M \\ s\notin t}} p_s U_s''(y_s)/\lambda\right], \quad t \notin S, \quad \text{where}$$

(12-76) S and M are those corresponding to $P = a_t$.

From either (12-75) or (12-76), $R_1(P) \leq \alpha < 1$. From (12-74), it must be that $p(M) < 1$, so that there are some states s not in M, and therefore the second term of $R_1(P)$ is positive. The inequality $R_1(P) \leq \alpha$ then implies

(12-77) $p(M) < \alpha$ if $\alpha < 1$.

It will be helpful to give something of an interpretation of $R_1(P)$. M can be partitioned into the two sets S and $Q \frown S$, so that $p(M) = p(S) + p(Q \frown S)$. Also $U_s''(y_s) = \lambda$ for $s \in S$, so that

$$\lambda p(S) = \sum_{s\in S} p_s U_s''(y_s).$$

If $s \in Q \frown S$, then $P - a_s > 0$, while $j_s = 0$, so that

$$i_s = j_s + \max (P - a_s, 0) = P - a_s,$$

and therefore $y_s = a_s + i_s - P = 0$. At the same time, $\lambda > U_s''(y_s) = U_s''(0)$.

$$\lambda p(Q \frown S) = \sum_{s\in Q-S} p_s[\lambda - U_s''(0) + U_s''(y_s)],$$

$$= \sum_{s\in Q-S} p_s[\lambda - U_s''(0)] + \sum_{s\in Q-S} p_s U_s''(y_s),$$

$$= p(Q \frown S)\{\lambda - E[U_s''(0)|Q \frown S]\} + \sum_{s\in Q-S} p_s U_s''(y_s).$$

Substitution into (12-74) yields

$$R_1(P) = R(P) + p(Q \frown S)\{1 - E[U_s'(0)|Q \frown S]/\lambda\},$$

where $R(P)$ is defined in Theorem 3 as the ratio of expected to maximum marginal utility of income at the optimum policy. From an earlier remark recall that if $U_s'(0) = +\infty$ for all s, then Q is a subset of S, so that $Q \frown S$ can have no elements, and $R_1(P) = R(P)$, which is continuous, so that the optimal P is determined by (12-75).

Finally, is the policy that satisfies (12-75) or (12-76) in fact feasible? It may be recalled that one of the hypotheses of Theorem 4 was that expected benefits, which are αP, be at least equal to expected premium waivers. In the notation used, we want to make sure that $F \geq 0$. But if $P = 0$, then $E = \alpha P = 0$, and certainly $F = 0$. Further, as P increases, with $E = \alpha P$, the total derivative of F is given by

$$dF/dP = (\partial F/\partial P) + \alpha(\partial F/\partial E) = \alpha - p(Q)$$

from (12-68). But for P not exceeding the optimum $dW/dP \geq 0$, which in turn is equivalent to $R_1(P) \leq \alpha$, and therefore implies $p(M) < \alpha$. Since Q is a subset of M, $p(Q) \leq p(M) < \alpha$, so that $dF/dP > 0$ at all P up to and indeed somewhat beyond the optimum P. Since $F = 0$ when $P = 0$, $F > 0$ throughout this interval, and the P chosen as optimum by (12-75) or (12-76) is indeed feasible.

THEOREM 5. *Suppose that the utility of income depends in general on the state of the world and that the individual can choose any insurance policy with nonnegative payments with a given ratio, $\alpha \leq 1$, of expected benefits to premium. For any P, consider the optimal policy defined in Theorem 4 for premium P and expected benefits αP. For that policy, let R(P) be the ratio of expected to maximum marginal utility of postinsurance income, $\lambda(P)$ the critical marginal utility, and N the set of states defined in Theorem 4(a), those for which the insurance payment is positive but exactly equals the premium waiver, and*

$$R_1(P) = R(P) + p(N)\{1 - E[U_s'(0)|N]/\lambda(P)\}.$$

(a) *No insurance is taken out if and only if the expected benefit-premium ratio does not exceed the ratio of expected to maximum marginal utility of preinsurance income — that is, $\alpha \leq R(0)$.*

(b) *If $R(0) < \alpha$, then the optimal premium level always exists and is defined by the condition*

$$R_1(P) \leqq \alpha \leqq R_1(P + 0).$$

(c) *The function $R_1(P)$ is monotone increasing. Hence, if $R_1(P) = \alpha$, condition* (b) *certainly holds. Also, a discontinuity at P can occur only if both* (1) $P = a_s$, *the preinsurance income, for some state s, and* (2) $U'_s(0) < \lambda(P)$ *when $P = a_s$. Hence, for any other P, the condition $R_1(P) = \alpha$ is necessary as well as sufficient that P be optimal.*

(d) *If any of the following conditions hold, then in every state where a premium waiver is paid, the insurance payment exceeds the premium waiver* (Q *is a subset of S*), *and therefore $R_1(P) = R(P)$ at the optimum:* (1) $\alpha \leqq R$ *(min$_s$ a_s);* (2) *the utility function for income is independent of the state of the world;* (3) $U'_s(0) = +\infty$, *all s. Since R(P) is increasing and continuous, the optimality condition would then be simply $R(P) = \alpha$.*

(e) *If the offering is not actuarially fair, so that $\alpha < 1$, then the probability of being in a state for which the insurance payment is positive is less than α.*

(f) *If the offering is actuarially fair ($\alpha = 1$), then the optimal policy is defined as the set of postinsurance incomes that maximizes expected utility subject to the condition of actuarial fairness (expected value of preinsurance income equals expected value of postinsurance income). These postinsurance incomes can be realized with nonnegative insurance payments by raising the premium sufficiently high.*

8. Comparative Statics: The Effect of Changing the Benefit-Premium Ratio

It was shown how to determine the optimal insurance policy when the expected benefit-premium ratio is some given α. It is of interest to observe how the optimal policy will change with changes in that parameter. To avoid unnecessary complications, we will essentially return to the situation of Theorem 3. That is, we ignore the possibility of premium waivers; or, to be more precise, in any state in which insurance is paid, it is assumed that the amount paid exceeds the premium waiver. Alternative conditions for validity of this assumption are given in Theorem 5(d).

The optimal policy for any given α is completely characterized by two parameters, the critical marginal utility of income, λ, and the premium, P. These can be regarded as defined by the two equations (12-30), with $E = \alpha P$, and (12-49), provided, of course $\alpha > R(0)$, so that we are in the interior case.

These equations are rewritten somewhat.

In (12-49) recall that $U'_s(y_s) = \lambda$ for $s \in S$. Then (12-49), or, equivalently, the equation $R(P) = \alpha$, can be written

$$\alpha\lambda = \sum_{s \in S} p_s U'_s(y_s) + \sum_{s \notin S} p_s U'_s(y_s) = \lambda p(S) + \sum_{s \notin S} p_s U'_s(y_s),$$

or

(12-78) $[\alpha - p(S)]\lambda = \sum_{s \notin S} p_s U'_s(y_s).$

In (12-30), substitute the definition of $V_s(\lambda, P)$ from (12-26):

$$\sum_{s \in S} p_s[(U'_s)^{-1}(\lambda) + P - a_s] = \alpha P,$$

or

$$\sum_{s \in S} p_s[(U'_s)^{-1}(\lambda) - a_s] + p(S)P = \alpha P,$$

or, finally,

(12-79) $\sum_{s \in S} p_s[(U'_s)^{-1}(\lambda) - a_s] = [\alpha - p(S)]P.$

Note that from Theorem 5(e) or Theorem 3(c), $\alpha - p(S) > 0$. We will study the dependence of λ and P on α through (12-78)–(12-79) over an interval in which S is constant. Since λ and P are continuous functions of α even at points where S changes, this analysis will give us a correct qualitative picture for all changes. For S fixed, let

(12-80) $\beta_S = \alpha - p(S) > 0,$

(12-81) $\psi_S(P) = \sum_{s \notin S} p_s U'_s(y_s),$

(12-82) $\Phi_S(\lambda) = \sum_{s \in S} p_s[(U'_s)^{-1}(\lambda) - a_s].$

Since $y_s = a_s - P$ for $s \notin S$, it is indeed true that $\psi_S(P)$ is a function of P alone (and not of λ or α, for S fixed). Since U'_s is a decreasing function, it follows from (12-81) and (12-82) that

(12-83) $\psi'_s(P) > 0,$

(12-84) $\Phi'_S(\lambda) < 0.$

Equations (12-78) and (12-79) can be written in the compact form

(12-85) $\beta_S \lambda - \psi_S(P) = 0,$

(12-86) $\Phi_S(\lambda) - \beta_S P = 0.$

As long as S is fixed, a change in α is equivalent to a change in β_S. Hence, differentiate the equations (12-85)–(12-86) with respect to β_S.

(12-87) $\beta_S(d\lambda/d\alpha) - \psi'_S(P)(dP/d\alpha) = -\lambda,$

(12-88) $\Phi'_S(\lambda)(d\lambda/d\alpha) - \beta_S(dP/d\alpha) = P.$

Equations (12-87)–(12-88) constitute a pair of linear equations in the comparative statics relations $d\lambda/d\alpha$ and $dP/d\alpha$. The determinant of this system is easily seen to be

(12-89) $D = -\beta_S^2 + \psi'_S(P)\Phi'_S(\lambda) < 0$

from (12-83)–(12-84). Solving by Cramer's rule yields

(12-90) $d\lambda/d\alpha = [\lambda\beta_S + P\psi'_S(P)]/D,$

(12-91) $dP/d\alpha = [\beta_S P + \lambda\Phi'_S(\lambda)]/D.$

From (12-80), (12-83), and (12-89), $d\lambda/d\alpha < 0$ unequivocally. Hence, since $U'_S(y_s) = \lambda$ for $s \in S$, y_s will be increasing for all insured states.

The variation of P with respect to α is not completely defined as to sign by purely theoretical considerations. We know, of course, that for α sufficiently small, $P = 0$, while for $\alpha = 1$, P can be indefinitely large. Hence, broadly speaking, the premium demanded will increase with the ratio of expected benefits to premiums. However, there could in principle be intervals in which an increase in α is accompanied by a decrease in P, though only under unlikely conditions.

We first note that, from (12-80) and (12-84), the two terms in the numerator of (12-91) are of opposite signs. From (12-89), the sign of $dP/d\alpha$ is opposite to that of this numerator, which we now proceed to interpret. From (12-31) and (12-32), we see that

$$\lambda\Phi'_S(\lambda) = -\sum_{s \in S} p_s T_s.$$

From (12-80) and the budget equation,

$$\beta_S P = \alpha P - Pp(S) = \sum_{s \in S} p_s(i_s - P).$$

Hence,

(12-92) $dP/d\alpha > 0$ if and only if $\sum_{s \in S} p_s(T_s - i_s + P) > 0.$

Certainly a sufficient condition for (12-92) to hold is that $T_s > i_s - P$ for all insured states s. Under the assumption of risk aversion, $T_s > 0$, so that certainly $T_s > i_s - P$ when $i_s \leq P$. For the case $i_s > P$ (the states where there is insurance beyond that needed to cover the premium), it is convenient to use the concept of relative risk aversion, introduced in (12-33). Then $T_s > i_s - P$ if and only if

(12-93) $R_{Rs}(y_s) < y_s/(i_s - P) = 1 + [a_s/(i_s - P)].$

Now if insurance is relatively minor compared with incomes, the right-hand side of (12-93) is very large, and the inequality is likely to hold. It can fail to hold, however, for states in which the insurance payment is large compared with preinsurance income and for which the relative risk aversion is large. This can happen in the medical context. Consider a state of illness in which the marginal utility of income is high up to some relatively large figure and then drops off sharply; further income has little value for either medical or nonmedical purposes. Then the right-hand side may not be much above one, while the left-hand side is large. But if this situation holds only for a set of states of relatively low total probability, we may expect (12-92) to hold even if (12-93) fails for a few states. It is certainly true that (12-93) holds if relative risk aversion never exceeds one, but this seems to be a strong assumption.

If the marginal utility of income is independent of the state, then y_s, $T_s(y_s)$, and $R_{Rs}(y_s)$ are the same for all insured states. From (12-92), by an argument like that leading to (12-93), a necessary and sufficient condition for $dP/d\alpha > 0$ is that

$$R_R(y) < 1 + [E(a_s|S)/E(i_s - P|S)].$$

It is easy to see that (12-92) can fail to hold. Consider, for example, the case where S contains a single element. Then it is only necessary to construct a case in which the inequality in (12-93) is reversed, while (12-78) and (12-79) hold. Hence, as remarked, the pure theory does not exclude the possibility that P falls as α increases for some ranges. In those ranges, note that $y_s = a_s - P$ is increasing in the noninsured states, while in the standard case of increasing P, the individual is getting worse off in the noninsured states. In those states, the ratio $U_s'(y_s)/\lambda$ is less than one, but the numerator is increasing if P increases, and the denominator is decreasing, so that eventually such a state moves into the insured category. Similarly, in an insured state, $y_s = a_s + i_s - P$ is increasing. If P is increasing, i_s must certainly be increasing and can never fall to zero, so that a state, once insured, cannot subsequently become uninsured in the standard case.

If, however, P decreases, it is conceivable that in an insured state i_s may fall to zero, and a state that is insured at one value becomes uninsured at a higher value. However, the postinsurance income associated with any state must be higher at higher α than it was when insured. Let $y_s(\alpha)$ and $\lambda(\alpha)$ be postinsurance income in state s and critical marginal utility as functions of α. Suppose state s is insured at some benefit-premium ratio α, and let $\alpha' > \alpha$. Then

$$U_s'[y_s(\alpha)] = \lambda(\alpha), \qquad U_s'[y_s(\alpha')] \leq \lambda(\alpha') < \lambda(\alpha),$$

so that $y_s(\alpha') > y_s(\alpha)$.

THEOREM 6. *Consider the optimal policy defined in Theorem 5 for any given expected benefit-premium ratio α. Assume that the premium waiver, if paid at all, is always smaller than the insurance payment (as would be true under any of the hypotheses of Theorem 5d). Then the critical marginal utility of income, λ, decreases as α increases, and therefore the postinsurance income for any insured state increases with α as long as that state remains insured. If it ceases to be insured at some higher value of α, it still must be true that postpremium income exceeds the postinsurance income at any lower benefit-premium ratio for which that state was insured.*

The premium is zero for sufficiently small α and can be regarded as indefinitely large when $\alpha = 1$. It is not necessarily monotonic increasing with α; it increases if and only if

$$E(T_s - i_s + P|S) > 0.$$

A sufficient condition that P increase with α is that the relative risk aversion for any insured state s at income y_s be smaller than

$$1 + [a_s/(i_s - P)].$$

If the utility of income is independent of the state, then the necessary and sufficient condition for the premium to increase with the benefit-premium ratio is that the relative risk aversion in any insured state (it is the same for all such states) not exceed $1 + [E(a_s|S)/E(i_s - P|S)]$.

9. Comparative Statics: The Effect of Changing Probabilities

The benefit-premium ratio is not the only parameter of the optimal choice of insurance policy. The probabilities of the different states are also parameters, and we may consider how the optimal policy would be different if the parameters were different. Such an effect may be useful to study for several reasons: it may be that, with changing knowledge or changing circumstances, such as alterations of medical techniques or public health measures, the probabilities of different states change; or one might want to know the sensitivity of the policy to errors in estimating the probabilities.

As in the preceding section, the basic technique is the differentiation of Eqs. (12-85)–(12-86), defining the optimal policy with respect to the parameter under study, in this case p_s, the probability of state s. There is a slight complication; the parameters p_s being probabilities, their sum must always be equal to one. Hence, one probability cannot be changed without changing one or more others. In what follows, it will be understood that if p_s is altered, then all other probabilities $p_t(t \neq s)$ are changed so as to keep their values relative to each other, while ensuring that the sum of the probabilities adds up correctly.

From a purely formal viewpoint, we can consider the parameters p_s in the insurance optimization to be independent parameters, if we ignore their interpretation as probabilities. It will be mathematically useful to follow this interpretation as a step in deriving the effects corrected by having other probabilities change appropriately. That is, we first consider the solution to the problem stated in (12-3)–(12-8), of maximizing

$$(12\text{-}3) \qquad \sum_s p_s U_s(y_s)$$

subject to

$$\sum_s p_s i_s = \alpha P$$

as a function of the parameters p_s, taken to be independent. As we know, a solution can be completely characterized by the choice of the critical marginal utility, λ, and the premium, P, and we consider the variation of these two magnitudes with respect to the variables p_s. From these derivatives, in turn, we derive the derivatives when a change in any one p_s is offset by changes in others to preserve the sum at unity.

The first step, then, is to differentiate (12-85)–(12-86) with respect to p_s. The result depends on whether $s \in S$ or not. First suppose $s \in S$. In (12-85),

p_s only appears in the factor $\beta_S = \alpha - p(S) = \alpha - \Sigma_{s \in S} p_s$. Hence, differentiation of (12-85) with respect to $p_s(s \in S)$ yields

$$\beta_S(\partial\lambda/\partial p_s) - \psi'_S(\partial P/\partial p_s) = \lambda \quad (s \in S).$$

In (12-86), p_s appears in β_S and also, from (12-82), in one term of the sum defining Φ_S. In the latter, p_s is multiplied by

$$(U'_s)^{-1}(\lambda) - a_s = y_s - a_s = i_s - P.$$

Hence, differentiation of (12-86) with respect to p_s yields

$$\Phi'_S(\partial\lambda/\partial p_s) - \beta_S(\partial P/\partial p_s) = -(y_s - a_s) - P \quad (s \in S).$$

We can solve these two equations $\partial\lambda/\partial p_s$ and $\partial P/\partial p_s$ by Cramer's rule. By comparison with (12-87) – (12-90), it is easy to see that

(12-94a) $\partial\lambda/\partial p_s = -(d\lambda/d\alpha) - (y_s - a_s)\psi'_S/D \quad (s \in S),$

(12-94b) $\partial P/\partial p_s = -(dP/d\alpha) - (y_s - a_s)\beta_S/D \quad (s \in S).$

Now differentiate with respect to $p_s(s \notin S)$. In (12-85), p_s enters only in the term ψ_S, where it has coefficient U'_s.

$$\beta_S(\partial\lambda/\partial p_s) - \psi'_S(\partial P/\partial p_s) = U'_s \quad (s \notin S).$$

In (12-86), p_s does not appear at all for $s \notin S$.

$$\Phi'_S(\partial\lambda/\partial p_s) - \beta_S(\partial P/\partial p_s) = 0 \quad (s \notin S).$$

Solution yields

(12-95a) $\partial\lambda/\partial p_s = -\beta_S U'_s/D \quad (s \notin S),$

(12-95b) $\partial P/\partial p_s = -U'_s\Phi'_S/D \quad (s \notin S).$

The next step is to adjust the effect of a change in one probability for the fact that others have to change simultaneously. Write

$$q_s = 1, q_t = p_t/(1 - p_s) \quad \text{for } t \neq s.$$

Then the condition that the relative values of $p_t(t \neq s)$ remain constant is equivalent to the condition that q_t remain constant, since $1 - p_s = \Sigma_{t \neq s} p_t$. Then

$$p_s = q_s p_s, p_t = q_t(1 - p_s) \quad \text{for } t \neq s.$$

For constant q_t's, we can consider the total derivative of λ with respect to

p_s; call it λ'_s.

$$\lambda'_s = \sum_t (\partial\lambda/\partial p_t)(dp_t/dp_s) = q_s(\partial\lambda/\partial p_s) - \sum_{t \neq s} q_t(\partial\lambda/\partial p_t)$$

$$= (\partial\lambda/\partial p_s) - [1/(1 - p_s)] \sum_{t \neq s} p_t(\partial\lambda/\partial p_t)$$

$$= [1/(1 - p_s)][(\partial\lambda/\partial p_s) - \sum_t p_t(\partial\lambda/\partial p_t)].$$

This result assumes slightly simpler form if the independent variable is taken to be not p_s, but its transform, $- \ln(1 - p_s)$. Let

(12-96) $\lambda_s = d\lambda/d[- \ln(1 - p_s)] = (1 - p_s)\lambda'_s = (\partial\lambda/\partial p_s) - \sum_t p_t(\partial\lambda/\partial p_t).$

Note that $- \ln(1 - p_s)$ is monotone increasing in p_s. Hence, the sign of λ_s indicates whether an increase in p_s with compensating proportional changes in all other probabilities increases or decreases λ. λ_s is the effect on λ of a given proportionate decrease in the probability that s will not occur.

One can calculate the term $\sum_t p_t(\partial\lambda/\partial p_t)$ from (12-94a) and (12-95b), but in fact it is easier and more revealing to argue more directly. The term in question is clearly the effect on λ of a shift in all p_s's in the same proportion. Such a shift has two effects: it multiplies the maximand (12-3) by a constant, and it multiplies the left-hand side of the budget constraint,

$$\sum_t p_t i_t = \alpha P,$$

by a constant. The first shift has no effect at all on the choice of the maximizing variables and, in particular, on λ. The second has exactly the same effect as a decrease of α in the same proportion. Hence,

(12-97) $\sum_t p_t(\partial\lambda/\partial p_t) = - \alpha(d\lambda/d\alpha).$

We can therefore calculate λ_s by substituting (12-97) and (12-94a) or (12-95a) into (12-96).

(12-98a) $\lambda_s = - [(1 - \alpha)(d\lambda/d\alpha) + (y_s - a_s)\psi'_s/D]   (s \in S),$

(12-98b) $\lambda_s = \alpha(d\lambda/d\alpha) - (\beta_S U'_s/D)   (s \notin S).$

If we substitute (12-90) into (12-98a) and simplify, we find

(12-99) $\lambda_s = (-1/D)\{(1 - \alpha)\lambda\beta_S + [(1 - \alpha)P + (i_s - P)]\psi'_s\}   (s \in S).$

From (12-89), $D < 0$; from (12-83), $\psi_S > 0$, so that certainly $\lambda_s > 0$ if

$(1 - \alpha)P + (i_s - P) = i_s - \alpha P \geqq 0$. Since an increase in λ implies a decrease in y_s for all $s \in S$,

(12-100) $i_s \geqq \alpha P$ implies that an increase in the probability of s, all other probabilities changing proportionately, leads to a fall in postinsurance income in every insured state.

Note further that the right-hand side of (12-99) is an increasing function of i_s. Since $i_s \geqq 0$ for insured states,

(12-101) $\lambda_s \geqq (-1/D)[(1 - \alpha)\lambda\beta - \alpha P\psi'_s]$ $(s \in S)$.

If the right-hand side of (12-101) is positive, then certainly $\lambda_s > 0$ for all $s \in S$. We can also say that there is a critical level of i_s such that among insured states, $\lambda_s > 0$ if and only if i_s exceeds that level; this critical level is, of course, a function of all the parameters of the problem. Given the parameters, and therefore the value of P, we can equivalently say there is a critical level of i_s/P with the stated property. This critical level may be zero and, from (12-100), must be less than α.

Now substitute (12-90) into (12-98b) and simplify to find

(12-102) $\lambda_s = (-1/D)[(U'_s - \alpha\lambda)\beta_s - \alpha P\psi'_s]$ $(s \notin S)$.

We immediately note that $U'_s \leqq \alpha\lambda$ implies $\lambda_s < 0$. Also the right-hand side of (12-102) is increasing in U'_s, so that there is a critical level of U'_s such that $\lambda_s < 0$ if and only if U'_s is below that limit. We can speak equivalently of a critical level for $(U'_s/\lambda) - 1$, and then we see that this critical level must be greater than $\alpha - 1$. Finally, since $U'_s \leqq \lambda$ for all $s \notin S$, it follows from (12-102) that

(12-103) $\lambda_s \leqq (-1/D)[(1 - \alpha)\lambda\beta_S - \alpha P\psi'_S]$ $(s \notin S)$.

If the right-hand side of (12-101) and (12-103) is positive, then $\lambda_s > 0$ for all $s \in S$ and for all $s \notin S$ for which $(U'_s/\lambda) - 1$ is sufficiently close to zero. If that right-hand side is negative, then $\lambda_s < 0$ for all $s \notin S$ and for all $s \in S$ for which i_s/P is sufficiently small. Define therefore

$k_s = i_s/P$ for $s \in S$

$\quad\;\, = (U'_s/\lambda) - 1$ for $s \notin S$.

Note that $k_s \geqq 0$ for $s \in S$, $k_s \leqq 0$ for $s \notin S$. Then all the preceding can be summed up by saying that there is a critical level, k_0, such that $\lambda_s > 0$ if

$k_s > k_0$, $\lambda_s < 0$ if $k_s < k_0$. Further, k_0 may be positive or negative or zero but is necessarily bounded by $\alpha - 1 < k_0 < \alpha$.

The effects of changing probabilities on the premium P can be studied similarly. The following analogues of (12-96) and (12-97) hold:

$$P_s = dP/d[-\ln(1 - p_s)] = (\partial P/\partial p_s) - E(\partial P/\partial p_s),$$

$$E(\partial P/\partial p_s) = -\alpha(dP/d\alpha).$$

Substitute from (12-94b) and (12-91).

$$(12\text{-}104) \quad P_s = -[(1 - \alpha)(dP/d\alpha)] - \beta_S(y_s - a_s)/D$$

$$= (-1/D)[(1 - \alpha)\lambda\Phi'_S + \beta_S(i_s - \alpha P)] \quad (s \in S).$$

From (12-84), $\Phi'_S < 0$. Hence, $P_s < 0$ if $i_s \leqq \alpha P$. Since P_s increases with i_s, we can say, by reasoning like that just used, that there is a critical level, k_1, such that for insured states, $P_s > 0$ if $i_s/P > k_1$, $P_s < 0$ if $i_s/P < k_1$, and $k_1 > \alpha$.

From (12-95b) and (12-91),

$$(12\text{-}105) \quad P_s = \alpha(dP/d\alpha) - (U'_s\Phi_S/D)$$

$$= (-1/D)[(U'_s - \alpha\lambda)\Phi'_s - \alpha\beta_s P] \quad (s \notin S).$$

If $U'_s \geqq \alpha\lambda$, then $P_s < 0$. Since P_s decreases as U'_s increases, it follows that there is a critical level, k_2, such that for uninsured states $P_s < 0$ if $(U'_s/\lambda) - 1 > k_2$, $P_s > 0$ in the opposite case; further, $k_2 < \alpha - 1$. Hence, we can summarize by saying that there are two critical levels, k_1 and k_2, such that $P_s < 0$ if $k_2 < k_s < k_1$, $P_s > 0$ if $k_s > k_1$ or $k_s < k_2$; further, $k_1 > \alpha$, $k_2 < \alpha - 1$. It can also be seen from (12-105), since $U'_s > 0$, that $P_s \leqq \alpha(dP/d\alpha)$ for $s \notin S$; hence, if $dP/d\alpha < 0$, $P_s < 0$ for all $s \notin S$ so that $k_2 = -1$.

The actuarially fair case ($\alpha = 1$) has not been covered by the discussion to this point. In this case, as we know, the optimal premium is essentially indeterminate, and all attention is concentrated on λ, which is determined by (12-50). Clearly, multiplication of all coefficients p_s by a common factor leaves the solution, λ, unchanged, so that

$$\sum_s p_s(\partial\lambda/\partial p_s) = 0.$$

Then, from (12-96), $\lambda_s = \partial\lambda/\partial p_s$. Differentiation of (12-50) yields

$$\left[\sum_t (p_t/U_t'')\right](\partial\lambda/\partial p_s) = -(i_s - P).$$

In this case, $\partial\lambda/\partial p_s$ has the same sign as $i_s - P$, so that $k_0 = 1$.

There is one curious implication of this remark: if a state is net insured (that is, $i_s > P$) for some set of probabilities, it will remain net insured if its probability alters, with all other probabilities changing in proportion. To see this, suppose state s is net insured for some set of probabilities. If p_s falls, λ falls, so that i_s rises, and $i_s - P$ increases, the state becoming even more heavily net insured. If p_s rises, i_s indeed falls. But it cannot fall to a value below P, for if it did, λ would start falling, and therefore i_s could not fall. Another way of seeing this is to note that if $i_s = P$ at some set of probabilities, then λ must be constant for any change in p_s. If we write (12-50) as

$$p_s(i_s - P) + \sum_{t \neq s} p_t(y_t - a_t) = 0,$$

then, since the first term is zero, the second term is also. If p_s changes, and the p_t's change proportionately ($t \neq s$), then if λ remains constant, all y_t's remain constant, both terms remain zero, and therefore the equation remains satisfied. Hence, if $i_s > P$ (or $i_s < P$) for some set of probabilities, no change in p_s alone can bring i_s into equality with P.

THEOREM 7. *Consider the optimal policy defined in Theorem 5. Assume that the premium waiver, if paid at all, is always smaller than the insurance payment (as would be true under any of the hypotheses of Theorem 5d). In the following, when it is asserted that the probability of a state rises, it is understood that the probabilities of all remaining states fall in proportion to each other so as to preserve the sum of probabilities at one. Let $k_s = i_s/P$ if s is an insured state, $= [U_s'(y_s)/\lambda] - 1$ if s is an uninsured state.*

(a) There is a critical level, k_0, for which $\alpha - 1 < k_0 < \alpha$, such that if $k_s > k_0$, then postinsurance incomes in all insured states fall if p_s increases, while if $k_s < k_0$, they rise with an increase in p_s.

(b) In the actuarially fair case, all states are insured and $k_0 = 1$, so that postinsurance incomes fall with an increase in the probability of a net insured state (one for which the insurance payment exceeds the premium) and rise with the increase in the probability of a state with negative net insurance.

(c) There are two critical levels, k_1 and k_2, such that the premium paid increases with the probability of any state with either $k_s > k_1$ or $k_s < k_2$,

where $k_1 > \alpha$, $k_2 < \alpha - 1$, and decreases with an increase in the probability of any state for which $k_1 < k_s < k_2$.

(d) *Statements (a) and (c) can be partly restated as follows: Among insured states, an increase in the probability of any state for which the insurance payment is at least equal to the expected insurance payment decreases postinsurance incomes in all insured states, while an increase in the probability of any state for which the insurance payment does not exceed the expected insurance payment decreases the premium paid. Among uninsured states, an increase in the probability of any state for which the ratio of the marginal utility of postpremium income to the critical marginal utility is at least equal to the benefit-premium ratio decreases the premium paid, while an increase in the probability of a state where the ratio of marginal utility of postpremium income to the critical marginal utility does not exceed the benefit-premium ratio increases postinsurance income in every insured state.*

(e) *If the premium decreases as the benefit-premium ratio increases, then the premium decreases with an increase in the probability of any uninsured state.*

(f) *In the actuarially fair case, any change in the probability of any given state s leaves unchanged the sign of $i_s - P$.*

Remark. For completeness, I record the exact expressions for k_0, k_1, and k_2 implicit in the preceding analysis, with some substitutions from (12-85) and (12-86).

$$k_1 = \alpha + (1 - \alpha)E(U'_s|\tilde{S})/PE(U''_s|\tilde{S}) \quad \text{if positive,}$$

$$= \alpha - 1 - \alpha PE(U''_s|\tilde{S})/E(U'_s|\tilde{S}) \quad \text{if negative,}$$

$$k_1 = \alpha + (1 - \alpha)E(T_s|S)/E(y_s - a_s|S),$$

$$k_2 = \alpha - 1 - \alpha E(y_s - a_s|S)/E(T_s/S).$$

10. Comparative Statics: The Effect of Changing Initial Incomes

To complete the discussion, consider the one remaining set of parameters, the initial incomes a_s. Again, differentiate expressions (12-85) and (12-86). First consider a_s for $s \in S$. This parameter does not enter (12-85) at all, so that its differentiation leads to

$$\beta_S(\partial\lambda/\partial a_s) - \psi_S(\partial P/\partial a_s) = 0.$$

But a_s does appear in Φ_S, and $\partial\Phi_S/\partial a_s = -p_s$. Differentiation of (12-86) yields

$$\Phi'_S(\partial\lambda/\partial a_s) - \beta_S(\partial P/\partial a_s) = p_s,$$

so that we may easily calculate

$$\partial\lambda/\partial a_s = p_s\psi'_S/D < 0 \quad (s \in S),$$

$$\partial P/\partial a_s = p_s\beta_S/D < 0 \quad (s \in S).$$

If $s \notin S$, then a_s appears in ψ_s, since $y_s = a_s - P$, so that $\partial\psi_s/\partial a_s = p_sU''_s$; a_s does not appear at all in (12-86). Hence differentiation yields

$$\beta_S(\partial\lambda/\partial a_s) - \psi'_S(\partial P/\partial a_s) = p_sU''_s,$$

$$\Phi'_S(\partial\lambda/\partial a_s) - \beta_S(\partial P/\partial a_s) = 0,$$

which can be solved to obtain

$$\partial\lambda/\partial a_s = -p_sU''_s\beta_S/D < 0 \quad (s \notin S),$$

$$\partial P/\partial a_s = -p_sU''_s\Phi'_S/D > 0 \quad (s \notin S).$$

Clearly, $y_t = a_t - P$ falls as a_s rises in any uninsured state other than s. What about $y_s = a_s - P$?

$$\partial y_s/\partial a_s = 1 - (\partial P/\partial a_s) = (D + p_sU''_s\Phi'_S)/D$$

$$= (-1/D)\left[\beta_S^2 + \left(\sum_{t \notin S} p_tU''_t - p_sU''_s\right)\Phi'_S\right]$$

$$= (-1/D)\left(\beta_S^2 + \Phi'_S \sum_{\substack{t \notin S \\ t \neq s}} p_tU''_t\right) > 0$$

with the aid of (12-89), (12-81), (12-84), and the fact that $U_t < 0$.

Finally, in the actuarially fair case, we use (12-50) in the form

$$\sum_s p_s(U'_s)^{-1}(\lambda) = \sum_s p_sa_s,$$

and it is obvious that an increase in any a_s decreases λ.

THEOREM 8. *Consider the optimal policy defined in Theorem 5. Assume that the premium waiver, if paid at all, is always smaller than the insurance payment (as would be true under any of the hypotheses of Theorem 5d).*

(a) An increase in the initial (preinsurance) income in any state increases post-insurance income in every insured state.

(b) *An increase in the preinsurance income in any insured state decreases the premium paid.*

(c) *An increase in the preinsurance income in any uninsured state increases the premium but not so much that the postpremium income in that state is reduced.*

References

Arrow, K. J. 1963. Uncertainty and the welfare economics of medical care. *American Economic Review 53*, 941–973.

Arrow, K. J. 1965. *Aspects of the theory of risk-bearing.* Yrjö Jahnssonin säätio, Helsinki.

Ehrlich, I., and Becker, G. S. 1972. Market insurance, self-insurance, and self-protection. *Journal of Political Economy 80*, 623–648.

Eisner, R., and Strotz, R. 1961. Flight insurance and the theory of choice. *Journal of Political Economy 69*, 355–368.

Gould, J. P. 1969. The expected utility hypothesis and the selection of optimal deductibles for a given insurance policy. *Journal of Business 42*, 143–151.

Hirshleifer, J. 1970. *Investment, interest, and capital.* Prentice-Hall, Englewood Cliffs, New Jersey.

Pashigian, B. P., Schkade, L. L., and Menefee, G. H. 1966. The selection of an optimal deductible for a given insurance policy. *Journal of Business 39*, 35–44.

Pratt, J. W. 1964. Risk aversion in the small and in the large. *Econometrica 32*, 122–136.

Ramsey, F. P. 1931. Truth and probability. *The Foundation of Mathematics and Other Essays,* K. Paul, Trench, Trubner and Co., London.

Samuelson, P. A. 1947. *The foundations of economic analysis.* Harvard University Press, Cambridge, Massachusetts [enlarged ed., 1983].

Smith, V. L. 1968. Optimal insurance coverage. *Journal of Political Economy 76*, 68–77.

Wilson, R. 1968. The theory of syndicates. *Econometrica 36*, 119–132.

Zangwill, I. 1969. *Nonlinear programming: A unified approach.* Prentice-Hall, Englewood Cliffs, N.J.

13   Risk Perception in Psychology and Economics

The growth in cognitive psychology, indeed partly stimulated by the active efforts of some economists, especially Jacob Marschak (1974, essays 4–10, 12, 14, 15, and 26), has coincided with a great attention to risk bearing as a factor in public policy, in areas such as occupational health and nuclear power plant safety. The work of the psychologists has called into doubt many of the analytic tools of the economists, particularly expected-utility theory and Bayesian probabilities. At the same time, these tools have been used far more strongly than ever before in the "rational expectations" models of macroeconomic fluctuations. In this chapter, originally a presidential address given before the Western Economic Association in 1981, I sought to relate at least some aspects of the experimental evidence with tests of the rational expectations hypothesis.

The concept of rationality has been basic to most economic analysis. Its content has been successively refined over the generations. As applied to the static world of certainty, it has turned out to be a weak hypothesis, not easily refuted and therefore not very useful as an explanation, though not literally a tautology. But recent decades have seen the development of stronger versions applied to a world in which time and uncertainty are real. Among its most important manifestations have been criteria for consistency

Reprinted from *Economic Inquiry,* 20 (1982):1–9. This research was supported by the Office of Naval Research Grant ONR N00014-7-C-0685 at the Center for Research on Organizational Efficiency, Stanford University.

in allocation over time, the expected-utility hypothesis of behavior under uncertainty, and what may be termed the Bayesian hypothesis for learning, that is, the consistent use of conditional probabilities for changing beliefs on the basis of new information. These hypotheses have been used widely in offering explanations of empirically observed behavior, though, as not infrequently in economics, the theoretical development has gone much further than the empirical implementation. These hypotheses have also been used increasingly in normative analysis, as a component of benefit-cost studies (therefore frequently referred to as benefit-risk studies). The value of reducing mortality rates from diseases, for example, has been studied by assuming that choice of occupations is made *inter alia* by comparing wage differences with mortality differences (Thaler and Rosen, 1976; Viscusi, 1979).

Hypotheses of rationality have been under attack for empirical falsity almost as long as they have been employed in economics. Thorstein Veblen long ago had some choice sarcastic passages about the extraordinary calculating abilities imputed to the average individual in his or her daily economic life by economists. More recently, Herbert Simon and his colleagues have produced much evidence of the difficulties of human beings in arriving at rational choices even in rather simple contexts (for a survey, see Simon, 1979).

The rationality or irrationality of choice has become a leading interest of the branch of psychology called cognitive psychology. This field of inquiry studies the capacity of human beings for perception and judgment. In the last twenty years it has become a major field of psychological research, in contrast to earlier work which tended to emphasize either the role of emotions or mechanistic models for learning. In good measure, the expected-utility hypothesis provided an important starting point for these studies, in the sense that it provided a refutable hypothesis and indeed one for which the testing of implications was rather straightforward. The economist Jacob Marschak was a major link between the formal developments of John von Neumann and Oskar Morgenstern (1947, appendix, pp. 617–632), which had such great influence on economic theory, and the experimental work of the psychologists (see the papers reprinted in Marschak, 1974, vol. 1). The earliest experiment testing the expected-utility hypothesis seems to be that of Mosteller and Nogee (1951); for a particularly fine study, see Davidson, Suppes, and Siegel (1957). Herbert Simon's exploitation of the analogy between information processing in computers and that in human beings has also been very influential.

Recently, the controversy over nuclear power and its effects has sharpened interest in the way individuals form risk judgments and act on them. In particular, it has proved very difficult to reconcile changes in public opinion attendant on new events with Bayesian learning models in any form. There has been renewed testing of expected-utility theory; one striking result has been the series of stunning experiments on the so-called preference reversal phenomenon by Lichtenstein and Slovic (1971). The subject is offered the choice between a pair of gambles. He or she is also asked to name, for each gamble, what is the certainty equivalent, that is, the amount of money payment for certain which is indifferent to having the gamble. In many cases, the preferred gamble is found to have a *lower* certainty equivalent. This is a flat contradiction to transitivity in a fairly straightforward way. More recently Grether and Plott (1979) have replicated the experiments; they found themselves unable to develop any explanation consistent with the usual postulates of rationality.

A striking real-life situation has given grounds for doubt as to the validity of the expected-utility hypothesis. Since 1969 the United States government has offered flood insurance at rates which are well below their actuarial value. The intention was to relieve the pressure for the government to offer relief when floods occurred. Under the usual hypothesis of risk aversion, any individual should certainly be willing to take a favorable bet, even more because it offsets an otherwise fluctuating income. Yet until the government increased the pressure by various incentives, very few took out this insurance. A careful study by Kunreuther (1978) failed to uncover any reason consistent with the usual explanations of economic rationality. The main distinguishing characteristic of those who took out flood insurance was acquaintance with others who took out such insurance. This might be taken as an explanation in terms of information costs, but the information seems so easy to acquire and the stakes so large that this hypothesis hardly seems tenable.

Experiments and very special forms of insurance might be regarded as exceptions to a hypothesis which has turned out to be useful in more central features of economic life. Securities and futures markets might be taken as better exemplars. I have followed some of the research in these fields as someone interested in the extension of general equilibrium theory to transactions over time and under conditions of uncertainty. In these fields there have been rich theoretical developments and equally rich empirical studies. The two types of research have not directly followed on each other, but there has certainly been a strong resonance between them. There are many aspects of the literature which bear strongly on rational behavior and on the rationality of the allocations brought about by these markets, for example, studies of the extent to which the market price fully reflects all the information available to those in the market. But I wish here to concentrate on the rational behavior of the participants.

One standard implication of rationality which has been drawn repeatedly in current research, both empirical and theoretical, is that the price of a security or futures contract at any moment is an unbiased predictor of the price at a future moment, as adjusted for discounting and, possibly, uncertainty. This implies that the price change from the present to the future is uncorrelated with current price. This, it is argued, is a rationality condition, but it is one based on rational learning from experience. For if it were not true, the individual observing the correlation could use the information to forecast the price change and therefore increase his or her wealth.

This argument presupposes that full use of available information, in this case an observed correlation presumably derived from past experience, is an aspect of rationality. It is assumed, then, that the rational individual will recognize any correlation to be found in the data.

Stewart's study of the grain futures market (1949) brought some rather discouraging evidence on this assertion. Stewart divided the participants in the market into three categories: large hedgers, primarily millers; professional speculators; and nonprofessional speculators, typically small. The first group lost, as was to be expected; they were in effect buying insurance, and their behavior was compatible with rational risk aversion. The second group made money; this was to be expected if only because they could not have survived otherwise. But the third group lost, which was especially surprising since they should be able to share with the professionals in receiving the net payments of the hedgers. In fact, the third group would have done better if each time they decided to enter the market for a fixed commitment, they flipped a coin to determine whether to go long or short.

This observation certainly suggests an inability to recognize a rather simple empirical regularity, namely that outside speculators typically lose. Why did they enter the market at all?

Stewart's data, incidentally, were drawn from direct examination of customers' accounts rather than indirect inferences calculated from market prices. To the best of my knowledge, his study has not been replicated and perhaps could not be with present privacy restrictions.

In the securities and futures markets, there are typically arbitrage possibilities. That is, there is a set of connected markets which provide substitute outlets for purchase or sale. Thus, ultimately a futures contract can be compared with a spot position; a long-term bond is an alternative to a planned sequence of investments in short-term notes, or a short-term note is an alternative to purchase and planned future sale of a long-term bond; stock purchases and sales can be arbitraged with both bond and note transactions and with future dividend payments by the firms. Since the holder is presumed to be interested solely in the money income (certain or uncertain) and not in the instrument from which it is derived, rationality has strong implications for the prices at which these instruments can sell. In the case of bonds, for example, under conditions of certainty about future short-term interest rates, the long-term interest rate must be effectively an average of them. More generally, the possibilities of arbitrage between long- and short-term interest-bearing securities give rise to strong implications for the whole term structure of interest rates. But these implications are not always borne out in reality. Many years ago, Macaulay (1938, pp. 29–32) examined simultaneous offers of bonds of varying maturities by the city of Detroit and by the New York Central Railroad and computed the implicit forecasts of one-year interest rates. Both series were quite irregular and differed sharply from each other as to pattern as well as level. He concluded that it would be difficult indeed to believe that the yields were the result of any deliberate forecasts.

Recently there has been a proliferation of new futures markets, mostly on financial instruments—Treasury bills, foreign exchange, and mortgage rates. It was expected that they would increase the efficiency of resource allocation, in particular because rational behavior on the part of participants would pool the information available and cause a futures price to be a best forecast, relative to the information available to the market. There has been considerable disappointment. Cagan (1981, pp. 170–172), quoting a large number of studies, holds that the futures price is no more accurate as a predictor of the future spot price than is a simple extrapolation from the current spot price. This, by itself, might mean only that there is no private information, that indeed all the information available at the present time is public knowledge and already reflected in the current spot price. But then, since there is little knowledge about the future, there is also little change in that knowledge from one day to the next. Yet prices on these financial futures markets are highly volatile. Indeed, this is an impression which many students of these markets and practitioners in them seem to have.

To put the matter slightly differently, when participants in the market behave rationally, prices should change only when there is new information.

The change in price from today to a future date, say one or two years off, will be the sum of a large number of daily changes, each reflecting new information as of that day. Rationally, it is clear from this that the change in any one day should be small, since it is merely one small piece of information among many. Hence, it seems intuitively clear that daily variations in the futures and securities markets are excessive relative to the daily changes in information.

Indeed, probability theory supplies necessary relations among the variances of prices at different times or of prices in different markets related by arbitrage possibilities. Consider the simple case of a security or futures contract which is valued today only for the purpose of selling tomorrow. If the market is efficient, then the price today is, as previously noted, the expected value of the future price. Both present and future prices are random variables. Then it is easy to see that the variance of today's price must be less than that of the future price, since by the unbiasedness hypothesis the future price is the sum of today's price and the price difference, the latter being a random variable with mean zero uncorrelated with today's price.

There have been several studies suggesting that when tests of this general type applied to arbitrage situations, the proposed inequalities are violated. Especially noteworthy are Shiller's studies of the bond and stock markets (1979, 1981). For example, in the bond market, the variability of long-term interest rates is too great to be explained as resulting from changing rational anticipations of future short-term rates.

I suggest that these failures of the rationality hypothesis are in fact compatible with some of the specific observations of cognitive psychologists. I am drawing especially on the work of Tversky and Kahneman (1974, 1981). They and others have identified several heuristic devices by which individuals form cognitive judgments and note that, while each has useful properties, each can also lead to biases in judgment.

One is the *representativeness* heuristic. The individual judges the likelihood of a future event by the similarity of the *present* evidence to it. There is a tendency to ignore both prior information, what the Bayesian would call probabilities, and the quality of the present evidence, for example, the size of the sample used to present evidence. Let me illustrate by quoting an experiment. "Subjects were presented with several paragraphs, each describing the performance of a student teacher during a particular practice lesson. Some subjects were asked to *evaluate* the quality of the lesson . . . Others were asked to *predict* the standing of each student teacher five years after the practice lesson. The judgments under the two conditions were identical" (Tversky and Kahneman, 1974, p. 1126).

This typifies very precisely the excessive reaction to current information which seems to characterize all the securities and futures markets. It is a plausible hypothesis that individuals are unable to recognize that there will be many surprises in the future; in short, as much other evidence tends to confirm, there is a tendency to underestimate uncertainties. In the case of the student teacher, clearly there are many grounds for uncertainty in projecting the quality of one lesson into a forecast of performance five years hence: even in the present, the student teacher undoubtedly varies in performance from one time to the next, so that the one lesson may actually not be good evidence for present performance; and certainly the student teacher's performance will change in unpredictable ways under the influence of five years' maturity and experience. The best point forecast may well be the mean performance of all teachers, perhaps modified very slightly in the direction of the quality of the single lesson, just as the current weather is useless in improving on the statistical normal in predicting weather ten days hence.

The business world's concern about profit and loss statements reflects its awareness that the stockholding public uses the representativeness heuristic. There are frequently some choices as to how to represent gains and losses, especially as to their timing. The alternatives have no bearing on the true value of the firm and therefore should have no bearing on the value of the firm's stock; but in fact they are seriously explored with regard to the effect of the profit and loss statement on stock prices. The recent liberalization of depreciation allowances created a dilemma for some firms; to receive the tax benefits, it was necessary to report larger depreciation and therefore reduce reported profits or, in some cases, turn them into losses. Even though there was by any standards a clear net gain to the firms, some of them were by no means happy with the change.

The experiments cited also have direct evidence on the insensitivity of judgments to sample size. This is true among professionally trained groups as well as laymen. Indeed, the use among all statistical research workers, including econometricians, of a fixed level of significance regardless of sample size reflects this bias, even though it has been understood since the work of Neyman and E. S. Pearson some forty-five years ago that optimal statistical testing of hypotheses should depend on a balancing of type I and type II errors.

Incidentally, the apparent inability to recognize the importance of sample size is again a contradiction to the implication of efficient markets and rational expectations theory, noted above, that economic agents will discover any profitable relation. The unreliability of small samples is demonstrated in any individual's experience; but we are apparently not programmed to group these instances appropriately and so do not make the general inference.

The drawing of inferences depends then on preconceptions, which may be true or false. The cognitive psychologists refer to the "framing" of questions, the effect of the way they are formulated on the answers. A fundamental element of rationality, so elementary that we hardly notice it, is, in logicians' language, its *extensionality*. The chosen element depends on the opportunity set from which the choice is to be made, independently of how that set is described. To take a familiar example, consider the consumer's budget set. It is defined by prices and income. Suppose income and all prices were doubled. Clearly, the set of commodity bundles available for purchase is unchanged. Economists confidently use this fact to argue that the chosen bundle is unchanged, so that consumer demand functions are homogeneous of degree zero in prices and income. But the description of the budget set, in terms of prices and income, has altered. It is an axiom that the change in description leaves the decision unaltered.

The cognitive psychologists deny that choice is in fact extensional; the framing of the question affects the answer. Let me draw a dramatic illustration from some unpublished work on choice of medical therapy by McNeil, Pauker, Sox, and Tversky (1982). McNeil and some of her colleagues have had a program, which economists should applaud, of introducing the patients' values into medical decision making. In this study the comparison was being made between two therapies, surgery and radiotherapy, for the treatment of certain forms of cancer. A therapy defines a set of probabilities of survival after varying lengths of time. In general, surgery has a distinct risk of mortality during the operation but a better survival rate thereafter. Different groups of individuals, including a group of physicians, were presented with the probabilities of survival during treatment, for one year and for five years for each of the two therapies. With these data, 84 percent of the physicians preferred surgery, 16 percent radiation therapy. Then another group was presented with the same data expressed differently: the probabilities of dying at each stage were given instead of the probabilities of survival. At each stage the probability of dying is, of course, merely 1 minus the probability of survival, so that the two formulations are not merely logically equivalent but can be transformed into each other by a trivial calculation. Yet the proportion of physicians choosing surgery over radiation therapy dropped from 84 percent to 50 percent.

This experiment suggests the possibility that the implications of information in the market may change with alternative frames of reference, which may themselves change because of all sorts of outside and irrelevant events. In the modern era of high technology, a "breakthrough" by a firm may enhance estimates of its prospects, even among sophisticated investors, well beyond any objective measure of possible profits. The extraordinary prices paid for stock in new firms planning to use recombinant DNA technologies are surely due to the framing of the prospects in terms of technological possibilities rather than the profit perspectives for the firm.

Any argument seeking to establish the presence of irrational economic behavior always meets a standard counterargument: if most agents are irrational, then a rational individual can make a lot of money; eventually, therefore, the rational individuals will take over all the wealth. Hence, rational behavior will be the effective norm. There are two rebuttals to the counterargument. (1) Not all arbitrage possibilities exist. For example, corporate profits, even though they may be down, are very distinctly positive in real terms after all necessary adjustments, including taxes. Yet there seems no way by which the average investor in corporate securities can get a positive real rate of return. (2) More important, if everyone else is "irrational," it by no means follows that one can make money by being rational, at least in the short run. With discounting, even eventual success may not be worthwhile. Consider, for example, a firm that engages in research and development which depresses the current profit and loss statement. Irrational investors look only at this information, and therefore the price of the stock is below the expected value of future dividends based on the profitable outcomes of the research and development. In a perfectly working market with rational individuals, stock prices would gradually rise as the realization date approached, but prices in the actual market would be constant. A rational investor would understand the future value of the stocks, but he or she could not realize any part of this gain during the gestation period. Although the rational investor may get rewarded eventually if the stock is held long enough, he or she is losing liquidity during an intervening period which may be long. Hence, the demand for the stock even by the rational buyers will be depressed. As Keynes argued long ago, the value of a security depends in good measure on other people's opinions.

I hope to have made a case for the proposition that an important class of intertemporal markets shows systematic deviations from individual rational behavior and that these deviations are consonant with evidence from very different sources collected by psychologists.

References

Cagan, P., "Financial Futures Markets: Is More Regulation Needed?" *Journal of Futures Markets,* vol. 1, pp. 169–190, 1981.

Davidson, D., Suppes, P., and Siegel, S., *Decision Making: An Experimental Approach,* Stanford University Press, 1957.

Grether, D., and Plott, C., "Economic Theory of Choice and the Preference Reversal Phenomenon," *American Economic Review,* vol. 69, pp. 623–638, 1979.

Kunreuther, H., et al., *Disaster Insurance Protection: Public Policy Lessons,* Wiley, 1978.

Lichtenstein, S., and Slovic, P., "Reversal of Preferences between Bids and Choices in Gambling Decisions," *Journal of Experimental Psychology,* vol. 89, pp. 46–55, 1971.

Macaulay, F. R., *Some Theoretical Problems Suggested by the Movements of Interest Rates, Bond Yields and Stock Prices in the United States Since 1856,* National Bureau of Economic Research, 1938.

Marschak, J., *Economic Information, Decision, and Prediction,* D. Reidel, 1974.

McNeil, B., Pauker, S. J., Sox, H. C., and Tversky, A., "On the Elicitation of Preferences for Alternative Therapies," *New England Journal of Medicine,* vol. 306, pp. 1259–62, 1982.

Mosteller, F., and Nogee, P., "An Experimental Measurement of Utility," *Journal of Political Economy,* vol. 59, pp. 371–404, 1951.

von Neumann, J., and Morgenstern, O., *Theory of Games and Economic Behavior,* 2nd ed., Princeton University Press, 1947.

Shiller, R. J., "The Volatility of Long-Term Interest Rates and Expectations Models of the Term Structure," *Journal of Political Economy,* vol. 87, pp. 1190–1219, 1979.

Shiller, R. J., "Do Stock Prices Move Too Much to be Justified by Subsequent Changes in Dividends?" *American Economic Review,* vol. 71, pp. 421–436, 1981.

Simon, H. A., "Rational Decision Making in Business Organizations," *American Economic Review,* vol. 69, pp. 493–513, 1979.

Stewart, B., "An Analysis of Speculative Trading in Grain Futures," U.S. Department of Agriculture Technical Bulletin no. 1001.

Thaler, R., and Rosen, S., "The Value of Saving a Life: Evidence from the Labor Market," in *Household Production and Consumption* (ed. N. Terleckyj), National Bureau of Economic Research, 1976.

Tversky, A., and Kahneman, D., "Judgement under Uncertainty: Heuristics and Biases," *Science,* vol. 185, pp. 1124–31, 1974.

Tversky, A., and Kahneman, D., "The Framing of Decisions and the Psychology of Choice," *Science,* vol. 211, pp. 453–458, 1981.

Viscusi, W. K., *Employment Hazards: An Investigation of Market Performance,* Harvard University Press, 1979.

Index

Actions, 173; admissible and dominant, 31, 63–64; valuation by consequences, 177
Adaptive choice model, 67, 70–73, 78–80
Adaptive expectations, 138
Alchian, A. A., 38
Allais, M., 61, 133
Allen, R. G. D., 101
Anderson, O., 139
Anderson, T. W., 76–77
Archimedean property, 70
Arrow's conjecture, 153–154

Bayes, T., 13–14; theorem, 14
Bayesian probabilities, 11–12, 17
Beardslee, D., 69
Becker, G. S., 212
Behavior under uncertainty, 174–179
Beliefs: probabilistic, 179, 194; equidivisibility of, 199, 206
Benefit-premium ratio, 247–251
Benson, P. H., 121
Bernoulli, D., 5, 23, 59, 127, 174, 178, 215; utility indicator, 180
Bernoulli, J., 14
Bet, 193
Brady, D., 81, 123
Bronfenbrenner, J., 140
Brumberg, R., 127
Budget constraint, 57
Buffon, G. L. L., 16
Bush, R. R., 71

Cagan, P., 137–138, 265
Cash balances demand, 159
Chernoff, H., 33, 35, 69
Choice function: defined, 102; rational, 103–105
Choices: transitivity of, 6, 118, 120–121; vs. decisions, 56; potential vs. actual, 58–59; multipersonal, 77–81
Coleman, J. S., 79
Commodity bundles, 43, 56–57; rationed, 45
Consumer price index, 85–86. *See also* Price index
Consumption, complements in, 57
Coombs, C. H., 66, 69, 76, 78
Cournot, A. A., 16, 62
Cramer, H., 25
Cramer, J. S., 139–140

Davidson, D., 70, 130, 262
Debreu, G., 77
Default risk of securities, 9, 24
de Finetti, B., 34, 60, 64, 129, 174
Demand: homogeneity, 110, 119; time-series analysis, 119–120
Demand function, 117; as choice function, 101; integrability, 101n, 111; estimation, 109–116
Differentiability in homogeneous systems, 1–4
Differential equations, 67, 79

Diminishing marginal utility of income, 23–24
Divisia, F., 93; index number, 93–94
Domar, E., 25
Dominance of actions, 177. *See also* Actions
Duesenberry, J., 81, 123
Duopoly, 62
Dynamic choice, 124–127, 136–143

Edwards, W., 55, 142
Ehrlic, I., 212
Eisner, R., 217
Engel curve, 87–91
Estes, W. K., 71–73, 140–141
Events: defined, 174; vanishing sequence, 175; null, 177, 202; subtraction axiom, 195
Expectations: influence on behavior, 136–137; formation, 137–140; adaptive, 138
Expected utility, 23, 26–28, 60, 68–69, 128–129, 149, 209–211; theorem, 179–193. *See also* Experimental tests
Expenditure equivalence curve, 89–90
Experimental tests: expected utility, 69–70, 130–132, 262–263; learning models, 70–73; game theory, 80–81; transitivity, 120–122; formation of expectations, 139
Extensionality, 268

Festinger, L., 67, 80–81, 124
Firm size, 10
Fisher, I., 10, 12–13, 20, 24–25
Fisher, R. A., 20
Flood, M., 72–73, 80, 141
Framing, 268
Friedman, M., 8, 13, 28–29, 61, 127, 132, 138, 148
Friedman, R., 81, 123
Friend, I., 140
Frisch, R., 90n
Futures markets, 263–266

Gambler indifference map, 36
Gambling, 8–9, 23, 29
Game theory, 32, 62–63, 80–81
Georgescu-Roegen, N., 101n, 102
Goodman, L. A., 77–78
Gould, J. P., 212
Grether, D., 263
Guttman, L., 74–76

Hardy, C. O., 9, 20
Harsanyi, J., 63, 78
Hart, A. G., 6, 9, 59
Hausner, M., 70
Hicks, J. R., 13, 25, 59, 78, 101, 125
Hirshleifer, J., 217
Hoffman, P., 80–81, 124
Hofsten, E. von, 96–98
Holzman, M., 134–135
Homans, G., 79
Homogeneous functions, 1–4
Hotelling, H., 101
Houthakker, H., 101, 109
Hurst, P., 131
Hypothesis testing, 11, 31

Income: marginal utility, 23–24, 28; permanent, 125, 126–127
Income function, 20, 35
Index numbers, 86–99; chain, 92–94. *See also* Price index
Indifference curve, 26, 43–54
Insufficient reason, 14–15, 35
Insurance, 8–9, 29, 212–260; state-independent utility, 218–223; state-dependent utility, 223–227; optimal amount, 232–236; benefit-premium ratio, 247–251; probabilities, 252–258; initial income, 258–260
Interdependence of values, 57
Inventories, 9

Jureen, L., 120

Kahneman, D., 266
Kalecki, M., 10
Kalisch, G., 81
Katona, G., 56n, 126, 136
Keynes, J. M., 12, 15, 18, 25–26
Klein, L., 95
Knight, F., 6, 10, 17–19, 29–31, 59, 61
Kolmogorov, A. N., 8
Kries, J. von, 15
Kuhn, H. W., 63–64
Kunreuther, H., 263

Lange, O., 13, 25
Large numbers, law of, 16
Laspeyres price index, 87
Latent structure analysis, 73–76

Lawrence, D., 80–81, 124
Lazarsfeld, P., 73–74
Learning, 70–73, 140–143
Lehmann, E. L., 31
Leser, C. E. V., 110
Lichtenstein, S., 263
Likelihoods, 14
Lottery, compound, 26–27
Luce, R. D., 133–134

Macaulay, F. R., 265
Marginal utility of income, 23–24, 28
Markowitz, H., 61, 132
Marschak, J., 25–26, 68–69, 78, 133–134, 262
Marshall, A., 13, 23
May, K. O., 122
McNeil, B., 268
Meneffe, G. H., 212
Menger, K., 23–24, 188, 209
Miller, N., 135
Milnor, J., 69, 81
Minimax principle, 32, 63, 68
Minimax regret, 33, 68
Mises, R. von, 12
Mixture: of probability distributions, 27; of income functions, 35
Modigliani, F., 127, 137
Monotone continuity of perference, 175–176
Monotone decreasing sequence of events, 175
Monotony of preference, 194–195
Moore, O. K., 63, 134
Morgenstern, O., 5, 7, 26, 60, 63, 174, 262
Mosteller, F., 70–71, 130, 262
Motivation, 134–136
Mueller, E., 136
Musgrave, R. A., 25

Nash, J., 62–63, 81
Neglect of small probabilities, 16–17
Nering, E. D., 81
Nerlove, M., 138
Neumann, J. von, 5, 7, 26, 60, 63, 174, 262
Neyman, J., 7, 20, 31
Niehans, J., 32
Nogee, P., 70, 130, 262
Null event, 177, 202

Oligopoly, 62
Ordering, 6, 56–57, 77, 102; of probability distributions, 24, 27
Ordinal theory of risk bearing, 26, 28
Overreaction to new information, 265–267

Palm, C., 30
Papandreou, A., 121
Pareto, V., 26, 56
Partition, 177
Pashigian, B. P., 212
Pauker, S. J., 268
Pearson, E. S., 7, 20, 31
Perfect scale, Guttman's, 74–76
Permanent income, 125; tests of, 126–127
Plott, C., 263
Pratt, J., 152
Preference: conditional, 176–177; reversal of, 263
Price index, 86–99; defined, 86; bias, 87; Laspeyres, 87; quality changes, 96–98
Principle of insufficient reason, 14–15, 35
Probabilistic beliefs, 179, 194; atomless, 178–179, 199, 206
Probabilistic choices, 133–134
Probability: classical vs. Bayesian, 11–12, 17; posteriori, 14; a priori, 14, 35; subjective, 34, 60–61, 68–69, 130–131, 148. *See also* Neglect of small probabilities
Probability distributions: ordering, 24, 27; mixture, 27
Probability measure, 197–198
Profit as reward for risk, 9–10, 29–30
Psychology, cognitive, 134–136, 262–263, 266–270

Quadratic utility, 28, 153
Quandt, R., 134

Radner, R., 69
Raiffa, H., 66
Ramsey, F. P., 7, 26, 34, 60, 68, 128, 129, 174, 193, 212
Rashevsky, N., 78–79
Rationality, 7, 261–270; of choice functions, 103–105
Regret, 33, 68
Representativeness, heuristic, 266–267
Resource limitations, jointness, 57–58

Revealed preference, 101–104, 107
Risk, 24–30; profit as reward, 9–10, 29–30;
    measurable, 18, 29–30; mean-variance
    characterization, 25, 28
Risk aversion, 147–163, 228; absolute,
    151–152, 228; Arrow's conjecture,
    153–154
Risk bearing, ordinal theory, 26, 28
Rose, A., 122
Rosen, S., 262
Ross, E. A., 10
Rotter, J. B., 139
Roy, R., 101
Rubin, H., 35, 95, 218n
Ryan, T., 209–211

Saint Petersburg paradox, 9, 16, 23, 188
Samuelson, P. A., 1n, 101
Saturation point, 44
Sauerlender, O., 137
Savage, L. J., 5, 8, 13, 28–29, 32–34, 61,
    64, 68, 129, 132, 148, 174
Savings, 123–124
Schkade, L. L., 212
Securities, default risk, 9, 24
Security markets, evidence on rationality,
    263–266
Sequential analysis, 61–62, 143
Sequential choices, 61
Shackle, G. L. S., 7, 17, 21–22, 36, 61
Shapley, L. S., 81
Shiller, R. J., 266
Siegel, S., 70, 130, 131, 141, 142, 262
Simon, H., 56, 66–67, 79, 262
Slovic, P., 263
Slutsky, E., 101; conditions, 112–113, 119
Smith, V. L., 212
Social welfare function, 64
Sox, H. C., 268
Standardized focus-loss, 36
States of nature, 60, 173
Statistical inference, 11, 59–60, 68
Stewart, B., 264
Stone, R., 120
Strategy, 61; mixed, 63
Strotz, R., 217

Structure analysis, latent, 73–76
Substitutes in consumption, 57
Suppes, P., 70, 130, 262
Surprise, potential, 21–22, 36–37

Thaler, R., 262
Theil, H., 139–140
Thompson, G. L., 71
Thrall, R. M., 66, 70
Thurstone, L., 120–121
Time series analysis of demand, 119–120
Tintner, G., 1–4, 24
Tobin, J., 124, 160–161
Tornquist, L., 29
Transitivity of choice, 6, 118; tests of,
    121–122
Tucker, A. W., 63–64
Tversky, A., 266, 268

Uncertainty: expressed as probability,
    11–13, 60–61; postulates of behavior,
    174–179
Unfolding technique, 76
Utility: bounded, 188–193, 209–211;
    state-dependent, 215–218
Utility function, 65, 77, 118; quadratic, 28,
    153; ordinal vs. cardinal, 66; boundedness,
    150, 209–211
Utility theory, 117–118
Uzawa, H., 102

Valavanis-Vail, S., 69
Values, interdependence, 57
Vanishing sequence of events, 175
Ville, J., 93–94, 101
Villegas, C., 194, 206
Viscusi, W. K., 262

Wald, A., 7, 20, 32, 61, 63, 68, 143; price
    index, 90
Wallis, W. A., 5
Welfare economics, 63–64
Wold, H., 45, 77, 120

Zero-sum two-person game, 32, 63
Zeuthen, F., 78